Seneca Falls and the Origins
of the Women's Rights Movement

PIVOTAL MOMENTS
IN AMERICAN HISTORY

Series Editors
David Hackett Fischer
James M. McPherson

James T. Patterson
Brown v. Board of Education:
A Civil Rights Milestone and Its Troubled Legacy

Maury Klein
Rainbow's End:
The Crash of 1929

James M. McPherson
Crossroads of Freedom:
The Battle of Antietam

Glenn C. Altschuler
All Shook Up:
How Rock 'n' Roll Changed America

David Hackett Fischer
Washington's Crossing

John Ferling
Adams vs. Jefferson:
The Tumultuous Election of 1800

Colin G. Calloway
The Scratch of a Pen:
1763 and the Transformation of North America

Joel H. Silbey
Storm over Texas:
The Annexation Controversy and the Road to Civil War

Raymond Arsenault
Freedom Riders:
1961 and the Struggle for Racial Justice

Seneca Falls
and the Origins *of the* Women's Rights Movement

Sally G. McMillen

OXFORD
UNIVERSITY PRESS

2008

OXFORD
UNIVERSITY PRESS

Oxford University Press, Inc., publishes works that further
Oxford University's objective of excellence
in research, scholarship, and education.

Oxford   New York
Auckland   Cape Town   Dar es Salaam   Hong Kong   Karachi
Kuala Lumpur   Madrid   Melbourne   Mexico City   Nairobi
New Delhi   Shanghai   Taipei   Toronto

With offices in
Argentina   Austria   Brazil   Chile   Czech Republic   France   Greece
Guatemala   Hungary   Italy   Japan   Poland   Portugal   Singapore
South Korea   Switzerland   Thailand   Turkey   Ukraine   Vietnam

Published by Oxford University Press, Inc.
198 Madison Avenue, New York, NY 10016

www.oup.com

Oxford is a registered trademark of Oxford University Press

Library of Congress Cataloging-in-Publication Data
McMillen, Sally Gregory, 1944–
Seneca Falls and the origins of the women's rights movement / by Sally G. McMillen.
p. cm.—(Pivotal moments in American history)
Includes bibliographical references and index.
ISBN 978-0-19-518265-1
1. Feminism—United States—History—19th century.
2. Woman's Rights Convention (1st: 1848: Seneca Falls, N.Y.)   I. Title.
HQ1418.M36 2008
305.420973'09034—dc22   2007031638

1   3   5   7   9   8   6   4   2

Printed in the United States of America
on acid-free paper

To my students

Contents

Editor's Note

When Thomas Jefferson wrote in the Declaration of Independence that "all men are created equal," he meant to limit this observation to the male half of the human race—at least with respect to equal membership in the polity. And not even all of them, since almost 20 percent of Americans were enslaved in 1776, and Jefferson did not consider them to be equal members of the social order.

Three-quarters of a century later, a women's rights meeting in the town of Seneca Falls, New York, adopted a Declaration of Rights and Sentiments written by Elizabeth Cady Stanton affirming that "all men and women are created equal." During the last two decades of the seventy-two years that separated these famous declarations, a ferment of reform had begun to challenge old institutions and old ways of thinking. Two of the most egalitarian and far-reaching reform movements had profound consequences for the future of America: abolitionism and women's rights. The antislavery movement provoked an increasingly strident proslavery counterattack that polarized the country and led to a revolution that abolished slavery and started the country on the road to racial equality before the law—a revolution that we know as the Civil War. The women's rights movement was at first almost equally polarizing but relatively nonviolent. It also brought about a more gradual revolution that made women equal before the law and increasingly equal in other spheres of American life as well. The valley of the Mohawk River and the Erie Canal in which Seneca Falls is nestled was the antebellum "Burned-Over District" of New York State where the fires of this and other reform movements swept through the landscape and left it forever culturally changed. From there the transformation that brought equal rights to American women in the twentieth century spread across America.

Sally McMillen frames this story around the careers of four remarkable women: Lucretia Mott, Elizabeth Cady Stanton, Lucy Stone, and Susan B. Anthony. Their lives spanned the decades from the 1830s to Susan Anthony's death in 1906, while Stanton's and Stone's daughters carried on the struggle to and beyond the Nineteenth Amendment that gave women the vote in 1920. At the beginning of this period, women yielded ownership of their property to husbands when they married, could not vote or serve on juries, were largely excluded from higher education, and were denied access to many occupations and professions. By its end, women had become part of the American polity in the ways that Elizabeth Cady Stanton had demanded in her Declaration of Rights and Sentiments at Seneca Falls in 1848.

This is a dramatic story, a moving story, a powerful story, and a story that has not ended. Sally McMillen's narrative conveys the drama and importance of the landmark events and the remarkable people that drove this story. The Seneca Falls Convention of 1848 was indeed a pivotal moment in American history—not just the history of women, but of all Americans.

James M. McPherson

Seneca Falls and the Origins
of the Women's Rights Movement

INTRODUCTION

Seneca Falls, New York, seems an unlikely site for a pivotal event in American history. Surrounded by beautiful, rolling farmland, the town sits alongside the Genesee Canal, only a few miles off the New York State Thruway. Waterloo lies three miles to the west and is about the same size as Seneca Falls. Several miles to the east sits the town of Auburn. But Seneca Falls, located in what today is called the Finger Lakes District of New York, is where in July 1848 five women initiated a social revolution and inaugurated the women's movement. Except for tourists who visit the site today to pay homage to the origins of the women's rights movement, the town is a quieter place now than it was in 1848. Seneca Falls underwent significant alterations in the early twentieth century with the widening of the Cayuga-Seneca Canal, which eliminated more than a hundred industrial and commercial buildings and sixty homes. A visitor may find it hard to imagine the radical movement and controversial issues that five women generated in this tranquil setting.

Today, the Seneca Falls Convention of July 1848 feels like an obscure event for most Americans. Students of American history probably have some familiarity with it, but most people have never heard of it. Yet this meeting changed the way American society (and much of the Western world) thought about and treated women in the mid-nineteenth century. It unleashed a complicated, lengthy struggle that continues to this day. At Seneca Falls, for the first time, women and men gathered for the sole purpose of articulating female grievances and demanding women's equality. As Susan B. Anthony observed in the early 1880s, "Woman had not been discovered fifty years ago."[1] Before Seneca Falls, no one could imagine that anyone would dare challenge, in such an organized manner, women's subservience or their legal, social, and political oppression. Before 1848, the nation's laws, traditions, and religious doctrines sustained women's subordinate status and codified their lack of legal and political rights. This Convention, though it lasted only two days, put everything into question and fostered a commitment to transform the country into a true democratic republic.

The Seneca Falls Convention took place during an exciting period in the nation's history when many people were seeking to rectify the nation's wrongs. Unlike other reform issues that galvanized concerned Americans—education, antislavery, prison reform, world peace, and intemperance—women's demands were deemed the most radical. No women's rights movement existed before 1848, nor had there ever been much appetite to question women's status. While a handful of Americans such as Abigail Adams and Margaret Fuller expressed open dismay about women's submission and their lack of basic rights, such comments were rare and inchoate.

That all changed with Seneca Falls, which produced the "Declaration of Rights and Sentiments," setting forth eighteen injustices women endured and articulating a series of resolutions to address those wrongs. When the Convention ended, a group of women (and a few men) were inspired to organize women's rights meetings, lecture, write, and petition elected officials to persuade them that women deserved all the rights of citizenship, including the most radical demand of all: female suffrage.

Seneca Falls led to a significant shift in Americans' perceptions of women, their status, and the rights they deserved. Women set out to force male politicians to alter state and national laws that legitimized women's secondary position, to challenge ministers who continued to use the Bible to justify female subordination, and to convince men to rethink their monopoly on political power and give women the right to vote and to hold public office. Reformers challenged society's deep-seated assumptions about women's innate inferiority and their dependence on men. Yet arguably, their biggest challenge was to convince women themselves that they deserved better, that they needed to fight oppression and demand their rights. So deeply ingrained were ideas about women's inferiority that seventy-two years would pass after Seneca Falls before the Nineteenth Amendment was added to the U.S. Constitution, giving women the right to vote.

This book focuses on the principal players and some of the seminal events that occurred in the years just prior to Seneca Falls and in the decades that followed.

Four remarkable women were central to the nineteenth-century women's movement. They provide the framework for this book.

The eldest stateswoman and a principal organizer of the Seneca Falls Convention was the Quaker minister Lucretia Coffin Mott. She absorbed a profound belief in women's equality throughout her childhood. Born on Nantucket Island into a faith that preached and lived human equality, Lucretia never doubted her ability to excel. Along with her sisters, she attended a coed boarding school, which was unusual for that time, giving her an education equal to that of her brothers. Her mother inspired her conviction that women could do anything they set their minds to achieve. Because Lucretia's father was often away, her mother made almost all the decisions relating to their home and the family's mercantile business. Here, women were the full and equal partners of men, a lesson that inspired Lucretia's later preaching and the way she conducted her life.

Elizabeth Cady Stanton, the driving intellect of the women's movement, a principal organizer of the Seneca Falls Convention, and the primary author of the Declaration of Rights and Sentiments, embraced women's equality with a passion. Elizabeth became keenly aware of women's inferior status as she grew up. Her only surviving brother died when she was eleven; she became determined to fill a void in her family and to excel at any activity normally reserved for men. She chafed against restrictions that confined her merely because she was female. Her rebellious spirit was evident from the start. An English teacher required her to read "The Wife" by Washington Irving, a poem that rhapsodized about a vine (wife) that entwined and sustained an oak tree (husband), an all-too-obvious metaphor demonstrating a married woman's dependent status. Elizabeth later recalled that she threw the poetry book aside and rushed out of the schoolroom in tears. When her teacher asked what was wrong, she retorted that assigning such "degrading" and invidious readings was insulting to women.[2] Elizabeth could not bear to think of women as anything but equal partners of men.

Two other important figures in the women's rights movement provide a framework for this book, though they were not present at the Seneca Falls Convention: Lucy Stone and Susan B. Anthony. Lucy learned firsthand the meaning of hard work on her family's farm, watching how hard her mother labored and how few rights she enjoyed. Lucy objected to her church's refusal to allow her to vote on matters of faith merely because she was female. She challenged scriptural passages that articulated a subordinate, silent role for women and vowed to learn Hebrew and Greek so that she could more effectively challenge the original biblical texts. Lucy objected to the fact that her brothers benefited from a college education while her parents insisted that her academy education was more than adequate to secure a husband. Eventually she acquired an education that very few women of the antebellum period (approximately 1820 to 1860) achieved, earning a college degree when she was twenty-nine. Lucy would become one of the nation's most famous and spellbinding lecturers of the mid-nineteenth century.

Finally, Susan B. Anthony, the tireless campaigner of the women's movement, grew up in a reform-minded family. Her father was raised a Quaker, and both he and Susan's mother subscribed to human equality. Deeply interested in reforms of the day, they committed themselves to abolition and temperance and insisted on educating their sons and daughters for useful lives. Thus, Susan gained a sense of purpose from the time she was a young girl. Her initial reform interests paralleled those of her parents. When she later received wages well below what less experienced male teachers earned, she felt a profound sense of injustice. A major impetus for her interest in women's rights was a speech she read by Lucy Stone in which Lucy objected to the common practice of women being identified on their tombstones merely as "relicts" of their husbands. Susan vowed that she would never be perceived as a piece of property.

These four singular individuals and other leaders of the nineteenth-century women's rights movement worked for decades to secure their rights. Though they did not achieve all that they hoped during their lifetimes, they had an enormous impact and were able to see that their efforts made a difference. Celebrating the thirtieth anniversary of Seneca Falls in 1878, Elizabeth honored those who were first involved in the movement. "At the very start we claimed full equality with man," she said.

> Our meetings were hastily called and somewhat crudely conducted; but we intuitively recognized the fact that we were defrauded of our natural rights, conceded in the National constitution. And thus the greatest movement of the century was inaugurated. I say greatest, because through the elevation of woman all humanity is lifted to a higher plane of action.... We already see the milestones of a new civilization on every highway.

Two years later, Susan B. Anthony called the Seneca Falls Convention "the grandest and greatest reform of all time—and destined to be thus regarded by the future historian."[3]

Like the women in this book—Lucretia, Elizabeth, Lucy, and Susan—I have long been interested in women's issues and know that these four made my life's path far easier than theirs.[4] Raised in Southern California, where gender differences were rarely an issue, I grew up with the unspoken assumption that women could accomplish whatever men could. My paternal grandmother, a second-generation Californian, could not attend high school; her father argued that riding into Pasadena on horseback was too arduous for a young woman. She continued to educate herself, read avidly, and drove a car as soon as her family purchased one. She raised three sons in the foothills above Pasadena, rode horses her entire life, and shot rattlesnakes in her backyard. My maternal grandmother graduated from Grinnell College in Iowa, taught high school English, and saved her earnings to travel solo through Europe in 1910. When my mother was two, my grandmother took her by train from Des Moines to Los Angeles to escape cold weather and the confines of close living in her mother-in-law's household. My grandfather visited and promised them their own house when they returned home.

I read constantly as a child, often novels and biographies about remarkable women. My mother encouraged me to excel in school. My father and older brother treated me as an equal, letting me play on the neighborhood football and basketball teams, teaching me to throw spiral passes and free throws, and encouraging my participation in school sports. Attending an all-female college exposed me to smart, motivated women. My graduate work in history focused on the southern United States, where our family moved in 1978, and in particular on its fascinating women.

The impetus for this book began with a casual conversation I had with the Civil War historian James McPherson, when he visited Davidson College a few years ago to deliver a lecture. In speaking with him after his talk, I inquired about current projects. He mentioned that he was co-editing a series, Pivotal Moments in American History, for Oxford University Press. I asked about titles in the series. He named the books that had been written and those nearing completion. Surprised at what I did not hear, I responded, "But you have nothing on women!" He looked at me and asked, "Do you have any ideas?" "Well, as a start," I answered, "Seneca Falls."

Exploring Seneca Falls and the women's rights movement[5] has been an exciting adventure. I assumed I knew a good deal about the women and the events initiated at Seneca Falls, but while writing this book I discovered the story to be far more complex and rich. Most of all, it has given me the opportunity to become familiar with a group of inspiring, visionary women and men. Had I lived in their day, I feel certain I would have joined their cause.

The structure of this book is chronological. It begins with an overview of American women's world before Seneca Falls. Chapter 2 examines reform efforts during the antebellum period, a framework for understanding what happened at Seneca Falls. It was during these years that Americans began to address some of the nation's considerable problems, including slavery, alcoholism, and limited educational opportunities. The antislavery movement, however, had the greatest impact, for through it women began to equate their own oppression to that of slaves. This equation outraged many. Seneca Falls itself is the subject of chapter 3. Chapter 4 looks at the nascent women's rights movement of the 1850s, as women lectured, wrote, held annual conventions, and petitioned to demand their rights. Chapter 5 examines the impact of the Civil War on the women's movement; the profound disappointments women faced during the early years of Reconstruction when former male slaves gained the rights women had long been seeking; and a split in the movement in 1869 when leaders, in disagreement over issues and often at odds with one another, created a schism in the women's movement. The final chapter covers the years up to 1890, when two women's rights organizations fought on several fronts— and sometimes with each other—to win suffrage; the problems they confronted; and the changes they brought about. This book ends with the two organizations reuniting in 1890 and a second generation of women taking over. While suffrage was not yet a reality, the seeds planted at Seneca Falls in 1848 had grown into a national women's movement that ultimately uplifted the lives of half this nation's population.

I

SEPARATE SPHERES

Law, Faith, Tradition

O h, my daughter, I wish you were a boy," Judge Daniel Cady allegedly uttered to eleven-year-old Elizabeth, following the death in 1826 of her twenty-year-old brother Eleazar, Cady's only surviving son. Now he had only daughters to raise. Whether or not he spoke these exact words, Elizabeth Cady Stanton later invoked them in written records of her life, identifying this as the moment when she first vowed to achieve all that men could. To her father, Elizabeth allegedly responded, "I will try to be all that my brother was."[1] If the story is apocryphal, the sentiment was not, and Elizabeth would indeed eventually accomplish more during her lifetime than did most men. Judge Cady may have been expressing his sorrow at the loss of a male heir to carry on the family name. But perhaps he hoped to inspire his energetic, precocious daughter to succeed in a man's world.

Born in 1815 into a privileged family in Johnstown, New York, Elizabeth throughout her childhood and adolescence tried to live up to her father's wish and excel at everything boys could do. She learned Greek and mathematics and became a skillful chess player and an accomplished equestrian. Though college was not an option for women at that time, she received an excellent education. Her schooling and her family's influences and expectations help explain how she was later able to become a principal organizer of the Seneca Falls Convention of 1848, principal author of its "Declaration of Rights and Sentiments," and the intellectual leader of the women's rights movement.

In a Massachusetts household a few hundred miles away, Hannah Matthews Stone apparently commented, following the birth in 1818 of Lucy, her sixth child, "Oh, dear! I am sorry it is a girl. A woman's life is so hard!"[2] Of course Lucy Stone never heard her mother utter those words, but throughout her childhood she witnessed how hard her mother worked—and how thanklessly. Francis Stone, Lucy's father, refused to look beyond traditional ideas of gender. As soon as they were old enough, Lucy and her sisters performed many of the chores needed to run the Stone household and farm. They helped to plant crops, gardened, hauled firewood, sewed, canned food, and drove cattle. To bring in additional income, Lucy and her sisters also did piecework for a local shoe factory.[3] Though dutiful, Lucy was a proud, independent, and willful child, with an easily aroused temper.

From an early age, Lucy was well aware of gender inequity. She abhorred the restrictions she endured, yearning for more education and the opportunities available to men. Her brother Luther earned praise from their parents for his academic achievements; Lucy never garnered such praise, even though her abilities equaled his. She resented the fact that she could not vote in her local Congregational church. At sixteen, when she wanted to extend her schooling, her parents denied her request, judging that she had obtained more than enough education to find a good husband. But marriage held little appeal for Lucy. She understood the laws that limited married women's lives and realized that her mother had no control over family money: any request usually met with a denial from Lucy's father. Reflecting patriarchal attitudes of the time, laws governing marriage, and traditional ideas about gender relationships, Francis Stone believed that men ruled their wives, their children, and the household. As Lucy recalled later, "There was only one will in our home, and that was my father's."[4]

Living in far different circumstances while Elizabeth and Lucy were coming of age were female slaves who had none of the opportunities that Lucy and Elizabeth—despite their frustrations—enjoyed. By this time, for the most part, slavery was confined to the South. Northern states had engaged in gradual emancipation following the formation of the new nation and, by the 1820s, had eliminated slavery. For instance, the antislavery and women's rights activist Sojourner Truth finally gained her freedom just before New York's abolition law went into full effect in 1827. Yet in the South during the antebellum period, whites became increasingly wedded to slave labor. The region's principal cash crops, such as cotton, tobacco, and sugar cane, made slavery extremely profitable. By the late antebellum period, the region was the country's major exporter of raw goods.

Slaves in the South, male and female, could anticipate a lifetime of servitude for themselves and their children. Forced to work from sunup to sundown and yield body and mind to an owner's bidding, slaves knew little about freedom and opportunity, other than to yearn for both. They were property, pure and simple. An owner could punish them for the slightest infraction. They could be sold at a moment's notice, placed in a stranger's possession, often far from their home and family of origin. The mother of the famous fugitive slave and abolitionist Frederick Douglass was sold to another plantation owner when he was a young boy, and she had to sneak away at night to visit her son.

While slavery often brought wealth to slaveholders, it brought a life of misery and oppression to the enslaved. Several clauses in the U.S. Constitution condoned slavery, and most southern states enacted laws that severely restricted slaves' freedom of movement. A number of states forbade slaves to learn to read and write lest they absorb ideas that might foster thoughts of freedom and equality. Slave women were especially vulnerable. Many were victims of sexual exploitation and had little power and no legal recourse to resist the sexual advances of any man. A young North Carolina slave woman, Harriet Jacobs, went into hiding for years to escape the sexual overtures of her predatory master until she finally was able to escape to Philadelphia in 1842. Like Jacobs, slave women faced the most degraded status—enslaved in a land of the free; black in a country that privileged white; and female in a world controlled by men.[5]

Beginning in the 1820s, the slavery divide between North and South led to increasingly rancorous political debates. Southerners sought to expand slavery into western states and territories, arguing that slaves were merely property and that people had the right to take their property wherever they moved. Though hardly of one mind on this issue, many northern politicians tried to prevent slavery's spread westward. A growing division over the issue wracked Congress and the nation during the later years of the antebellum period. While most Americans accepted slavery as long as it remained in the South, a growing number of northern abolitionists began to decry its very existence.

Like their slave counterparts, free black women, whether residing in the North or South, often lived bleak lives. Many were single mothers who made ends meet by working as domestic servants, laundresses, or cooks. Most lived in poverty, apart from whites. Some states and cities passed laws that codified the separation of the races. The city of Boston segregated blacks from whites on its streetcars, and Philadelphia prohibited blacks from riding on its omnibuses. Northern churches segregated themselves by race, and many public buildings and public spaces were off limits to blacks. Northern free black men and women, however, managed to take matters into their own hands. They organized their own churches and self-help groups and gained access to a rudimentary education in schools that were organized and run by individuals or churches in their own communities.

Life as a woman in antebellum America seems alien to us today. Women were considered inferior to men, a fact rooted in tradition, law, and scripture. Their rightful place was in the home, where they were to serve as devoted wives and mothers, and they were therefore deemed unfit to operate as political beings and unable to enjoy the benefits of citizenship afforded men.[6] Very few women acquired a college education, secured a well-paid job, or pursued a fruitful career. Other than marrying well, they could do little to enhance their economic status. The ideal woman was presumed to be pure, delicate, pious, and maternal; the expectation was that she would marry, reproduce, raise her children, create a comfortable home, and find fulfillment through her family. Judge Cady's and Hannah Stone's regrets that their daughters were not boys and Lucy's parents' decision to limit her education were not unusual reactions for the period.

Their secondary status notwithstanding, women did play a central role in developing, civilizing, and advancing this nation long before the United States gained its independence from Great Britain. During the colonial period, they made significant contributions to family and community. They worked alongside their husbands, since family survival demanded that chores be shared by all. Women helped to plant, sow, and harvest crops. As Lucy would do decades later, they raised hogs and chickens, planted gardens, sewed, milked cows, and tended orchards. This need for shared male and female labor remained a constant theme as families moved to the frontier, where the participation of all family members proved essential.

Scholars still debate the nature of white women's standing during the colonial period. Some argue that they enjoyed a somewhat higher legal status before the American Revolution than they did after it, while others have concluded that wives in early America lived under significant legal restrictions. Their status was that of "perpetual dependents," reflecting laws that the American colonies inherited from England, statutes that remained in effect for decades.[7] Nonetheless, most historians concede that colonial women achieved some standing in their families and communities because their contributions were so essential. A woman might perform chores in the home but also assist her husband in running a newspaper, operating a ferry or store, or serving as the community's midwife and health provider. A widow might oversee her late husband's estate or serve in the role of deputy husband to conduct business in his absence. Dinah Nuthead of St. Mary's, Maryland, took over her husband's printing business when he died around 1694, moved it to the new colonial capital at Annapolis, and gained a license to print assembly publications. Eliza Lucas Pinckney helped to revitalize colonial South Carolina's agrarian economy in the 1740s by successfully experimenting with the indigo plant. Laurel Ulrich's study of the Maine midwife Martha Ballard exposes the busy life of someone who played a key role in her late-eighteenth-century community.[8] In the fairly fluid society of the American colonies, husbands and wives engaged in mutually supportive roles by performing work in the home and the field. But this cooperative approach did not translate into equal rights for women; instead, it reflected the realities and uncertainties of colonial life. As the historian Marylynn Salmon has said, "The legal position of women may well have been hindered as much as helped by the unsettled conditions of American life."[9]

On occasion, colonial women even challenged their status and the prevailing laws, as Anne Hutchinson and Mary Dyer did, but they paid a dear price for their bold behavior. In 1637, Hutchinson defied Puritan ministers in the Massachusetts Bay Colony by asserting her right to interpret ministers' sermons and lead discussions about them with both men and women. She was brought to trial the next year for her assertiveness, and though she defended herself brilliantly in court, she and several of her family members were banished from the Bay Colony. The Quaker Mary Dyer continued to visit New England even after Puritans in Massachusetts passed a law that prohibited Quakers from entering the Colony under threat of death. She was hanged for her defiance in 1660.

A few men did question women's secondary status before and during the American Revolution, but their utterances stand out as unique. As the nation began to rebel against its subservience to Great Britain, a handful of men began to ponder women's subordinate status to men. "Are not women born as free as men? Would it not be infamous to assert that the ladies are all slaves by nature?" questioned James Otis in 1764. In his "Occasional Letter on the Female Sex" written in 1775, Thomas Paine objected to the fact that throughout most of history, women, almost without exception, had been "at all times and all places, adored and oppressed." While he stirred patriotic passions among colonists, Paine never went so far as to suggest political and economic equality for all.[10]

A handful of assertive women raised similar concerns. Mercy Otis Warren, sister of James Otis, held meetings in her home and corresponded with a number of illustrious men, including Thomas Jefferson and John Adams. She argued that " 'inherent rights' belonged to all mankind and had been conferred on all by the God of nations."[11] Abigail Adams admonished her husband, John, while he was serving in Philadelphia as a delegate to the Second Continental Congress: "Remember the Ladies," she wrote in March 1776,

> and be more generous and favourable to them than your ancestors. Do not put such unlimited power in the hands of the Husbands. Remember all Men would be tyrants if they could. If perticuliar [*sic*] care and attention is not paid to the Laidies [*sic*] we are determined to foment a Rebelion [*sic*], and will not hold ourselves bound by any Laws in which we have no voice, or Representation.[12]

Despite such audacity, her words indicate that Abigail recognized that it was up to men to improve women's lot. She could do little more than importune her powerful husband. John Adams apparently was amused but also a bit worried. He confided to his fellow Massachusetts lawyer John Sullivan that any effort to accommodate a variety of potential voters could lead to chaos and controversy—and perhaps the terrifying possibility of female suffrage. "There will be no End of it," he warned. "New Claims will arise. Women will demand a Vote."[13]

In any case, the republican government created in 1787 accorded American women neither citizenship nor a political role in the new democratic republic. Jefferson's words in the Declaration of Independence that "all men are created equal" were not up for debate at this time. Despite ringing sentiments about the glories of democracy, female participation in the public sphere probably declined in the late eighteenth century. What gradually emerged was a concept that identified separate spheres for men and women. Men were supposed to engage in larger issues regarding the state and world while women were supposed to deal with home and family. Gender roles thus became more rigidly defined, and expressions of patriarchy solidified. By the early nineteenth century, women's place in the home and the centrality of their maternal responsibilities were more forcefully articulated. The pervasiveness of this separate sphere ideology and the fact that the majority of Americans embraced it helps to explain why the struggle for women's rights would prove so protracted and so difficult.

American women's dependency and secondary status were so apparent that they often surprised travelers who visited the United States during the antebellum period. Their condition seemed inconsistent with the ideals of a nation that touted its democratic character. The Scottish reformer and writer Frances Wright, the British writer Harriet Martineau, and the Frenchman Alexis de Tocqueville were among the many European visitors who shared insights into life in the United States and observed this contradiction. Wright initially expressed enthusiasm about her two-year visit, and in 1821 she published sympathetic reactions in her book *Views of Society and Manners in America*. She returned to the United States in 1824 and stayed several years, lecturing widely and establishing a biracial utopian community, Nashoba, in western Tennessee. Wright was one of the first women in this country to speak to mixed audiences, addressing them on women's rights, marriage, free love, and universal education. Marriage, she felt, demeaned women, and she observed how few opportunities were open to married women in this country. Her advocacy of free love and racial equality proved too radical for most Americans. Martineau visited the United States between 1834 and 1836, and in her book *Society in America* she observed that the nation's democratic government, based on the Declaration of Independence, derived its power from the consent of the governed. Yet, she wondered, "How can the political condition of women be reconciled with this?" In *Democracy in America,* Tocqueville observed the pronounced differences in the legal standing of single and married women. When American women married, he noted, they seemed to retreat into submission, overwhelmed by the demands of running a household and bearing and rearing children. Tocqueville concluded that "a woman forfeits her independence forever when she embraces matrimony." The idealization of the separate spheres of influence and activity defining men's and women's existence struck him as unique. But Tocqueville also felt that American women exhibited an intelligence and independence rarely found in European women.[14]

Several factors help explain the widespread acceptance of the ideology of separate spheres. First of all, as we have seen, the nation needed women to ensure the survival of the new republic by supervising their homes and families. A concept the historian Linda Kerber has dubbed "republican motherhood" developed in the early national period. Mothers had an important role to play in the new nation's future. They were to devote their energies to raising and educating the next generation, especially their sons, to become virtuous, civic-minded citizens. Motherhood assumed a lofty status—at least as it was articulated in print. A woman's superior moral nature would shape and uplift her family, and she would serve as a shining example to her children.[15]

Few women challenged what seemed to be the natural order; most accepted their exalted domestic and maternal roles, which society continually reinforced. Stories, scripture, poems, advice manuals, sermons, and novels extolled the virtuous mother and dedicated homemaker. Reflecting popular thought of the time, an 1836 essay in the *Southern Literary Journal* celebrated her well-delineated role: "His aspirations are for thrones and large dominions; she is queen of the household; her diadem is the social affections; her scepter, love."[16] A woman was to shun the political world for fear it would sully her delicacy and purity. She should not participate in the rough-and-tumble of politics and business, but confine any activities beyond the home to religious and benevolent causes. Whether such utterances were written to reconcile women to their assigned sphere or simply reflected their willing acceptance is unclear.

Women even authored some of the writings that celebrated female inferiority and dependency. In *Observations on the Real Rights of Women*, published in 1818, Hannah Crocker urged women to "sooth [*sic*] the turbulent passions of men" and "steer them safe to the haven of rest and peace." Crocker insisted that women not assert themselves in the political, legal, or religious arena. Mothers' rightful duties were to care for their children and raise their sons to be virtuous and God-fearing, so that they could "shine as statesmen, soldiers, philosophers, and christians." By contrast, she added, "It must be woman's prerogative to shine in the domestic circle, and her appropriate duty to teach and regulate the opening mind of her little flock." Mrs. A. J. Graves wrote in 1841, "*Home* is [woman's] appropriate sphere of action." Should she leave her rightful sphere "to mingle in any of the great public movements of the day, she is deserting the station which God and nature have assigned to her." In her diary, a young Georgian, Ella Gertrude Clanton Thomas, thanked God for her many blessings, "but none do I so sincerely thank thee as for *my husband*... for true to my sex, I delight *in looking up* and love to feel my woman's weakness protected by man's superior strength."[17]

One of the most influential maternal advisors of the antebellum period was a man: the minister John S. C. Abbott. His popular book *The Mother at Home,* published in 1833, lauded a wife's domestic role. "The mothers of our race must be the chief instruments in its redemption," he avowed.[18] Women were more virtuous, moral, and pious than men, and apparently all the more so by relying on a man's greater strength, intellect, and worldly understanding. Indeed, the concept of separate spheres comforted most American women—and obviously pleased men.

Another factor that helped to reinforce this ideology was a nation experiencing the nascent stages of industrialization and an emerging market economy. In the first decades of the nineteenth century, more men, particularly in the Northeast, began to abandon farming and to take paid jobs in the nation's burgeoning towns and cities—as lawyers, merchants, brokers, factory workers, businessmen, storekeepers, newspaper writers and publishers, bakers, and doctors. Family duties shifted. The gradual introduction and growth of factories, initially in the New England states, reflected a nation becoming more self-sufficient. The separation of home and wage work widened the gap between male and female duties, especially among the growing middle class. As more men took paid jobs in the public arena, female labor in the home became ever more important. Women engaged in hours of unpaid labor each day, cooking and baking, washing clothes, ironing, mending, cleaning lanterns, sewing clothes and linens, gardening, nursing the sick, and raising their children. Nonetheless, the expanding wage economy and factory production did confer some benefits on women. Many families could now purchase items formerly produced by their own labor—woven cloth, soap, candles, and milled flour, among others— freeing women from incessant work.

Instrumental in disseminating the message of separate spheres were the many periodicals and newspapers published in the antebellum period directed to a growing number of literate women who now had more leisure time to enjoy them. A profusion of novels, poems, and essays exalted women's role in the home and glorified motherhood. Authors, both male and female, also produced a stream of advice manuals instructing young women and mothers on how to behave properly and find fulfillment in their sacred assigned role. For instance, in the introduction to *Mrs. Parker's Domestic Duties, or Instructions to Young Married Ladies*, published in 1836, its author urged new wives to recognize the enormity of their responsibilities in overseeing their family and household. At no time should wives regard this as an onerous "duty" but rather see their new respon- sibilities as a "source of happiness."[19]

The most popular women's magazine of the nineteenth century was *Godey's Lady's Book,* edited by Sarah Jane Hale. In 1860, its circulation peaked at 150,000, making it one of the most widely read magazines in the country. Hale, born in 1788, benefited from a solid education, thanks in part to a brother who outlined a course of study for her. She taught school until she married at the age of twenty-five. When her husband died nine years later, Hale found herself with few resources and five children to raise. She made a living by selling her poems and short stories until a publisher asked her to serve as editor of *American Ladies' Magazine.* In 1837, she became editor of *Godey's.* While Hale promoted female education, good health, exercise, proper diet, and expanded job opportunities, she also embraced traditional ideas about women's proper role. She showed little patience with those who strayed from their rightful place in the home and professed radical views in public. Rather, she celebrated the concept of separate spheres and well-defined roles for wives and mothers. Females were more pious and thus morally superior to men, she affirmed. *Godey's* and other women's magazines had a profound impact on female readers and solidified the im- portance of female submission. For instance, one article included a "Code of Instruction for Ladies." It outlined a wife's proper behavior, including admo- nitions never to contradict her husband, never to respond if he was abusive, never to give him advice unless he asked for it, never to censor his morals and behavior, and never to make him feel that he had done anything wrong.[20]

Religion was a major factor in American life that also served to reinforce women's inferior status. It played a dominant role in early New England, where religious dissenters like the Puritans wielded enormous influence in colonial communities. The Anglican Church was powerful in the colonial South, while greater religious diversity began to characterize the middle colonies, with their mix of Quakers, Catholics, Lutherans, Anglicans, and, by the late eighteenth century, recent Protestant sects such as Presbyterians, Baptists, and Methodists. Religion was at the core of life in America, whether organized or not, for a strong belief in God and the afterlife helped to offset the uncertainties of colonial life and the ever-present fear of death. It provided a sense of order and community. Most people read and reread the Bible. If an American owned a single book, that book was the Bible. Communities held ministers in high esteem and considered them arbiters of moral authority. Many people dutifully attended church. (In some communities, attendance was required, at least among God-fearing citizens who followed the rules.) Women were especially pious, and they soon began to outnumber men as churchgoers, making up as much as three-fourths of all congregants in some churches by the mid-eighteenth century. The messages articulated by clergymen in their sermons and religious tracts articulated the ideal: that women were to be virtuous, pious, obedient, and submissive but, at the same time, strong and hard-working—"good wives," as the historian Laura Ulrich has described New England women. Ministers might celebrate the equality of men's and women's souls and their place in heaven, but they upheld the importance of separate spheres and female inferiority on earth.[21]

Female submission was proclaimed to be part of God's order. In church, women were to sit in silence and never dream of occupying the pulpit. Numerous examples from scripture supported this, though as reformers like Lucretia Mott would later point out, just as many scriptural citations celebrated female strength and independence. Such admonitions as that of Genesis 3:16 applied only to wives, not husbands: "Unto the woman he said, I will greatly multiply thy sorrow and thy conception; in sorrow thou shalt bring forth children; and thy desire [shall be] to thy husband, and he shall rule over thee." Clearly, marriage was an institution that bound wives to submission. These biblical tenets and the use of them to sustain women's inferior status would galvanize those like Lucretia, Elizabeth, and Lucy. When her mother explained scripture to her, Lucy sought to understand the original biblical script, sensing that the words had been skewed. These women and others would begin not only to challenge scriptures' relevance but also to question the translation of the Bible and the majority of preachers who articulated conservative views of women.[22]

Marriage and the laws that established wives' secondary status in the early nineteenth century were also factors that had a significant impact on solidifying female inferiority. Reformers would later challenge these laws and their negative effect on women—no one with greater energy and determination than Elizabeth Cady Stanton. Women's legal status was based on Blackstone's law, a codification of English common law that became the basis for the legal system throughout most of the United States and its territories.[23] Two categories defined a woman's status. A married woman was a *feme covert*, or "covered woman"; a single woman was a *feme sole*. According to Blackstone, "By marriage, the husband and wife are one person in law: that is, the very being or legal existence of the woman is suspended during the marriage, or at least is incorporated and consolidated into that of the husband; under whose wing, protection, and *cover*, she performs every thing [*sic*]."[24] A wife was a dependent and remained so throughout her married life. According to Blackstone, a white man became independent at twenty-one and was then accorded both political and legal rights. A wife never gained such privileges, whatever her age. Indeed, a wife had no legal existence apart from her husband. She could not claim possessions, even those she brought into her marriage; all her possessions belonged to her husband. He had rights to her wages or any money she might earn. A wife could not sign contracts in her own name or claim custody of her children in the rare instances of divorce or legal separation. Yet the majority of women yearned to wed, and most did, despite the fact that, according to Blackstone, a *feme sole* retained the rights a woman lost when she married. A single woman could claim rights a wife could not: retain her own property and wages, write and sign contracts, run a business, and operate independently. A widow also had legal custody of her children. A single woman could write her own will and dispose of her possessions as she saw fit.

During the seventeenth and much of the eighteenth centuries, marriage was often based on pragmatic concerns: to increase family property holdings, to procreate and produce heirs, and to bind families together. If love was not part of the initial equation, the assumption was that affection would develop over time. Parents played a significant role in helping their offspring select a suitable partner by assessing a future spouse's economic standing, family background, and character. Either by luck or sustained effort, some women found a suitable husband. Others were less fortunate.

The choice of a husband was an important one. Marriage was perceived to be a sacred, nearly indissoluble bond between husband and wife, a mutual commitment to create a family. A husband's principle responsibility was to support his wife and children; a wife's was to stand behind her husband, to bear and nurture their children, and to create a harmonious home. Wedding vows codified a woman's secondary status. A bride promised to "love, honor, and obey" her husband; a groom uttered no similar promise to obey his wife. Advice manuals addressed to young women urged them to select a partner wisely, because severing the marital bond was extremely difficult.

The ideal was marriage, and few women in the antebellum period made a conscious decision to avoid it. Despite the legal advantages of remaining single—or a "spinster," as a single woman was often called—this condition had its drawbacks. Many regarded it as a woman's worst fate. Marriage was part of the natural order, and those who never married and bore children were more pitied than admired. Being single fostered other problems, since women enjoyed few opportunities to earn a decent living. Professional women were virtually unknown at this time, and the most interesting and financially rewarding occupations generally remained closed to women. Single women often had to live as dependents with their parents or siblings rather than alone. Engaging in a sexual relationship outside marriage was scandalous and always risky. Bearing a child out of wedlock was socially unacceptable for a white woman, bringing shame on herself, her family, and her community. She faced the threat of banishment from church and home. A single woman who discovered she was pregnant might resort to a self-induced abortion rather than face such disgrace. For slave and free black women, the social stigma associated with being single or bearing an out-of-wedlock infant was less severe, for black communities were far more accepting of unmarried women bearing children than were white ones.

Of course, some like Susan B. Anthony never married—either out of choice, an inability to find the right partner, or their sexual orientation. Susan remained a spinster her entire life and spent her final years living with her sister. As a *feme sole*, she had the freedom to lecture, travel, and devote herself to the women's rights movement. Elizabeth and Emily Blackwell, who trained as physicians and later became Lucy's sisters-in-law, never married.

As young women, Lucy and her friend Antoinette Brown vowed not to marry, for they abhorred marriage laws. Both were unique, being among the first women in the nation to earn college degrees, and they had big dreams for their futures, Lucy as a public lecturer and Brown as a preacher. Marriage, they agreed, would undermine their ability to be active, independent women. As Brown wrote Lucy in 1847, "Let us stand alone in the great moral battlefield with none but God for a supporter. . . . Let them see that woman can take care of herself & act independently without the encouragement & sympathy of her 'lord & master,' that she can think & talk as a moral agent is priveleged [*sic*] to. O no dont [*sic*] let us get married." Two years later, Lucy urged her friend to read Edward Mansfield's *Legal Rights, Liabilities and Duties of Women* (1845), a lay guide to legal and civil rights and laws on domestic relations. Despite her vow to remain single, Lucy was ambivalent, admitting that living without the love and companionship of a man would be a sacrifice. "But nothing is so bad as to be made a *thing*, as every married woman now is, in the eye of Law." Lucy hoped that the common law that determined wives' inferior status could be altered, though she doubted this would happen in her lifetime.[25]

Obtaining a divorce during the antebellum period, while not impossible, was rare. The process could be a prolonged and costly undertaking, and its outcome highly unpredictable. Legally ending a marriage required extensive resources, stamina, and supportive family members. Grounds for doing so were limited: bigamy, desertion, an unconsummated relationship, adultery, and sometimes extreme cruelty. There were two levels of divorce. An absolute divorce allowed both parties to remarry; the more common approach was known as a "bed and board" divorce, similar to what today we call a legal separation. This allowed the couple to live apart but not to remarry. Either way, the path was difficult. Ministers and church governing boards sometimes intervened in the domestic relationships of their congregants, punishing members who abandoned their families, committed adultery, or engaged in abusive behavior. Most women in unhappy marriages had no choice but to remain married, often because they lacked the financial means to survive without a husband.[26]

Each state and territory enacted its own laws regarding divorce. For instance, not until after the Civil War and the writing of a new state constitution did South Carolina allow an absolute divorce under any circumstances. Throughout the antebellum period, no married couple living there could sue for divorce. New York was almost as restrictive. In general, it was easier to win an absolute divorce in the New England states than in the South. Southerners clung tightly to the importance of family and blood relations. Ending a marriage was not only about the dissolution of a couple but the undoing of one's place in the white South's well-defined social hierarchy and the severing of important kin ties that marriages created. The historian Thomas Buckley has argued that divorce in the South was generally regarded as a "fundamental assault" on society. Couples were supposed to remain united, survive the trials and tribulations of life, and provide stability for their children. Therefore, extended family members sometimes did everything possible to ensure that a couple, however unhappy, stayed together.[27]

No one could predict what might sway a legislature or judge to award a divorce. Some were sympathetic; others believed that family and patriarchal authority trumped individual happiness and were reluctant to sever that bond.

Even wives who were victims of serious battery or serial adultery might not gain support from a judge. Historians have found cases of severe physical abuse that failed to win anyone's sympathy. Yet, interestingly, a wife was more likely to prevail if a husband committed adultery openly than the other way around. Judges or legislators were less understanding of men whose wives committed adultery because they believed husbands should be able to control their wives and not rely on the courts. But the double standard usually prevailed, and a husband, if he were discreet, might engage in an extramarital relationship without suffering major repercussions. A wife who did the same could unleash serious social consequences. Women were to serve as the moral compasses of their families, and adulterous affairs, if discovered, could make them outcasts. Success in divorce proceedings often depended less on the strength of the evidence than on a person's economic status and family connections. Few women had the resources, knowledge, or time to maneuver the complicated channels of divorce on their own. Couples in unhappy marriages often found other ways to cope by leading separate lives.

No divorce laws or procedures, of course, applied to slave women. While female slaves were the most oppressed of all women in antebellum America, ironically they enjoyed more freedom in their personal relationships than did whites. Since slave marriages were not legally sanctioned (though a majority of slave couples did marry), a relationship could end merely by a spouse's leaving or the couple deciding to live apart. Invariably, slave children, if not sold by their masters, resided with their mothers. Most free black women never considered seeking a legal divorce. The majority could not afford either the time or money to pursue one. The easiest solution was to live apart from their husbands.

Reflecting the nation's patriarchal attitudes, antebellum laws provided some protection to widows after the death of their spouses. Because most wives spent their married lives as dependents, they had little experience earning a living, much less supporting their children. A husband's death could be a major shock and result in a family's economic decline. But under laws known as "dower rights," a wife automatically received a third of her late husband's estate. She could receive more if he so designated that in his will, but she was not to be given less. A widow was allowed to use her dower during her lifetime, though she could not sell her husband's estate. On her death, the estate passed to their children. The dower was a practical legal response to the fact that most men did not write wills, so widows and children might be left without any assurance of support. Communities did not want to be financially responsible for men's dependents, and the dower existed, in part, to relieve them of that obligation.

Familiarity with the laws governing marriage and divorce and understanding how seriously they circumscribed women's lives had an impact on future female reformers. Lucy's Aunt Sally, her maternal grandfather's half sister, lived with the family for several years because her husband had abandoned her and their two sons, leaving them without property or possessions. Lucy's aunt had no recourse but to turn to her extended family, and she lamented her loss and dependency. Another profound lesson Lucy learned about wives' inferior status was witnessing the situation of their neighbors. By all accounts, Mrs. Lamberton was an "excellent" mother, but married to a worthless drunkard who abandoned his wife and children for weeks at a time. Lucy's mother often prepared baskets of food to feed the family. With his pregnant wife's due date nearing, Lamberton left home. Weeks later, her father appeared, determined to rescue his daughter and grandchildren from such tragic circumstances. Lamberton heard of the plan and was there waiting for his father-in-law. He forbade him to take his wife. A confused Lucy asked her mother why a father had no right to intercede and protect his own daughter. Throughout her life, this unhappy scene remained etched in her mind.[28]

Similarly, as a young girl, Elizabeth learned about the many laws that restricted wives. Disturbed by what she learned when reading portions of the *Revised Statutes of the State of New York* in her father's law office, she marked every page on which she found a law that limited the rights of women. Her plan was to cut out these pages, believing that once removed from the *Statutes*, the laws would disappear. When Judge Cady learned of Elizabeth's intentions, he told her that such a scheme would benefit no one, because law offices throughout the state contained copies of the *Statutes*. As an adult, Elizabeth found more effective means to try to reform marriage and divorce laws.[29]

Because women lost claim to all their possessions on marriage and therefore were financially dependent on their husbands, state laws did provide one means to protect their property. Before marrying, some women or their fathers had the foresight to create what was termed a "separate estate" to protect these women's assets on marriage. Separate estates, created through equity courts, set aside a wife's property from future claims that her husband or creditors might make. Widows with financial means who remarried might set up a separate estate to protect what they brought into a subsequent marriage. Occasionally a separate estate was established to protect a wife's property from creditors if the family fell on hard times or if the husband overextended himself. Yet only the well-to-do could afford such legal procedures; the less privileged rarely enjoyed this protection.[30]

Women during the antebellum period could not vote, hold public office, or serve on juries. On the issue of female suffrage, popular sentiment prevailed: voting was a privilege, not a right, of citizenship. Most Americans assumed that women did not need to vote; husbands and fathers would represent them well. On occasion, the issue came up for discussion. For instance, a delegate at the 1829 Virginia State Convention suggested that women be considered the equal of men and be allowed to vote. Another delegate, Samuel Moore, immediately countered that horrifying thought, claiming that although women were the equal of men, they could not vote because they had never demanded that right. And suffrage, he gallantly insisted, was a burden women should not have to bear. "Their interests are so completely identified with our own, that it is impossible that we can make any regulation injuriously affecting their rights," he declared. Did women not have "unlimited confidence in our sex?" he queried rhetorically, perhaps hoping no one would answer.[31] The issue of determining who deserved the right to vote would resonate for decades, as women and African Americans began to see suffrage as central to their rights as citizens. At this point white men were unwilling to relinquish any power.

One significant exception gave women full suffrage rights during the revolutionary and early national periods—at least temporarily. In 1776, New Jersey took the unique step of allowing all inhabitants who owned a certain amount of property and who had lived there for a year the right to vote. Surprisingly, the law did not exclude women, and it passed with little debate. Until 1807, a number of women and African Americans in New Jersey were allowed to vote. While this broad suffrage act remained in effect, the state government did not collapse, women did not adopt masculine traits, and marriages did not dissolve in record numbers, all of which opponents of female suffrage predicted could happen. But in 1807, the state legislature, responding to a case of voter fraud, decided that it was time to restrict voting to white males.

That the world of politics was such a male enclave offered additional rationale to exclude women. Few places were as gender exclusive as the staging area for political elections. Because voting for the most part had always been a male prerogative, saloons, public halls, and even livery stables, where few women dared venture, served as polling places. Election days were rowdy, sometimes even violent. Candidates and their supporters encouraged the free flow of liquor, dispensing drinks to anyone who voted for their party. Men swore and caroused, and on occasion fistfights broke out. Little wonder that most American women had scant desire to venture into this chaotic space dominated by drunken males, much less cast their votes. One of the many arguments activists would later use to demand female suffrage was that their presence would clean up elections and make the process far more decorous.[32]

Finally, central to understanding the pervasiveness of the separate sphere ideology must be an appreciation for the reality of women's lives. One need only read details about the daily existence of most women during the antebellum period to realize how confined, busy, and exhausted they were. In the nineteenth century, all but the most privileged labored constantly without pay. They bore, nurtured, and nursed their children and guided their development. The amount of work they accomplished was staggering. Family laundry could consume an entire day. Cooking over an open fire or on a wood-burning stove to prepare meals for a large family was labor-intensive. Nursing sick children during a time when childhood illnesses were common and often life-threatening meant sleepless nights and days of attentive nursing. The majority of women spent much of their lives at home with their families. Few had time to ponder— much less voice concerns over—gender equality, the rights of citizenship, just laws, and female suffrage.

In addition, a constant worry all Americans faced during this period was the pervasiveness of poor health and its debilitating impact on their lives. Endemic and epidemic diseases were common. Medical and scientific knowledge was rudimentary at best, and the medical profession had little understanding of how to treat and cure most diseases. Medical assessments of a disease or injury were based on physical observation. The most popular treatment that antebellum physicians utilized involved "heroic" medicine, employing medications and methods that would provoke a dramatic reaction in the patient. The "cures" employed, such as leeching, bloodletting, and drugging, often did more harm than good. Until the scientific community discovered the true nature of contagion and sepsis, no one understood bacteria, the importance of cleanliness, and why people became sick. In the first half of the nineteenth century, even the mildest disease or infection could lead to chronic suffering and an early death. Nursing of family members, a task that usually fell to mothers, was constant and demanding. Family correspondence from this period reveals how consumed people were by the task of maintaining their own and their families' physical well-being. Many regarded poor health as a normal state; an extended period free from illness was cause for celebration.

Women faced unique health problems. It is easy to forget that constant childbearing was the norm during this period, and many parturient women experienced traumatic deliveries and little, if any, sound medical attention. For most women, delivery was a harrowing, painful experience. Nearly all women bore their babies at home—an environment that was far cleaner and safer than the nation's few urban hospitals. The majority did little to control their number of pregnancies, and the few known methods of birth control were of limited effectiveness. Though childbirth was risky, most mothers welcomed the birth of each live child. Children were usually considered an asset, especially in farm families, which needed many helping hands. Travelers from abroad confirmed the high fertility rate among American women and the large size of families. According to the 1790 federal census, the average American woman bore slightly more than seven live children. Because miscarriages were fairly common, the number of pregnancies a woman experienced was usually higher. And while women celebrated the birth of any healthy infant, many would have welcomed some control over the number they bore and the spacing between them. Typical was the writer Caroline Dall, who moaned after finding herself pregnant yet again after one full-term pregnancy and one or perhaps two miscarriages in only two and a half years of marriage, "Oh that I could have been spared a little longer!"[33] Most married women could anticipate being pregnant or nursing a baby for twenty to twenty-five years during their prime adult years. Lucretia Mott had six children. Elizabeth Cady Stanton bore seven children and, like many others during this period, experienced at least one miscarriage. On the other hand, Lucy Stone and Abby Kelley Foster, in part because they married in their mid- to late thirties, each had only one child.[34]

Despite widespread acceptance of the doctrine of separate spheres and the severe limitations on women's lives, lines were never rigid. For instance, the ideology had little to no meaning in slave and poor farm families. Most male and female slaves performed field work, and both were constantly subjected to their masters' bidding. Male slaves could claim little power even at home, for they were not their family's principle breadwinners—masters held that position. Female slaves had little time or energy to perform domestic chores in their cabins, and most were denied much quality time to spend with their children. In free black and in many poor white families, both men and women worked hard to make ends meet. Separate spheres also had little meaning to many in rural America, where husbands and wives shared the burdens of farm life.

And positive changes in women's lives were becoming evident, giving a glimmer of hope to some women that their status might improve and the restrictions on their lives might wane. For one thing, expectations about marriage shifted by the early nineteenth century. More young men and women sought marriages based on companionship and love. Parents still might affect the selection of a spouse, but they were losing the influence they once wielded. For instance, Judge Cady strongly objected to Elizabeth's desire to marry Henry Stanton, because beyond his profound interest in politics and antislavery, Henry seemed to have no career plans and, in the judge's eyes, showed little promise of ever earning a steady income. Elizabeth, having broken off their relationship once, went ahead and married Henry anyway.

A growing number of couples began to perceive marriage as a relationship of true equals. Achieving a companionate marriage, which implied some sense of equality between husband and wife, was not necessarily easy during a time when patriarchal ideals remained strong. A wife was supposed to be the dependent partner, the man head of the household. Nevertheless, a few couples rewrote their wedding vows to reflect that ideal. In their wedding ceremonies, Quakers traditionally avoided any words that implied female subservience. A number of reform-minded individuals followed suit. When Elizabeth married in 1840, she removed "obey" from the ceremony. Lucy and the abolitionist Abby Kelley Foster did the same when they wed. The reformer and congressman Robert Dale Owen wrote a marriage contract with his wife Mary Jane Robinson that articulated his view of her as his equal. Owen removed all "relics of a feudal, despotic system" that gave him power over his wife. Most people who knew Lucretia and James Mott regarded their marriage as an example of a loving, companionate relationship. The Motts shared similar ideals, including Quaker values and an abhorrence of slavery. Lucretia later explained that in a true marital union, "there is no assumed authority or admitted inferiority; no promise of obedience. Their independence is equal, their dependence mutual, and their obligations reciprocal." After nearly forty years of marriage, Lucretia maintained that she and James had "loved each other with perfect love." Perhaps it was James who understood the key to their happy marriage, claiming that in the rare instances when they disagreed, "it always turns out that she was right, and I was wrong." Throughout their lives, James supported his wife's reform efforts and public lecturing, even when those put the family in harm's way.[35]

Divorce laws also began to alter, partially due to persistent reformers like Elizabeth and others who saw divorce as key to achieving gender equality. Gradually, divorce proceedings, which had been conducted and heard by state legislatures, became easier as they were moved from the legislatures to the courts, where judges had charge of the cases, simplifying the process and limiting a couple's public exposure. Like a few other positive changes that women experienced, this step was not taken to ease their trauma. State legislatures had become overburdened with too many divorce petitions and acrimonious cases, and politicians felt they had better ways to spend their time. Some lawyers supported the move as well, sensing that politicians had been slighting their cases and ignoring the issues.[36]

The number of divorces rose throughout the antebellum period. Several states revisited the issue of divorce and began to provide additional reasons to sue for divorce and easier methods to succeed. The trend toward companionate marriages also may have affected this increase, because heightened expectations about marriage meant a greater possibility for disappointment, especially among women, who sued for divorce more often than did men. A few judges who ruled on divorce petitions began to pay heed to the good will and happiness of the couple. If a husband and wife were truly miserable or incompatible, it made little sense to maintain the marriage at any cost. For instance, in 1849, Connecticut expanded its laws and allowed judges to grant divorces for any misconduct that "permanently destroys the happiness of the petitioner, and defeats the purpose of the marriage relation."[37] Some midwestern states shortened their residency requirements for obtaining a divorce. Mormons in the Utah Territory were fairly open to divorce, especially when a wife sought one, sustaining their belief in happy marriages to ensure harmonious family life. Interestingly, Mormons were less willing to award husbands a divorce, since under polygamy, men had the option of marrying additional wives.

Another perceptible change for women, though only in a nascent stage at this time, was birth control. Family planning and the ability to control fertility were ideas still foreign to most Americans, and birth control was an issue rarely aired in public. But by mid-century, a growing number of women or couples, especially in the urban Northeast, were engaging in means to control the size of their families.[38] These efforts were having some impact, for by 1850, the federal census showed that the number of live children borne by the average woman had fallen to 5.4. The decline in fertility varied by region. In rural America, where children were an important source of farm labor, families still tended to be large.

One of the most important changes in men's thinking about women was the growing debate over women's marital property rights. By the late 1830s and early 1840s, legislatures in a handful of states and territories considered granting married women rights to their own property and guardianship of their children. The first successful attempt occurred in 1839 in what might seem an unlikely state—Mississippi. The legislature there, however, did not enact its marital property bill out of concern for women. Rather, the new law was meant to protect family property from potential losses due to spendthrift husbands, or, in many cases, wildly fluctuating cotton prices. By establishing a wife's property as separate from a husband's assets, a creditor could not claim that property as payment for her husband's debts, thereby increasing the chances that a family could survive a serious economic downturn.

Other states debated this issue but at this point ultimately were wary of acting. For instance, the Virginia legislature discussed a married woman's property act in the 1840s, but voted it down before the end of the decade, alleging that it might threaten the institution of marriage by giving wives the right to control their own property. A writer for the *Richmond Whig* asserted that a wife's dependence on her husband was sacrosanct, for that relationship "inspires affection, generates confidence, and promotes domestic fidelity." He enumerated the potential horrors that might result if wives had access to their own property. "This invasion of the family circle—this interference between man and wife—between the father and his children—which annihilates that salutary subordination of the one sex to the other...has made American and English women the purest specimens of humanity."[39] To men's thinking, female dependency created the ideal domestic relationship for both husbands and wives.

In New York State, Judge Thomas Hertell, a lawyer, reformer, and state assemblyman, introduced a proposal in 1836 asking that wives have the right to claim their own property. His bill attracted the attention of Ernestine Potoski Rose, a Jewish immigrant from Poland who would become a major force in the women's rights movement. She circulated a petition to gain signatures in support of Hertell's bill. Results were truly disheartening: all of five signatures. At this point, most people opposed—or were indifferent to—such change and refused to sign the petition. Judge Hertell tried again in 1840, and again his proposal met defeat.[40]

Allowing wives to control their property raised an important related question concerning the meaning of citizenship, which helps to explain why this issue fostered such heated debate. The conventional wisdom was that those who owned property were most vested in their government and thus should be able to vote. Those who owned no property should not. Some states required that a man possess a certain amount of property or assets in order to hold public office. Yet some property owners, including women and men who were not white, were not accorded the full rights of citizenship. Women who owned land and therefore had to pay taxes could not vote or hold office. If a wife had the right to her own property and paid taxes to support the government, should she not have the right to vote and participate in that government? At this juncture, an affirmative answer was unthinkable. Many men feared the next step: if wives gained a right to claim their own property and thus became more independent, husbands might lose all control over them. As states began to eliminate property qualifications for male voters, officials developed new rationales for preventing women from claiming the same right, arguing that females were unable to make sound political decisions and that voting threatened femininity and domestic harmony. Legislators also upheld clauses in their state constitutions that specifically designated voters as male.

Another significant change undermining the concept of separate spheres was women's growing presence in the paid labor force. As the nation industrialized and economic opportunities increased, more women, too, left the home to become wage laborers. They earned money by working in textile and shoe factories, sewing piece goods at homes or in urban sweatshops, selling homegrown produce, making hats, working as seamstresses and mantua makers, editing newspapers, teaching, writing books, essays, and poems, and lecturing. Though far more males participated in the wage economy than did females, women were becoming more visible in a number of occupations by the mid-nineteenth century.

Female wage workers were most perceptible in manufacturing; by 1850, they made up nearly a quarter of that labor force. Their presence was particularly evident in the Northeast, which first witnessed the construction of huge textile mills. New factory towns such as Waltham and Lowell, Massachusetts, seemed to spring up overnight as the United States began its transition to the industrial age. The Boston Associates, a group of successful New England businessmen, recognized a lucrative future in the factory system and began to construct textile mills in the 1820s and 1830s. To meet the demand for laborers, they hired native-born, middle-class farm girls from the region. Factory owners created unique communities for these young women, promising to preserve morality by housing them in protected, all-female environments. An older female supervisor lived in each multistoried dormitory they constructed, to maintain security and ensure proper behavior. The girls had strict rules and curfews to observe. They were expected to attend church on Sunday, the one day of the week when they did not have to work. Traveling lecturers occasionally visited factory communities to enlighten the workers. Some girls attended night classes. Young women in Lowell even created, wrote, and published their own newspaper, the *Lowell Offering* (1840–1845). Females were vital to the early success of these factories; single women made up the largest percentage of workers in all northeastern textile factories. The girls earned $1.50 to $3.00 per week, about the same pay a female schoolteacher received.[41]

Initially, factory girls found the work appealing and the opportunity to earn money exciting. Most had never had their own spending money or lived in settings beyond their homes. Many felt a sense of pride, for example, in sending wages home to help support their families, buying their own clothes, or paying a brother's tuition. Living among like-minded young women opened a new world to them. Close, often intimate, female friendships that were typical of the time developed in these dormitory settings. Initially the labor system proved fairly flexible, and a number of girls went in and out of the factories, working for several months there and then living at home or teaching school, moving back and forth between two worlds.

But as the years passed and the number of textile factories increased, competition intensified. The labor system became more restrictive and demanding. In order to maintain a profit, factory owners had to cut corners. They forced laborers to work longer hours and oversee more machines. They instituted a bonus system that rewarded male supervisors who increased the productivity of employees working under them. Some young women joined forces to challenge these injustices, objecting to their low pay and deteriorating work conditions. In 1824, girls in Pawtucket, Rhode Island, protested a reduction in their wages, as did female mill workers four years later in Dover, New Hampshire. Efforts to win a ten-hour workday in Pittsburgh achieved mixed results: owners decreased work hours but then cut workers' pay. In 1834 and again in 1836, hundreds of young women in Lowell went on strike to protest wage cuts that brought no commensurate reduction in what they paid for room and board. The girls' protest ultimately made little difference other than to give them a slightly longer lunch break. They struck again in the 1840s. Such responses revealed their shared concerns and a determination to improve their situation, a forerunner to the powerful labor movement late in the century. Their protests at this juncture ultimately proved ineffective, since factory owners had the upper hand and saw no reason to offer concessions. More important, the composition of the workforce shifted dramatically. Immigrants from Ireland and central Europe, who were coming in droves to the United States in the 1840s, moved into factory jobs, grateful to find work and willing to labor for low wages. They and their children began to replace middle-class farm girls in the workplace. By 1860, Irish women made up nearly a quarter of the nation's mill workforce.[42]

One must remember, however, that women rarely took paid jobs to advance themselves in lucrative careers. Inevitably, they received unequal treatment. Wages women earned were well below what men were paid for the same work. A female factory worker, even with years of experience, earned less than her male coworkers, and she could never ascend to a position of responsibility or one in which she supervised male employees. In addition, women were excluded from the most rewarding or esteemed professions such as law, medicine, the military, and the ministry, and from jobs deemed inappropriate for women. Such situations made a number of women increasingly troubled by unequal treatment and limited opportunities. Demands for fair wages and greater job prospects would become major issues at Seneca Falls.

Finally, one of the most profound, long-term changes in women's lives was the growing interest in education. During the colonial period, education was seen as useful for males but as having limited bearing on females, who, presumably, were going to devote their futures to raising children and managing their households. Those girls who did learn to read and write often were taught by family members or by attending a summer school or what was called a "dame school." Daughters in elite families might be sent abroad to a finishing school or be instructed by a private tutor or governess.

In the years following the American Revolution, people began to show a genuine interest in female education and to promote its importance. In this period, arguments to augment women's schooling focused on the importance of motherhood. If mothers were to raise their children (i.e., sons) properly and serve as their first instructors, they needed to be schooled, at least in the basics. An education would also make them better companions for their husbands. A popular female essayist and author of the early national period, Judith Sargent Murray, argued that if the new nation was going to survive and thrive, women needed a sound education. In her 1790 essay "On the Equality of the Sexes," Murray insisted that differences between the sexes were not innate, as many people believed, but the result of the superior education males received. Better-educated women could play a central role in the new nation. Murray subscribed wholeheartedly to the concept of republican motherhood. If the United States was to serve as a model democratic republic, Murray asserted, it had to educate both men and women.[43]

The British writer Mary Wollstonecraft was the most famous advocate of female education and women's rights in the early national period. In her *Vindication of the Rights of Woman*, first published in England and then in the United States in 1792 and widely read and discussed in both, she declared that women could best serve their families, communities, and country if accorded equal rights, including access to the same education available to men. They needed to be equal partners with men and operate under the same laws. She insisted, "If she be not prepared by education to become the companion of man, she will stop the progress of knowledge and virtue, for truth must be common to all." A number of Americans read and admired Wollstonecraft's writings. Lucretia called this work "my pet book," recognizing this brilliant woman as far ahead of her time. She expressed with "great moral courage" the rights all women deserved, Lucretia asserted.[44] Such ideas began to have a greater impact as more people recognized the importance of educated women.

During the antebellum period, common schools in lower grades were often coeducational, but academies and seminaries for older students were typically single sex. Most people thought it imperative to separate boys and girls in the classroom once they passed early childhood. One of the earliest and most notable female schools founded in the late eighteenth century was the Young Ladies' Academy of Philadelphia, which opened in 1787. Men established it, ran it, and taught there, but they were determined to provide girls with a rigorous education. Its founders included the physician, writer, and politician Benjamin Rush, who wrote an essay entitled "Thoughts upon Female Education" in 1787, insisting that women needed to be well prepared for their central role: raising and educating their children and instructing sons "in the principles of liberty and government."[45] This school offered a substantial curriculum to develop female intellectual abilities. Salem Academy, founded in Winston-Salem, North Carolina, in 1772 by Moravians who held strong beliefs in education, was another example of a successful female academy. It became a boarding school in the early nineteenth century, attracting girls from across the nation with its demanding curriculum and exceptional art and music programs. A number of dame schools offered a less demanding curriculum that focused on basics, providing some academic courses but also classes in the fine and domestic arts, aimed at women's future roles as mothers and, ideally, as ladies.

But even as the idea of educating women became more accepted, not everyone embraced this concept as part of the natural order. Some Americans remained unconvinced that women were men's intellectual equals, and they objected to the idea of educating them to the same degree as men. For example, a writer for the *Southern Quarterly Review* noted, "They are physically unable to tax their mental organs as severely, and as continuously as men.... The application of women to study can neither be so intense, nor of such duration, as that of men."[46] The female brain was allegedly less developed. Many deemed women frivolous, unable to perform well in an academic setting, and unable to reason. Battles still had to be fought to gain widespread support for the equal education of women.

By the mid-nineteenth century, the United States would witness a dramatic increase in the number of middle- and upper-class white females attending school, and a significant increase in both female literacy and the number of academies opening to meet that need. As women began to awaken to the intellectual challenges of an education, they yearned for more. They longed to live in a world that put them on an equal footing with men. Their exposure to new ideas and an exciting array of academic courses gave them entry into a larger, more rewarding world beyond their homes. It is little wonder that Lucretia, Elizabeth, Lucy, Susan, and other leaders of the women's rights movement were well educated and continued to engage in intellectual pursuits throughout their lives. They regarded education as a critical step in women's fight for equality. Advancing female education to be on a par with what was available for men would become a major issue at Seneca Falls and beyond.

In the early years of the antebellum period, women existed in a society that heralded them as angels in the home but treated them legally, politically, and socially as second-class citizens. Yet a few positive changes began to uplift women's lives and open new opportunities. Increasing public discussion of such issues as education, marital property rights, and easier access to divorce engendered in some women's minds the hope that they might enjoy the full rights of citizenship and all the opportunities available to men. By mid-century, Lucretia, Elizabeth, Lucy, Susan, and others would begin to ponder how they might change their world, improve the legal status of all women, and develop women's public voice. To this end, despite significant hurdles, by the second quarter of the nineteenth century a growing number of women began to participate in benevolent and reform efforts. They began to work to improve and transform institutions, challenge injustices, and rectify wrongs. As they engaged in reform movements, they turned their dreams and frustrations into tools for fashioning a better world.

2

FASHIONING A
BETTER WORLD

From childhood, Lucretia Mott absorbed the ideals of human equality. "Among Quakers there had never been any talk of woman's rights—it was simply human rights," she observed.[1] Throughout most of her adult life, this demure but determined activist fought against injustice. A principal organizer and the most famous participant at the Seneca Falls Convention, she was one of the first women to speak out publicly on the causes of antislavery and women's rights. Like thousands of Americans during the antebellum period, her commitment and actions were part of a larger movement to reform and improve the nation.

Lucretia was born on Nantucket Island in January 1793, the second of five children of Thomas and Anna Coffin. She developed a loathing of slavery as a child when she heard and read about the horrors of slavery at home, in Quaker meetings, and in school. As for the injustices females faced, Lucretia later recalled, "I grew up so thoroughly imbued with woman's rights that it was the most important question of my life from a very early day." On Nantucket, "the Women have long been regarded as the stronger part—This is owing in some measure to so many of the men being away at sea." Her father was often absent from home on long whaling voyages. Thus, her mother made most of the family decisions, ran a small shop, and purchased everything needed to run both home and business. Quakers were unique in believing in coeducation. Girls like Lucretia and her younger sister Martha (who would also play a role in the movement) considered themselves the intellectual equals of boys. When the Mott family moved to Boston in 1804, Lucretia attended the coeducational Nine Partners School, near Poughkeepsie in Dutchess County, New York.[2]

Lucretia Coffin Mott,
1879 (Sophia Smith
Collection, Smith College)

After completing her schooling, Lucretia worked as an assistant teacher at Nine Partners. Here she met James Mott, a grandson of the school's superintendent. They married in 1811, vowing, following Quaker fashion, to be "true and loving," and denying any hint of female obedience. They settled in Philadelphia. Over the next sixteen years, Lucretia bore six children (five of whom lived to adulthood) while James worked as a wholesale merchant. The Motts, like a number of Quakers, participated in the Free Produce Movement, whose followers refused to consume any product produced by slave labor. Because they eschewed sugar and cotton, James changed his mercantile trade from cotton to wool. Lucretia taught part-time at a local Quaker school. In 1818, she began to speak at Quaker meetings and three years later had become an influential Quaker minister. James supported her activities and growing prominence.[3]

Lucretia was one of the most respected and best-known women of her day, speaking passionately when riled but genteel in her everyday demeanor. Her intimate knowledge of the Bible allowed her to counter ministers who often cited scripture to support the subordination of women. Lucretia began to travel and address audiences on abolition. Her extemporaneous speeches were, it was said, memorable. The former slave Frederick Douglass first heard her speak in Lynn, Massachusetts, and recalled, "In a few moments after she began to speak, I saw before me no more a woman, but a glorified presence, bearing a message of light and love." Douglass found Lucretia's thoughts inspiring. "Whenever and wherever I have listened to her, my heart has always been made better and my spirit raised by her words." But Lucretia also stirred controversy, especially when she delivered her antislavery message to mixed audiences of men and women. At one point an angry mob threatened to set fire to the Mott home.[4]

Lucretia was merely one of many Americans who made their marks during an exciting period in this nation's history. Cries for reform were pervasive, and more and more Americans dedicated themselves to rectifying society's ills. Ralph Waldo Emerson observed this in 1841, commenting that "in the history of the world, the doctrine of Reform had never such scope as at the present hour."[5] Optimism and a belief in human agency motivated many Americans to try to uplift society, for its many inequities and social problems seemed at odds with the tenets of a democratic nation. Individuals and organizations sought to perfect human behavior, end injustice, and improve the nation's institutions. Lucretia's efforts on behalf of women's rights and abolishing slavery reflected this commitment to reform. The Seneca Falls Convention of 1848 fit within this larger world of upheaval and reform.

The United States was only one among several nations experiencing social and political upheaval in the first half of the nineteenth century. This was evident to Elizabeth Cady Stanton when she first visited England in 1840 and found the world to be "in a general hubbub."[6] Chartists in England led massive protests demanding broader male suffrage. Revolutions wracked several European nations in the late 1840s and early 1850s. In France, political unrest led to the removal of King Louis Philippe in 1848, the adoption of universal male suffrage, and the formation of a short-lived democratic republic. Uprisings in Austria, Prussia, the Germany Confederation, and Italy challenged the old order, inspiring calls for constitutional revisions and mass political participation. In 1848, Karl Marx wrote *Das Capital*.

The year 1848 was especially momentous in the United States. In January 1848, gold was discovered at Sutter's Mill in California. People worldwide caught "gold fever" and journeyed to the California foothills, hoping to make their fortunes. A devastating cholera epidemic hit the country in December, killing thousands of Americans over the next few years. And 1848 marked the end of the United States's two-year war with Mexico. The Treaty of Guadalupe Hidalgo ending that conflict gave the nation vast new territory in the west, expanding the size of the country by a third and extending its borders coast to coast. These new land acquisitions from Mexico, however, reignited debates over slavery and whether it should be permitted to spread to western territories and states. Within a few years, civil war would convulse the country over that question.

The United States also faced a plethora of concerns that demanded attention, though these were hardly new. Since the founding of the colonies, Americans had tried to address human depravity and rectify social and economic ills. What characterized antebellum attempts at reform, however, was the heightened level of commitment and the number of people and voluntary organizations engaged in these efforts. By the 1830s, industrialization, immigration, and urbanization were transforming the nation and creating unprecedented social problems. Cities seemed to be riddled with violence, crime, and disease. Immigrants pouring into the country often arrived ill and impoverished, bringing with them unfamiliar languages and customs. Their very presence challenged Americans' sense of identity, community, and strong Protestant roots. The absence of institutions to care adequately for the needy, the infirm, the physically impaired, and the illiterate worried others.[7]

A groundswell of religious enthusiasm, faith, and an accompanying message that religious duty demanded social engagement encouraged Americans to work to address the nation's problems. A major religious revival, the Second Great Awakening, took hold of the country in the early nineteenth century, sparking an intensity of faith and excitement that lasted for decades. Huge throngs participated in revivals and camp meetings. At these gatherings, a dozen or more ministers representing different denominations would deliver impassioned sermons, pray, proselytize, and exhort listeners to recognize their sinfulness, repent, experience a personal rebirth, and commit their lives to God. At camp meetings, which often lasted a week or longer, participants listened, prayed, sang, and often became physically agitated, even convulsed, as the spirit moved them. To an uninitiated observer, such scenes could be alarming. The British traveler Frances Trollope witnessed several revivals and camp meetings, including one in Indiana where she observed "hysterical sobbings, convulsive groans, shrieks, and screams." So violent were the physical manifestations that Trollope feared serious accidents might occur.[8] But revivals not only strengthened individual faith but proved a boon to organized religion, leading to a significant increase in the number of conversions and in Protestant church membership. Over time, camp meetings found a more formal, subdued expression through what were known as "protracted meetings," which were common up through the Civil War and continue to occur even today.

The perfectibility of humankind was a critical subtext of the Second Great Awakening. With enough human energy directed at addressing a problem, a solution seemed possible. Ministers urged parishioners to demonstrate the depth of their faith and reach out to help the needy and less fortunate. Some converts dreamed of the millennium and Christ's return to earth. To prepare for that moment, the world had to be free from sin and misery—a belief that encouraged people to participate in benevolent acts to rid the country of its social and economic problems. Whatever the motivation, the shared objective was to improve the human condition and fashion a better world so that the United States could serve as a beacon to other nations.

The Second Great Awakening had its greatest impact in the Northeast, especially in upstate New York. This area was so consumed by religious revivals that it became known as the "Burned-Over District." One of the most famous and charismatic ministers of the Second Great Awakening, Charles Grandison Finney, experienced a powerful religious rebirth and vowed to devote his life to God. In the mid-1820s, he held his first successful revivals in upstate New York. For years thereafter, he delivered his evangelical message to crowds in the Midwest, the Northeast, and abroad. He converted thousands by using direct, emotional language to emphasize God's love, the importance of conversion, and humans' capacity to conquer sin. A major theme in his sermons was individuals' responsibility to engage in benevolent acts.[9]

Two unique expressions of faith arose in New England and in this area of upstate New York. The minister William Miller attracted tens of thousands of believers (known as Millerites) by predicting Christ's second coming, thanks in part to clever promoters who distributed millions of pamphlets promoting Miller's ideas and sent out agents to publicize his findings. Using scripture, Miller calculated that Christ's return to earth would occur by March 1844, leading people nationwide to spend months anticipating the second coming. When March 1844 came and went, Miller admitted errors, reworked his calculations, and offered another prediction for October 1844. Mary Sherwood Bull of Seneca Falls heard Miller preach and remembered the moment. Local citizens fashioned special robes in which to ascend to Heaven. As she and her sister prepared for bed on the night Miller predicted Christ's coming, they asked their mother to wake them in order to "see the end of the world," believing it would "be more fun than a big fire." More illustrious individuals, including the reformers Angelina Grimké Weld and Sojourner Truth, also embraced Miller's beliefs. Of course, nothing happened that fall, and disillusioned believers turned their attention elsewhere.[10]

Far more successful was the Church of Jesus Christ of Latter-day Saints, or the Mormon Church, founded by Joseph Smith, only miles from Seneca Falls. While a young man, Smith experienced both a religious awakening and a "supernatural" experience. In 1823, he reported that the Angel Moroni appeared before him and told him of golden tablets hidden on a nearby hillside, which he later retrieved and translated in secret. These became the Book of Mormon, published in 1830. Smith attracted a number of followers but also stirred up uneasiness among locals who objected to his self-proclaimed ability to receive direct divine revelations and his defiance of local laws. Detractors forced Smith and his followers out of the region, and Mormons began a series of moves westward, seeking an earthly kingdom where they could practice their faith in peace. Smith experienced new revelations, including one in 1842 that allowed Mormons to practice polygamy. When Smith and his brother were killed by a mob in Carthage, Illinois, in 1844, Brigham Young became the sect's new leader. A revelation directed Young to lead Mormons across the country to the Great Salt Lake in Utah. There, through faith and a strong work ethic, they turned the desert into a thriving community.

A growing number of Americans experimented with other ways to cope with their changing, problematic world by seeking alternative lifestyles through communitarian living. Especially popular during the second quarter of the nineteenth century were intentional, or utopian, communities, which offered a means to live communally and adopt new values and codes of behavior. Each one promised an opportunity to lead a more fulfilling, perhaps even perfect, life far beyond the constraints of mainstream society. Typically, leaders of these communities were charismatic individuals inspired by a unique approach to religious or economic principles.

One communitarian society, the Shakers, established themselves in small villages and followed the teachings of the Englishwoman Sister Ann Lee. She envisioned herself as a female Christ figure and believed that evil in the world stemmed from sexual intercourse. Shakers, also known as Shaking Quakers, received their name from a ritual dance they performed. Men and women lived separately and practiced sexual abstinence, making the life of any Shaker community dependent on attracting new recruits. Despite their unusual beliefs, Shakers were an industrious group who thrived on a successful seed business. Some women, including an acquaintance of Lucy Stone, found the Shaker community a welcome escape from constant childbearing and sexually aggressive husbands.

Another well-known utopian society was the Oneida Community in upstate New York, founded by John Humphrey Noyes in the 1840s. In his search for perfection, Noyes advocated male sexual restraint, complex marriages, mutual criticism, eugenic breeding, and communal labor. Oneida is best known today for its flatware, but in the mid-nineteenth century, Noyes's radical ideas on marriage and sexuality alarmed mainstream Americans. Nevertheless, Oneida survived for more than thirty years, making it one of the nation's most successful communitarian societies. Brook Farm, a Transcendentalist social experiment in West Roxbury, Massachusetts, never achieved much success as a residential community, despite its famous supporters, including Bronson Alcott, Margaret Fuller, Henry David Thoreau, Elizabeth Peabody, and Ralph Waldo Emerson. The Brook Farm residents seemed to emphasize intellectual pursuits as much as they did hard work. Nonetheless, Elizabeth Cady Stanton was impressed when she visited Brook Farm, calling the community a "charming family of intelligent men and women." It peaked at about one hundred members, but was never more than marginally successful. When a fire destroyed its main building in 1846 and funding dried up, the community collapsed.[11]

New faiths and unique lifestyles were only two responses to the unsettled times. Some Americans became more open to new ideas. For instance, many had become disillusioned with mainstream medicine and its adherence to what were known as "heroic" practices. Medicine was still quite primitive; medical education often of questionable worth. Many people preferred to take charge of their own health rather than put themselves in the hands of a physician. Elizabeth was one such skeptic. While pregnant with her first baby, she wrote, "I have commenced the study of medicine. Having a great horror of both medical & theological quacks, I have come to the conclusion to take care of my own soul & body. I am examining Homeopathy."[12] For much of her adult life, especially while raising her children, she relied on her own good sense and alternative practices rather than doctors' standard treatments. Similarly, others preferred medical options such as herbal cures, hydropathy, and homeopathy. New approaches to diet also attracted a following, and a number of advisors— as well as some quacks—took advantage of this (and a gullible public) and promoted their "sure-fire" answers to good health, including Dr. Sylvester Graham's key to a healthful diet, his "graham" cracker.

Spiritualism, phrenology, and mesmerism also became popular, reflecting curiosity about the mysteries of human behavior and the unknown. Spiritualism, which held that the dead could communicate with the living through a medium, attracted a number of prominent Americans, including the reformers Wendell Phillips, Abby Kelley and Stephen Foster, Amy Post, Horace Greeley, the Grimké sisters, and the first lady, Mary Todd Lincoln. Two famous spiritualists, the sisters Kate and Maggie Fox of upstate New York, conducted public séances, duping and enrapturing audiences with tappings and knockings that allegedly were communications from the dead.[13] Phrenology was another fad, based on the belief that the measurements, bumps, and indentations of the cranial structure allowed one to understand a person's personality and behavior. Lucretia, Elizabeth, and Wendell Phillips evidenced a profound interest in phrenology. Lucretia attended lectures, read material on the subject, and for years corresponded with George Combe, a well-known Scottish phrenologist who undertook a study of her head.[14] In 1853, Elizabeth visited "Fowler and Wells' Phrenological Cabinet" in New York City, where Orson Fowler scrutinized her skull and wrote an exhaustive report detailing her character. She sent the report to her parents, obviously pleased because it often "hit the nail on the head." During a period of rudimentary scientific knowledge and little understanding of human behavior, this primitive form of psychology seemed as credible as anything else.[15]

Of course, most people did not join a utopian community or embrace a unique religious sect or medical alternatives. Instead, by the second quarter of the nineteenth century, a growing number of concerned Americans turned their energy to benevolent work and social activism. Many—at least among the privileged—found they now had the free time to do so. The nation's industrial revolution and market economy meant that the self-sufficient household was becoming a thing of the past. Families could purchase factory-loomed cloth, soap, milled flour, candles, bread, and shoes, giving many adults, especially women, time to pursue activities beyond the home. Thus it makes sense that a striking characteristic of antebellum reform was the number of women it attracted. Imbued with a desire to improve society, they devoted themselves to various causes. Such activism came naturally. Mothers had long been held responsible for ensuring the moral well-being of their families. Improving their community or righting an injustice was merely an extension of that responsibility.

Women, like men, established their own voluntary organizations to address particular problems, such as illiteracy, poor health, and poverty. They founded and funded schools for the poor and tried to assist destitute widows, orphaned children, and the physically impaired. In the nation's port cities, women established seamen's aid societies to assist lonely sailors. In many towns and cities, a Female (or Ladies') Charitable Society, such as the one organized in Morristown, New Jersey, in 1813, aided the "colored," the "Irish," and "our own people." Women also formed societies for self-improvement to advance their intellectual interests. They joined sewing circles to make clothing and linens for the poor.[16]

Benevolent work brought personal rewards to its practitioners, giving women socially acceptable outlets through which to participate in the public arena and to work and socialize with like-minded persons. They organized and ran their own meetings, lectured in public, and raised and budgeted money. They began to use the written word purposefully, keeping detailed minutes of their meetings, expressing their opinions in essays, petitions, letters, and reports sent to agencies and governmental bodies, and writing for and editing newspapers. Some, like Lydia Maria Child and Harriet Beecher Stowe, took their literary talents a step further and wrote books that changed people's thinking forever.[17]

Ministers encouraged female volunteerism, especially in activities centered around the church such as Bible study and prayer groups, maternal associations, and missionary organizations at home and abroad. Women organized and taught Sunday schools. They held bazaars and produced handcrafted items to raise money for worthy causes. Free black women in northeastern cities organized literary societies and benevolent associations through their churches and conducted charitable work for the needy. For instance, the Colored Female Religious and Moral Reform Society of Salem, Massachusetts, started in 1818, focused on mutual aid and self-help within the black community. These volunteer organizations imbued women with a sense that they were contributing to a greater good.

This interest in societal reform was most active in the Northeast and in urban areas farther west. While southern cities like Charleston, New Orleans, and Petersburg, Virginia, could boast of a number of benevolent societies that addressed poverty, intemperance, illiteracy, and depravity, the South's dispersed settlements often made it difficult for the region's largely rural population to gather and work for particular causes. And people in the South showed little willingness to alter their society's social structure, though not because the region was any closer to perfection than elsewhere. Slavery profoundly affected southerners' response to reform. Had white southerners taken a good, hard look, they would have identified slavery as the region's—and nation's—most glaring injustice. But most white southerners, whether or not they owned slaves, focused on the profits and prosperity slave labor brought their region. Any undertaking that threatened their "sacred institution" was shunned. By the early 1830s, especially after Nat Turner's bloody slave uprising in Virginia in 1831 and northern abolitionists' increasingly strident activism, southern whites became more defensive about slavery and their way of life. Tampering with any southern institution became suspect.

Americans identified the cities as the seedbeds for most of the nation's ills. Concentrated urban populations made problems more visible and thus stirred uneasiness. For those who subscribed to Thomas Jefferson's vision of a nation made up of hard-working farmers, rapid urban growth and the rise of industry were deeply troubling developments. For instance, Lowell, Massachusetts, which had not even existed in 1800, had nearly forty thousand residents by 1860. The same year, greater New York City boasted a million inhabitants, and Philadelphia reached a half million. Cities farther west—Chicago, Cincinnati, St. Louis, and San Francisco—attracted tens of thousands of people seeking a new life. Adding to this urban growth were many farm families who migrated to cities, drawn by opportunities for jobs and a more stimulating life.

Yet urban growth fostered problems, and concerned Americans blamed this on a decline in the nation's morals. In cities, prostitutes brazenly walked the streets, hung out in taverns and dance halls, and serviced clients in gaudy brothels. In 1832, a survey conducted by the minister John McDowall revealed that New York City was home to some ten thousand prostitutes, confirming what people feared.[18] Hundreds of Chinese women who were transported to California in the 1850s were enslaved as prostitutes to service the largely male population of the West. In response to this widespread problem, alarmed citizens began to organize moral reform societies. They tried to confine prostitutes to certain areas of towns or to close all brothels outright. Female reformers tackled the double standard by also holding men accountable. They threatened to stand outside brothels, write down names of anyone who frequented them, and publish the names in local papers. Members of the New York Female Moral Reform Society, established in 1834, visited brothels and jails, prayed and read scripture to arrested prostitutes, distributed Bibles, and raised money to establish homes where prostitutes could take refuge from life on the street and perhaps learn requisite skills to pursue other occupations.

Another means to address the nation's ills that captured widespread attention was education. Significant strides were made in the antebellum period to establish more private and public schools for both boys and girls. Horace Mann, who served as secretary of the Massachusetts Board of Education for twelve years, played a key role in these efforts. He promoted the radical idea that states had a responsibility to provide funding for public schools in order to educate all children, rich and poor alike. His "Report of the Massachusetts School Board," sent annually to the legislature beginning in 1838, called on the state to ensure all children access to a decent education. Some people dismissed his idea of educating the poor, who allegedly would have little use for anything beyond basic literacy, but others welcomed Mann's ideas. A rudimentary education would expose all children not only to academic courses but also to lessons in morals and good manners.[19]

Of special relevance to the beginning of the women's movement was the growing interest in female education, leading to the founding of hundreds of female academies and seminaries during the antebellum period and a significant rise in female literacy. A typical curriculum in female academies included modern languages, English, grammar, history, botany, chemistry, geography, natural philosophy, algebra, geometry, and courses in the fine and domestic arts. Classes in Latin and Greek taught at some seminaries duplicated what the finest boys' schools offered. Though most Americans justified female education as a means to enhance the maternal role, the educational experience had unanticipated consequences, opening young women's eyes to a larger, more intellectually exciting world. Demanding access to higher education would be a major theme at Seneca Falls and subsequent conventions, for well-educated women's rights leaders were all too aware of the disparity between their own educational attainments and the legal and political oppression most women endured.[20]

A number of women deserve credit for fostering the expansion of female schooling during this period. The educator and writer Catharine Beecher, the oldest sibling in the influential Beecher clan, spent much of her life advancing education. With her sister Mary, she founded the Hartford Female Seminary in 1823, and several years later, Cincinnati's Western Female Institute, which not only offered an excellent education but sought to bring New England values to this western city. Her dream was to train young women to become teachers who would work primarily in the West. Although she remained single all her life, Beecher felt well qualified to advise women on how to enhance their maternal skills. To her thinking, a sound education was vital to mothers' positive influence over their children. Though her interest in these issues was heartfelt, Beecher displayed little tolerance for assertive women who abandoned their assigned sphere to demand greater rights in public.[21]

Another influential educator, Emma Hart Willard, founded the Troy Female Seminary in Troy, New York, in 1821, known today as the Emma Willard School. She taught school for several years before marrying. When her husband lost nearly all his savings in a bank robbery, Willard opened a boarding school for girls. Her goal was to offer courses that matched those in the top male academies. In 1819, she lobbied the New York state legislature for funding, arguing that the state had an obligation to educate both males and females. "It is through the mothers, that the government can control the characters of its future citizens," she maintained.[22] Unmoved by her appeal, the legislature never allocated her the money. But with the completion of the Erie Canal in 1825 and bright prospects for the region's future, the town of Troy pledged Willard funding for her new school, and she set to work. Students at her seminary pursued rigorous courses in solid geometry, Latin, and physiology. Willard encouraged graduates to teach in other girls' academies and establish their own schools based on the Troy model. Elizabeth was one of the seminary's most famous alumnae; she attended for two years and graduated in 1832. Though she apparently experienced periods of boredom and disliked the all-female environment, Elizabeth later called Willard one of the most "remarkable" women of the age and recognized the intellectual and social impact her seminary had on females.[23]

Another ground-breaking school was Mount Holyoke Female Seminary, founded by Mary Lyon and opened in November 1837. Lyon had taught at several schools from the time she was in her teens. Emboldened by a profound religious transformation, she decided to establish her own school based on Christian principles. Lyon spent four years soliciting funds and seeking a site for her school. Town fathers in South Hadley, Massachusetts, sensing that such an institution could enhance their community, offered her $8,000 to establish her school there. With eighty students enrolled on opening day, Lyon's experiment in offering both domestic arts and challenging academic courses proved a success. Many students boarded on campus, relishing the all-female environment. Lyon created demanding admission standards and laid out a three-year course of study. She oversaw the curriculum, wrote several textbooks, and, until her premature death in 1849, served as principal. One of Mount Holyoke's most famous students was Lucy, who attended for one semester.[24]

By the 1830s and 1840s, efforts to expand women's schooling began to enjoy remarkable results. Unlike the reticent New York legislature, Pennsylvania lawmakers recognized the importance of female education and beginning in 1838 agreed to provide start-up funds to establish women's academies throughout the state. Several schools opened with the aid of that money. The Greenville Female Academy in South Carolina was founded with the assistance of state support. Churches, communities, and individuals put up money to found scores of women's academies, which varied in size and course offerings. Some were managed and taught by a single proprietor, with a few pupils drawn from the immediate vicinity, often boarding in the teacher's home. Others were more substantial. Catholics founded a number of female academies in Louisiana, Kentucky, and Maryland. The Methodist Church was especially active in fostering female education. In 1839, in Macon, for instance, it opened the Georgia Female College, which claimed to be the first state-chartered school to offer women a college degree.[25]

While coed colleges were almost nonexistent before the Civil War, a handful of schools experimented with this radical idea. The first college to commit to coeducation—and to accept black students—was Oberlin Collegiate Institute, founded in Ohio in 1833 by the Congregational Church. Four years after opening, the school began to accept a few women. Many heralded the practical benefits of this decision, for coeducation saved money by using the same facilities for men and women. Supporters like Horace Mann waxed positive on this approach, which he believed would "work both moral restraint and intellectual excitement."[26] He dismissed critics who argued that women would distract men students, insisting instead that they would enhance the total school experience. But coeducation did not upend all traditional ideas about gender. In October 1857, while president of the coed Antioch College, Mann refused to allow senior women the use of the school's chapel to demonstrate their oratorical skills before the public.[27] Oberlin administrators also clung to conservative notions and treated male and female students differently. As Lucy discovered while there, the school discouraged women from engaging in "unladylike" behavior and prohibited female students from speaking in public. Thus, she was denied the honor of reading aloud her prize-winning essay at commencement. Nor did Oberlin permit Antoinette Brown to earn a degree in theology, a field closed to women. Nonetheless, Lucy's years at Oberlin proved stimulating, and throughout her life, she argued that everyone should pursue the same course of study in coed schools. She criticized classes that only prepared women for motherhood. Colleges should offer everyone the same courses, "and after that it is at their option what they will choose."[28]

A few other institutions experimented with coeducation, such as Genesee Wesleyan Seminary and New York Central College, which opened or became coed in the 1850s, but in general, this experiment advanced slowly. People began to accept the fact that women were intellectually men's equals, but were less sure about the value of higher education for them. Some critics expressed uneasiness about men and women sitting together in the same classroom. Others dismissed higher education for women as a waste of time. Not until after the Civil War did institutions and universities, especially out west, become coeducational. It was well into the twentieth century before most private colleges and universities finally erased gender barriers.

Among this era's four principal women's rights activists, the only one to achieve her dream of a college education was Lucy, though it took years for her to earn her degree. After attending local schools as a youngster, she began teaching when she was sixteen and attended school intermittently as funds allowed. She learned about Mary Lyon's new female seminary and decided to attend, but her father refused to pay her tuition, insisting that his daughter needed no more schooling. So Lucy earned the money by teaching. She enrolled at Mount Holyoke in April 1839. Already, she held firm beliefs about women's rights and abolition and found that Lyon, despite her commitment to female

Lucy Stone (Sophia Smith Collection, Smith College)

education, had little tolerance for such radical ideas. Lyon wished to instill in her students the skills they needed to become good wives and mothers, or "man's helper, not his equal," as she put it. Lucy believed on the other hand that "for herself alone, woman should receive the highest mental cultivation of which she is capable." While at Mount Holyoke, Lucy began speaking on abolition and left copies of the radical antislavery newspaper the *Liberator* in the school's reading room. When Lyon discovered Lucy's actions, she condemned this inappropriate behavior.[29]

The following year, Lucy learned of three women who had graduated from Oberlin Collegiate Institute, and she decided to do the same. Her parents again objected. Oberlin had a reputation as a hotbed of controversy, due in part to its firebrand minister, Charles Finney, and its stance on abolition. This was exactly what Lucy wanted. Now twenty-five, she arrived at Oberlin in 1843, joining six other women and some five hundred male students. Despite its liberal reputation, the institution did not share Lucy's ardent views on abolition and female equality, and she soon stood out for her assertiveness and unshakeable belief in human equality. When Antoinette Brown enrolled at Oberlin during Lucy's third year, a school trustee warned her about Lucy—"a very bright girl, but eccentric, a Garrisonian, and much too talkative on the subject of woman's rights."[30]

Brown had enjoyed a far easier path to achieve her educational dreams. Born in 1825 in Henrietta, New York, one of ten children, she started school when she was only three, encouraged by parents with a deep faith and strong

Antoinette Brown Blackwell
(Oberlin College Archives,
Oberlin, Ohio)

antislavery sentiments. Brown was determined to become a minister. When she first spied Lucy at Oberlin, Lucy was seated at a long dining table, speaking nonstop "with much earnestness and with very positive convictions." They struck up an immediate and lifelong friendship, even though Brown sometimes found Lucy's radical opinions upsetting. Lucy worried that her friend's theological studies might curb her free spirit, and she had no use for Brown's indulgence in fine fashion. One Sunday, seeing Brown wearing a flowery hat to church, Lucy asked her why she dared put a flower pot on her head.[31] Seven years Brown's senior, Lucy became her role model. Together, they challenged the school on women's issues. Because Oberlin did not allow females to speak in public, they formed their own off-campus debating society, which they later claimed was the first one ever established for college women.[32]

Lucy became well known on campus for her quick mind and impassioned views. She tried to invite the radical abolitionists Abby Kelley and Stephen Foster to speak, but Oberlin's president refused to allow the controversial couple to lecture on campus. The town's antislavery society, however, extended them an invitation. As fellow students later recalled, Lucy was frequently the topic of conversation. They expressed admiration that she "had not only the ability but the moral courage" to challenge her professors. She openly professed her beliefs that females should be able to vote, run for public office, have access to all professions, and speak in public. Though many disagreed with Lucy, "All admitted that she was the most brilliant woman of her age they had ever met."[33]

Attending Oberlin proved an enormous financial struggle for Lucy, as it did for many students. She borrowed money, mended fellow students' clothes, cleaned houses, and taught at a school for free blacks. She often worked seven or eight hours a day, attending classes all the while. When she discovered that she earned only two-thirds of what less experienced male teachers were paid, she demanded equal wages. The faculty board that oversaw teachers' pay turned her down. Lucy threatened to resign. Her students learned of the situation, and they volunteered to give her what she deserved. The faculty board relented, and from that point forward, female teachers earned the same salary that men received of 12½ cents per hour. And Lucy's financial situation eased when her father softened his stance, impressed with his daughter's determination and upset to learn that she woke up at two o'clock each morning in order to study. He lent her the money she needed, as he had done for his sons, writing, "You can have what you will need without studying nights or working for eight cents an hour."[34]

It was in the teaching profession that women began to have a real impact, gradually feminizing that vocation. Many who acquired a sound education taught school for a few years before they married. By the Civil War, teaching had become a socially acceptable paid job for single, middle-class women. No standardized requirements existed for teachers, although some, like Susan B. Anthony, had to take a qualifying examination to be certified to teach in county schools.[35] It was not unusual for females as young as fifteen or sixteen to teach, so a number of them were no older than some of their pupils.

These expanded opportunities in teaching came about not because antebellum society became convinced that women should advance themselves professionally, but because teaching seemed a natural fit for women, who were deemed innate nurturers of children; teaching was an extension of those maternal skills. More pragmatically, schools were eager to hire women because they could pay them well below what a male teacher earned. Most females accepted wage inequity in silence, but low pay did not sit well with everyone. Susan recalled with bitterness that male teachers in the school where she taught earned $10 per week, and female teachers were paid only $2.50. Both Lucy and Lucretia were also outraged to discover that they earned only a part of what men received for the same work. A national study presented at an 1851 women's rights convention confirmed this inequity. For instance, in Connecticut, male teachers earned $20 per month in summer, $17.50 in winter, while female ones earned $8.69 per month in summer and $6.50 in winter. School administrators were invariably male.[36] Most occupations, of course, did not have wage in-equality, because at this juncture, so many of them remained closed to women.

Earning a professional degree was an even greater uphill battle, as Elizabeth Blackwell discovered. She was the oldest sister in the remarkable Blackwell family that emigrated from England to the United States in 1832. Like other women of her background, Blackwell taught school, but her dream was to become a doctor. Society, however, regarded medicine as an inappropriate field for women, even though they had long served as midwives and, as mothers, were responsible for their family's health care. A few enlightened men believed otherwise. Samuel Gregory, one of the founders of the Boston Female Medical College, lectured and wrote on the importance of educating and employing women physicians.[37] But he was an exception. Medicine seemed too gory and grubby for women's allegedly delicate natures. Moreover, it required training in the sciences, an area closed to women.

Nonetheless, a determined Blackwell applied to several proprietary medical colleges. All but one rejected her. Students at Geneva College in New York saw Blackwell's application and decided that a young man or a rival institution had submitted it as a joke. School officials admitted the applicant, and when Blackwell showed up in the fall of 1847, they let her stay and attend classes, though they required her to sit at the back of the classroom so as not to dis-tract the young men. Townspeople were less tolerant and ridiculed this young woman who dared to become a doctor. After graduating in 1849, Blackwell acquired additional professional experience in England, returned to the United States to open a clinic in the slums of New York City, and later, with her sister Emily, established a medical college for women. Looking back several years later, she deemed her accomplishments a "moral crusade" and true "justice" for her sex. Interestingly, Blackwell did not fully support female activism, despite the fact that one brother, Henry, later married Lucy, and another, Samuel, married Antoinette Brown.[38] Nevertheless, her example as the first woman in this country to earn a medical degree encouraged others, including her younger sister Emily, to do the same. Some medical colleges that opened after the Civil War—a few, like Blackwell's and Gregory's, designed solely for women—gave American women the opportunity to earn a medical degree. Most, however, refused to admit women or severely limited their numbers until the twentieth century.

The law and the ministry proved even harder professions to crack. A handful of women studied law on their own or under the tutelage of a male family member, but no woman was admitted to a law school or to the bar until after the Civil War. Other than Quakers and a few lesser-known religious sects, no major Protestant denomination considered hiring a female minister until mid-century, and even then, such appointments were rare. Clergymen in particular deemed the ministry a wholly inappropriate profession for women, believing they should not interpret the Bible or address mixed audiences. They cited scriptural passages to defend the exclusion of women from the pulpit and to confirm their innate inferiority. Antoinette Brown was one of a few women who succeeded. Yet despite her Oberlin undergraduate degree, strong faith, and determination, Brown received no call from a mainstream church until 1853. A struggling Congregational church in South Butler, New York, which had previously hired an African American and then a theology student as its ministers, finally invited Brown to preach. She was ordained in September 1853.

Even if they could not become ministers, women could still address moral issues, and many did so with astonishing energy and dedication. Of all antebellum reform efforts, the temperance movement attracted the widest support, as hundreds of thousands of women joined this cause, prompted by Christian ideals and a desire to improve human behavior. By the second quarter of the nineteenth century, they had justification for alarm, for the nation seemed awash in liquor. The average amount of absolute alcohol consumed by Americans of drinking age ranged from five to seven gallons a year, at least twice what it is today. Excessive drinking was a threat to civility and good health. Men had long been imbibing inexpensive ale and hard cider as a matter of course, armed with the defense that fermented beverages often were healthier alternatives than the local water supply. Men might fortify themselves with a drink at the beginning of each day. Alcohol was an accepted component of male socializing. Factory employees enjoyed a pint during work breaks. Alcohol was standard fare at holiday celebrations and social and political gatherings. The tavern was a favorite place for men to gather after work and on weekends. The impact of excessive drinking was becoming more apparent, especially in cities and as more men imbibed hard liquor. Eager to pinpoint offenders, the elite and middle class blamed the problem on immigrants, blacks, and the poor, though these groups hardly had a corner on the market.[39]

Nineteenth-century health advisors and dietary reformers such as Sylvester Graham warned of the dire economic, medical, and social consequences of excessive drinking. Women took the issue of temperance to heart. Too many men spent their hard-earned wages on alcohol, leaving their families with little money for necessities. Others returned home drunk and took out their aggression on wives and children. Women had few avenues to escape such behavior, for only a handful of states allowed a wife to sue for divorce because her husband was a drunkard. But problems moved well beyond the home. Alcohol exacerbated crime and violence and undermined the fabric of a virtuous society. A number of businessmen and factory owners supported the temperance cause. In an increasingly competitive world, they could no longer afford to tolerate employees who showed up late or were suffering from a hangover. Naturally ministers participated in and often led the temperance crusade, ever eager to ensure righteous behavior.

Initially, the temperance movement relied on persuasion as it sought to reduce the amount of alcohol consumed. Gradually, total abstinence and a ban on the manufacture and sale of all alcohol became the movement's goals. Organizations such as the American Society for the Promotion of Temperance, formed by concerned Boston clergymen in 1826, sprang up. The Washington Temperance Society, founded in 1840 by reformed alcoholics in Baltimore, held parades and cold-water picnics to promote sobriety.

The movement to eradicate alcohol attracted many women, including several who would become active in the women's rights struggle—Susan, Elizabeth, and Amelia Bloomer among them. They signed pledges never to marry men who drank. Others forced their husbands to sign "cold-water pledges," vowing never to let liquor cross their lips. Female societies sought to protect wives and children from inebriated husbands and fathers. To campaign effectively, women realized they needed a political voice to change laws and expand the causes for divorce so wives could escape drunkard husbands. To this end, they petitioned, lectured, and pressured state and local governments to pass laws to prevent the distribution and sale of alcohol and to permit divorces for alcoholism. Efforts began to reap results—the amount of alcohol consumed started to decline. In 1851, Maine became the first state to pass a law outlawing the production and sale of alcohol; twelve more states passed similar legislation by the mid-1850s. Then the first phase of the temperance movement peaked, as more Americans shifted their attention to abolition. Prohibition would reemerge as a key issue later in the century.

Amelia Jenks Bloomer was one of the most visible temperance activists of the antebellum period, later linked to women's rights and to a female fashion statement that bore her name. Born in 1818 in Homer, New York, she attended local schools and began to teach at age seventeen. After only one term, she moved to Waterloo, New York, and worked there as a governess. In 1840, she met and then married Dexter C. Bloomer, a lawyer, Quaker, and newspaper editor. The couple moved to Seneca Falls, New York, where they became active in the temperance crusade. With her husband's encouragement, Amelia began to write articles for local newspapers, including the temperance paper the *Water Bucket*. Though she attended the 1848 Seneca Falls Convention, she was not convinced that women's demands made sense. A year later, Bloomer became editor of a temperance newspaper, the *Lily*.[40]

It was temperance that first drew Susan into the world of reform. Her father had been involved in the cause for years, and Susan's elevated sense of rectitude and morality made the issue compelling. She was born in Adams, Massachusetts, into a large, supportive, and affectionate family in 1820, the daughter of a Quaker father and Baptist mother. Though Susan's mother, Lucy, never adopted her husband's faith, the family lived a simple life in accordance with Quaker tenets. When Susan was six, the family moved to Battenville, New York, where her father, Daniel, became a successful mill owner. She attended local schools and was also home-schooled by her father and a tutor after a male instructor at her district school refused to teach her long division because she was female.[41] Susan and a sister then attended Deborah Moulson's Quaker boarding school for girls outside Philadelphia. When their father's business failed in the depression of 1837, they left school, and Susan began supporting herself as a teacher.

In 1845, the Anthony family moved to the Rochester, New York, area. Though he was never able to achieve his earlier success, Daniel Anthony discovered there an exciting community of reformers and abolitionists. Frederick Douglass, William Lloyd Garrison, and Wendell Phillips were frequent guests in the Anthony home. Susan served as a governess and then taught at the Canajoharie Academy in upstate New York. In 1849, she began to weary of teaching, claiming that the profession offered her few challenges. But her dissatisfaction and the decision to leave probably stemmed as much from the arrival of a new principal, a nineteen-year-old man from Alabama who demanded "implicit obedience and the use of the rod" and resented contrary opinions.[42] Susan returned home to help run the family farm and engage in temperance and abolition work. Marriage was not something Susan sought, and as she aged, she became more defensive about her single status. "When I am crowned with all the rights, privileges, and immunities of a citizen, I may give some consideration to this social institution," she asserted.[43]

Susan gradually awakened to the injustices women faced, learning firsthand that male teachers outearned females. She joined a local chapter of the Daughters of Temperance in Canajoharie after recognizing that women were not allowed to speak to mixed audiences or serve in leadership positions in

*Susan B. Anthony, 1848
(The Schlesinger Library,
Radcliffe Institute,
Harvard University)*

men's temperance organizations. In March 1849, she delivered her first public speech to the Daughters of Temperance, using the type of rhetoric that would typify her future lecturing on women's rights, labeling drunkenness "the blighting mildew of all our social connections" and urging more women to unite to eradicate alcohol.[44]

Although temperance was deemed a worthy activity for women, their involvement generated mixed responses regarding the roles they should play. Men's temperance societies welcomed them as worker bees for the cause, but did not allow them to become full-fledged members, officers, or lecturers. Not until 1854 did the Sons of Temperance admit female members, and even then only on a limited basis. The many ministers involved in temperance had a decided influence on male organizations' reactions to women. To some clergymen's way of thinking, temperance was far too political for women; they should devote themselves to domestic or religious duties. Others agreed. For instance, New York legislators were unwilling to accept any temperance petitions signed by women. According to the *Lily*, Assemblyman Moses D. Gale commented that "the constitution of the female mind was such as to render woman incapable of correctly deciding upon those questions." As the minister Henry Mandeville of Albany explained, "When a woman goes out of her sphere, when she goes miles attended or unattended . . . I say she unsexes herself, is a hybrid, and I for one wish to do nothing in approbation of it."[45] Excluded from male organizations, women founded their own temperance groups, such as Martha Washingtonian Societies and the aforementioned Daughters of Temperance.

Even more upsetting was the purposeful exclusion of women from the World's Temperance Convention, a meeting organized by a group of men in 1853. When seven representatives from the New York State Female Temperance Society showed up, men contemptuously denounced their presence and told them to return to their "proper sphere." The president declared that "he would rather resign" than have them participate. It was "not fit that woman should be in such places." In response, Lucy, Susan, Antoinette Brown, William Lloyd Garrison, the minister Thomas Wentworth Higginson, and others organized the first "Whole World's Temperance Convention" to counter what they dubbed the "Half World's Temperance Organization" because it excluded women. These reformers' gender-inclusive convention met September 23 and 24, 1853, in New York City and attracted some two thousand people. They urged the passage of national legislation to curtail alcohol consumption and the creation of more "places of popular amusement and innocent excitement" as an antidote to drinking. A "Cold Water Banquet" was the perfect conclusion to this successful convention.[46]

While various reform movements gave women opportunities to organize, speak, and petition, the antislavery movement did the most to heighten women's awareness of their inferior status. They encountered enormous resistance as they began to work and lecture against slavery. This made them all too aware that they were as enslaved by men as the slaves they were trying to free. Little wonder that many of those who would lead the women's rights movement——Lucretia, Lucy, Susan, Wendell Phillips, William Lloyd Garrison, Abby Kelley Foster, Martha Wright, and others—were ardent abolitionists.

In the late eighteenth century, Quakers had become the first mainstream Protestant denomination to demand an end to slavery. Holding someone in bondage was anathema to this faith, which taught and tried to live by a creed promoting human equality. The Quaker John Woolman wrote one of the earliest denunciations of slavery in this country. He journeyed south twice and in 1756 began writing *A Journal of the Life, Gospel Labours and Christian Experience of that Faithful Minister of Jesus Christ, John Woolman*, published posthumously in

1774. He convinced members of his Philadelphia meeting to free their slaves and end ties to this inhumane institution.

More formal efforts to address the slavery question began with plans to colonize slaves and free blacks by sending them outside the country. Founded in Maryland in 1816 and attracting such men as James Madison and Henry Clay, the American Colonization Society spawned dozens of chapters elsewhere. White southerners saw colonization as a means to ship problematic free blacks and slaves to Africa. Northerners identified colonization as an opportunity to purchase the freedom of slaves and send them to Liberia, established in 1820 as a home for American blacks. The Society raised money to ship a few thousand blacks overseas, but ultimately colonization failed. For one thing, it proved expensive. Moreover, many died of disease or faced major struggles in fashioning new lives in strange places. Native Africans did not always welcome newcomers from the United States. Outraged by being forced to move elsewhere, a number of blacks in this country denounced the entire undertaking. Far better that whites erect black colleges, insisted Maria W. Stewart, than that "their money should be sunk in the ocean." Frederick Douglass decried this response to slavery as shameful. "From the beginning of the existence of this people, as a people, the colored man has had a place upon the American soil," he asserted.[47] Radical abolitionists like William Lloyd Garrison abhorred the colonization movement, which they regarded as a halfway measure in dealing with slavery.

More successful and enduring was the antislavery movement, which attracted a number of prominent Americans and generated an enormous amount of publicity and political debate. Interestingly, though the abolition movement occupies a central place in our nation's history, the cause never generated a mass following, attracting perhaps no more than 1 percent of the entire population. Its base of support lay in the Northeast and Midwest, though even in these regions, most people were either indifferent or opposed to abolition. But whatever their numbers, antislavery activists were relentless in their pursuit. They considered slavery a sin and a direct contradiction of God's will, and they used moral suasion to try to convince Americans and the federal government of the evils of the institution. From tiny villages to large cities, activists gathered signatures on petitions demanding that Congress legislate an end to slavery. Lecturers traveled widely to generate support for the cause. By the 1830s, activists had founded a number of antislavery societies. Several abolitionists—Wendell Phillips and Lewis and Arthur Tappan among them—brought wealth and stature to the movement. Others, like Lucretia, Abby Kelley, and William Lloyd Garrison, made names for themselves with their uncompromising stance opposing slavery. What most surprised abolitionists was the depth of opposition they encountered in the North. Violent mobs disrupted their lectures and conventions, pelted speakers with eggs and rocks, and threatened them physically.[48] Deep-seated racism and fears of what emancipation might mean were hardly confined to white southerners.

William Lloyd Garrison was one of the most famous radical abolitionists of the day, a man who decried the use of violent tactics but who generated violent responses in his writings and lectures. On one occasion, an angry mob carried him through the streets of Boston. Garrison represented the most extreme branch of the movement, uncompromising in his demand for an immediate end to slavery. Born in 1805 and raised in Newburyport, Massachusetts, by a single mother whose husband had abandoned the family, Garrison was apprenticed at a young age to a local printer and editor. Newspaper work and abolition became his lifelong passions. His antislavery stance led to his arrest for libel when he accused a prominent merchant of robbery and murder by engaging in the internal slave trade. During his forty-nine in jail, Garrison wrote about his situation and attracted the attention of the New Yorkers Lewis and Arthur Tappan, who posted his bail and began to fund his antislavery work. In 1831, Garrison began publishing the *Liberator*, a weekly newspaper. Its first issue clearly articulated his intent: "I do not wish to think, or speak, or write, with moderation."[49] And he did not. Garrison believed that working through the political system was useless, and he denounced the U.S. Constitution, and at one point even burned a copy of it, because it condoned slavery. He became an ardent supporter of women's involvement in the antislavery cause and of women's rights in general, and a close friend of many female activists.

While Quakers played a leading role in the antislavery movement, even they were not of one mind about how far to commit to the cause and how best to eradicate slavery. In 1827, a serious conflict developed between orthodox Quakers and the Hicksites, who were followers of the British Quaker and ardent abolitionist Elias Hicks. Hicksites were upset by conservative Quakers' growing reliance on scripture rather than on the "inner light." Furthermore, orthodox Quakers often did not welcome blacks as full church members and made them sit on separate benches in the backs of the meetinghouses. Hicksites, in contrast, welcomed blacks, tended to be strong critics of slavery, and sought a more democratic, rather than elder-driven, faith. After much soul-searching, Lucretia and James Mott left the orthodox branch to become Hicksite Quakers. Their decision fostered considerable criticism and severed several friendships.[50]

In the 1830s, black women began to play a prominent role in the abolition cause. A number of them in the North organized antislavery associations,

*William Lloyd Garrison
(Photography Collection,
Miriam and Ira
D. Wallach Division
of Arts, Prints and
Photographs, The New
York Public Library,
Astor, Lenox and Tilden
Foundations)*

including a group in Salem, Massachusetts, that established the nation's first
female antislavery society. Nine black women were among the founding
members of the biracial Philadelphia Female Anti-Slavery Society. In 1832 and
1833, twenty-nine-year-old Maria W. Stewart of Boston became the first African
American woman to speak in public to mixed audiences, urging free blacks
to work for abolition and establish their own schools. She noted that black
women were dependent not because of the same marriage laws and customs
that kept white women in a subordinate state but because they had little choice
but to work in poorly paid jobs. While sensitive to the hurdles that black men
faced in securing an education and finding decent employment, she urged them
to make more of themselves. Stewart spoke out, motivated by her strong faith,
and because "it is no use for us to wait any longer for a generation of well
educated men to arise. We have slumbered and slept too long already." Her
words stirred uneasiness among many whites and a number of black men who
did not welcome such assertions from a woman. In fact, the controversy Stewart
generated caused her to abandon her activism after less than a year in the public
eye and devote herself to education.[51]

White women in northern communities were also active in founding abolition societies, such as the New England Female Anti-Slavery Society. When
the American Anti-Slavery Society organized in Philadelphia in early December
1833, its male members did not invite women to join, even though hundreds of
committed female abolitionists lived there.[52] Within days, Lucretia, Lydia Maria
Child, and several others formed the biracial Philadelphia Female Anti-Slavery
Society. Taking this bold step, however, fostered anxiety. "At that time I had no
idea of the meaning of preambles and resolutions and voting," Lucretia admitted. "Women had never been in assemblies of that kind." The same year,
Child gave voice to her thoughts on abolition. With Garrison's encouragement,
she wrote *An Appeal in Favor of That Class of Americans Called Africans*, which became a widely read abolitionist tract. Child demanded immediate emancipation
and pointed out the depth of racial prejudice in the North, a view that won her
few friends there. Lucretia was thrilled with Child's book and urged her friends
to read this "noble work, & by a woman too."[53]

Ironically, it was two white southern women who, through their writing and
lecturing on abolition, publicly challenged society's traditional views on women.
Sarah and Angelina Grimké, born and reared in an elite, slaveholding family of
Charleston, South Carolina, were unique in the antislavery movement. While
growing up, the sisters were troubled by slavery and by masters who mistreated
their slaves, but they felt helpless to change the system. (They did ignore South
Carolina law by teaching their black maids to read.) After the death of their
father, a well-respected judge, Sarah moved to Philadelphia in 1821. Eight years
later, Angelina followed her north. They became Quakers, drawn to that faith's
belief in human equality.

After joining the Philadelphia Female Anti-Slavery Society in 1835, Angelina sent a letter to William Lloyd Garrison emphasizing the importance of
the antislavery cause. Impressed by the power of her "soul-thrilling epistle,"
Garrison published her piece in the *Liberator*.[54] Elders in the Philadelphia Society
of Friends expressed disapproval, and even Sarah found her sister's radical stance unsettling. But Angelina was determined to express her opinion. On hearing the British abolitionist George Thompson lecture the following
year, Angelina wrote *An Appeal to the Christian Women of the South*. "The *women of
the South can overthrow* this horrible system of oppression and cruelty, licentiousness and wrong," she insisted. She urged women to pray, read, petition,
and persuade southern men of slavery's many evils.[55] Angelina's tract had little
impact on southern women—other than to alienate family and friends in the
region—but her essay galvanized northern abolitionists.

In December 1836, the American Anti-Slavery Society commissioned the
Grimké sisters to lecture to female audiences in New York and New Jersey.

*Angelina Grimké Weld,
c. 1845 (The Schlesinger
Library, Radcliffe
Institute, Harvard
University)*

Angelina proved an especially powerful speaker and became renowned for her eloquence and passion. Initially, the sisters addressed women in the privacy of their homes, but their audiences grew, and soon they were speaking in meeting halls and churches overflowing with listeners of both sexes.

Sarah Grimké also went public, as it were; in late 1836 she wrote *An Epistle to the Clergy of the Southern States*. She used biblical passages to denounce slavery and identified selections that southern ministers misinterpreted to defend slavery. The Bible says "Let us make man in our image, after our likeness," but slave-owners, she asserted, instead have "seized with an iron grasp this God-like being, and torn the crown from his head." Sarah urged clergymen to remove "the sin which the Church is fostering in her bosom" and questioned how any man of the cloth could "sanction and sanctify this heart-breaking, this soul-destroying system?"[56]

In May 1837, responding to Congress's passage of the 1836 gag rule that tabled all antislavery petitions, approximately one hundred black and white women gathered in New York City for the first meeting of the National

Sarah M. Grimké
(Library of Congress)

Anti-Slavery Convention of American Women. They knew that by holding an interracial meeting, they were challenging society's views of acceptable female behavior. One delegate admitted, "To attend a Female Convention! Once I should have blushed at the thought."[57] Paying no heed to Congress's gag rule, women pledged themselves to collect a million signatures on petitions demanding that Congress abolish slavery in the nation's capital. They questioned why most churches avoided the antislavery cause and urged supporters to shun all products produced by slave labor. Delegates debated and then passed a resolution presented by Angelina to challenge woman's circumscribed sphere into which "corrupt custom & a perverted application of the Scriptures had placed her." Lucretia was present and gave a speech that intertwined themes of abolition and women's rights. Angelina introduced a resolution urging greater engagement in the antislavery struggle: "It is the duty of woman, and the province of woman, to plead the cause of the oppressed in our land, and do all that she can by her voice, and her pen, and her purse, and the influence of her example, to overthrow the horrible system of American slavery." Shortly after the convention, Angelina wrote a second tract, *An Appeal to the Women of the Nominally Free States*, describing the horrors of slavery and urging northern women to help eradicate it.[58]

The audacity of women expressing such bold thoughts in public—and especially in a biracial meeting—offended many Americans. While the *Liberator*'s coverage was predictably positive, several New York papers denounced the gathering as an "Amazonian farce." They mocked women for leaving their babies, sewing needles, and pots and frying pans at home in order "to discuss the weighty matters of state—to decide upon intricate questions of international policy."[59]

Having lectured effectively to audiences in New York and New Jersey, the Grimkés in 1837 were asked to speak in New England. Again, they denounced the South's reliance on slavery but, like Lydia Maria Child, also pointed out the North's collusion in the institution by allowing slavery and the slave trade to exist in the nation's capital, letting the southern domestic slave trade continue, supporting the Constitution's pledge to return fugitive slaves to their masters, admitting slave states into the Union, and allowing northern manufacturers and businessmen to profit from raw materials produced by slave labor.[60] The Grimkés' language stirred uneasiness, even antagonism, among their New England audiences.

The Grimkés' lectures deeply troubled New England's Congregational ministers. They found the sisters completely out of line, not only for such radical antislavery messages, but for daring to speak in public to mixed, or "promiscuous," audiences. Many ministers were feeling some loss of authority, threatened not only by the growing popularity of evangelical sects but also by these two sisters and other antislavery speakers who were supplanting them as moral authorities. They also worried lest these messages influence their female congregants, encouraging them to participate in antislavery activities and ignore benevolent work more befitting their sex. In July 1837, the Council of Congregational Ministers of Massachusetts responded to these concerns, issuing its "Pastoral Letter" protesting the Grimkés' audacity and criticizing their supporters. They warned the public of "the dangers which at present seem to threaten the FEMALE CHARACTER with wide-spread and permanent injury" by leading women away from their assigned sphere. "The power of woman is her dependence," they insisted, for "God had ordained her weakness and need of protection." Any woman who lectured in public, they said, loses that right to male protection, for "her character becomes unnatural." By contrast, those who accepted their rightful role in the home deserved universal approbation.[61]

The ministers' overall response to the Grimkés' activism illustrated the enormous challenge clergymen posed to female advancement. These outspoken women had assumed a role reserved for ministers. In men's eyes, Sarah and Angelina's assertiveness in the public arena promised social disorder, undermining the stability of American society. It is little wonder that reformers like

Elizabeth and Lucy would question and later denounce organized religion. Even Lucretia agreed that the church was a huge impediment to female equality. While she remained a Hicksite Quaker, at least in name, she concluded that the most "determined opposition" women encountered came "from the clergy generally, whose readings of the Bible are intensely inimical to the equality of women with men." The Bible was being "ill-used" to justify female inferiority.[62]

The "Pastoral Letter" infuriated those who supported a woman's right to speak in public. Lucy and her cousin "listened with great indignation" to the "Pastoral Letter" when it was read in their church in North Brookfield, Massachusetts. It had the opposite effect on these two young women from what the ministers had intended. This effort to silence women infuriated Lucy. Her cousin related that Lucy poked her every time she heard an offensive statement, causing her side to turn black and blue.[63] For Lucy, this moment was another turning point: "If I had ever felt bound to silence by interpretations of Scripture texts or believed that equal rights did not belong to women, that pastoral letter broke my bonds," she recalled years later. Others concurred. In response to the "Pastoral Letter," abolitionist Anne Warren Weston addressed the Boston Female Anti-Slavery Society, pointing out that ministers who used the Bible to justify slavery were using the same arguments to justify women's subordination. The Quaker poet and abolitionist John Greenleaf Whittier sympathized with the Grimkés and complimented their activism. "You are now doing much and nobly to vindicate and assert the rights of woman." Their lectures, he continued, were "practical and powerful assertions of the right and the duty of woman to labor side by side with her brother for the welfare and redemption of the world." Whittier not only defended the sisters but denounced the New England clergy in a fifteen-verse satirical poem that appeared in the *Liberator* on October 20, 1837. Among other biting lines, he wrote: "Now, shame upon ye, parish Popes! / Was it thus with those, your predecessors, / Who sealed with racks, and fire, and ropes / Their loving-kindness to transgressors?"[64]

While ministers were denouncing them, Sarah produced a treatise that revealed her feminist makeup. In *Letters on the Equality of the Sexes, and the Condition of Woman*, which ran in serialized form in the *New England Spectator* beginning in July 1837 and then in the *Liberator*, she offered an intellectual defense of women's rights. The sexual abuse slave women suffered at the hands of white men appalled her. She labeled men "irresponsible tyrants" for succumbing to lust and taking advantage of female slaves. White women should empathize with female slaves who had no recourse but to submit to the power of their masters. Citing examples from the Bible, Sarah also demonstrated women's strength and reminded her readers of the vital roles they had played in the past. She criticized laws that suppressed them, especially those that gave husbands so much control over their wives, urging that they be overturned. "Man has asserted and assumed authority over us. He has, by virtue of his power, deprived us of the advantages of improvement which he has lavishly bestowed upon himself." Under the nation's laws, a wife's relationship to her husband was like that of a slave to a master, for a wife could claim nothing of her own except what her husband allowed her to have. Like a slave, the law treated her with severity when she erred. Sarah importuned women to stand on an equal footing with men and accept the responsibilities God intended for them.[65]

Sarah also defended women's right to express themselves in public. Criticism of such behavior came "from those who, having long held the reins of usurped authority, are unwilling to permit us to fill that sphere which God created us to move in." Ministers were mistaken when they insisted that women's only power derived from their dependence, silence, and deference. But she admitted that blame should not solely fall on men, for many women basked in a state of dependency and a life of leisure. "If women felt their responsibility, for the support of themselves, or their families, it would add strength and dignity to their characters," Sarah argued. Then men might truly value women.[66]

Yet the Grimkés' behavior appalled far more people than it rallied. Most Americans accepted biblical evidence for women's subordination and silence in public settings. The apostle Paul had said, "Let your women keep silence in the church; for it is not permitted unto them to speak." Many women found the Grimkés' assertiveness shocking, including some female abolitionists who felt the sisters had gone too far. A few questioned whether women should work alongside men in the antislavery movement; others felt the debate over a woman's right to speak in public detracted from the antislavery cause. In a moment of metaphorical rapture, the minister Nehemiah Adams explained the problem: "If the vine, whose strength and beauty is to lean upon the trellis work and half conceal its clusters, thinks to assume the independent and overshadowing nature of the elm, it will not only cease to bear fruit, but will fall in shame and dishonor into the dust."[67] Catharine Beecher criticized the Grimké sisters in her 1837 *Essay on Slavery and Abolitionism with Reference to the Duty of American Females*, claiming that only men should speak in public. Women should yield to men's greater intellect and lovingly wield their moral authority in the domestic sphere, not at the lectern. A woman diminished her status by operating in the public arena.[68]

Angelina found Beecher's statements so unspeakable that she responded in a series of letters published in the *Liberator* beginning in May the same year. She asked why a woman, but not a man, generated criticism when she "begins to feel the promptings of ambition, or the thirst for power?" Angelina challenged traditional doctrine that declared man was strong while woman was only "to sit as a doll . . . to be admired for her personal charms, and caressed and humored like a spoiled child, or converted into a mere drudge." Beecher should consider how slaves might react to her denouncing women's involvement in opposing "the heinous crimes of our nation." Abolition was a crusade that everyone should embrace.[69] So transparent was Angelina's fury that even Theodore Weld and John Greenleaf Whittier took issue with her biting response to Beecher. To the two men, Angelina countered that it was not her letters to Beecher that aroused people but the "Pastoral Letter which did the mischief." Pleading for the men's support, she continued, "*The time* to assert a right is *the* time when *that* right is denied."[70]

By speaking to mixed audiences and enlisting women in the cause, the Grimké sisters had joined two reform issues: abolition and women's rights. Though they were initially taken aback by the controversy they had stirred, the Grimkés explained that they felt driven by a higher calling. Angelina confessed, "the Lord knows that we did not come to forward our own interests but in simple obedience to his commands." The sisters understood the storm they had unleashed, for as Angelina wrote to Weld, "We are placed very unexpectedly in a very trying situation, in the forefront of an entirely new contest—a contest for the *rights of woman* as a moral, intelligent & responsible being." Lecturing to mixed audiences pushed to the forefront the question of a woman's right to speak in public and, more broadly, her appropriate role in society. But the controversy and constant lecturing took their toll. In November 1837, exhaustion and poor health led Sarah and Angelina to withdraw from most public activism. Angelina did lecture twice more. On February 21, 1838, she spoke on the antislavery cause before the Massachusetts state legislature, becoming the first American woman to address an all-male elected body.[71]

It was more than exhaustion, however, that brought about the sisters' retreat from the public eye. In May 1838, Angelina married Weld. She had weighed the wisdom of marriage, fearing the restrictive laws that made wives into dependents. But she was drawn to Weld and their shared beliefs, and she realized she was prepared for this commitment. Angelina sensed that her passion about women's rights and abolition would not be easy on anyone and warned him, "Thou art trying a *dangerous experiment*, one which I do believe *no other man* would try, because I tho't *no other* understands my principles or myself."[72] When the two announced plans to marry, the public reaction was mixed. Many felt that Angelina would have a difficult time making the transition to domestic life; others commented on Weld's courage in marrying this outspoken woman. Female reformers worried quietly that marriage would end Angelina's vital work.

After a brief courtship, the couple married on May 14, 1838. Family members and white and black friends attended the simple ceremony held at the Philadelphia home of Sarah and Angelina's widowed sister Anna Frost. Weld professed his belief in a marriage of equals, noting that a husband should have no authority over his wife except that which was motivated by love. Angelina promised to love and honor him. Following Quaker tradition, the word "obey" was absent. A white and a black minister each offered prayers, and Garrison read the certificate. As expected, the Society of Friends expelled both sisters because Angelina had married outside her faith and Sarah had attended the wedding.

The Grimké-Weld wedding did little to soften public ire. The day after the ceremony, the second annual Anti-Slavery Convention of American Women convened in the Pennsylvania Hall for Free Discussion in Philadelphia. The handsome new meeting hall, with its exterior pillars resembling a Greek temple and modern interior gas lamps, had been funded and built by liberal reformers to provide meeting space for controversial speakers, given that so many churches and public halls refused them access. The week before the upcoming interracial forum, hecklers were in the streets denouncing it. Notices posted around the city urged people who cared about their jobs and the Constitution to attend and protest this convention of "amalgamators." Dedication ceremonies of the new building took place without incident. As the convention opened, however, some three thousand protestors filled the aisles and galleries of the hall and began to smash windows. The women found it almost impossible to conduct their meeting.[73] As Angelina, Maria Weston Chapman, and Abby Kelley tried to speak, hissing and shouting drowned them out. Kelley attempted to denounce the North's collusion with slavery and how much of the region's wealth had resulted from it. Protestors threatened speakers with bricks and rocks. The president of the Pennsylvania Hall came forward and asked the mayor to provide police protection. The mayor refused, claiming that the female abolitionists had brought this chaos on themselves.

When the meeting opened the following day, the hall's director stepped in and urged black women to leave. Angelina rose to speak. The mob began to smash windows and to heckle her. She persisted for over an hour. Garrison later described the scene: "Her eloquence kindled, her eye flashed, and her cheeks glowed, as she devoutly thanked the Lord that the stupid repose of that city had at length been disturbed by the force of the truth." Philadelphia's mayor turned up and tried to quell the unruly crowd, now estimated at fifteen thousand, but without success. Finally authorities forced everyone out of the building, and the mayor secured the doors. Nonetheless, mobs broke into the hall, opened the gas jets, and set the auditorium on fire, burning the new building to the ground. The next morning, a few white women met at a local schoolhouse and vowed to continue their struggle. A month later, Lucretia emphasized the "deep interest" generated among the participants, who had discussed a "rich feast" of ideas. Even the destruction of the hall could not discourage them from pursuing their cause.[74]

The Welds and Sarah moved to Fort Lee, New Jersey, and avoided most public activities. The sisters circulated antislavery petitions and helped Weld gather and publish a collection of articles into what became his bestselling book *American Slavery As It Is*, which appeared in 1839 and included personal testimony by many abolitionists, including the Grimkés.[75] Though often asked to rejoin the antislavery movement, the sisters remained out of the fray. Both seemed to relish domestic life. Angelina bore two sons, one in 1839 and another in 1841, bore a daughter in 1844, and suffered at least one miscarriage. She experienced lengthy bouts of ill health, and Sarah helped to raise the three children. In 1848, the Welds opened a boarding school on a farm near Belleville, New Jersey. Moving to an experimental community in Perth Amboy in 1854, they established a new school, Eagleswood, which attracted several children of abolitionist parents, including two of the Stantons' sons.

The Grimkés' impact on antislavery and women's rights was considerable. Antislavery activists often visited the Weld home. Though he never met the sisters, Frederick Douglass felt their powerful influence, realizing how much they had done to open doors for others. Yet many found their sudden retreat from public life puzzling. Years later, Henry Blackwell commented on their decision, wondering how the sisters could give up so much. "It is entirely unaccountable how one who is struggling in the waves to rescue a drowning child, can leave it to contend alone, and feebly, with the devouring elements," he observed. He hoped the three Weld children, now the focus of Sarah and Angelina's lives, would someday do good in the world. Similarly, Lucretia regretted that the Grimkés no longer provided leadership for the causes of antislavery and women's rights. "I have little hope of them, after such a flash and such an effectual extinguishment."[76]

Though not as well known as the Grimkés, Abby Kelley did not shrink from public activism. She, too, was one of the early antislavery advocates who lectured to mixed audiences and challenged society's acceptance of women's secondary role. Kelley was born into a Quaker family in 1811 and grew up on a farm near Worcester, Massachusetts. She attended local schools and then a

Abby Foster Kelley
(American Antiquarian
Society)

Quaker boarding school in Providence, Rhode Island. Like many young women of her background, Kelley taught school near home for several years. In 1836, she moved to Lynn, Massachusetts, to teach and there became involved in temperance, pacifism, dietary reform, and Garrison's uncompromising approach to the antislavery cause. At the convention in Pennsylvania Hall, she delivered her first major public address. Theodore Weld and others who heard her speak urged her to become a professional lecturer—a career she began in 1838 under the auspices of the American Anti-Slavery Society. Kelley's passion, eloquence, and bold opinions attracted large, mixed audiences and inevitably provoked controversy. In May 1840, at the annual meeting of the American Anti-Slavery Society, Garrison and his followers elected her to serve on the organization's all-male business committee. The idea of a woman holding this position appalled several members, and they demanded that she tender her resignation. Kelley refused. Two ministers on the committee then resigned to protest her nomination, and several Society members, including Henry Stanton, walked out and formed a new organization, the American and Foreign Anti-Slavery Society.[77] This event had little impact on Kelley, who continued to lecture in her uncompromising, direct style. But it did help to create a major fissure in the antislavery movement.

The 1830s and 1840s were a critical period in setting the stage for women's participation in a larger world, generating their interest and involvement in key reform movements. They established a significant role for themselves through their work in the public sphere—efforts that sometimes brought personal rewards and visible results. In some cases, their work encouraged unanticipated resistance, public outrage, and even violence. Through their activism, they challenged traditional ideas that insisted on their silence and their place in the home. Yet at this juncture, trying to alter society's view of women's role in the public sphere often proved costly. As Susan observed years later, one had to risk a great deal in order to bring about change. "Cautious, careful people always casting about to preserve their reputation and social standing," she wrote, "never can bring about a reform."[78] These words would resonate for decades, as women became increasingly aware of their unequal place in society and the wrongs inflicted on them solely due to gender. Within the framework of their growing social activism emerged an understanding of the injustices they endured. In the summer of 1848, a few brave women willingly would shed caution and convention as they risked their reputations to fight back.

3

SENECA FALLS

S tanding before a crowd packed into Wesleyan Chapel in Seneca Falls, New York, thirty-two-year-old Elizabeth Cady Stanton proclaimed: "We hold these truths to be self-evident: That all men and women are created equal." The intent of her statement was clear—to give new meaning to Jefferson's often-quoted phrase from the Declaration of Independence. For the first time in an organized public setting, women found their voices and directed their attention to the injustices that for centuries had defined and circumscribed their lives. Here, a group of women was insisting that they were men's equal. This was a momentous assertion, a momentous event. The July 1848 Seneca Falls Convention and its Declaration of Rights and Sentiments formally initiated the struggle for women's equality and justice.

This two-day meeting could have been an event of little significance, merely one of scores of conventions held in towns and cities across the country addressing one of several reforms. Despite how few details are known about the event, it was of enormous consequence, for it motivated a group of women (and some men) to demand justice and to seek the rights of citizenship for half the nation's population. It provided the impetus to hold future meetings and inspired activists to circulate petitions, write letters and essays, and lecture in public. The concerns discussed at Seneca Falls hardly seem radical now. Today, no one questions the right of American women to vote, serve on juries, hold public office, claim their own possessions, earn equal wages, acquire a good education, have access to divorce, and pursue meaningful work. In 1848, however, these revolutionary demands required that American society upend the way it perceived and treated women.

The Seneca Falls Convention might seem remarkable just for its location—in a small community in upstate New York, but a town in the throes of industrialization. One might consider Boston, New York, or Cincinnati more suitable for this significant event. But the locale was not random, since four of the five who organized the Convention lived in or near Seneca Falls. Just as remarkable was the document the Convention produced. The Declaration of Rights and Sentiments offered a comprehensive recitation of the wrongs women suffered and a list of resolutions demanding change. Signed by one hundred of the approximately three hundred people who attended the Convention, the Declaration emboldened some people who were there and many who were not to demand full citizenship. For years to come, the Declaration would serve as the basic text for the women's rights movement and be reintroduced at future meetings. Most important, this Convention was the first time so many Americans met in a public setting to discuss the radical idea of female equality.

Pivotal moments often have a catalyst. The event generally acknowledged to have prompted the Seneca Falls Convention occurred in London eight years earlier. In June 1840, eight female delegates from the United States accompanied a large group of male delegates to the World Anti-Slavery Convention.[1] (Also attending the Convention were Elizabeth Cady and Henry Stanton, he as a delegate and she as his new bride.) The eight had been invited to attend the Convention as representatives of the American Anti-Slavery Society and the Massachusetts and the Philadelphia Female Anti-Slavery Societies—a controversial decision supported by some men who believed that women should be full participants in the antislavery movement. Their presence in London was expected to arouse controversy. As he set sail for this meeting, William Lloyd Garrison acknowledged that "the 'woman question' will inevitably be brought up," and he anticipated that the female delegates might not be seated. "It is, perhaps, quite probable, that we shall be foiled in our purpose;—but the subject cannot be agitated without doing good." Garrison admitted that including women as equal participants in such a convention was unheard-of in Europe, but he was never one to avoid a challenge.[2] The eight women were also skeptical and anticipated some resistance. Indeed, most British and American male delegates opposed their involvement. They worried that the women would prove a distraction from the fundamental topic at hand and undermine the proceedings. More important, they felt it was both unseemly and unfeminine for women to share this public event with men.

As the Convention opened, this issue consumed the entire first day's proceedings. In an unusually understated manner, Elizabeth later commented that the topic "created some little discord."[3] A handful of men, led by the young

American lawyer and rising star in the antislavery movement Wendell Phillips, defended the women's right to be seated. This marked Phillips's initial foray into women's rights. He was born into a prominent Boston family in 1811. His father, a judge who became mayor of Boston, died when Phillips was eleven. His mother had high hopes for her brilliant son. Educated at Boston Latin School and Harvard College, Phillips showed enormous talent but had little direction. Like many well-educated young men of his day, he studied law but had no real affinity for it. When he met Ann Terry Greene, he found his soul mate. Though Greene was also from a wealthy, well-connected Boston family, Phillips's mother was less than enthusiastic about this match, for Greene had a reputation as a strong Garrisonian abolitionist and women's rights advocate. But Phillips wooed and won her, and they wed in 1837. Now he found his calling—embracing his wife's commitment to reform. Inspired by Charles Finney's impassioned preaching, Phillips felt driven by his Christian duty and perhaps by a sense of entitlement to try to uplift American society. In 1837, he became an agent for the American Anti-Slavery Society, beginning a long, illustrious career as a lecturer, generous contributor, and successful fund-raiser. Soon Phillips became a major presence in the abolition movement, bringing, according to his biographer, Irving Bartlett, "wealth, social position, and great talent to the cause."[4]

But a mysterious, undiagnosed illness that made Ann Phillips a partial invalid for most of her life marred the Phillipses' marriage. Though she was often bedridden and in pain, friends claimed that Ann never lost her wit, sense of commitment, or vivid personality. The couple had no children and likely only limited sexual intimacy, but they apparently were devoted to one another. They eventually adopted a lifestyle that allowed Wendell to throw himself into reform. In 1839, the young couple set sail for Europe and remained there until they attended the London World Anti-Slavery Convention the following year.[5]

It was Ann Phillips, one of the eight female delegates, who insisted that her husband take a lead in the debate to seat them. She jotted a quick note to him: "Wendell, Please to maintain the floor—no matter what they do don't give up yr. right to." Phillips and a few men stepped forward and argued in what was described as a "spirited manner" that women were full-standing members in American antislavery societies. It was not "just or equitable" that they, who had traveled across the Atlantic and left their families behind, be excluded. "What a misnomer to call this a World's Convention of Abolitionists, when some of the oldest and most thorough-going Abolitionists in the world are denied the right to be represented in it by delegates of their own choice," argued another defender,

Wendell Phillips (Photography Collection, Miriam and Ira D. Wallach Division of Arts, Prints and Photographs, The New York Public Library, Astor, Lenox and Tilden Foundations)

George Bradburn. To deny them seats would silence them and leave the convention bereft of their wise counsel.[6]

Far more vocal were the majority of male delegates who insisted that women not be seated. Interestingly, the minister Henry Grew, whose daughter Mary was a delegate, was among them. "The reception of women as a part of this Convention would, in the view of many, be not only a violation of the customs of England, but of the ordinance of Almighty God," he intoned. Others agreed, pointing out that female involvement in the abolition movement aroused controversy; hundreds of men had abandoned the American Anti-Slavery Society to object to their presence. British delegates who shared similar attitudes reminded Americans that the British had long supported abolition in the United States, inferring that their opinion on this matter should hold sway.[7] At the end of the day-long debate, a vote was taken. Ninety percent of male delegates voted against seating the women. As a result, the eight had to observe the proceedings from an area curtained off from the main hall, invisible and silent. Phillips, James Mott, and a few other men submitted a formal written protest, but a majority in the convention tabled that complaint, refusing to include it in any records of the proceedings.

Garrison, who arrived in London four days late because of bad weather at sea, immediately joined the women to protest their exclusion. He refused to add his name to the list of delegates in attendance and would not participate in the convention. Never one burdened by humility, Garrison declared that had he been present for the debate, "we could have carried our point triumphantly." Despite the defeat, he felt some elation that this effort had unleashed a discussion on the "woman question," controversy that he believed was already resonating from one end of Britain to the other. James and Lucretia Mott were less sanguine, equating the injustice to "a prejudice similar to that which exists in America against color and against women too."[8] Lucretia tried to meet with several female British abolitionists to gain their support, but they exhibited no desire to become involved in the controversy. Ultimately Lucretia concluded that the debate was less about men's worries over female participation than over concerns that men "would be ridiculed in the morning papers." Daniel O'Connell, an Irish Catholic delegate who had supported the women, agreed. The main reason male delegates voted to exclude them was "the ridicule it might excite," a reaction O'Connell deemed "an unworthy, and indeed a cowardly motive."[9]

Writing about the event years later, Elizabeth expressed only limited gratitude to Phillips for spearheading this effort. What stuck in her mind was his statement to the convention after the vote was taken. Adopting the high ground, or perhaps tendering a gracious gesture, Phillips said that those who supported female participation did not resent the outcome and would now move forward and "act with the utmost cordiality." He added, "I have no doubt the women will sit with as much interest behind the bar as though the original proposition had been carried in the affirmative." Elizabeth wondered why Phillips assumed they would willingly tolerate their exclusion. His comment convinced her that even the most enlightened men could not truly identify with women's plight. She also denounced ministers in attendance and the influential role they played. "The clergy with few exceptions were bitter in their opposition," she recalled. "Although, as Abolitionists, they had been compelled to fight both Church and Bible to prove the black man's right to liberty, conscience forbade them to stretch those sacred limits far enough to give equal liberty to woman."[10]

News of what happened in London crossed the Atlantic. Sarah Grimké read about the controversy. She feared the debate might harm the antislavery movement by detracting from the principal issue—an interesting response from someone whose actions a few years earlier had fostered a similar debate. But on balance, Grimké decided that what had happened in London would heighten Americans' awareness of the importance of women's involvement in the antislavery cause. "The Convention had no right to reject the female delegates; as members of the A.S.S. they were entitled to a seat, unless it could be proved they were not persons," she concluded.[11]

Crucial to the development of the women's rights movement, the London convention proved a turning point in Elizabeth's and Lucretia's lives, initiating an enduring friendship and shared commitment to women's rights. Up to this point, Elizabeth had been on the periphery of reform work, enjoying a fairly indulged life after she left Troy Female Seminary—visiting friends and extended family, riding horseback, reading, and entertaining. (Apparently well before her marriage to Henry, Elizabeth and her brother-in-law Edward Bayard, who at the time was married to Elizabeth's older sister Tryphena, had developed an intimate friendship, and in 1838, he proposed to her that they run away together. Reason prevailed; Elizabeth rejected him.) Her interest in abolition developed primarily through her cousin Gerrit Smith and now through her husband, Henry. But the London convention and the injustices perpetrated against the eight delegates caused a "burning indignation that filled my soul," she wrote, adding that nothing could convince her to believe that heaven had ordained the inferiority of women. Garrison, who was boarding in the same London house as the Motts and the Stantons, ascertained that Elizabeth, along with her cheerful, lively demeanor, was "a fearless woman" who, he said, "goes for woman's rights with all her soul."[12]

Lucretia and Elizabeth shared similar reactions to the exclusion of female delegates in London and, more important, similar ideas about women's secondary status. Their sense of mutual respect was immediate. More than twenty years younger, Elizabeth was in awe of the remarkable Lucretia. Decades later, she wrote that she found her "the greatest wonder of the world—a woman who thought and had opinions of her own," someone "emancipated from all man-made creeds, and not afraid to question anything." Elizabeth called Lucretia an older, "peerless" woman, and she took "great delight in her society." The next year, Lucretia described Elizabeth as "bright, open, lovely," and admitted, "I love her now as one belonging to us." Apparently Elizabeth became a quick convert, for when she returned home she subscribed to the *Liberator*. In 1841, she spoke at a local temperance convention and "infused into my speech an Homeopathic dose of woman's rights, as I take good care to do in many private conversations." To Lucretia, Elizabeth confessed, "The more I think on the present condition of woman, the more am I oppressed with the reality of her degradation. The laws of our Country, how unjust are they!—Our customs how vicious! What God has made sinful, both in man & woman,—custom has made sinful in woman alone."[13]

The two continued to correspond, although eight years would pass before they acted on an idea they may have discussed in London: to hold a convention to demand women's rights. Their lives between that first meeting and the Seneca Falls Convention were busy. Children, weddings, grandchildren, entertaining, and corresponding with a wide circle of friends kept Lucretia occupied. She continued to preach and lecture on antislavery and helped to found a new organization to provide relief to impoverished women in Philadelphia. In 1844, her seventy-three-year-old mother, with whom she had been extremely close, died unexpectedly, causing Lucretia's own health to suffer. On returning home from Europe in December 1840, the Stantons lived with Elizabeth's family in Johnstown, New York, for nearly two years while Henry studied law. In the fall of 1842, they moved to Boston. During those eight years, Elizabeth gave birth to three boys and was busy with maternal and domestic responsibilities and Boston's stimulating social and cultural life.

Between the 1840 London convention and Seneca Falls, women's rights began to generate some attention. Margaret Fuller's influential treatise *Woman in the Nineteenth Century* was published in 1845. Fuller, who became one of the most famous Americans of her day, was brilliant and well read; her ambitious father had provided her with an exceptional education and allowed her full access to his library. By the age of nine, Fuller was reading Latin texts and writing to her father in Latin. She participated in the Transcendentalist movement, edited its magazine, the *Dial*, for a year and a half, and established friendships with well-known literary figures, including Ralph Waldo Emerson, Nathaniel Hawthorne, Bronson Alcott, Elizabeth Peabody, and Henry David Thoreau. While living in Boston, Fuller hosted "Conversations" in her home with some of the city's brightest minds. In 1844, Horace Greeley hired her as literary editor for his popular *New York Tribune*, thus making Fuller the nation's first female journalist.[14]

Although Fuller did not advocate female suffrage, her book addressed many issues later included in the Seneca Falls Declaration of Rights and Sentiments. Susan B. Anthony credited Fuller's treatise with having a more profound influence on the beginning of the women's movement than any other publication. Lydia Maria Child admired Fuller's bold thoughts, confessing that she would not have dared to express some of Fuller's ideas, "But they need to be said, and she is brave to do it." Fuller rejected the indulged lifestyle she believed typified too many privileged women. Nothing contained more "despicable frivolity" than the "novels which purport to give the picture of English fashionable life." Ignoring the domestic and family concerns that filled popular female literature, Fuller's book critiqued a society that separated men and women into public and private spheres and thus limited women's rights and opportunities. Female education often failed to expand their opportunities, primarily because it sought to make women "better companions and mothers for the *men*." She encouraged female self-reliance and self-fulfillment. To Fuller, marriage resembled a form of slavery, for "there exists in the mind of men a tone of feeling toward women as toward slaves." In 1846, Fuller traveled to Europe and reported on the social and political tumult occurring there. While returning home from Italy with her young son and Italian husband in 1850, she died a tragic death in a shipwreck off Long Island. Her premature demise stunned friends and admirers; her writings inspired women reformers for years.[15]

Another pivotal work was Elisha Powell Hurlbut's *Essays on Human Rights, and Their Political Guaranties*, also published in 1845. It is likely that Elizabeth read these essays, for Hurlbut became a judge of the New York State Supreme Court the same year as Daniel Cady, and his work remained in print for years. These writings placed Hurlbut among a small group of men who publicly supported women's rights. Understandably, he emphasized legal issues, arguing for individuals' inalienable rights, rejecting Blackstone's laws, and, according to the historian Ann Gordon, offering "a scathing portrait of male domination." He defined common law as "the law of the male sex gathering unto themselves dominion and power at the sacrifice of the female." Once married, a woman experienced "civil death," and Hurlbut denounced laws that conferred wives' entire estates to their husbands. "Hath not woman a *right* to be ever regarded as a free moral agent?" he asked. The fact that women had no say in divorce and custody laws argued for their involvement in government.[16]

Other men began to express opinions on gender equality. Of particular note was a sermon entitled "The Rights and Condition of Woman," delivered by the Unitarian minister Samuel J. May, Jr., in November 1845. May was born into an elite Boston family and educated at a public grammar school and Harvard College. He found his calling as a Unitarian minister, though his liberal beliefs frequently put him at odds with other ministers and his parishioners in Syracuse, New York. May became involved with several reform issues, including temperance, the peace movement, and public education. A meeting with Garrison drew him into the radical arm of the antislavery struggle, and he became an advocate of women's rights. As male delegates gathered to revise the state constitution, he felt compelled to address his church. Temperance was one issue on the docket, and May believed that women should have a voice in this matter. Since women were usually the victims of drunken husbands or fathers, May recognized the irony of preventing at least half the population from voting on temperance.[17]

May became the first minister representing a mainstream denomination publicly to support female enfranchisement. He reminded parishioners that women had no opportunity to choose the form of government under which they lived—men alone framed it. He countered the many arguments used to justify women's inferior status and exclusion from the political process. Some men insisted that women's physical stature rendered them incapable of political involvement. To that, May queried, "Why should this consign them to mental, moral or social dependence?" Moreover, he wondered why anyone objected to women speaking in public when they had something significant to say. "To me, it is as grateful to hear words of wisdom and eloquence from a woman as a man." Characterizing the voting process as too contentious, indecorous, and acrimonious, men used this as another reason to exclude women; May's solution was that men act in a more refined manner when voting. Many argued that women who engaged in the political process would neglect their families; May suggested that mothers and fathers share childrearing duties. "Women are coaxed, flattered, courted, but they are not respected by many men as they ought to be; neither do they respect themselves as they should." He concluded: "These circumstances operate powerfully to depress, and oppress women—to make them too dependent—to leave them at the mercy of men." Equal rights for all would correct this injustice.[18] May's sermon appeared in newspapers and in tract form the following year. Lucy found May's arguments so persuasive that she bought multiple copies to send to family members and friends.

In 1846, New York held its convention to revise the state constitution. Among the issues being considered, aside from temperance, were married women's property laws and universal suffrage. Legislators expressed skepticism about extending property rights to married women: that issue also suggested the

need to redefine gender relationships. If wives gained access to their own property, what other rights might they demand? Since property ownership implied
independence, women might make their own decisions or challenge their husbands and therefore foster family rivalry. Some might even assume they deserved the right to vote. Effectively turning the tide against majority support, the
delegate Charles O'Conor, a bachelor lawyer, argued that wives achieved wealth
and status through their husbands and that men were well qualified to vote for
them.[19] A wife should accede to her husband's demands and willingly relinquish
all her property. Laws and traditions sustained wives' dependence on husbands
as a central tenet of marriage.

These debates generated interest well beyond Albany. On August 15, 1846,
the delegate Alpheus S. Greene presented a petition to the convention written
and signed by six courageous women from Jefferson County, New York. These
women had followed the convention proceedings and discussed the issues being
raised. Their petition demanded that all governments should "derive their just
powers from the consent of the governed" and accused New York state's
government of failing to do that. The state taxed women as citizens but then
gave them no voice or representation. The six demanded that men revise the
state constitution so as to "extend to women equal, and civil and political rights
with men." As a gesture of their independence, the five married women signed
the petition using their given first names rather than identifying themselves
through their husbands' first names. Ultimately, their petition and the debates in the
constitutional convention came to naught, for the assembly opposed making any
change in married women's property laws.[20]

Individual campaigns were another channel for female activism. Lucy's
letters from Oberlin to her family expressed her strong views on women's rights,
and in November 1846, she announced her intention to become a public lecturer and labor "for the restoration and salvation of our sex." Lucy's mother
disapproved, as did her sister Sarah, expressing disappointment that Lucy would
forgo true happiness as a wife and mother and reject teaching, for which she
had a proven talent. Sarah insisted that women were not "groaning under half
so heavy a yoke of bondage as you imagine. I am sure I do not feel burdened by
anything man has laid upon me, because I can't vote. But what care I for that?
I *would* not if I could." Lucy could not let such comments rest without responding, and she sent her sister a copy of Samuel May's sermon to reinforce
her views. The next year, she began lecturing for the Massachusetts Anti-Slavery
Society.[21] Renting a tiny room in Boston with two other girls, she scrimped to
pay for food as she traveled and lectured. No one had heard of this young
country girl. She often posted her own handbills advertising her lectures and

confronted men who taunted her and pelted her with paper wads, rotten fruit, and, in one instance, a hymnal.

Later that year, Lucy experienced a moment of revelation that caused her to also speak on women's oppression. One day while walking through the Boston Common, she stopped to admire Hiram Powers's famous statue "The Greek Slave" and broke into tears, realizing how this image also symbolized female oppression. From that moment forward, in all her antislavery speeches, Lucy also pleaded for equal rights for women. When a worried Samuel May, Jr., now an agent for the Society, questioned her on the wisdom of introducing this controversial issue, Lucy responded, "I was a woman before I was an abolitionist."[22]

Only months before the Seneca Falls Convention, property rights for married women resurfaced as a key concern in both New York and Pennsylvania and finally gained majority support. After twelve years of debating the issue, the New York state senate and assembly passed into law the Married Woman's Property Act on April 7, 1848. Aiding the cause were petitions signed by hundreds of men and women, urging the legislature to change the law. A few weeks later, the Pennsylvania state legislature enacted a similar measure, which Lucretia and other women had supported with a petition campaign. Both states addressed a major injustice by allowing wives the right to claim property they brought into a marriage and retain additional property they acquired during marriage. A husband's creditors could no longer seize a wife's property to pay his debts.[23] These state laws represented significant advances in women's rights; both served as models for other states in the years ahead and no doubt planted hope in women nationwide.

But it was the Seneca Falls Convention that truly changed history. Two slightly different accounts exist of how the actual suggestion to hold a convention was made. In the *History of Woman Suffrage* and in her later writings, Elizabeth attributed the idea to female delegates' exclusion from the 1840 World Anti-Slavery Convention, recalling that she and Lucretia "walked home arm in arm afterwards" and "resolved to hold a convention as soon as we returned home." In their correspondence and during a meeting of the two in Boston in 1841, Lucretia and Elizabeth continued to discuss women's rights. According to Lucretia's version, Elizabeth was the "moving spirit of the event" because she conceived the idea of the convention. She reminded Elizabeth of the circumstances: "Thou must do thyself justice. Remember the first Convention originated with thee. When we were walking the streets of Boston together in 1841 ... thou asked if we could not have a Convention for Woman's Rights."[24] Whenever and wherever the idea first germinated, these two conceived it, inspired by events at the London convention. In July 1848, they would finally translate their idea into action.

Seneca Falls, the setting for this convention, a small town in what today is called the Finger Lakes District of New York state, was undergoing significant changes. As mentioned earlier, it was situated in the heart of an area that was on fire with various reform movements: revivalism, spiritualism, communitarianism, temperance, Millerism, Mormonism, and abolition. The town and surrounding area had attracted a number of families who moved there for its rich farmland, natural resources, and easy access to points east and west, thanks to the recent construction of several canals and railroads. Like so many other towns in the Northeast, Seneca Falls was an agrarian community transforming into an industrial one. The town was aptly named for waterfalls that generated power for its factories. With the completion of the Erie Canal, an engineering marvel of its time, the Great Lakes and cities in the Midwest were opened to the East Coast, and travel time was reduced from a few weeks to a few days. The completion in 1828 of a connecting canal from Seneca Falls to the Erie Canal prompted expansion of the town's commerce. The Auburn and Rochester Railroad, finished in 1841, gave another boost to local transportation. The towns of Auburn and Waterloo were now only a short train ride away, and the cities of Rochester to the west and Syracuse to the east now likewise only a few hours away. New woolen mills, flour mills, and sawmills, built by enterprising businessmen who sensed the area's potential, dotted the Seneca River. By the 1840s, a number of businesses lined Seneca Falls' main street, including a millinery shop, several dry goods stores, two distilleries, an iron pump company, and two hotels. To serve its four thousand inhabitants, the town had its own newspaper, the semiweekly *Seneca County Courier,* and the townspeople enjoyed reading the *New York Tribune*, which arrived each week. Five churches welcomed worshipers, including the Wesleyan Chapel on Main Street, completed by local Methodists in 1843.[25]

A number of Quakers had moved to the region in the 1820s and 1830s, many from Pennsylvania and New Jersey, creating a community of like-minded people and a stronghold of antislavery sentiment. In December 1847, Frederick Douglass and his family settled in Rochester, where he began publishing his newspaper, the *North Star*. The fugitive slave Harriet Tubman would make her home in Auburn in the 1850s. Frances and William Seward, both strong abolitionists, lived there as well. (He would become a leader in the Republican Party and later Abraham Lincoln's secretary of state.) Rochester, the largest city in the

East view of Seneca Falls village.

East View of Seneca Falls Village (Archives of Seneca Falls Historical Society)

region, boasted three sizeable antislavery organizations by the late 1830s—one for men, another for white women, and one for black women. People active in the abolition movement hosted controversial lecturers like Garrison and Abby Kelley and sent at least a dozen petitions to Congress demanding an end to slavery. Several homes served as way stations on the Underground Railroad.[26]

The area in and around Seneca Falls had a strong community of reform-minded women. In 1842, five of them, including Mary Ann M'Clintock, Amy Post, and Abby Kelley, organized a fair in Rochester to raise money to support antislavery activities. Seneca Falls hosted one the following year. Temperance garnered substantial community support. Citizens established a temperance society for men and another for women, and in February 1842, a temperance paper, the *Water Bucket*, began publication there. Only two months later, Seneca Falls voted to prohibit the sale of alcohol, creating an immediate and positive impact on the community. Drinking and crime dropped significantly. Most businessmen and factory owners welcomed the new law, which promised greater worker productivity and a sober citizenry. And, as mentioned earlier, Millerism caught hold of several hundred citizens in 1843 and 1844 as they awaited Christ's anticipated return.[27]

While a number of Seneca Falls residents were strong abolitionists, support for the cause was hardly universal. The town experienced some unrest when antislavery lecturers visited in 1842 and again in 1843. Abby Kelley spoke in

Seneca Falls in August 1843, decrying the evils of slavery. Her six lectures, delivered to mixed audiences, elicited responses similar to those the Grimké sisters had stirred up years earlier. Because of her radical reputation, ministers refused Kelley the use of their churches. A local abolitionist and town leader, Ansel Bascom, finally agreed to let her speak from the stoop of his home. As Bascom's daughter Mary later recalled, Kelley "harangued the people assembled in his orchard," trying to convince listeners to join the movement. Seneca Falls' Methodists divided over their commitment to antislavery. In March 1843, several militant members abandoned their original church because it refused to adopt a strong stance against slavery, and they organized a new Wesleyan Methodist Church.[28] They built the Wesleyan Chapel, which welcomed all speakers and their causes—including women's rights.

The suggestion to hold a women's rights convention surfaced at an afternoon tea party—a popular type of social gathering enjoyed by privileged women. Jane C. Hunt, who lived in a handsome brick home on the east side of Waterloo, hosted the event on July 9 or 10, 1848 (the exact date is uncertain). She had invited to tea her good friend Martha Coffin Wright of Auburn and her famous older sister, Lucretia, who was visiting. Hunt also invited another friend and relative by marriage, Mary Ann M'Clintock of Waterloo, as well as Elizabeth, who was now living in Seneca Falls.[29] All but Elizabeth were Quakers, Garrisonians, and formerly from the Philadelphia area. Lucretia had come the farthest distance. She and James had been traveling in upstate New York to attend the Genesee Yearly Meeting of Hicksite Friends and to visit Seneca Indians on their New York reservation. (Quakers had long been concerned about the poor treatment of Native Americans and had established a school and model reservation for the Seneca tribe.) The Motts also toured several settlements of fugitive slaves living in the area before coming to stay with Lucretia's sister Martha and her family.

The Stantons had moved to Seneca Falls only a year earlier. Elizabeth, now the mother of three sons, arrived in the spring of 1847; Henry joined the family ten months later. Though stimulated by life in Boston, Henry had failed to achieve the financial or political success he desired. Seneca Falls offered new possibilities. He also worried about his health, living in a city where consumption, the disease that had caused his mother's death, was endemic. He sought a wholesome, commercially vibrant community, populated by sympathizers with the antislavery cause, which meant a great deal to him. Probably also figuring in the decision to move was Judge Daniel Cady's offer of a house he owned. Interestingly, Cady deeded the home to Elizabeth rather than to Henry; he continued to harbor doubts about his son-in-law's financial stability.[30] The rambling house stood on two acres of land on a hill with a view of the river and of several of the town's factories. It was located near the main road that connected Waterloo, Seneca Falls, and Auburn, but on the opposite side of the river from many of the town's equally large homes.

This was not an easy move for Elizabeth. The demands of motherhood and household chores overwhelmed her, and she had trouble finding dependable domestic help. The house needed attention, since it had not been lived in for

Elizabeth Cady Stanton with sons Daniel and Henry, 1848 (Library of Congress)

five years, so Judge Cady gave Elizabeth money to oversee major renovations. Henry's delay in moving and several illnesses that afflicted the Stanton boys made the family's first year in Seneca Falls all the harder on Elizabeth. She may have suffered a miscarriage. Even after Henry arrived, he was of little help, for he traveled frequently. Legal cases drew him afield, as did political interests, including his two terms in the New York state legislature and his work on behalf of the Free Soil and Republican parties. Elizabeth's privileged upbringing probably made her myriad responsibilities seem all the more difficult. But years later she interpreted these struggles as significant: "I now fully understood the practical difficulties most women had to contend with in the isolated household." The discontent she felt "with woman's position as wife, mother, housekeeper, physician, and spiritual guide" awakened in her another reason to improve their lot.[31]

Elizabeth had thrived in Boston, and she found adjusting to Seneca Falls a "depressing" and startling change, as she noted years later.[32] She missed friends and intellectual stimulation. This well-educated, bright, energetic woman had relished Boston's bustle and its many reform activities and cultural outlets. Seneca Falls was far quieter. She tried to keep abreast of news through the *Seneca Falls Courier* and the *New York Tribune*. Certainly debates in the New York state legislature on extending property rights to married women caught her attention. Through Henry's reform interests, she gained constant exposure to abolition and politics. But there is no doubt that she was primed for a greater cause. In July 1848 that opportunity arose.

At Jane Hunt's tea party, the five probably chatted about family and community happenings, but soon their conversation turned to a discussion of injustices against women. Elizabeth recalled that she "poured out, that day, the torrent of my long-accumulating discontent, with such vehemence and indignation that I stirred myself, as well as the rest of the party, to do and dare anything."[33] According to Hunt family lore, Jane's husband Richard briefly joined them and asked why they didn't do something to address their concerns. It was one thing to complain, quite another to take action. The five women resolved to hold a convention that would meet while Lucretia was still in the area. Her presence was critical in order to attract a crowd.

Among the others present that afternoon, the one who would become a lasting and visible presence in the women's rights movement was Lucretia's younger sister, Martha Coffin Wright. She was six months' pregnant at the time, carrying her seventh and last child at the age of forty-one. She had lived most of her adult life in upstate New York. Her first husband had died in 1826, leaving her with an infant daughter to raise. While teaching school in Aurora she had

*Martha Coffin Wright
(Sophia Smith Collection,
Smith College)*

met David Wright, a lawyer. They married in 1829. Four years later, when visiting Lucretia in Philadelphia, Martha had met Garrison and become committed to the antislavery cause. She and Lucretia were present at the founding of the American Anti-Slavery Society in 1833. The Wrights' large home in Auburn became a center for antislavery discussions and a way station for fugitive slaves escaping via the Underground Railroad. Martha also became conversant with the laws and practices that limited married women's legal and economic status. She was well aware of low wages paid to women, and she protested when she learned that the family seamstress earned only half of what they paid a man to do outdoor work. A witty and gifted writer, Wright made light of her pregnant condition at the Convention. "I plead guilty to being very stupid & dispirited at Seneca Falls—the prospect of having more Wrights than I wanted tending materially to subdue the ardor & energy that wd. doubtless have characterized me 'at another time.' "[34]

Both the M'Clintocks and Hunts were Hicksite Quakers and long active in the antislavery movement. Jane Clothier Hunt was the fourth wife of Richard P.

Hunt, a merchant and mill owner, investor in the Waterloo Woolen Mill, and the wealthiest resident of Waterloo. He had moved there from Westchester County, New York, in 1821, opened a successful dry goods store, and later purchased land and built a commodious brick house. His third wife was Sarah M'Clintock Hunt, probably the niece and ward of Thomas M'Clintock, Mary Ann's husband. Jane Hunt had a young son, and two weeks before entertaining her four guests at tea, she had given birth to a baby girl. Mary Ann M'Clintock's husband owned a moderately successful pharmacy business in Waterloo where the family had moved in 1837 from Philadelphia. Thomas also served as an officer of the American Anti-Slavery Society. Both homes probably served as way stations on the Underground Railroad.[35]

With only days to organize the Convention, the five women immediately set to work. One of them contacted the minister of the Wesleyan Chapel to secure space for their meeting. The notice sent to the *Seneca County Courier,* which first appeared on July 11, announced a convention "to discuss the social, civil, and religious condition and rights of woman." It mentioned Lucretia because of her fame. Rather than signing their names at the bottom of the announcement, the five organizers declared that the meeting was "called by the Women of Seneca County, New York." They saw this not as a personal effort but an event representing the shared concerns of all.[36]

A few other newspapers ran the announcement, including the *Ovid (NY) Bee* and Douglass's *North Star.* News also spread by word of mouth, especially among the region's large Quaker community. Elizabeth Cady Stanton and Elizabeth M'Clintock invited a few well-known reformers and antislavery activists, including Lydia Maria Child, Maria Weston Chapman, and Sarah Grimké, even though they lived far away. M'Clintock contacted Frederick Douglass, and he quickly responded that he would attend. Nevertheless, the five experienced some trepidation, wondering if anyone would show up and whether protestors would upset the proceedings, as had happened at a number of antislavery meetings. No public convention on this scale had ever been held to discuss the injustices and oppression American women endured. This was an exciting and bold, but risky, venture.

The women also had to establish an agenda and compose a statement of purpose. They immediately began to consider their goals, though as Elizabeth later recalled, "they felt as helpless and hopeless as if they had been suddenly asked to construct a steam engine." She began creating an outline of injustices and accompanying resolutions for change. With his legal background, Henry Stanton helped Elizabeth locate particular laws to ground their concerns in reality.[37]

A second meeting took place, this time at the M'Clintock home, on Sunday, July 16, to discuss a draft Elizabeth had been composing. Sitting around a mahogany table in the parlor were only three women—Mary Ann M'Clintock, her daughter Elizabeth, and Elizabeth Cady Stanton. Lucretia was unable to attend because James was ill.[38] Their task was now to transform the draft into ringing statements that befit the revolutionary nature of their cause. They examined different declarations written for antislavery, temperance, and peace conventions, but nothing seemed quite right. They pored over statute books and institutional constitutions and pondered customs and religious dictates. After considering several possibilities, one of them began to read the Declaration of Independence. Suddenly they had their model. According to Elizabeth's account, they had no trouble adjusting the Declaration of Independence to suit their purpose. They modified its preamble for their opening statement and substituted injustices imposed on women by men for the eighteen grievances perpetrated by George III against the colonists. Even though these privileged women acknowledged that they had never been subjected to the full brunt of the wrongs they set forth, they could identify with those who had. While no records reveal the details of this second meeting, Elizabeth was probably the principal author of the Declaration, with the assistance of others. They named their document the Declaration of Rights and Sentiments, the same name given the founding document of the American Anti-Slavery Society. Eleven resolutions were added to address their grievances.

The press announcement had started to circulate. How people in the region responded to this news is unknown, but some must have been startled, others excited, and a good many just plain curious. Two days before the meeting, Lucretia wrote Elizabeth, expressing both optimism and caution. "The Convention will not be so large as it otherwise might be, owing to the busy time with the farmers, harvest, &c—But it will be a beginning & we may hope it will be followed in due time by one of a more general character."[39] Her words proved prescient. Among those who attended, some were drawn to a cause with which they could readily identify; some were attracted by the presence of Lucretia Mott; and others came out of curiosity or boredom. Reporters represented at least three newspapers: the *Seneca County Courier*, the *North Star*, and Auburn's *National Reformer*.

The meeting caught the attention of both admirers and detractors. During a period when public entertainment was limited, lectures, meetings, and debates on almost any topic attracted crowds. This convention promised to address something daringly radical. Charlotte Woodward, a nineteen-year-old glove maker at the time, recalled decades later that on reading the notice, she "ran from one house to another in her neighborhood, and found other women reading it, some with amusement and incredulity, others with absorbed interest." Encouraged by at least six friends who agreed to accompany her, Woodward decided to attend the first day, when only women were allowed. Religion was a factor in attracting an audience. Quakers made up the largest denomination represented, though a number of Episcopalians, Congregationalists, Methodists, and Wesleyan Methodists also attended.[40]

On Wednesday, the first day of the Convention, Lucretia and her sister rode the train from Auburn to Seneca Falls, having arranged to spend the night with the Stantons. According to an account by someone who was present, the day dawned bright and clear, with the temperature reaching ninety degrees. Elizabeth's sister Harriet Cady Eaton brought her young son Daniel. Elizabeth approached the day with trepidation, feeling responsible for what was about to unfold and nervous because she had never before spoken in public. She later admitted that she felt like "abandoning all her principles and running away." But there was no time for second thoughts. Organizers brought several copies of the Declaration of Rights and Sentiments, the Resolutions, and volumes of the statutes of New York in case they needed to consult state laws. People were waiting outside Wesleyan Chapel when the women arrived, for the building was locked—a detail they had overlooked. No one had a key, so Daniel Eaton crawled through a window and opened the door from the inside. One girl who attended remembered the chapel's dusty windows, wooden pews, and gallery extending around three sides of the interior. The audience was more varied than the organizers had intended. Only females were supposed to attend that first day, but a few young mothers like Harriet Eaton brought their children. Approximately forty men showed up. The five women decided to allow them to stay, although they were asked to listen rather than talk that first day. Mary Ann M'Clintock, Jr., was appointed to take notes of the proceedings.[41]

By eleven o'clock, an hour later than planned, the meeting was under way. On the platform at the front of the chapel sat the principal organizers, including the four M'Clintock daughters. Elizabeth described their purpose to the assembled crowd, asserting that her sense of "right and duty" motivated her to take up the cause of women's rights. This was a woman's responsibility, for only she could "understand the height, the depth, the length, and the breadth of her own degradation." Elizabeth argued that no more important question stood before the public. For too long, women worldwide had been degraded, mocked, and scorned. "So long has man exercised tyranny over her, injurious to himself and benumbing to her faculties, that few can nerve themselves to meet the storm: and so long has the chain been about her that she knows not there is a remedy." Elizabeth boldly insisted these attitudes had to change. She encouraged female listeners to remain steadfast as they pursued their rights. Following this inspiring address, Lucretia, "the moving spirit of the occasion," spoke and encouraged everyone to join the cause. Elizabeth then introduced the Declaration of Rights and Sentiments, reading it through and then slowly rereading it paragraph by paragraph so comments could be made and changes incorporated. The first session adjourned at 2:30.[42]

The Declaration of Rights and Sentiments (see Appendix A) began with the words "all men and women are created equal," a clarion cry for the women's rights movement. It listed the injustices women endured due to "repeated injuries and usurpations on the part of man toward woman, having in direct object the establishment of an absolute tyranny over her." Man denied woman access to the vote; forced her to submit to laws over which she had no voice; prevented her from being represented in elected bodies; enacted laws for marriage that made her "civilly dead"; removed a wife's rights to property and wages; created divorce laws that caused her to lose guardianship of her children; forced a wife to promise to obey her husband; allowed the government to tax her property; prevented her access to the most lucrative professions such as law and medicine; paid her lower wages than a man received; denied her the opportunity to attend college; insisted on her subordinate role in the church; established a different set of moral codes for men and women; and claimed it was man's right to assign woman to a specific, domestic sphere. The Declaration laid the responsibility for these injustices squarely on men.

While radical in most respects, the document reflected its time as well as the socioeconomic status of those who composed it. From today's perspective, its undemocratic, even uncharitable thoughts are rather jarring. The document elevated white women above male immigrants, free blacks, and the destitute who lacked the advantages many middle-class women possessed. The Declaration argued that men withheld rights from women but gave the same rights "to the most ignorant and degraded men—both natives and foreigners." It acknowledged that the nation's political and legal culture treated all women unjustly, but then it cited specific issues that were relevant primarily to middle- and upper-class white women, such as the lack of any opportunity to attend college or pursue a lucrative career. The Declaration also failed to acknowledge that wives in New York, Pennsylvania, and Mississippi could claim their own property and that Oberlin Collegiate Institute was coeducational.

One of the more intriguing assertions in the Declaration concerned a woman's lack of confidence, claiming that society systematically undermined her so as "to lessen her self-respect, and to make her willing to lead a dependent and abject life." The Declaration also attacked the double standard, arguing that a different "code of morals for men and women" existed and that society expected women to act as models of virtue. It insisted that the pursuit of happiness mentioned in the Constitution was a right everyone should enjoy. Women needed the same rights as men "to promote every righteous cause by every righteous means." Laws and customs that kept them in a dependent state must be overturned.

During the afternoon session that first day, Elizabeth again addressed the audience. "The world has never yet seen a truly great and virtuous nation, because in the degradation of woman the very fountains of life are poisoned at their source," she asserted.[43] The Declaration was read again and changes made. Then eleven Resolutions that laid out concrete ideas on how to improve women's lives were presented and discussed for the first time. One Resolution demanded that women become the equal of men. Another said that the "virtue, delicacy, and refinement of behavior" demanded of women should also be required of men. Other Resolutions asked that the domestic sphere assigned to women be enlarged and that laws impeding female equality be changed, since they countered "the great precept of nature." The Resolutions strengthened the Declaration of Rights and Sentiments by demanding that women should have the same rights and responsibilities as men and participate in the life of the nation as equal human beings.

Following the reading of the Resolutions, Lucretia shared a humorous piece written by her sister Martha, in which she challenged the idea that wives should always obey their husbands and do so with a "smiling countenance." After cleverly examining the daily burdens of overworked mothers, she questioned why written advice was "so lavishly bestowed on the wife" but not on the husband. Then Elizabeth M'Clintock, daughter of Mary Ann, delivered a speech. That evening, Lucretia placed women's grievances within a larger context by describing the progress of other reform movements. She urged men in the audience to aid in the struggle for women's rights. Eliab W. Capron, the editor of Auburn's *National Reformer*, later remembered her talk as "one of the most eloquent, logical and philosophical discourses we ever listened to."[44]

Word had spread that something exciting, even revolutionary, was happening at Seneca Falls, and a larger crowd appeared the second day, including more men. Those in attendance commented on the throng, and latecomers like Amelia Bloomer only managed to find a seat upstairs. James Mott chaired the morning meeting, since no woman could imagine a female presiding before a mixed audience. The minutes of the previous day were shared, and Elizabeth reread the Declaration of Rights and Sentiments. Several individuals addressed the Declaration, including Ansel Bascom, who had participated in New York State's recent constitutional convention and now spoke at length about the new married women's property act. After some discussion, the audience adopted the Declaration unanimously.

Now the eleven Resolutions were reread, and individually each came up for a vote. The most controversial issue, and the only one to face opposition, was the ninth: "Resolved, that it is the duty of the women of this country to secure to themselves their sacred right to the elective franchise." Henry, who had assisted Elizabeth with some of the legal issues, had expressed surprise at his wife's insistence that women should demand the right to vote. "You will turn the proceedings into a farce," he warned her. According to family lore, Henry was so upset by this radical demand that he left town.[45] In any case, among the five husbands of the organizers, he and David Wright were the two who did not attend the Convention or sign the Declaration of Rights and Sentiments. A number of people at the Convention apparently agreed with Henry and believed that Resolutions should only address the "social, civil, and religious," but not the political, rights of women. Several Quakers, including the Motts, found the demand for suffrage troubling, and Lucretia warned her friend Elizabeth, "Why Lizzie, thee will make us ridiculous."[46] On principle, Quakers tried to avoid partisan politics and believed that women should wield their influence elsewhere. Others argued that fathers or husbands adequately represented them at the ballot box. In their thinking, women's moral superiority and domestic influence were too precious to sacrifice merely for the right to vote. But Elizabeth was adamant, believing that with the vote, they would gain additional rights and be able to affect future legislation.

It was Frederick Douglass who saved the day. Born in 1818, Douglass was the son of a slave mother and a white father who grew up knowing oppression firsthand. As a young slave, he served several masters. While working in the Hugh Auld household in Baltimore, he learned to read and write. He was hardly tractable, and when he was in his teens, Auld sent him to a slave breaker to teach him to obey. Here, Douglass dared to fight back and assert his humanity. In 1838, he was able to escape bondage, borrowing the papers of a free black seaman and secretly making his way to Boston. A few years later, the American Anti-Slavery Society hired him as a lecturer, and Douglass riveted northern audiences with his personal accounts of the slave experience. His *Narrative of the Life of Frederick Douglass*, which he wrote and published in 1845, became a bestseller in the United States and abroad and made him the most famous and respected African American in the United States. Eventually British abolitionists helped him purchase his freedom and funded his antislavery newspaper, the *North Star*.[47]

Douglass now spoke up, arguing that he could not claim the right of suffrage for himself if he would not allow women that same right. The world, he felt, would be a far better place if women were as politically involved as men. "In this denial of the right to participate in government, not merely the

*Frederick Douglass
(American Antiquarian
Society)*

degradation of woman and the perpetuation of a great injustice happens, but the maiming and repudiation of one-half of the moral and intellectual power of the government of the world." His arguments and personal efforts in fighting injustice and enslavement convinced many in the audience that suffrage was essential. This Resolution and all others passed. From this point forward, Douglass became an ardent advocate of women's rights. Years later, he proudly recalled the moment. "When I stood up for the rights of woman, self was out of the question, and I found a little nobility in the act." Douglass expressed a sense of satisfaction that he had been "sufficiently enlightened" to take this stance and felt "glory" in having done so.[48]

After another break in early evening, the Convention reconvened. Thomas M'Clintock now presided and asked the audience to comment on what had transpired earlier in the day. No one spoke up, so Elizabeth enumerated the laws that kept women in a subordinate state. Thomas M'Clintock read sections of Blackstone's laws to emphasize woman's current legal subservience to man. Mary Ann M'Clintock, Jr., delivered a talk, calling on women to shake off their lethargy and demand a change in their status. Douglass presented an "excellent and appropriate speech" to reiterate his support for women's rights. An hour-long speech by Lucretia, later described as consisting of "most beautiful and spiritual appeals" closed the evening. Five women, including Elizabeth and Mary Ann and Elizabeth M'Clintock, were appointed to prepare minutes of the proceedings for publication in the *North Star*.[49]

As the Convention drew to a close, one final debate ensued over whether both women and men should sign the Declaration of Rights and Sentiments. A compromise was reached to include signatures of both, but on different sheets of paper. Sixty-eight women added their names; thirty-two men signed separately. Most of those who signed were not illustrious; they varied in economic status from wealthy to poor. A quarter of them were Quakers, and the rest were from several different religious backgrounds; only one Presbyterian and no Catholics signed. Most lived in the immediate vicinity, though a few had come from as far away as Rochester. Only four of the signers—Elizabeth, Lucretia, Douglass, and Wright—would achieve national fame. Douglass was the only known African American signatory. All but one signer were dead by the time the Nineteenth Amendment became part of the U.S. Constitution in 1920. Charlotte Woodward Pierce was still alive, though probably too infirm to vote in the presidential election that year.[50]

Organizers of the Convention felt elated by what had transpired. The excitement the meeting generated far surpassed their expectations. As the *North Star* reported, "ability and dignity" marked the Convention, adding, "There were frequently differences of opinion and animated discussions; but in no case was there the slightest absence of good feeling and decorum." Elizabeth characterized the event as one "dignified" by a "religious earnestness."[51] A well-attended meeting addressing such radical ideas that did not fall prey to protestors and violence was worthy of note. Undoubtedly it helped that this first convention met in a small, fairly isolated community and convened with little advance notice.

Several Quaker women from Rochester were so excited about the issues raised at Seneca Falls that they decided to hold a convention two weeks later in their city's Unitarian church. Its stated purpose was "to consider the rights of woman, politically, religiously, and industrially." Some people who had been at the Seneca Falls Convention attended this Rochester meeting, including Lucretia, Elizabeth, Amy Kirby Post, Douglass, and Mary Ann M'Clintock. Lucretia had not planned to attend, but Post's entreaties convinced her that her presence was essential. Also in the audience were Susan B. Anthony's parents and two sisters, who afterward shared their impressions with her. Smaller and less noteworthy than the Seneca Falls Convention, the Rochester meeting nonetheless punctuated the growing sense of excitement and dedication among reformers. Something had started at Seneca Falls that would not be stopped.[52]

Moreover, the Rochester convention lay to rest the idea that men had to preside over conventions with mixed audiences. Taking a most radical step, Abigail Bush stepped to the podium to chair this meeting. So accustomed were women to having men preside that even Elizabeth and Lucretia initially opposed Bush's leadership, fearful that it would doom their effort. They quickly became converts, however, for at the end of the first session, as Bush remembered decades later, Lucretia approached her and "folded me tenderly in her arms and thanked me for presiding." Recognizing Bush's ability and right to take charge, Elizabeth apologized and chided herself for such "foolish conduct." As she explained, "My only excuse is that woman has been so little accustomed to act in a public capacity that she does not always know what is due to those around her."[53]

This meeting initiated a practice subsequent conventions followed: opening the floor to all. Several people in the audience took the opportunity to speak. The newly married Rebecca Sandford, described as a "young and beautiful stranger," addressed the crowd, saying that when she had learned about this convention she had delayed travel with her husband in order to attend. She argued that women would not abuse the right of suffrage but instead enhance the political process and the legal system by their political participation. Taking the opposite stance, at least three men in the audience objected to female suffrage. Other attendees addressed ideas articulated in the Declaration of Rights and Sentiments, discussing women's economic and political rights and working women's right to fair wages and to a decent education. Two seamstresses shared their firsthand experiences with economic oppression, noting that they could barely survive on earnings of 31 to 38 cents a day and $1.50 charges for weekly board. As a postscript to their remarks, Lucretia noted, "Our aim should be to elevate the lowly and aid the weak," and Elizabeth commented that wages for domestic servants were far too low, considering the amount of work they performed. Douglass and his coworker William C. Neill at the *North Star* declared their support for women's rights. Elizabeth M'Clintock read Maria Weston Chapman's satiric poem "The Times That Try Men's Souls." Its first verse depicted a world turned upside down: "Confusion has seized us, and all things go wrong / The women have leaped from 'their spheres' / And instead of fixed stars, shoot as comets along / And are setting the world by the ears." Participants voted to support married women's property rights, fair wages, equal access to education and employment, and greater female authority in the home and church. They approved dropping the word "obey" from marriage vows, for as Lucretia explained, Quakers long ago had eliminated that word in their wedding ceremonies without disasters befalling their marriages. The audience endorsed female suffrage and added that it should be given without regard to "complexion" or gender.[54]

The issue of religion arose when a Mr. Colton of Connecticut delivered a lengthy commentary, declaring that he "loved the ladies as well as they loved themselves" but "would not have woman excel her proper sphere" for "the strife and contention of the political world." Citing scripture, Colton insisted that no woman had the right to occupy the pulpit or demand equality. After he sat down, Lucretia went on the attack and with "great sarcasm and eloquence" countered that the church was partly responsible for women's degraded status. Too many misconceptions about their proper role emerged from the mouths of clergymen rather than from actual words in the Bible. Using her extensive knowledge of scripture, Lucretia argued that the Bible had "none of the prohibitions in regard to women" he had quoted. She urged Colton to reread his Bible and locate the many passages that revealed female strength and significance.[55]

Overall, the Rochester convention was a success. The *North Star* commented on the meeting and the injustices it addressed, predicting, "The time cannot be far distant when this monstrous wrong will be remedied, and woman restored her dignity." Both the proceedings and female leadership impressed the *Rochester Daily Advocate*, which concluded that with such "eloquent and determined champions," the women's cause "must triumph in the end."[56]

Buoyed by the success of the Seneca Falls and Rochester meetings, Elizabeth was eager to move forward. She wrote the abolitionist and reformer Amy Post and raised a major question facing female activists: "Our conventions both went off so well that we have great encouragement to go on. What are we next to do?—We have declared our right to vote—The question now is how shall we get possession of what rightfully belongs to us?" She suggested that women inaugurate a petition campaign in several states to demonstrate what she assumed to be widespread support for women's equality.[57] From July 1848 forward, Elizabeth would devote much of her life to fighting for justice and female suffrage, although family demands would tie her down, and her public appearances would be few until after the Civil War. Her major weapons were her daring ideas and compelling rhetoric. Lucretia continued her fight for abolition and women's rights by lecturing, writing, and lending her star power to meetings and conventions.

Soon other activists joined Elizabeth and Lucretia, and all of them realized the need for publicity, whether negative or positive. To that end, Elizabeth Cady Stanton and Elizabeth M'Clintock began to write letters and essays to publish in various newspapers, demanding their rights. Stanton circulated the published minutes of the Seneca Falls Convention. She also suggested that they hire lecturers to spread the message, doing what antislavery agents had been engaged in for years. Elizabeth quickly identified Lucy Stone, who in only a year's time had established a reputation as an eloquent, effective lecturer for the Massachusetts Anti-Slavery Society. At the time, Elizabeth may have been unaware that Lucy was already including women's rights messages in her speeches.

The response to the Seneca Falls Convention was immediate, although not as wholly positive as its organizers had anticipated. Predictably, local ministers denounced the Convention, the Declaration of Rights and Sentiments, and the Resolutions. Elizabeth felt betrayed, for apparently several clergymen had attended the meeting but said nothing on the second day when organizers had encouraged comments from the floor. Instead, ministers sat in silence; "but afterwards the pulpits throughout the town were used to denounce [women] and they could not be allowed, of course, to reply, she explained."[58] Such cowardly behavior in Elizabeth's mind proved that ministers preferred to profess their opposition before sympathetic parishioners.

Media reactions to the Seneca Falls Convention were mixed. Douglass's *North Star* was predictably supportive, calling the meeting "one of the most interesting events of the past week" and the speakers "brilliant talents and excellent dispositions." Sensing that derision and criticism would follow such a radical event, Douglass added with a note of cynicism: "A discussion of the rights of animals would be regarded with far more complacency by many of what are called the wise and good of our land, than would be a discussion of the rights of woman. It is, in their estimation, to be guilty of evil thoughts, to think that woman is entitled to rights equal with man." While some people realized that blacks deserved the same rights as all "members of the human family," the same individuals had "yet to be convinced that woman is entitled to any." Also waxing positive was Auburn's *National Reformer*, which regarded the convention as a symbol of the progressive age. The paper congratulated women for their speechmaking and felt that their abilities far surpassed those of the men in Congress.[59]

The *Seneca County Courier* in its July 21 issue characterized the meeting as "respectable in numbers and highly respectable in character" and identified Lucretia as the most prominent luminary present. "The lady is so well known as a pleasing and eloquent orator, that a description of her manner would be a work of superserogation," it gushed. It described her speech on the first evening as "eminently beautiful and instructive," and the Resolutions as "spirited, and spicy" as well as "radical." Anticipating what would happen when the Declaration of Rights and Sentiments and the Resolutions became public, the paper predicted, accurately, "Some will regard them with respect—others with disapprobation and contempt." These declarations would be revolutionary, the *Courier* said, "to those who are wedded to the present usages and laws of society."[60]

A number of newspapers offered a more neutral assessment, including Nashville's *Daily Centre-State American*. Undoubtedly borrowing comments found in another paper, this paper seemed more impressed with the behavior of the audience than with the issues discussed. It reported approvingly that the Convention had had a "respectable audience" and "the most perfect order was preserved throughout." The editor Horace Greeley provided readers of his *New York Tribune* with a complete report of the Convention. Though not excited about the demand for female suffrage, he conceded that if enfranchising women was a natural right, they should have it.[61]

Other papers were less charitable—a response that surprised some women, especially Elizabeth. As she later recorded in her memoir, "No words could express our astonishment on finding, a few days afterward, that what seemed to us so timely, so rational, and so sacred, should be a subject for sarcasm and ridicule to the entire press of the nation."[62] Those who attended the Convention were derided as "women out of their latitude" and encouraged to spend their time more productively by tending to domestic duties. The *Philadelphia Public Ledger and Daily Transcript* said an assertive woman was a "nobody. A wife is everything"—and expressed relief that "the ladies of Philadelphia ... are resolved to maintain their rights as Wives, Belles, Virgins, and Mothers, and not as Women." Some newspapers dubbed female participants "Amazons" for demanding "some new, impracticable, absurd, and ridiculous proposition." The *New York Herald* ridiculed the idea of women demanding political rights, suggesting that the next step might be someone like Lucretia imagining that she was qualified to run for president. The *Syracuse Recorder* dismissed the meeting as "excessively silly," and the *Oneida Whig* wondered, if women continued to assert such "unnatural" demands, who would cook men's dinners and darn their stockings?[63]

While the greatest interest and agitation for women's rights was in the Northeast and Midwest, southern papers also responded to the Seneca Falls Convention. One might expect condemnation or, at best, indifference from a region that embraced women's secondary role in that society's well-defined social hierarchy. Indeed, several southern newspapers ridiculed the women at Seneca Falls. Others, however, reported favorably on the Convention. One historian who examined press coverage of the event found that 42 percent of the national press opposed the Convention, 28 percent were neutral, and 20 percent approved of it. In the South, of the twenty-three newspapers that mentioned the Seneca Falls meeting, fifteen (65 percent) offered either a neutral or favorable account, a greater percentage than elsewhere.[64] Yet as subsequent women's rights conventions were held throughout the 1850s, southern newspapers became more critical and more defensive about southern women, who, they claimed proudly, were happily occupying their rightful place in the home.

Individual reactions were no less varied. Some of those who signed the Declaration later withdrew their names in the face of family or community censure. According to legend, when Judge Cady heard about the Convention and Elizabeth's role in it, he immediately boarded a train for Seneca Falls to see if his daughter was "insane." In a more public venue, when the Boston lawyer and writer Richard H. Dana, Sr., visited Philadelphia the following year to lecture on Shakespeare, his "Address on Woman," in which he planned to analyze the Bard's female characters, turned into a denunciation of women who tried to make a name for themselves by speaking in public, demanding rights, and writing on controversial topics. He praised those who adhered to scriptural tenets and maintained silence in public.[65]

Incensed by these demeaning remarks, Lucretia responded to Dana in a public lecture that she delivered on December 17, 1849. A reporter took down her extemporaneous speech, and it was edited and published the following year as "Discourse on Woman." Lucretia characterized Dana's lecture, which she had heard, as "fraught with sentiments calculated to retard the progress of woman." She defended women's right to participate equally with men in all endeavors. Rather than identifying man as the sole oppressor, she also blamed women's inferior status on social custom. She argued for the expansion of female education and celebrated the recent entry of a few women into professions such as medicine and science. Laws limiting married women's rights and impeding their political participation needed to be overturned. Though herself not a strong advocate of female suffrage, Lucretia insisted that women should enjoy that option if they so desired it. She celebrated the appearance of a "new generation of women" who would no longer allow themselves to be "degraded into a mere dependent."[66]

A number of women disagreed with what transpired at these conventions or condemned them outright. Elizabeth Blackwell was less than enthusiastic about the demands for women's rights and blame for female oppression being placed wholly on men. Responding to an admirer who saluted her achievements in medicine, Blackwell noted that she had little patience with women who accepted the limitations on their sphere of activities or women who spent their days in idle pursuits. Most, she felt, were "feeble, narrow, frivolous at present:

ignorant of their own capacities." She did not feel that they suffered at the hands of men. Rather, female oppression "has arisen naturally, without violence, simply because woman has desired nothing more, has not felt the soul too large for the body." In a fit of self-interest, Blackwell later disparaged those involved in the women's rights cause, fearing her medical career might suffer because of "the vulgarity of the radical movement."[67]

Catharine Beecher offered reactions in *The True Remedy for the Wrongs of Woman*, published in 1851. She agreed that women had suffered many wrongs. Giving them the right to vote, however, would not address the problem. Their power was in the domestic sphere. Reiterating a favorite theme, Beecher argued that women needed to be better educated so they could succeed as mothers and wives. A sound education also would allow them to enter teaching, a profession perfectly suited to them. They should avoid politics and careers in which they competed with men. If women wanted to influence the world, they could do so discreetly, behaving in a ladylike manner rather than making unseemly demands in public.[68]

The Seneca Falls Convention also generated discussion of women's issues in other public venues, such as an Education Convention that met in Philadelphia in 1848, with Horace Mann presiding. Elizabeth reported that "much was said for Woman" and that many attendees raised the issue of unequal pay for male and female teachers. Though family pressures weighed heavily on Elizabeth, in September 1849 she delivered an address on women's rights at a Quaker meeting in Waterloo, New York, a talk she identified as her "first speech" and one she would present several more times. Here, she reiterated much of what the Declaration of Rights and Sentiments articulated. On women's right to vote, Elizabeth challenged critics. How would men feel if they were subject to laws over which they had no influence? She believed that men tried to make women feel delicate and weak in order to make them reliant on male protection, entrapped by a sense of inferiority and dependence into believing that men were serving their best interests.[69]

After the Seneca Falls and Rochester conventions, a group of women recognized how critical it was to maintain the momentum. But that was not easy. When Lucretia returned to Philadelphia late in the summer of 1848, her excitement soon gave way to realism. She explained to Elizabeth in October that she was attempting to awaken interest in holding a women's rights meeting in Philadelphia, but it was "far more difficult than we found it out West." Few women felt comfortable speaking in public, and finding venues that welcomed women's rights meetings proved a challenge. Some ministers were already turning against Lucretia. A Massachusetts minister had warned his parishioners that she was "the worst of women." She hoped Elizabeth would take charge of future meetings. "You are so wedded to this cause, that you must expect to act as pioneer in the work." The future activist Paulina Wright had not attended either convention but wrote Elizabeth to identify another concern. What she detected was "the stolid indifference of women. They hug their chains because they hate responsibility," Wright moaned. "I find more apathy and indifference with the women than the men."[70]

In thinking back on the Seneca Falls Convention and its significance, recollections varied. To Lucretia, the Seneca Falls and Rochester meetings, as important as they were, were only two events during a busy time in her life. Seneca Falls was an extension of her larger work, for she had been discussing women's issues for years in Quaker meetings and other public venues. Writing to the newspaper editor Edmund Quincy in late August 1848, she reported that she had "attended two Conventions called to consider the relative position of woman in society" that had been "greatly encouraging; and give hope that this long neglected subject will soon begin to receive the attention that its importance demands." Elizabeth, on the other hand, viewed Seneca Falls as the beginning of the women's rights movement and herself as a central figure. In this assessment she was correct, although it sometimes led her toward self-dramatization. Years later, in the *History of Woman Suffrage*, she called Seneca Falls "the greatest movement for human liberty recorded on the pages of history—a demand for freedom to one-half the entire race."[71] Yet interestingly, Elizabeth's memoir, *Eighty Years and More*, nearly five hundred pages long, includes only two sentences that describe the entire Convention. As is the case with a number of events in the nation's past, especially when written records are scarce, the few actual details we have of this two-day meeting pale in comparison to what it soon came to represent—and what it represents today.

Arguably, one of the Convention's greatest effects was on those who were touched by women's rights issues for the first time. Catherine Ann Fish Stebbins attended both the Seneca Falls and Rochester conventions. After marrying and moving to Michigan in the 1850s, she participated in other conventions, served on the board of the National Woman Suffrage Association, and engaged in civil disobedience by trying to register to vote in 1871.[72] Another attendee, Emily Collins of South Bristol, New York, later wrote, "From the earliest dawn of reason I pined for that freedom of thought and action that was then denied to all womankind.... But not until that meeting at Seneca Falls in 1848, of the pioneers in the cause, gave this feeling of unrest form and voice, did I take action."[73] She subsequently organized an Equal Suffrage Society, and its members sent petitions to the New York state legislature, demanding equal rights, including suffrage. Her husband supported her efforts throughout their thirty-five years of married life. When the Collinses moved to Louisiana, she continued her efforts there. This was exactly what those first activists hoped to inspire in all women, especially as they now embarked on their work to achieve the demands they articulated at Seneca Falls.

4

THE WOMEN'S MOVEMENT
BEGINS, 1850–1860

I n entering upon the great work before us, we anticipate no small amount of misconception, misrepresentation, and ridicule," the authors of the Seneca Falls Declaration of Rights and Sentiments solemnly intoned, "but we shall use every instrumentality within our power to effect our object." The final paragraph of the Declaration laid out action for the years ahead: to "employ agents, circulate tracts, petition the State and national Legislatures, and endeavor to enlist the pulpit and the press in our behalf." The five women who organized the Seneca Falls Convention expressed hope that it "will be followed by a series of Conventions, embracing every part of the country."[1] Though Elizabeth had noted that "the thorns of bigotry and prejudice" would impede their efforts, little did she or other women anticipate the challenges they would face to win their most radical demand—women's suffrage—or how much time it would take.

Two years after Seneca Falls, Elizabeth Cady Stanton sensed growing interest in women's issues. Before the 1848 conventions, newspapers and lecturers had ignored women's rights. "Now," she observed, "you seldom take up a paper that has not something about woman; but the tone is changing—ridicule is giving way to reason. Our papers begin to see that this is no subject for mirth, but one for serious consideration.... We have every reason to look hopefully into the future."[2] Optimism abounded as a new decade dawned and a group of committed activists sought to alter society's perceptions of women and to change state and national laws that had long constrained their lives.

This first decade after Seneca Falls was crucial to the future success of the movement. Between the 1848 Seneca Falls Convention and the start of the Civil War in 1861, women held a number of meetings to articulate the injustices they faced, offer resolutions for change, and persuade others that their cause was worthy. They gained confidence as they took charge and found their public voices. Friendships developed. Women lectured widely, formed ad hoc committees to study issues relevant to women, and reported their findings. They conducted petition campaigns, edited newspapers, raised money, wrote letters and essays, and occasionally engaged in acts of civil disobedience. In all these activities, the movement operated without elected officers or a national association. Acting alone or as part of an appointed committee, individuals organized each state and national meeting. No overall theme defined any of these conventions. No treasurer kept a budget or calculated how money was raised or spent. Despite the absence of organizational structure, however, the movement in its early years achieved some success in acting on resolutions articulated at Seneca Falls. The conventions and numerous activities generated an air of excitement and fostered in reformers the possibility of change as they worked together to advance their cause.

This seemingly rudderless approach was a matter of choice. Most reformers preferred individual initiative over formal association. Several women feared that an official structure would create division in their ranks and stifle creative thinking. Lucy opposed a formal organization, which she felt could restrain goals and force views on constituents that many might oppose. A number of women showed skepticism toward structured associations; after all, men's organizations had rarely served them well. And Antoinette Brown pointed out that forming an organization could generate multiple rivals, foster agitation, and accomplish "comparatively little."[3]

Throughout the 1850s, the most visible and meaningful activities of the movement were the many conventions held at the county, state, and national levels. Their goal was to inform people of the injustices women faced and to discuss how to change the nation's laws and perceptions of women. As they had at Seneca Falls, those who attended these meetings did so for different reasons. Some came to listen and learn, others to be inspired or entertained, and others to deride and protest. Most conventions followed a similar pattern, lasting one to three days, highlighted by invited speakers and extemporaneous comments and speeches from the floor. A core group of individuals typically took charge and performed most of the labor. Ad hoc committees studied key issues and reported their findings. Each meeting required extensive planning: selecting a suitable date and location; renting a hall or church; soliciting sponsors, lecturers, and entertainers who could attract a crowd; and preparing advance publicity and follow-up publications of the proceedings. In a period before recording devices existed, written minutes of conventions depended on secretaries or reporters to

Yᵉ MAY SESSION OF Yᵉ WOMAN'S RIGHTS CONVENTION—Yᵉ ORATOR OF Yᵉ DAY DENOUNCING Yᵉ LORDS OF CREATION.

Woman's Rights Convention, 1850s (Library of Congress)

document speeches and activities as they transpired. These notes are often the only extant records of conventions, aside from occasional newspaper accounts.

The first National Woman's Rights Convention, which set the tone for future meetings, was held in Worcester, Massachusetts, on October 23 and 24, 1850. Excited by the two New York conventions of 1848 and a convention held in Salem, Ohio, earlier in the spring, women activists now sought a wider audience. After the American Anti-Slavery Society meeting in Boston in the spring of 1850, someone raised the idea of creating a formal women's rights movement and convening a national meeting. Eight women, including Lucy, Abby Kelley Foster, Paulina Wright Davis, and Harriot Hunt, one of the nation's first female physicians, met to discuss the idea. They then wrote friends and supporters to encourage greater participation.

Paulina Wright Davis, who would become a major presence in the first decade of the movement, served as the principal organizer of this first national convention. Born in upstate New York in 1813, she was only seven when both her parents died. Raised by a strict aunt, she became a faithful churchgoer and frequent participant in religious revivals, but she soon began to bristle under the church's restrictive views of women. At the age of twenty, Paulina married a successful merchant, Francis Wright. They settled in Utica, New York, and became active in the antislavery movement. Francis's death in 1845 left Paulina a widow with substantial wealth. She then studied physiology and toured the East Coast, presenting lectures on female anatomy and shocking audiences by demonstrating her points on a life-size female manikin imported from France. Four years later, she married a wealthy widower and Rhode Island state senator, Thomas Davis, who supported his new wife's causes.[4] Childless, she enjoyed freedom to pursue her own interests.

Davis invited prominent Americans to serve as sponsors and speakers at the Worcester Convention. The list of lecturers read like a who's who of antebellum reformers: Lucretia, Lucy, William Ellery Channing, William A. Alcott, Wendell Phillips, Harriot Hunt, Stephen and Abby Foster, William Lloyd Garrison, Sojourner Truth, Ernestine Rose, and Frederick Douglass, among others. Unlike the hastily arranged Seneca Falls Convention, the

Paulina Wright Davis
(The Schlesinger Library,
Radcliffe Institute,
Harvard University)

Worcester meeting benefited from advance publicity sent to papers weeks before the event. Those who felt "sufficient interest in the subject to give an earnest thought and effective effort" to women's rights were urged to attend this meeting. Though Davis and others worried about poor attendance, representatives from nine states filled Worcester's Brinley Hall that first morning. Several newspapers estimated that up to a thousand people were in the audience by day's end, with men in the majority. Elizabeth, several months' pregnant, included her name as a sponsor and sent a letter to be read during the proceedings.[5]

Excitement was palpable as the meeting began. In her lengthy opening remarks, Davis expounded on the boldness of this undertaking, calling the cause a "radical and universal" reformation and an "epochal movement." Women's demands for equal rights promised no less than "the emancipation of a class, the redemption of half the world, and a conforming re-organization of all social, political, and industrial interests and institutions." At the same time, Davis sought to reach as many supporters as possible and to maintain a sense of decorum. She urged everyone to adopt a tone of "courtesy and respectfulness" and to avoid offending anyone as they pursued their goals.[6] This suggestion did not sit well with Abby Kelley Foster, who frequently faced hostile audiences when lecturing on abolition. Foster took the opposite stance, encouraging women to employ dramatic methods if necessary to achieve their goals. Even Lucretia found Davis's comments too "tame," but unlike Foster, she encouraged "spiritual" rather than "carnal" weapons.[7] At times, she felt confrontation might be needed to demand women's rights. And one should not blame woman's ills on abstract principles, but on man. "Where there is oppression," Lucretia maintained, "there is an oppressor."[8]

As would be the case at future conventions, speakers and members of the audience addressed a panoply of issues. Channing, a Unitarian minister, presented resolutions demanding higher education and greater employment opportunities for women. He called for a standing committee to gather statistics about women's status and to publish its findings. One man in the audience suggested that fathers share childrearing duties and that cooking and housekeeping be simplified so mothers could engage in public activities. All colleges, trades, and professions should open their doors to women, another participant insisted. Harriot Hunt raised the need for female medical education. Antoinette Brown, a minister, shared examples of women's key roles in the Bible and quoted scripture that supported gender equality. The convention also passed a resolution declaring that slave women were "the most grossly wronged and foully outraged of all women" and should be accorded the same rights white women sought.[9]

This first national convention marked Lucy's official entry into the women's movement, though she barely made it to Worcester. The weeks leading up to the convention were exhausting and life-threatening for her, preventing her from carrying out her plans to assist Davis in organizing this exciting enterprise. Weeks earlier, she had traveled to Illinois, where she had nursed her infirm brother Luther, only to witness his death from cholera. After settling his finances, she accompanied her pregnant sister-in-law, Phebe, home. Three days into their travels, Phebe prematurely delivered a stillborn son. While nursing her back to health, Lucy contracted a nearly fatal case of typhoid fever and was in and out of consciousness for three weeks. Eventually the two women were able to resume their journey home. When Lucy arrived in Worcester, she was exhausted and dispirited, fearing the convention might prove a failure. Instead, she found eager crowds and excited participants. She managed to speak briefly on the second day, urging women to petition their state legislatures to demand suffrage and marital property rights.[10] Much applause followed her insistence that no gravestone should ever identify a wife merely as a "relict" of her husband. Like Lucy, speakers and organizers were thrilled with their first national convention.[11]

A few months later, another noteworthy event took place: the meeting of Elizabeth Cady Stanton and Susan B. Anthony. In mid-May 1851, Susan was visiting Amelia and Dexter Bloomer in Seneca Falls in order to hear Garrison and George Thompson, a radical British abolitionist who was on a speaking tour of the United States. After the lectures, Bloomer introduced the two women. Susan knew of Elizabeth because Susan's parents and sister Mary had attended the 1848 Rochester convention. For her part, Elizabeth later recalled the moment she met Susan. "There she stood, with her good, earnest face and genial smile... the perfection of neatness and sobriety." Distracted by her three energetic sons, Elizabeth did not invite Susan home, although she later said, "I liked her thoroughly."[12]

Subsequent events brought these two together, initiating a friendship and working partnership that would last half a century. They complemented one another. Elizabeth's exuberance, optimism, and passion were balanced by Susan's self-discipline, independence, and tireless dedication. Henry Stanton later commented to his wife on this relationship: "You stir up Susan & she stirs the world." During the years when Elizabeth's domestic and family responsibilities consumed her, Susan became the legs of their relationship. Elizabeth's daughter Harriot later wrote that Susan, though less talented as a writer or speaker than Elizabeth, threw herself into the cause. "In writing we did better work together than either could alone," Elizabeth observed. "While she is slow and analytical in composition, I am rapid and synthetic. I am the better writer, she the better critic."[13]

Throughout the 1850s, women's rights activists held their annual meetings in different cities—Syracuse, Cincinnati, Cleveland, Philadelphia, Worcester, and New York City—in order to reach a wide audience and attract media attention. Until the outbreak of the Civil War, they held a national meeting every year except 1857. Speeches and debates formed the heart of these meetings. Audiences could count on hearing uplifting lectures covering familiar but vital topics: suffrage, wage inequities, education, unjust marriage laws, and the lack of occupational opportunities. For instance, a highlight of the 1851 National Convention at Worcester was Paulina Davis's speech drawn from the findings of an ad hoc committee on female education. She described women's limited options when pursuing educational or professional training. Society still regarded "intellectual culture" as "unwomanly" and preferred to keep females in a state of ignorance and dependence. The committee's report included a resolution that demanded public funding to support female colleges and give women the same educational opportunities available to men.[14]

Convention speakers enjoyed some freedom to discuss subjects of their choosing in ways that suited their styles. At the second Worcester meeting, Abby Foster spewed forth a testimony to the persecution she had suffered. "My life has been my speech. For fourteen years I have advocated this cause by my daily life. Bloody feet, sisters, have worn smooth the path by which you have come hither," she declared. Though this blunt, highly personal message offended some people, an admiring Lucy later described it as "hot with the feeling which was in her heart" in addressing the "wrongs done to women," and called it "the speech of the convention."[15] One topic of interest was prostitution, which Abby H. Price of Hopedale, Massachusetts, first addressed at the 1850 Worcester meeting. Too many women had to compromise themselves, Price argued, falling prey to sexual predators because they lacked educational and job opportunities, as well as the legal and political rights to live honorably. Far more startling were comments uttered at New York City's 1858 National Convention, when the abolitionist and communitarian Stephen Pearl Andrews introduced various approaches to marriage and advocated free love. Even more shocking was his insistence on the right of women to control "the cares and sufferings of maternity," or what Martha Wright later descried as "unwilling maternity." By raising the highly personal issue of birth control in a public setting, Andrews created a "sensation" in the audience and among women reformers. The brief *New York Times* report said his discussion about, euphemistically, "questions affecting the existing system of matrimonial relations" was the only unique speech of the convention.[16]

Some speeches dealt with more abstract ideas. At the sixth National Woman's Rights Convention in Cincinnati, Lucy attacked the concept of separate spheres and its odious impact on circumscribing women's lives. "They will be found to have no basis except in the usages and prejudices of the age," she noted. Each individual should determine his or her own sphere and ignore the dictates of others. Using the Grimké sisters as examples of those who had been active in the public sphere, she noted that the two were now enjoying home and family life, a choice they had made, not one made for them. Another topic that fostered debate throughout the decade was whether women were similar to or different from men. Women activists cleverly argued both sides of the question. If they were the same as men, they deserved the same rights, including the right to vote. If they were different, they should be able to vote in order to add their unique opinions to help govern the nation. In either case, preventing women from voting denied half the population the advantages of a democracy.[17]

Spontaneous speeches arose in reaction to comments from the floor. No one was more skillful at extemporaneous responses than Lucy. When a heckler interrupted the proceedings at the 1855 Cincinnati convention, calling female speakers "a few disappointed women," Lucy seized the moment and responded with what became one of her most famous speeches. Yes, Lucy agreed; she was, indeed, a "disappointed woman." "In education, in marriage, in religion, in everything, disappointment is the lot of woman. It shall be the business of my life to deepen this disappointment in every woman's heart until she bows down to it no longer." Nearly every form of employment, she asserted, had been closed to her when she was seeking her livelihood. "The same society that drives forth the young man, keeps woman at home—a dependent" and ultimately creates "a horrible perversion of the marriage relation."[18]

Reputations could blossom at conventions, for they offered a stage and media attention for both famous and less-known personalities. Among the former was Sojourner Truth. This tall, elderly former slave spoke at several gatherings, recounting her own experiences and offering her views on slavery and women's rights. Originally named Isabella, Truth was born into slavery around 1799 in New York State and served under several masters. In 1815, she married and subsequently bore five children. Her freedom came just before New York's emancipation law went into effect in 1827. Truth then worked as a maid for various families, experienced a profound religious conversion, and was drawn to spiritualism and Millerism. For a few years she belonged to a liberal utopian society, and then she joined the antislavery movement. Being illiterate, she dictated her memoir, *The Narrative of Sojourner Truth*, which was published in

1850. She made a huge impression at the first Worcester convention and had an even greater impact at the Ohio Woman's Rights Convention in Akron the following year. In Worcester, Truth declared: if woman had been the original cause of sin and upset the world, "give her the chance to set it right side up again." In Akron, she described the backbreaking work she had performed as a slave woman, labor as demanding and exhausting as that performed by any man. Using simple language and scripture, Truth urged man to give woman the rights she deserved. The recording secretary called her talk "one of the most unique and interesting speeches of the Convention."[19]

Debates often arose unexpectedly. At the 1854 Philadelphia Convention, one of the more spirited ones occurred between Lucretia and the minister Henry Grew, who had been among those who had opposed seating women delegates in London. Before a racially diverse crowd, Grew raised strong objections to

Sojourner Truth (Chicago History Museum)

speakers who demanded equal rights for women. He cited examples from the Bible that supported women's proper, subordinate role. An incensed Lucretia went on the attack, accusing him and other clergymen of selectively using the Bible to serve their own needs in order to keep women in their place. "The pulpit has been prostituted, the Bible has been ill-used," she noted. "Instead of taking the truths of the Bible in corroboration of the right, the practice has been, to turn over its pages to find examples and authority for the wrong," she thundered, offering her own citations from the Bible to prove Grew incorrect. Garrison finally had to intercede. Nearly everyone attending the convention agreed, he avowed, that all were equal in the eyes of God. This debate was further proof of Lucretia's innate ability to put someone in his place. Phillips recalled her response to a comment he once uttered. "She put, as she well knows how, the silken snapper on her whiplash, and proceeded to give me the gentlest and yet most cutting rebuke."[20]

Because the movement lacked any formal organization, conventions became the setting for activists to air pragmatic concerns. In September 1852, at the third National Woman's Rights Convention in Syracuse, the idea of establishing a national organization arose and led to "spirited discussion." Overwhelmingly, women opposed any type of formal organization, although Elizabeth Smith Miller suggested they follow the lead of Ohio women and create state associations. Even that idea generated little enthusiasm. Davis's thoughts on the subject were unequivocal. "I hate organizations," she responded. "They cramp me." Lucretia sensed trouble and urged that the current pattern continue. "Congregational independence will thus be preserved, and the seeds of dissolution be less likely to be sown," she advised. Angelina Grimké Weld concurred: "We need no external bonds to bind us together, no cumbrous machinery to keep our minds and hearts in unity of purpose and effort." If they organized, a prescient Wendell Phillips predicted, "you will develop divisions among yourselves." The discussion ended; no national women's organization formed until the Civil War.[21]

At the 1854 national meeting in Philadelphia, it was suggested that women establish a newspaper to serve as the official voice of the movement. Opponents, including Lucretia, predicted that a paper would also foster division. She worried about the expense involved, given the outstanding debt they faced, incurred from printing convention proceedings. Lucretia felt the popular press was providing substantial coverage of the movement. Instead, a committee formed to distribute women's essays, tracts, and convention proceedings to newspapers nationwide.[22]

Another contentious subject was religion and what role it should play at these meetings. At Syracuse in 1852, Antoinette Brown, one of the more devout

Ernestine Rose, c. 1853
(The Schlesinger Library,
Radcliffe Institute,
Harvard University)

reformers, articulated the right of women to become ministers, claiming that the Bible contained no command to prevent their doing so. Ernestine Rose then stood up, arguing that they should not rely on written authority to settle any dispute, especially the Bible, because it offered such contradictory views of women. The next year in Cleveland, Brown opened the meeting with a prayer, later followed by a long speech on the proper interpretation of scripture. Her prayer sparked a vigorous debate on the role of religion. Those who objected to prayer, such as Abby Kelley and Stephen Foster, did so on the grounds that the majority of clergymen opposed women becoming preachers and had tried to impede woman's progress at every turn. The outcome of this discussion is unclear, although several subsequent conventions opened and closed with prayers.[23]

In speeches and convention proceedings throughout the 1850s, the Seneca Falls Convention and all it had inspired were popular themes. In June 1852, Mary Anne W. Johnson, who chaired Pennsylvania's first state women's rights convention, highlighted Seneca Falls and the brave individuals who organized that pivotal meeting. "In the summer of 1848, in the village of Seneca Falls, a small number of women, disregarding alike the sneers of the ignorant and the frowns of the learned, assembled in Convention and boldly claimed for themselves, and for their sex, the rights conferred by God and so long withheld by man," Johnson intoned. "The seeds of truth which that Convention planted in faith and hope...germinated apace and brought forth fruit."[24] Lucy and Paulina Davis paid homage to Seneca Falls in their addresses at the Cleveland meeting, reminding everyone that only five years earlier, women in upstate New York had organized the first women's rights convention. Frances Gage, serving as that convention's chair, also uttered a tribute to "a band of earnest men and women" at Seneca Falls who defied criticism to articulate women's demands. William Channing proposed that they write a new "Declaration of Rights and Sentiments," an idea that generated little support. Instead, Lucretia read the original document aloud. Some discussion ensued on amending its statement about coed colleges, since institutions such as Oberlin and Centre College now existed. At the 1855 convention, Martha Wright, as acting president, entertained the audience with a brief history of the movement, highlighting Seneca Falls as the place where women first became aware of "our own strength, our own capacity, our own powers."[25]

Especially thrilling to American reformers was the international impact of their movement. Prompting great excitement was an essay, "The Enfranchisement of Women," written by the Englishwoman Harriet Taylor Mill, wife of John Stuart Mill, which appeared in the *Westminster Review* and then in the *New York Tribune* in July 1851. Mill heralded American women who deserved recognition for holding a successful women's rights convention at Worcester and inspiring women worldwide. She insisted that women should be full participants in government and treated as the intellectual equals of men. Wendell Phillips thanked her for laying out "with singular clearness and force" the arguments of their cause. Lucretia called Mill's piece "one of the best essays on Woman's Rights that I have seen," and she was especially delighted that a woman had written it.[26] She sent a copy to Elizabeth, noting that "no man can write on Woman's wrongs, as an *intelligent* sufferer of our own sex can.... It is beautifully written. I wish it could be reprinted & extensively circulated." Lucretia also mailed a copy to Garrison and asked him to publish it in the *Liberator*. Lucretia's wish came true; Mill's essay was reprinted as a tract the following year and was sold for decades.[27]

Reformers often situated their struggle within a global context. Despite limited transatlantic connections, a number of activists corresponded with women overseas, followed events abroad, and read speeches and tracts that were sent to their conventions. At the second national convention, William

Channing read a letter from two French women who were imprisoned in Paris for promoting socialism and demanding their right to vote and to hold public office. The two reassured American reformers, "Your socialist sisters of France are united with you" in demanding equal rights. Harriet Martineau wrote from England, complimenting American women on the "earnestness and sound truth" found in their addresses at the 1850 Worcester convention. With her European background, Ernestine Rose's presence invariably brought attention to women's status abroad. At the first national meeting in Worcester, Rose acknowledged the many women worldwide who were demanding their rights. In 1856, after Thomas Higginson proposed that they extend sympathies to British women who were seeking equality, Rose added another resolution to support French women demanding their rights and fighting despotism as well.[28]

At a New York state convention in 1853, Paulina Davis proposed appointing a committee to establish more formal contact with European women, share objectives, and seek cooperation. Garrison immediately seconded her proposal, for it "shows the universality of our enterprise," he proclaimed. Women worldwide should cooperate in this "glorious struggle." Toward the end of the meeting—and over the din of an unruly crowd—Matilda Francesca Anneke, the editor of a German women's rights newspaper, addressed the convention in her native tongue while Ernestine Rose translated. Anneke explained that because real freedoms were unknown in her country, Germans looked to American women for inspiration.[29]

And reformers looked to men for inspiration as well, for apparent to everyone was the critical role a number of men were playing in the women's rights movement. These men were visible at conventions—on the podium and in the audience—as well as on the lecture circuit. Their presence and dedication revealed their deep interest in female equality. For instance, as Lucy recalled years later, early on she approached Garrison in despair, wanting to make their cause a national one but lacking both money and support. Garrison reassured her that women's rights was as rich in truth as was the antislavery movement; the latter was succeeding, and so would theirs. As already mentioned, Frederick Douglass was a frequent participant, as was Wendell Phillips, another steadfast ally and one of the most eloquent orators of his day. At the second Worcester meeting, Phillips delivered a speech entitled "Shall Women Have the Right to Vote?"—it was considered one of his most impressive and later reprinted as a tract. In it, he called women's enfranchisement "the cornerstone" of the movement. Though men would help women win the right to vote, "we do not seek to protect woman, but rather to place her in a position to protect herself." While arguments for female suffrage remained central to his talk, Phillips also decried man's desire to circumscribe any woman's life, for she should be given the chance "to prove what she can do; to prove it by liberty of choice, by liberty of action." If given the same opportunities to excel that men enjoyed, women would become men's equals. In conclusion, he heralded women's rights as "the most magnificent reform that has been launched upon the world."[30]

Henry Blackwell, who would become a major participant in the movement after the Civil War, delivered his first women's rights address in Cleveland. Apparently feeling a need to state the obvious, he identified himself as the "son of a Woman and the brother of Women." Though admitting this was a female crusade, "I feel that it is mine, also." For over an hour, he lectured on the need for women's equality, denounced a husband's right to control his wife's property, and paid tribute to Mary Wollstonecraft's "noble character." Providing the audience with a quick history lesson, Blackwell cited examples of influential female figures—England's Queen Elizabeth I, Queen Isabella of Spain, France's Joan of Arc, America's own Harriet Beecher Stowe, and others—who provided irrefutable evidence of women's capabilities. Perhaps to impress Lucy, whom he was wooing, he called for "higher ideas of marriage" and urged men to seek female partners whose intellect and interests were "well developed." Though his heart was in the right place, Blackwell's ramblings failed to win universal approval. At least one newspaper commented that he "forgot it was a women's convention."[31]

The openness of these conventions in the 1850s created a welcoming environment but also made them vulnerable to unruly crowds. Typical was advance publicity for the Syracuse convention: "Our platform will, as ever, be free to all who are capable of discussing the subject with seriousness, candor, and truth." Such lofty ideals did little to discourage detractors. Inclusiveness attracted disorderly, often angry throngs of men who had no tolerance for female equality. The 1852 Syracuse meeting was the first time that "coarse and ribald speech" disrupted the proceedings. J. B. Brigham, a schoolteacher, challenged women's rights speakers and defended the concept of separate spheres, insisting that women should never venture beyond the home for fear of becoming masculine. The Congregational minister Junius Hatch of Massachusetts upset the proceedings by cynically questioning whether women's rights conventions ever recognized the authority of the Bible.[32]

Syracuse proved a model of order compared to the two-day "mob convention" held in New York City's Broadway Tabernacle the following year. A crowd of men showed up both evenings to dispute women's demands for equal rights. The *New York Herald*'s headline, "Strong-Minded Women are Getting Up Their Pluck," likely provoked tensions. Garrison's opening remarks also fueled passions by labeling opponents of women's rights "malignant, desperate, and satanic." Lucy's speech highlighted the advances women had made over the past few years: presiding over their own meetings, running their own businesses, and attending medical school. Someone hissed after she mentioned that a woman had even been ordained a minister, and Lucy responded calmly that men should know better than to hiss. The words of God were the same whether uttered by a man or a woman. When Lucy said that women should be men's equals, the crowd erupted with boos and laughter. The commotion broke up the convention that first night.[33]

The following day's proceedings began on a calm note, but the situation became chaotic by evening. Two men in the audience cited scripture, defending women's proper place in the home and presenting a litany of reasons to prove that they should never vote. In response, several women labeled the men ignorant bigots and derided their misuse of the Bible. Tensions heightened as more protestors arrived and tried to drown out speakers with hissing and heckling. Phillips took charge. "Go on with your hisses," he shouted. "Geese have hissed before now." He added that such bad behavior proved that women deserved suffrage, for "the men here, at least, are not fit for exercising political rights." Ernestine Rose managed to close the convention before violence erupted. Later characterized as "indescribable confusion," such disturbances troubled a number of women, though Lucretia complimented them for their dignified behavior throughout the disruptions.[34]

No national meeting convened in 1857. Lucy, who had married Henry Blackwell in 1855, was a new mother. Antoinette Brown had married Samuel Blackwell in 1856 and given birth to a daughter as well. Ernestine Rose was ill, and Susan was lecturing for the American Anti-Slavery Society, traveling on her own throughout New York state. Lucretia, now sixty-four years old, opposed holding a convention and hoped they could let it "slide." To Lucy she admitted, "We have had so many, & such a repetition of the same speakers, that I fear they are costing more than they come to."[35] As enthusiasm and anyone to organize a meeting were lacking, none was held.

The last three national women's rights conventions before the Civil War all met in New York City. It was a convenient setting for both speakers and audience—as well as for ardent opponents of women's rights. The 1858 national meeting at Mozart Hall became a free-for-all, as speakers, including Garrison, Sarah Grimké, and Martha Wright, upped the ante by immediately raising controversial issues. Eliza W. Farnham's comments on the superiority of women elicited audience ire. Everyone from radical thinkers, free-love proponents, and hidebound traditionalists used the opportunity to make their cases.

But in typical Quaker style, Lucretia defended the convention's openness, feeling that a free exchange of ideas gave vitality to the meeting.[36]

The most divisive national convention and the last one held before the Civil War met on May 10 and 11, 1860. This time it was disagreements among female leaders that threatened to undermine the proceedings. Attending her first national women's rights convention, Elizabeth was determined to discuss marriage and divorce, subjects that had consumed her thinking for over a decade. Privately, she felt that marriage too often was "nothing more nor less than legalized prostitution," and New York State had some of the most restrictive divorce laws in the nation. Beforehand, Lucy questioned the wisdom of raising these issues, since they affected both males and females and, as state concerns, seemed inappropriate subjects for a national meeting. Rejecting what she called the "common herd" mentality and ever eager to add "zest" to the proceedings, Elizabeth ignored all advice. On the second day of the convention, she spoke at length on marriage and divorce, arguing that the institution of marriage benefited only men. Wives had no choice but to accept laws that codified their subjugation. To her thinking, marriage should resemble a business contract between two partners and not be bound by restrictive laws. She presented a dozen resolutions on divorce, including a demand for more liberal laws, and startled the audience when she described children born into a loveless marriage as "of unlawful birth."[37]

The audience was shocked, as were prominent female reformers. Elizabeth had gone too far. Antoinette Brown Blackwell agreed that laws on marriage served men advantageously, but she insisted that if society elevated the morals of everyone, husbands and wives would function as equal partners. Marriage was a sacred, indissoluble institution. Blackwell countered Elizabeth with thirteen resolutions of her own to show why couples should stay together. The entire discussion so upset Phillips that he managed to strike it entirely from the record. Only Susan and Ernestine Rose defended Elizabeth and challenged Blackwell, claiming that "marriage has ever been a one-sided matter, resting most unequally upon the sexes. By it, man gains all—woman loses all; tyrant law and lust reign supreme with him—meek submission and ready obedience alone befit her." Women needed liberal divorce laws, they maintained, to free them from the chains of unhappy marriages.[38]

While conventions were a natural venue for speechmaking, so, too, was the lecture circuit. Public oratory was a major form of popular entertainment in the mid-nineteenth century, and skilled speakers were held in high esteem. Communities regularly invited speakers, and lyceums sponsored debates and annual lecture series. Agencies represented some of the nation's most famous public speakers, including Lucy, Elizabeth, and Frederick Douglass, who earned between $75 and $100 for each engagement. These were more than talks; they were performances, blending humor, historical anecdotes, factual data, and oratorical flourishes. Even when merely read, their speeches inspire and entertain today.

Lucy became the best known female lecturer of her day, and everyone who heard her acknowledged that she possessed an innate gift. She devoted most of her attention to women's rights after she ceased lecturing for the American Anti-Slavery Society in 1851. By the mid-1850s, Lucy was one of the most famous women in America. Even those who rejected her radical message admitted that she was a powerful speaker. "Wherever she goes the people *en masse* turn out to hear Lucy Stone, and are never weary of her stirring eloquence," commented the *Cayuga (NY) Chief*. For months on the lecture circuit, Lucy spoke every evening, traveling as far west as Wisconsin and as far south as Kentucky. Wherever she went, she had an ability to sway her audience. So persuasive was her speech at the 1853 Syracuse convention that the editor of the *Syracuse Weekly Chronicle,* who had opposed women's rights, found his hostility dissipating as he listened to her. "Whether we like it or not, little woman, God made you an orator!" he exclaimed. Editors in St. Louis were prepared to criticize Lucy but were "greatly delighted" not only with her message but her clear, forceful, and compelling delivery. Elizabeth claimed that Lucy's eloquence had "electrified large audiences all over the country." An admiring Susan wrote after Lucy's two-day speaking engagement at Metropolitan Hall in New York City: "If the reports are to be relied on, you made two most convincing speeches." She predicted that Lucy's speeches "Woman's Rights" and "The Legal Disabilities of Woman" would soon be known worldwide. The *Frederick Douglass Paper* (formerly the *North Star*) rhapsodized that Lucy had "carried her audience above the earth, thrilled their hearts, and made herself their favorite." A number of prominent women, including the reformer and writer Julia Ward Howe and the author Helen Hunt Jackson, later admitted that they joined the movement after hearing Lucy speak.[39]

Public lecturing, however, was a demanding profession that only attracted a small core of reformers. Most activists felt little desire to face hostile crowds, much less any crowd; others experienced stage fright. Family demands kept many women housebound. While enthusiastic crowds could energize a speaker, audiences were just as likely to be small, indifferent, or unruly. Though two decades had passed since the Grimké sisters stirred controversy, women appearing before mixed audiences to demand justice tended to arouse considerable ire. Susan remarked with some bitterness on society's inconsistent responses to women's public appearances. Female actresses and singers came onstage with bare arms and necks and garnered much praise. But when a demurely dressed woman stood before the public and demanded the right to vote, people labeled her masculine and denounced her for moving beyond her assigned sphere.[40] Angry listeners sometimes bombarded lecturers with stones, eggs, books, and rotten fruit to protest their message. In one instance, Lucy had to ask a stranger to escort her out of a lecture hall to protect her from an angry mob.

This was exhausting, stressful work. Bad weather, especially in winter, could delay plans and cause railroads and steamships to cancel scheduled trips. Traveling by carriage sometimes meant painful progress through sleet and snow in temperatures well below zero. Susan endured freezing sleigh rides when lecturing in upstate New York in January 1855. At one point, she was stuck in fifteen-foot snowdrifts. Hotel rooms were frequently crowded, cold, and uncomfortable; meals were unpredictable. Abby Kelley Foster and Lucy each wrote of sharing bedrooms with strangers and being bitten by fleas. The best laid plans often went awry. Speakers might show up in town only to discover that no hall had been rented and no advance announcements sent out. They then had to scurry to find any available church, tent, or private building for their lecture and place handbills around town to announce the event. And there was no guarantee that anyone would come. Foster reported that one night's audience consisted of six people.

Lecturing took a physical toll; many female speakers suffered poor health and exhaustion. Lucretia sometimes lost her voice; stress caused her to suffer from dyspepsia. Lucy had to deal with periodic migraine headaches that forced her to curtail speaking engagements. She had planned to speak at the Albany convention in February 1854 but instead went home. "I am more than half sick," she admitted to Susan. "I am completely exhausted by long & hard field service. And my back is giving me so much pain that I am going home to rest." After moving to Iowa, Amelia Bloomer found public speaking a challenge because of that state's sparse settlements and "tedious" travel services. "Even my ardor in the cause of woman chills at the thought" of stage rides in temperatures of twenty-five below zero, she confessed. The indefatigable Susan, who earned the nickname "Little Napoleon" for her stamina and persistence, complained of exhaustion and sometimes took time off to recuperate. These women understood the demands of this work and readily empathized with one another. A solicitous Susan urged Lucy not to overdo lecturing but to "take some quiet rest" so that she would live a long life, for "there is a vast deal of work for you to do." Months later, Susan again insisted that Lucy take care of herself. "Your whole nervous and mental energies have been most unduly taxed this winter....Do get rested and well. Then work more moderately. All the women are growing old and ugly-looking before their time."[41]

Some lecturers brought problems on themselves. Foster and others developed a well-deserved reputation for long-windedness. Garrison finally insisted that she share the stage with others. He couched his criticism by warning that she was injuring her health but added, "All our lecturing agents err in this— they speak too often and too long—and you probably more than any other." Foster was losing her audience and taxing everyone's patience. "If all our agents would abridge their speeches in half, I am satisfied the effect produced would be much greater." He urged her to wear a watch and confine her remarks to one hour.[42] On occasion, Lucretia reminded Antoinette Brown that she had exceeded her allotted time and needed to share the stage with others.

Lecturers without an agent usually decided where and when to speak and what to say. Many paid their own expenses; some barely broke even. Caroline Dall, who committed herself to public speaking in the late 1850s, systematically developed three lectures each season and delivered these in towns and cities throughout New England. She later had them published. In the 1860 federal census, she even listed herself as "lecturer."[43] Some speakers traveled long distances to locations where they sensed a need or felt they could have an impact; others preferred large urban crowds, which could mean generous contributions. Proximity often determined the choice of venue. When Lucy and Henry briefly resided in the Midwest, Lucy toured Wisconsin, lecturing on women's rights to indifferent, often hostile audiences. While in Ohio in 1856, she spoke at the trial of the slave woman Margaret Garner, who was in prison. During her flight from slavery, when slave catchers had been about to catch up with her, Garner had killed her three-year-old daughter. Lucy insisted that if she were in a similar situation with nothing to live for, "I would with my own teeth tear open my veins."[44] While Lucy's appearance generated no income there, it reflected her commitment to the antislavery cause and justice.

Lecturers also varied in style and message, from those as blunt and fiery as Abby Kelley Foster and Ernestine Rose to the fashionably dressed Elizabeth Oakes Smith, known for her "sweetness, strength, and beauty." Several men, including Wendell Phillips and William Channing, traveled widely to lecture on women's rights. "We need every possible shade and variety of lecturers and workers in this great movement," Paulina Davis observed.[45]

Speakers enjoyed the freedom to address whatever topics they fancied. Though Elizabeth rarely spoke in public during the 1850s, when she did, she usually generated controversy. In her mind, it was better to create a reaction than merely to utter what people wanted to hear. She had little tolerance for apathy. For instance, her interest in temperance was prompted in part by a desire to inject women's rights into that issue. In January 1852, she spoke to the Woman's State Temperance Meeting in Albany, urging members to demand the right to vote. Only if they had a voice in the law could they change it. She argued that drunkenness should be grounds for divorce and decried any wife who tolerated a drunken husband. Reflecting her own sentiments toward organized religion, she asked these women to "withdraw from all societies and churches, under the exclusive jurisdiction of Man, where Woman is not allowed to speak or not recognized as an equal in counsel." Her leadership as president of the New York State Woman's Temperance Association was short-lived; a number of members were so upset by her speech that she was not reelected the following year.[46]

Elizabeth prepared one of her most effective addresses for male delegates who were gathering in February 1854 to revise New York State's constitution. Before handing copies of her essay to the men, she read it aloud at the women's rights convention being held in Albany at the same time. In it, she discussed women's legal vulnerability, their subordinate status, and the injustices they endured. She asked the delegates to create a new set of laws that would advance women:

> We demand the full recognition of all our rights as citizens of the Empire
> State. We are persons; native, free-born citizens; property-holders, tax-payers;
> yet are we denied the exercise of our right to the elective franchise. We
> support ourselves, and, in part, your schools, colleges, churches, your
> poor-houses, jails, prisons, the army, the navy, the whole machinery of
> government, and yet we have no voice in your councils. We have every
> qualification required by the constitution, necessary to the legal voter,
> but the one of sex.

Despite changes that had been made to the state's constitution in 1848, laws still penalized wives. Marriage was a contract, Elizabeth argued, but one unlike any other because it could not be dissolved by mutual consent. She challenged anyone who disparaged female reformers as a few "sour, disappointed old maids and childless women," pointing out that the majority of women supported their efforts, for "the mass speak through us." Most wives longed to claim their own wages, possessions, and guardianship of their children. She deplored laws that placed women in the same category as lunatics, criminals, and blacks. Using an argument she would repeat often after the Civil War, Elizabeth declared: "You place the negro, so unjustly degraded by you, in a superior position to your own wives and mothers." Though her eloquent essay failed to persuade legislators to extend greater rights to women, it was published as a tract and was sold for years.[47]

To appeal directly to men in power, a few women addressed legislative bodies. Lucy appeared before the Massachusetts Constitutional Convention in May 1853, demanding that women have a voice in forming laws and receive the same rights as men. As taxpayers, they deserved suffrage. They were as well or better educated than many of the men who voted, and they possessed mental abilities equal to men's. Legislators debated Lucy's forceful points but quickly dismissed them, concluding that women could make their opinions known through petitioning and thus had no need to vote. More significantly, since only two thousand women in the state had signed a petition demanding suffrage, the men assumed that few desired that privilege. In February 1855, Susan, Antoinette Brown, and Ernestine Rose addressed the Hearings Committee of the New York state assembly and presented signed petitions demanding female suffrage. As the governor prepared to sign the more expansive 1860 Married Woman's Property Act, Elizabeth spoke to a joint session of the state legislature's Judiciary Committee. She insisted that expanded rights would do women little good unless they had a voice in their government. Returning several months later, she asked the committee to revise and expand the state's limited grounds for divorce. As matters stood in New York, a wife had few legal means to leave an abusive or neglectful husband. If one of the duties of government was to ensure every citizen a level of happiness, Elizabeth insisted, men in power had a responsibility to revise the laws governing marriage and divorce. However passionate her words, they had little impact. New York would not revise its divorce laws for decades.[48]

The popular press also played a critical role in spreading women's messages, producing both positive and negative coverage. A handful of reporters were present at most conventions. The invention of the telegraph increased newspapers' ability to gather and disseminate information, as well as borrow and print stories from one another, a practice common at this time. A few papers printed convention proceedings in their entirety, while others provided a synopsis or editorial comments. Several mainstream papers even created special "ladies' sections" to cover women's issues.[49]

Newspapers' reactions to women's rights concerns depended on the sentiments of their editors. Some were openly hostile, while men like Douglass were unabashedly supportive of the cause. Horace Greeley, the editor of the *New York Tribune*, the nation's most popular and influential newspaper, maintained a good relationship with Elizabeth and provided generous coverage on women's rights before the Civil War. Two other papers in the city, the *New York Herald* and the *New York Observer*, were far less charitable. Every so often, an event might prompt an editor to alter the tone of his paper. After attending the second national convention at Worcester, the minister Henry Bellows, editor of the *New York Christian Enquirer*, admitted that he had approached women's rights with "distrust and distaste." He was so impressed that he declared the 1851 convention "the most important meeting since that held in the cabin of the *Mayflower*."[50]

Several newspapers provided positive coverage of the conventions. The *Lily*, Amelia Bloomer's paper, claimed that the 1850 Worcester meeting "went off 'gloriously' and none but those blinded by ignorance or prejudice could find it in their hearts to ridicule all that was said or done." Worcester's *Massachusetts Spy* reported on the decorous spirit of the crowd and the "forensic talent" displayed by speakers at that meeting. The *Frederick Douglass Paper* called the 1852 Syracuse meeting a "glorious" convention that, it said, "has done much good, not in regard to woman's rights only, but in regard to all human rights." Douglass could hardly contain himself, touting speeches by Lucretia, Paulina Davis, and Ernestine Rose and describing these women as "deep thinkers, and well-stored with the truths of philosophy, and history, and eminently gifted with powers of eloquence." Of special note was Lucy, who "carried her audience above the earth, thrilled their hearts, and made herself their favorite. She was greatly cheered." Even Douglass's coverage of Elizabeth's 1854 essay for New York's constitutional delegates was positive, despite the fact that she placed female suffrage ahead of black men's right to vote. His paper did no more than call this "a slight blemish" and urged everyone to read her piece. The *Syracuse Journal* described that city's convention as "the most dignified, orderly, and interesting deliberative body ever convened in this city." The paper complimented women who had organized the convention and who had performed their duties so admirably. Those who delivered speeches were of "decided ability" and used "compact logic, eloquent and correct expression" to argue their points.[51]

A number of papers took equal delight in ridicule. The *New York Herald* called the first national Worcester convention a "motley mingling of abolitionists, socialists, and infidels of all sexes and colors." The second annual meeting was dubbed a "Hens Convention" and an "Insurrection in Petticoats." Reporting on the Syracuse convention from abroad, the *London Times* described the event as a "petticoat Parliament" and referred to those in attendance as both "pretty girls" and "Amazons of the New World."[52] Frances Gage denounced *Harper's* for its "violent and uncompromising" views of the cause. Using "ridicule and satire, to make the whole movement odious," the editor of *Harper's* maintained that no woman had cause to complain, for her lack of legal rights was just and proper. Should she gain political power, she would lose "her womanly character." The *Middletown (CT) Constitution* derided all demands for gender equality, painting unimaginable images of a world turned upside down, fearing that a "petticoat government" would result. Soon women might lead armies and naval fleets and become governors and politicians.[53] The 1860 national meeting in New York elicited more than its share of media ire. Elizabeth's proposals on divorce suggested that marriage might become a mere business negotiation, allowing wives to move in and out of marriage at will. The *New York Evening Post* called such views "suicidal," and the *New York Observer* denounced the entire convention as "infidel and licentious." If carried out, Elizabeth's ideas would turn the world "into one vast brothel."[54]

Some newspapers criticized individual reformers with biting, even cruel comments. Susan proved a popular victim. The *Utica (NY) Evening Telegraph* assessed her speeches on temperance and concluded, "We were inexpressibly disgusted with the impudence and impiety evidenced in her lecture. Personally repulsive, she seems to be laboring under feelings of strong hatred towards male men, the effect we presume, of jealousy and neglect." The *Telegraph* challenged Susan's insistence that no wife could ever love a drunken husband and denounced her advice to mothers that they not drug their babies with alcoholic stimulants. It questioned how a spinster like Anthony knew anything about motherhood and "the thousand delights of married life."[55] Several newspapers criticized Susan's appearance, voice, and stage presence when she and Elizabeth later lectured in the Far West.

Despite their compelling speeches and extensive media coverage, women's only access to any semblance of political power was through petition drives. During the 1850s, women conducted numerous petition campaigns to demand equal rights and suffrage. They established networks of volunteers to conduct each campaign. Every volunteer covered assigned neighborhoods or streets, walking from house to house to obtain signatures. Printed sheets instructed the uninitiated on how to conduct this work. Collecting names, however, was difficult and, for some, repugnant work. As Sarah Pugh admitted after one petition campaign, "I never undertook anything that was so entirely distasteful to me." Results were often discouraging, for most people refused to support such radical demands. Doors frequently remained shut or, if opened, might be slammed in a volunteer's face, accompanied by nasty comments or personal insults.[56]

The best time to conduct petition drives was while states were revising their constitutions or debating relevant issues such as female suffrage or married women's property rights. In the spring of 1850, for instance, Ohio women activists timed their first convention to precede a meeting of delegates to revise the state's constitution. This was an opportune moment to demand that they "secure to all persons the recognition of Equal Rights, and the extension of the privileges of Government without distinction of sex or color." Though the Ohio women collected eight thousand signatures, their petitions did not sway delegates. When the resolution to remove the word "male" from the statement on suffrage came up for a vote, it was defeated seventy-two to seven.[57] New York women activists in 1854 circulated two petitions, "Woman's Right to Suffrage" and "Just and Equal Rights of Women," and organized a convention in Albany to present their petitions.[58] In 1852, Clarina Howard Nichols spearheaded a petition campaign demanding that the Vermont state legislature give women the right to vote on school board issues. Again, all these demands fell on deaf ears.

At the first Worcester convention, women vowed to undertake a major petition campaign for suffrage in several states. Elizabeth oversaw the drive in upstate New York. A few months after volunteers collected signatures, Henry Stanton, now in the state senate, submitted two petitions but reported to Elizabeth that fellow senators were unimpressed and "tried to throw ridicule upon them." In 1850 and again in 1853, Massachusetts activists circulated suffrage petitions and submitted them to the state legislature. Of the two hundred thousand women living in the state, only two thousand signed the petitions, although fifty thousand women had recently supported a temperance petition. The legislative committee virtually ignored their effort, reasoning that since governmental powers derived from the consent of the governed and so few women supported suffrage, Massachusetts men had every right to prevent women from voting. Indiana women activists drafted and gathered signatures on petitions for their legislature in 1858 and again in 1859, asking that they have "the same rights in property that are enjoyed by men," including the right to suffrage.[59]

A few activists engaged in petition drives single-handedly. In the winter of 1854–55, Susan undertook a challenging adventure, traveling alone through fifty-four counties in New York State, holding meetings, lecturing, and collecting signatures on a petition demanding more generous marital property laws. On her own, Lucy lectured and circulated petitions across Wisconsin, though she found almost no support for women's suffrage. Apathy and resistance were the chief enemies of petition campaigns. The drives also had limited impact on legislators, but women persisted, hoping to prove widespread support for their just cause.

Finding little satisfaction through legal and political channels, women also engaged in acts of civil disobedience with growing frequency. If any governmental act galled them, it was "taxation without representation," a grievance American patriots had held against the British decades earlier. It was included in the injustices listed in the Declaration of Rights and Sentiments. Though they could not vote, for years women had paid taxes on property they owned. Elizabeth raised this complaint in her letter addressed to the 1850 Ohio women's rights convention. In forming the nation's government, men "have taken from us the very rights which they fought, and bled, and died, to secure to themselves," she asserted. In 1852, Harriot Hunt, who had long been paying Boston property taxes, protested this injustice and did so for years thereafter, accompanied by much publicity. The fact that Boston's tax money supported two boys' academies but offered no such funding for girls' education heightened her frustration. Elizabeth's letter to the 1852 Syracuse convention urged women to stage a mass protest and to refuse to pay taxes until given the right to vote. Among fourteen resolutions William Channing presented at the 1853 Rochester state convention, one claimed that it was "a gross act of tyranny and usurpation, to tax women without their consent." The issue came up again at the ninth national convention in New York City.[60]

This concern, in particular, touched Lucy, a property owner and taxpayer. When her city property tax came due in November 1857, she refused to pay, believing that since she had no voice in town government, she was under no obligation to do so. She wrote the tax collector of Orange, New Jersey, the following January, hoping he would recognize the error and change the law. The current policy "is not only unjust to one half of the adult population, but is contrary to our theory of government," she declared.[61] The town identified only one error—Lucy's unpaid taxes. Because she refused to pay, the town seized the family's household goods and sold them at public auction. Fortunately, a sympathetic neighbor purchased the items and allowed Lucy to buy them back.

Another public assertion of female independence was the challenge to traditional attire. Fashion was (and is) a key issue for what it revealed about society's image of an ideal woman and females' perceptions of themselves. In the mid-nineteenth century, female clothing, at least that worn by the middle and upper classes, was both physically constricting and voluminous. One doctor estimated that an outfit could weigh as much as twelve pounds. From the time they were adolescents, females wore binding undergarments that constricted their internal organs and conformed their bodies to a desirable hourglass figure. Stiff corsets and whalebones, bustles, hoop skirts, and tight lacing created shapely proportions. Illustrations in *Godey's Lady's Book* and *Harper's* depicted layers of petticoats and long dresses made from yards of material, discreetly covering legs and ankles, as symbols of high fashion. Such clothing made it difficult to move easily, reinforcing society's idealization of women as sedentary, ornamental creatures.

Godey's Unrivaled Fashions (Library of Congress)

For several years, dress reform had been a concern; not everyone regarded current fashion as a good thing. A number of physicians and advisors of women, including Catharine Beecher, campaigned to alter female clothing and to eliminate whalebones and corsets. In her essay "Dress of Women" in *Letters on the Equality of the Sexes*, Sarah Grimké observed that fashion was not always imposed on women against their will. Many donned "gewgaws and trinkets" in order "to gratify the eye of man." After all, men did not bedeck themselves in silks and ribbons. "God created me neither a bird nor a flower," she insisted. She empathized with poor women who spent their hard-earned wages on fashionable attire in order to please an employer. To Sarah, the solution was simplicity of dress. An article in the *Lily* discussed health problems associated with current fashion. Using language that might have led any well-dressed female to pause, the piece noted that "excessive heat induced by an inordinate amount of clothing" led to "spinal affections," and excessive pressure caused "torpidity of the liver and portal circulation, accompanied by constipation." The Savannah (GA) *Magnolia* was equally critical of women who compressed their "waists, and the vital organs beneath it, to the equal violations of the laws of nature." Nothing was "more detrimental to health and beauty, than the system of tight lacing."[62]

The British actress and abolitionist Fannie Kemble may have been the first woman in this country to challenge fashion by donning pantaloons, or the "Turkish dress," causing a slight stir in the late 1840s. Female residents of Brook Farm wore a type of pantaloons under their dresses, and a few magazines devoted to medical issues and health reform promoted simple attire. But again, Seneca Falls was where women first attracted attention by shortening their dresses, removing whalebones from undergarments, and wearing pantaloons. Elizabeth Smith Miller, Elizabeth's cousin and a committed feminist, introduced the style in early 1850. She had worn the Turkish dress while traveling in Europe and now did the same when visiting Seneca Falls. Within days, Elizabeth copied Miller's dress. She found the new style comfortable and practical. As someone who encouraged physical activity, Elizabeth could enjoy freedom of movement that the new outfit afforded. Others imitated the costume. Elizabeth's housekeeper, Amelia Willard, soon wore bloomers. The next year, female textile workers in Lowell adopted the costume, "not only a very becoming, but an extremely convenient and useful dress for them." As the *Lily* noted, "We welcome the factory girls of Lowell...to all the comfort and convenience of the short, *loose* dress," encouraging them to reject tight bodices. By fall of 1851, a group of Lowell women had formed the "Lowell Bloomer Institute," vowing to emancipate themselves from the "whimsical and dictatorial French goddess *Fashion*" and to dress "according to the demands and proffers of *Nature*."[63]

The *Lily* did much to promote the new costume, so much so that eventually the outfit was christened with the editor's name. Amelia Bloomer's paper ran dozens of articles on the costume, asserting a woman's right to reject cumbersome dresses and tight lacing and to wear pants. By the summer of 1851, pictures and descriptions of the attire appeared in the *Lily*. The paper dramatized the dire consequences of wearing tight whalebone bodices, commenting that "the health of untold thousands has been sacrificed, and countless numbers of fair and lovely beings have committed suicide and gone down to early graves, from their desire to secure that admiration of men." Bloomer defended the outfit, noting that since it required fewer yards of material, it was less expensive, and skirts would no longer drag in mud and snow. Women could show off their natural figures, breathe freely, and enjoy vigorous exercise. To promote the new fashion (and the *Lily*), Bloomer offered a free pattern to all new subscribers, and she printed letters from satisfied readers who affirmed the costume's many benefits. Several physicians endorsed the outfit. Composers and lyricists created music to celebrate or mock the new fashion statement, producing such pieces as "The Bloomer Polka," "The Bloomer's Complaint," and "The New Costume Polka."[64]

The New [Bloomer] Costume Polka (sheet music) (Library of Congress)

More women began to don bloomers in public. It took Elizabeth six months to convince Susan to try the outfit, perhaps because, as her letters reveal, Susan appreciated fine fashion and beautiful clothes. Lucy, on the other hand, immediately embraced the new style. When lecturing at antislavery and women's rights conventions, she donned bloomers. Elizabeth even had a special white bloomer ballgown designed to wear to dances when she visited Henry in Albany.[65]

Activists had mixed feelings about the bloomer outfit. Elizabeth Smith Miller's father, the radical abolitionist and reformer Gerrit Smith, urged all women to discard "the kingdom of fancy and fashion and foolery" in favor of this sensible attire. So committed was Smith that he became actively involved in the Dress Reform Association, insisting that demanding equal rights was a waste of time if women remained encumbered by their clothing. But such enthusiasm was hardly universal. Wendell Phillips, who prided himself on his liberal outlook, felt embarrassed for those who adopted the unattractive outfit. Jane Swisshelm tried bloomers but decided she wanted nothing to do with them; she found such attire "immodest, inconvenient, uncomfortable, and suicidal" and felt that wearing it would ruin her reputation. Davis refused to wear bloomers in public, for "if I put on this dress, it would cripple my movements in relation to our work at this time and crucify me ere my hour had come." To her, dress reform was merely a "fragment" of their larger work.[66]

Public outcry was immediate; few Americans welcomed this aberration of traditional female clothing. Women who wore bloomers seemed defiant, masculine, and tasteless. *Harper's* had a field day deriding bloomers. The January 1852 issue contained portraits of weird-looking male creatures modeling a form of bloomers. In contrast, the magazine flatteringly displayed women looking radiant in traditional hoopskirts, layered petticoats, and ruffles. The following month, *Harper's* parodied Hamlet's soliloquy: "To wear or not to wear the Bloomer costume, that's the question...To don the pants:—For pants! Perchance the boots! Ay, there's the rub." Indeed, the outfit was not particularly flattering and revealed more of women's legs than society found tasteful. Members of the New England Anti-Slavery Society who hired Lucy as a lecturer were aghast at her new costume. They regarded bloomers as a distraction and an embarrassment to their cause. Susan admitted that audiences and reporters now paid more attention to her clothing than her impassioned views. Judge Daniel Cady expressed displeasure with his daughter's new attire, saying that no one of "good sense and delicacy" would wear bloomers. Neil Stanton, away at boarding school, asked his mother not to wear pants and a short skirt when she visited.[67]

The bloomer experiment ultimately failed. Elizabeth began to have second thoughts and returned to dressing in a more conventional, feminine style. She made the transition slowly, first wearing a dress that fell within an inch of her boot tops but attracted less attention. When she spoke to the Albany state convention in 1854, she wore traditional garb. Lucy received so much negative press that she began carrying both long and short dresses while on the lecture circuit, selecting the style most appropriate to her audience. Elizabeth advised Lucy to follow her lead. "We put it on for greater freedom; but what is physical freedom compared with mental bondage? By all means, have the new dress made long." Susan gave up bloomers reluctantly, for doing so meant that she was accepting society's rigid definition of her. She admitted to Lucy, "I have let down some of my dresses and am dragging around with long skirts. It is humiliating to my good sense of cleanliness and comfort."[68]

Just as the press found good copy in covering women's rights events and fashion, activists were becoming savvy about the role of the media, and they made good use of it. Well-educated, well-read, and articulate, these women understood the power of free speech. They wrote and sent material to newspapers sympathetic to their cause, including the *Liberator*, the *Frederick Douglass Paper*, the *New York Tribune*, and women's papers such as the *Lily* and the *Una*. Elizabeth and Martha Wright were especially clever writers who submitted humorous as well as biting essays to a number of papers. Elizabeth was a blunt stylist. Her essays, written in longhand, have few editorial changes. Typical of her sometimes acerbic approach was an article celebrating the fact that the New York state legislature in 1850 finally allowed married women the right to deposit and withdraw money from banks without their husbands' permission. Elizabeth concluded, "Only think of it! A *woman*!! Be she married or single, can now deposit her *own* money in a bank, and draw it *all* out again *herself*." In another essay, "I Have All the Rights I Want," she leveled a blistering attack at those who were indifferent to or opposed equal rights. An 1860 essay reiterated her uncompromising sentiments about marriage:

> I would have woman repudiate marriage utterly and absolutely, until our tyrants shall revise their canons and their codes, and by the talisman of justice transform the *"femme [sic] covert"* into an equal partner.... If woman were sufficiently developed to love and appreciate freedom, nothing could tempt her to accept the kind of marriage man now offers.[69]

Being housebound, Elizabeth relied on others to gather information she needed for her writing. In preparing her 1854 speech for the New York state legislature, she asked Susan to locate "the most atrocious laws" that restricted women's lives. "While I am about the house, surrounded by my children, washing dishes, baking, sewing, I can think up many points, but I cannot search books," she explained. The next year, Elizabeth considered writing a history of the women's rights movement and shared her idea with Lucretia. On learning of the project, Lucretia offered to supply documents and suggested what to include, urging that the book begin with the Grimké sisters, the New England clergy's "Letter of Protest," and Sarah's book *On the Equality of the Sexes*. But Lucretia warned Elizabeth, "Thou wilt have hard work to prove the intellectual equality of Woman with man—facts are so against such an assumption, in the present stage of woman's development." Despite good intentions, Elizabeth's history project did not become a reality for nearly three decades.[70]

Women edited newspapers that often covered rights issues. One of the first was the monthly *Lily* of Seneca Falls, which started as a temperance paper six months after the Seneca Falls Convention. To the paper's initial motto on its masthead, "A Ladies' Journal, devoted to temperance and literature," was soon added "Devoted to the Interests of Woman." Those living in the Northeast and Midwest made up its readership, but at least one Virginia subscriber circulated her copy among friends, causing "no small amount of merriment—more especially amongst the Ladies, who had never heard of such a thing as Woman's rights, until they saw The Lily, nor did we so much as know that we had rights."[71] Elizabeth soon became a regular contributor, using the pseudonym "Sunflower" and writing such pieces as "Women Voting and Holding Office," "Confessions of a Housekeeper," "The Model Wife," and "Woman's Rights and Woman's Wrongs According to Law." When the Bloomers moved to Ohio at the end of 1853, the *Lily* went with them. In 1855, Mary Birdsall of Richmond, Indiana, became its new editor and owner, with Bloomer listed as corresponding editor. When Birdsall became ill the following year, the paper folded.

Another influential but short-lived paper associated with the women's movement was Paulina Wright Davis's paper the *Una*. The first issue appeared in February 1853 with a clear focus: "devoted to the elevation of woman." Davis had been pondering this venture for months, debating various titles and topics that would reflect well on the movement and attract broad readership. She started the paper because she felt that most mainstream newspapers and fashion magazines either provided inadequate coverage of the movement or misrepresented it. Her paper would add an impartial voice and "discuss the rights, sphere, duty and destiny of woman, fully and fearlessly."[72] Davis was frustrated with annual conventions, which she felt lacked a sense of purpose and were monopolized by individuals who grabbed the spotlight. She wanted another medium to deliver activists' messages but to do so in a respectable tone. In her view, refined, well-educated women like herself best represented the cause.

Davis spent several months developing a subscriber list. She hired proven writers like Elizabeth, Caroline Dall, Thomas Higginson, and others, and paid them well. Besides printing convention proceedings, the *Una* carried short stories and essays on such topics as the female intellect, the rights of women in different states, education, women's moral character, female employment, working women's industrial associations, legal injustices, and married women's property rights. Davis published the paper from her hometown, Providence, Rhode Island. Her husband promised to fund her paper for six months, at which point it was to become self-sustaining.

Even with advance planning, responsibilities soon overwhelmed Davis. Subscribers failed to materialize, and the stress began to affect her health. She explained to readers that the paper "overtaxed us both mentally and physically," and she realized she could not carry the burden alone. In a farewell note written in early 1855, Davis expressed disappointment that women had not supported the *Una* as she had hoped, although female indifference proved more than ever that a paper was needed to expose them to their oppression. "Slaves know no want of freedom till the soul begins its development through the light of truth," she commented. With hundreds of unpaid subscriptions and a muddled financial situation, the *Una* fell to Caroline Dall, who published it in Boston for several months before it folded in October.[73]

A handful of women published other newspapers that offered readers more than fiction and fashion. Elizabeth A. Aldrich edited a monthly Cincinnati paper, *Genius of Liberty*, published between 1851 and 1853, in which she sought to develop and strengthen the female community. The *Cayuga Chief*, a weekly in Auburn, New York, was published by Emma Brown and her brother. Other papers included Jane Swisshelm's *Saturday Visiter* [*sic*], from Pittsburgh, primarily an antislavery publication but with many articles supporting women's rights. The *Woman's Advocate*, edited by Anna W. Spencer in Philadelphia between 1855 and 1860, received praise from the *Lily*, which called it a "beautiful and excellent paper." The *Sibyl* began in 1856, edited by Lydia Hasbrouck in Middletown, New York, serving as the official journal of the National Dress Reform Association. In Vermont, Clarina Howard Nichols used the *Windham County Democrat* to express her views on reform issues, especially women's rights.[74]

Women also conveyed their messages by publishing and selling tracts and pamphlets. Journals, print media, and convention proceedings advertised these publications, which included the Seneca Falls Declaration of Rights and Sentiments, of course—as well as the sermon "A Discourse on the Rights and

Condition of Women" by Samuel May, Jr.; a collection of letters by Elizabeth Cady Stanton; "Protest against Taxation of Married Women," by Harriot Hunt; and "The Sanctity of Marriage," by Elizabeth Oakes Smith.[75]

Predictably, as women became more active in their pursuit of equality and their efforts began to translate into a real movement, they elicited more impassioned responses from the public, especially from ministers. Though the Declaration of Rights and Sentiments had expressed women's hope "to enlist the pulpit," most clergymen continued to express uneasiness, if not outright opposition, to women's bold demands and public presence. Typical of clergymen's opinions was that expressed by the minister John Weiss of New Bedford, Massachusetts, who in 1854 wrote "The Woman Question" for the *Christian Examiner and Religious Miscellany*. He sprinkled his essay with expressions of sympathy for women's economic status, and pointed out that education might have expanded female intellect, but the opportunities available to them were few. Women's rights conventions should discuss female labor, for decent pay was "the foundation of her prosperity and freedom." But his sympathy stopped there. Women should never lecture from the podium or pulpit or seek political or administrative positions; such acts were "fatal to finer and nobler" female character. Ambition in a woman belied her femininity, purity, and piety. She should never vote, since this would corrupt the home and foster marital discord. "Domestic love and peace are more valuable to a country, more closely implicated with its vital welfare, richer with the motives and elements of a spiritual transformation, than its best diplomacy or its most righteous votes," Weiss insisted. A woman owed "her success to the policy of a heavenly temper rather than to the contradictions of her votes. The country needs the pure and loyal home."[76]

Weiss was hardly alone. Other men dealt with female activism by mixing flattery with incontrovertible evidence to uncover the glories of women's domestic role and secondary status. If women could feel elevated by praise, presumably they would see no need to demand additional rights. In typical fashion, a committee of the New Jersey legislature responded with scripture and flattery to one woman's petition demanding equal rights. They dismissed her effort by flooding her with compliments. Woman "is often found to be our superior, and that in beauty and loveliness, and charms, we are compelled to bow before her and acknowledge our inferiority." But the right to govern and to reign supreme had always been man's prerogative. For a woman, "thy desire shall be to thy husband, and he shall rule over her." In closing, they added, "Whilst entertaining the highest respect and expressing the greatest confidence in lovely woman, and being now, as ever, [we are] ready to extend to them love, honor, respect, comfort, and protection."[77]

Throughout the 1850s, as political tensions heightened between North and South, white southerners grew increasingly hostile toward the women's rights movement, though most expressed relief that agitation remained in the North and that few southern women showed interest in such matters. A speaker delivering the commencement address at Laurensville Female College in North Carolina expressed his gratitude: "The madness, the frenzy, the absurdity of this spirit has not touched us here at the South. Woman has not unsexed herself here." Woman's "roaring, however terrific it may be in certain sections of our country, with us at least is any thing but lion-like. In our own Sunny South, at least, she 'aggravates her voice so,' that she 'roars as gently as any sucking dove' and 'as sweetly as any nightingale.'" The movement's close association with antislavery activists amplified its negative image in the region.

One of the most censorious southern critics of women's rights was the plantation owner and author Louisa Cheves McCord. She denounced the jarring, mannish discord unleashed by northern women, which to her thinking degraded the image of all women. In her poem "Woman's Progress," she wrote: "Oh! Let us be the woman of God's make; / No Mrs. Bloomer, Abby Kelley thing / Aping man's vices, while our weaker frame / knows not his harsher virtues. Let us be / Strong—but as Woman; resolute in right— / All woman— perfect woman." Southern papers added to the hue and cry. An 1852 essay in the *Southern Quarterly Review* warned of "passionate discourse" being expressed as "the softer sex mounted the rostrum." Women were sacrificing their "empire" in the home and their ability to influence men through a "sensitiveness" of feeling and "delicacy of thought" by abandoning their God-ordained sphere.[78]

In 1859, a particularly bold move by northern activists backfired in at least one southern state. Women attempted a new tactic, setting up a committee to send a memorial to all state legislatures, questioning where the Declaration of Independence gave white men exclusive power over women and blacks and demanding that states provide equal rights and privileges to all. Susan sent a copy of the memorial to former Alabama supreme court justice John J. Ormond to present to his state government. Though it is highly unlikely the state would have rendered a positive response under any circumstances, Susan's timing could not have been worse. The memorial fell into the hands of the state legislature at the moment when John Brown and his followers tried to occupy the U.S. arsenal at Harper's Ferry and initiate an uprising to overthrow white power in the South, outraging white southerners, including the people of Alabama. Ormond did his best to respond as a southern gentleman, but he made it clear that the Alabama legislature could no longer consider any request from the North, which it now saw as the South's worst enemy.[79]

Male opposition and negative press coverage were bad enough, but they were far less disheartening than the indifference and hostility of so many women. In trying to explain this phenomenon, many reformers probably agreed with Lucretia: "So circumscribed have been her limits that she does not realize the misery of her condition." Susan's assessment was harsher: "Woman is the greatest enemy of her own sex. She spurns the betrayed but feels flattered by the betrayer." At the 1851 Worcester national convention, Abby Kelley Foster blamed female oppression not only on man but also on everyone who did "not feel the full weight of her responsibilities." She had little patience with women who complained but did nothing to change their status.[80] In 1854, while preparing yet another petition campaign, a disheartened Elizabeth observed: "It is most humiliating to know that many educated women so stultify their consciences as to declare they have all the rights they want." Surely they did not understand the "barbarous laws" that confined them. Had women lost so much self-respect that they could not raise their voices to protest "such degrading tyranny"? She assumed that if they truly understood the injustices they endured, women would fight to end their oppression.[81] Many likened female apathy to the behavior of downtrodden slaves who felt so little hope that they simply accepted their oppression. Edmund Burke's statement "The happy slave must be a most degraded man" reflected women's situation all too well.

Thomas Wentworth Higginson tried to explain female indifference and opposition in his widely read 1859 essay "Ought Women to Learn the Alphabet," published in the *Atlantic*. From the moment they were born, he observed, females learned that they were inferior to men. Too few had the advantage of a sound education to question those lessons. "Systematically discourage any individual, or class, from birth to death, and they learn, in nine cases out of ten, to acquiesce in their degradation," he maintained. Women had not excelled because they did not yet have the opportunities that would allow them to do so.[82]

Yet it is understandable that most American women at this juncture did not embrace the movement. The well-educated, upper-middle-class reformers who led it usually directed their messages to others of similar background. The issues they articulated—better education, access to professions, control of marital property, and suffrage—had little to do with how most American women lived. The majority did not attend conventions or read radical newspapers—or any newspaper for that matter—and did not have the time or energy to question their status. Nor did they have much property to claim. Most were farm wives and mothers, working from sunup to sundown; their goal was to make it through each day. Those laboring in mills and factories suffered long hours

Thomas Wentworth Higginson (Print Collection, Miriam and Ira D. Wallach Division of Arts, Prints and Photographs, The New York Public Library, Astor, Lenox and Tilden Foundations)

and low pay. Sometimes they took action by striking to demand redress for injustices that directly affected them. But, as noted earlier, they rarely were able to force significant changes in their situation. Female indifference or resistance to the women's rights movement stemmed as much from the demands of women's daily lives as from a rejection of radical ideas that few had the time or energy to contemplate. And most wives depended on their husbands in order to survive. Challenging the marital relationship or demanding more independence was hard to fathom when alternatives were so few. For the majority of American women, changing their status was a frightening and unwelcome concept.

While external pressures on the movement were enormous, internal problems also took their toll. Disagreements, both public and private, surfaced. Some reformers complained about the excessive number of conventions and the absence of strong leadership. Paulina Davis had definite ideas on how to run conventions, and she exhibited little patience when a meeting fell short of her expectations. After the 1851 Worcester convention, she insisted that no location be used more than once. She also complained that two or three fiery female speakers "almost set me frantic." No person should speak more than twice in one day or for longer than half an hour. "If they could not say their say out in that time, they were not worth much," she grumbled.[83]

Women activists disagreed over which issues deserved top priority. Some remained unconvinced that suffrage was needed; others considered it essential in order to give women power to influence other issues. Still others were disenchanted with all partisan politics and happy to let a husband or father vote for them. The issue of expanding the grounds for divorce proved divisive. Though the Declaration of Rights and Sentiments included the issue, most women avoided public discussion of the subject until Elizabeth aired it in 1860. Some worried that if grounds for divorce were eased, husbands would find it easier to leave their wives and children without any means of support.

Jealousy, exhaustion, self-righteousness, and miscommunication often generated discord. Though revered as the most senior woman in the movement, even Lucretia was not always universally loved. Davis felt that she was past her prime, reiterating the same messages at every convention. Lucy showed irritation with Davis's "vanity and her jealousy" and hoped she would miss the 1855 national convention. Douglass came under criticism; even friends and admirers became alienated by his personal style, concluding that his years of enslavement had left him bereft of basic manners. As Susan expressed to Lucy in 1853, "Douglas[s] is uncovering what has long been lurking beneath a smooth exterior." He and Garrison had a falling out in the 1850s over the role each played in the antislavery movement. The Motts became upset with a tirade Douglass unleashed against Lucy when she lectured at Philadelphia's Music Hall, a building that excluded blacks. While James Mott regarded racial segregation as "very wrong & wicked," he felt that Lucy had every right to speak there. "I do not see we are required to exclude ourselves from everything which is wrongly denied others," he assured her.[84] In 1859, Douglass again publicly criticized Lucy, this time for allegedly inviting Illinois's Democratic senator, Stephen Douglas, to a Chicago women's rights convention. Like other ardent abolitionists, Lucy never would have considered inviting a senator who supported the westward extension of slavery, and she issued a public disclaimer of this wrongful accusation. Nevertheless, Douglass continued his attack, deeply upsetting Lucy, who decided the best action was to ignore his diatribe.[85]

Negative feelings toward one another sometimes undercut larger goals. Elizabeth disparaged Amelia Bloomer, urging Susan to use caution when acting on any of Bloomer's suggestions. "She has not the spirit of the true reformer," she warned. "At the first woman's rights convention, but four years ago, she stood aloof and laughed at us." Though Bloomer had joined the cause, Elizabeth found her commitment halfhearted, since she would not denounce the fugitive slave law or criticize clergymen for their conservative views on women.[86]

Bad moods and uncharitable comments should be understood in the light of what these reformers experienced in their daily lives. Personal events had a profound impact on their activism. The death of Elizabeth's father in October 1859 led to months of mourning and perhaps regret that she had never won his admiration or total approval. Four years earlier, she had written Susan after experiencing a "terrible scourging" from her father: "To think that all in me of which my father would have felt a proper pride had I been a man, is deeply mortifying to him because I am a woman."[87]

On the other hand, one of the happier, most surprising events of the decade was the marriage of Lucy to Henry Blackwell on May 1, 1855. She had long resisted marriage, determined to retain her legal status as a *feme sole*. To Henry, Lucy was a welcome challenge, for strong-minded women were the norm in his family.[88] Henry was born in England, but his family immigrated to the United States, eventually settling in Cincinnati. His father, Samuel, became active in abolition, befriending Garrison, Samuel May, Jr., Gerritt Smith, and others. When Samuel died of malaria, the Blackwell women supported the family by running a girls' school. Henry attended college for one year but apparently exhibited some instability, not sleeping for days on end and suffering periods of depression. Harriet Beecher Stowe, who had lived near the Blackwell family, called him a "wild boy." With borrowed funds, he invested in a sugar refinery, moved to New York City, where he worked as a bookkeeper, and then returned to Cincinnati, where he and his brother Samuel, Jr., invested in a hardware business.[89]

Blackwell first met Lucy when she came into his store to cash a check. Up to this point, his life had lacked focus, yet he yearned to marry. He explained to his sister Emily that in order to make his way in the world, he needed an "intelligent, go-ahead lady with a fortune to back her go-aheadativeness." Lucy was hardly a lady of fortune, though she was already famous, smart, and earning a solid income from lecturing. Blackwell, seven years her junior, began his pursuit of her months later. He soon admitted that she was a "born locomotive" and hard to pin down. Within an hour after their first formal meeting, Blackwell had proposed. His campaign to win her involved writing long, passionate letters. Henry expounded on the joys of married life, especially marriage to a man like himself who would sacrifice anything to please her. After sixteen months of relentless courtship and Henry's dramatic assistance in rescuing a fugitive slave,

*Henry Browne
Blackwell, c. 1880 (The
Schlesinger Library,
Radcliffe Institute,
Harvard University)*

Lucy finally gave in. Henry promised to let her live as an independent woman, to support her work, and to consider her his equal. They married at her parents' home in West Brookfield, Massachusetts, and wrote their own vows, excluding "obey" and proclaiming their shared belief in a partnership of equals. On Henry's suggestion, they wrote and then published a "Protest," a statement objecting to laws that allowed a husband to claim a wife's property and earnings, that suspended a wife's legal existence, and that upheld a father's claim as guardian of any children.[90] After residing in Cincinnati and following Lucy's lecturing in Indiana and Wisconsin, the couple settled on a farm in New Jersey.

Marriage often diminished a woman's enthusiasm for reform work, as it had for Angelina Grimké Weld, and activists understandably grew worried about Lucy's commitment to the cause. Susan treasured Lucy's friendship and feared she would leave the movement. Lucy was irritated by her friend's prediction. "Do not do me the injustice Susan of suspecting liabilities *now* for me which are not called for by my free will," she wrote her. Susan also reacted negatively when another close friend, Antoinette Brown, married Henry's brother Samuel the following January. Well aware of Susan's feelings, Elizabeth reminded her of all that Lucy and Antoinette had contributed to the cause. "Let them rest awhile in peace and quietness and think great thoughts for the future," she urged. Constant engagement in public life was not good for anyone. "You need rest too, Susan," Elizabeth admonished. "Let the world alone awhile."[91] For Susan, letting the world alone was not possible.

The press had a field day over Lucy's marriage. "How the newspapers sneer and insinuate and talk about Lucy's repudiating her principles, and make merry over her protest," the reformer Frances Gage commented. She defended Lucy's marriage, claiming that Lucy had never publicly rejected the institution; what she opposed were unjust marriage laws. Gage expressed delight with the couple's "Protest," which she felt would generate discussion and alert Americans to women's subordinate status when married.[92]

The boldest statement Lucy made was not her marriage but her decision to keep her maiden name. For several months, she used Blackwell, but in July 1856, she reconsidered. Since no man would ever consider taking his spouse's last name as his own, why should she? A number of reformers—Elizabeth Cady Stanton and Abby Kelley Foster among them—used their own full names when addressed formally. Years earlier, Elizabeth had expressed antipathy toward women who used "Mrs." followed by their husbands' first names, likening them to slaves who had to take their masters' names, leaving them no claim to their own identity. This custom, she explained, was "founded on the principle that white men are lords of all." Lucy went a step farther; for the remainder of her life, she was Lucy Stone. This was not an action she took lightly, for she consulted several lawyers to understand the legal repercussions. Elizabeth and Susan were thrilled by her decision.[93]

Even more than marriage, motherhood transformed reformers' lives and circumscribed their commitment to the cause. Some mothers pondered whether to remain at home raising their children, as Angelina Grimké Weld had done, or continue their work. Lucretia's situation was easier than most, since her lecturing and reform work began when her children were fairly self-sufficient and relatives living nearby could assist with child care. The birth of Alice Stone Blackwell in September 1857 altered Lucy's life for several years. Initially she hired a nurse so she could continue traveling and lecturing, but she found the woman inattentive. Lucy then retired to full-time mothering. She believed her first duty was to raise her daughter. Her sister-in-law Antoinette Blackwell later observed that Lucy was "an almost too careful and self-sacrificing mother."[94]

Following a different path was Abby Kelley, who married Stephen Foster in 1845 and bore their only daughter, Alla (Paulina), more than a year later. Nursing the baby tied her to home, a commitment Abby initially found satisfying. Writing to her husband when Alla was only a few months old, she commented, "She has so thoroughly entwined herself about me that I fear it would send me in pieces to take her away." By the time Alla was three, however, Abby and Stephen switched roles. He acknowledged that his wife was the better lecturer and more committed to reform causes than he. Stephen and various relatives cared for Alla while Abby traveled and lectured. During adolescence, Alla suffered "a diseased spine," probably a severe case of scoliosis, which required her to wear a metal corset and to exercise for hours each week. In the first year of Alla's treatment, Abby canceled all lecturing in order to tend to her, but then Stephen took over once again.[95]

Among all women's rights leaders, Elizabeth was the most profoundly affected by motherhood. After the Seneca Falls Convention, many assumed she would lead the movement, but this was not to be. Henry was no help at home, was absent for several months each year, and was never around when she gave birth to their children—seven in all. Elizabeth was not a typical mother of her day. She encouraged her children's high-spirited antics and promoted exercise, fresh air, and healthful food. A devoted mother, she took joy in her rambunctious and apparently rather spoiled brood. Her delight in motherhood came from the challenge of raising healthy, energetic children and the ease with which she bore them. As she wrote after her last child was born, "I would not have one less than seven in spite of all the abuse that has been heaped upon me for such extravagance." Unlike most mothers, who experienced health problems during and after childbirth, Elizabeth delivered six of her seven babies with little pain. She was ecstatic when, in October 1852, she bore her first daughter, Margaret. Sharing her happiness with Lucretia, she declared, "Rejoice with me all Womankind, for lo! a champion of thy cause is born. I have dedicated her to this work from the beginning." Throughout that pregnancy, she had sensed, she said, "I was cherishing the embryo of a mighty female martyr— Glorious hope!" Despite these sentiments, it was not Margaret but the Stantons' second daughter, Harriot, born in 1856, who would carry on her mother's work.[96]

Nonetheless, Elizabeth complained about the demands of motherhood and often yearned to escape the bedlam. When pregnant in early 1851, she apologized for missing yet another convention due to "a kind of biennial clumsiness to which I have been subject many years." Susan noted that Elizabeth could not attend the 1853 convention because she was weaning a baby and recovering from malaria. "She longs to be free from household cares, that she may go into the reform work," Susan concluded. That summer, Lucy wrote Elizabeth about the approaching convention but sympathized with her situation. "But, we shall sadly miss the brave, true words you have been wont to send us. When your children are a little more grown, you will surely be heard, for it can not be possible to repress what is in you."[97] At times, Elizabeth resented Henry's freedom to leave home at will, but she justified her situation to Susan. "I do long to be free from housekeeping and children, so as to have some time to read, and think, and write. But it may be well for me to understand all the trials of woman's lot, that I may more eloquently proclaim them when the time comes." In another instance, she referred to herself as "a caged lioness," tied down by "nursing and housekeeping cares." But her life eased in the early 1850s, when she hired sixteen-year-old Amelia Willard, who served the Stantons for thirty years. More than one person commented on Willard's contribution to women's rights by providing Elizabeth time to engage in the movement.[98]

Those without children, of course, could focus their time and attention on reform. Paulina Davis never bore children. Ernestine Rose had two children in the 1840s, but both died while they were young. As a spinster, Susan centered her life on women's rights work and, as noted, displayed little tolerance for her friends' decisions to marry and bear children. Although she and Elizabeth often collaborated, Susan felt frustrated that domestic and maternal duties tied down her friends. In May 1853, Susan fussed to Lucy that Elizabeth wanted to write, "but oh dear, Lucy, what can she do with *five* children & two raw Irish girls." Susan became even more upset when she learned that Lucy was to speak at a lyceum on women's future, the only female sharing the stage with several illustrious male orators. Susan feared she would be ill-prepared, for at the time, Lucy had charge of Alice and her household while Henry was away. Susan complained to Antoinette Blackwell that Lucy was "foolish" for serving as maid and mother, "tired and worn from such a multitude of engrossing cares" and thus unable to engage in "careful, close continued intellectual effort." When Blackwell bore a second daughter, Susan scolded her: "Now Nette, *not another baby* is *my peremptory command.*" She had trouble understanding why marriage and family duties diverted any woman from their cause. Her feelings were well known; Elizabeth reassured Nette, "In spite of all Susan's admonitions I do hope you & Lucy will have all the children you desire."[99]

Despite the negative jibes, female friendships sustained these women, and their feelings for one another often ran deep. Elizabeth had a wide circle of friends and extended family who often visited her in Seneca Falls. She initiated a "Seneca Falls Conversation Club" that met Saturday nights to debate various issues.[100] She and her cousin Elizabeth Smith Miller addressed one another with endearing nicknames in their correspondence and shared intimate confidences. Lucy's closest friends were Susan, Antoinette Blackwell, and her siblings. Lucretia formed friendships with an array of men and women, entertained frequently, and maintained an active correspondence, writing lengthy letters to friends and acquaintances at home and abroad. Susan felt deep affection for both Lucy and Antoinette.

Understandably, those involved in the movement often turned to one another for support. Facing indifference, public ridicule, negative press, and grueling work, they could empathize with each other's hardships, poor health, and personal sacrifices. Correspondence and personal interactions show the depth of their concern and support for one another. For a few years, when Lucy and Susan were close and before they became estranged, their letters displayed mutual warmth. Susan signed her letters with affectionate closings, such as "In Love" and "Lovingly," ever-solicitous about her friend and grateful that she and Lucy could depend on one another.

National events also encroached on these women's lives and interests. By the last half of the 1850s, politics consumed the nation and became increasingly volatile, as arguments over slavery threatened to tear the country apart. Women's rights activists stayed well informed about the complicated issues, especially the conflict over slavery's possible extension westward. They followed the passage of the 1854 Kansas-Nebraska Act, which gave men living in those territories the right to determine whether the territory would ultimately allow slavery or not. Both the North and South encouraged people to migrate and settle in Kansas in order to influence that territory's future. Armed conflict soon broke out there between Free Soil settlers and proslavery defenders. "Poor Bleeding Kansas—how the soul sickens," Susan wrote, as Americans watched two governments form, one at Topeka and the other at Lecompton, each claiming authority to govern the territory. Lucy insisted that even though women could not vote, "it is for *our interest*, to aid in securing justice for Kansas." The *Lily* followed the crisis, reporting on the heated "discord" in Kansas and calling anyone "characterless" who disdained interest in the situation. The paper asked why any woman would be indifferent, and then answered its own question in strong language: "Her *will* is so weak that it can't move her tongue to speak, so long and steadily have the chains pressed her soul's energies." Southerners began to threaten secession, and a group of abolitionists suggested the same, urging the North to sever all ties with the slaveholding South. By the end of 1856, the nation's volatile political situation caused a disheartened Elizabeth to write prophetically: "I am becoming more and more convinced that we shall be in the midst of violence, blood, and civil war before we look for it."[101]

The 1856 election between the Republican Party's first presidential candidate, John C. Frémont, and the Democrats' James Buchanan pulled women into the campaign. What encouraged their interest was not only the Republican platform, which opposed the extension of slavery westward, but Frémont's colorful, smart, outspoken wife, Jessie Benton Frémont. The daughter of the Missouri senator Thomas Hart Benton, Jessie was independent and well educated and did much to enhance her husband's military, literary, and political career. (She also elicited negative sentiments, for many placed her in the women's rights camp.) A campaign slogan heralded "Frémont and Jessie," and many women attended Republican rallies and parades and wore ribbons and buttons declaring "Frémont and Our Jessie" and "Jessie for the White House." Republicans sang songs that celebrated the woman they hoped would become First Lady: "Oh, Jessie Is a Sweet Bright Lady," "We'll Give 'Em Jessie," and "Jessie Frémont." Reformers considered postponing their 1856 women's rights convention because of the election, but decided to move ahead. "There will always be something of more importance than a *woman's* convention," Martha Wright observed, "if *we* are willing to think so." Despite female enthusiasm, Frémont lost his bid for the presidency. And as the 1860 election loomed, Elizabeth became disenchanted with all Republicans and was anything but excited by Lincoln's candidacy. His disappointing stance on slavery followed the Republican party line: to prevent its extension into the West but not to abolish it in the South.[102]

By the end of the decade, as the nation divided politically, the women's rights movement began to find itself on firmer ground financially. During the early years, money had been especially tight. Charging admission to lectures and meetings brought in revenue, but fees kept others away. As a compromise, speakers sometimes solicited donations or took up a collection after an event. Some, including Lucretia, Paulina Davis, and Ernestine Rose, never felt the pinch, for they relied on their husbands' incomes to support their work. Until the late 1850s, Lucy's comfortable earnings from lecture fees and donations allowed her to support her family and in-laws and lend Henry money for his various real estate schemes and business ventures. On occasion, Lucy and Lucretia helped to defray publishing costs of convention reports and tracts. Phillips generously funded special needs of the women's movement from his own and his wife Ann's substantial wealth.[103] Lydia Maria Child donated $1,000 to the cause.

But it was two generous male benefactors who finally put the movement on a firm financial footing. In 1858, the Boston merchant and philanthropist Francis Jackson gave an anonymous gift of $5,000. Jackson stipulated that Phillips serve as steward of his money. Another gift came the following year from Charles Hovey of Boston, who established a $50,000 trust fund to support the antislavery cause, free religion, and female suffrage. Garrison was thrilled, noting that this legacy had been given to "the most radical and unpopular reforms," and it created "a marked sensation, in various quarters."[104] These contributions gave women the sound financial base they needed in order to hold future meetings, pay lecturers, and publish tracts and convention reports.

As a new decade dawned, reformers were finally beginning to see results from their hard work. Attitudes about women began to shift. By 1860, some two dozen states had expanded marital property rights laws, either recognizing that women deserved such rights or, in other instances, sensing the need to protect wives' property to ensure their families' economic survival. In a few locales, women gained limited voting rights. Widows in Kentucky with children between the ages of six and eighteen could vote in local school-board elections. Michigan allowed women at school meetings to vote in county districts. Several more states eased their divorce laws, adding new grounds for divorce and shortening the waiting time to win one. A few women gained access to professions that had been closed to them, for example, Antoinette Blackwell in the ministry and Emma R. Coe in law. The Female Medical College of Philadelphia opened its doors in 1850, and Elizabeth and Emily Blackwell established their New York Infirmary for Women and Children in 1857. Before the Civil War, design schools for women opened in Boston and Philadelphia. Women were becoming better educated, gaining a greater public presence, and enjoying a few more rights.

But they still had a long road ahead to achieve the goals articulated in the Declaration of Rights and Sentiments. When the Civil War broke out in April 1861, everything changed. The women's rights movement subsumed itself into the greater cause of winning the war and eradicating slavery forever.

5

WAR, DISILLUSIONMENT, DIVISION

The Civil War had a profound impact on the women's movement. Once fighting broke out in April 1861, female reformers gave scant thought to the Declaration of Rights of Sentiments and the goals they had pursued throughout the 1850s. The outbreak of war caused the cancellation of the eleventh annual national convention, scheduled for that spring. In fact, no national women's rights convention met during the four-year war. A disappointed Susan questioned why they should not convene, believing that nothing should impede their crusade. On this, she had little support. Martha Wright cautioned, "When the nation's whole heart & soul are engrossed with this momentous crisis...it is useless to speak if nobody will listen." Susan confessed to being "sick at heart" in putting aside their work but admitted, "I can not carry the world against the wish and the will of our best friends."[1]

Women on both sides of the conflict were essential to the war effort. White women in the eleven Confederate states immediately rallied to support the southern cause. They sent men off in a blaze of glory, believing that it would take little effort to defeat vile Yankees. "My God! That such a race should blot the earth," was the response of Grace Brown Elmore, of South Carolina, to the enemy. For four years, these southern women drew on their strength and domestic skills to support the military effort. Plantation women oversaw the planting and harvesting of crops; farm wives took on that work themselves. They cooked, baked, sewed, cleaned, nursed family members, and learned to make do with less. Some, like Elmore, yearned to don a uniform: "Would that women might change their occupation, would that they could give the dastards their needles, and shoulder the musket."[2] Most slave women labored overtime on farms and plantations; others worked as laundresses, cooks, and aides in southern hospitals and in battle encampments. With nearly all the war fought on southern soil, many Confederate women endured the full brunt of military action and its accompanying hardships and tragedies. For those living near battlefields, the war experience became truly terrifying, as shells rained down on fields and houses. Union and Confederate troops invaded southern homes and took food, livestock, and farm implements. Many families fled and took refuge in areas far from the line of fire, living with relatives or renting any available accommodations, putting additional pressure on communities for declining resources. By 1863, the northern blockade of southern ports, government confiscation of basic supplies for military needs, and disrupted supply lines created acute food shortages in many areas of the South. Food riots in several southern communities in the summer of 1863 revealed the desperate situation many families faced. Women became all too accustomed to mourning and burying their dead. Though Union women also lost loved ones and experienced the vagaries of a wartime economy, southerners dealt more directly and constantly with the hardships of war.

Northern women engaged in work they knew well, dedicating themselves to charitable pursuits and domestic projects to support the troops. Northern relief efforts were better coordinated than southern. Following Lincoln's call for seventy-five thousand troops in April 1861, Dr. Elizabeth Blackwell stepped forward to articulate the need to organize relief efforts and create and train a capable nursing corps. She held a well-attended meeting in New York City on April 26, 1861, to present her ideas. From this gathering emerged the largest women's wartime organization, the Woman's Central Association for Relief. Two months later, the United States Sanitary Commission was formed in order to centralize, coordinate, and motivate civilian relief efforts, especially domestic production. As might be expected, influential men, including Henry Bellows and Frederick Law Olmsted, oversaw this commission, and hundreds of men served as paid agents. Below them, female volunteers organized themselves into some seven thousand local soldiers' aid associations and performed most of the charitable work. Women met periodically to sew, knit, roll bandages, and collect food and medical supplies.[3] "Stitch, stitch, stitch" was how Caroline Dall described her days as she made soldiers' hats and uniforms, and Louisa May Alcott wrote of joining three hundred others "all sewing together at the hall for two days." Despite their dedication, no doubt some shared Alcott's sentiments: "If I was only a boy I'd march off tomorrow."[4]

Women also organized bazaars, held public readings, and produced tableaux and elaborate dramatic productions to present to paying audiences.

Sanitary fairs, organized and run by women in Chicago, New York, Philadelphia, Boston, and other cities raised hundreds of thousands of dollars to purchase military and medical supplies to support the Sanitary Commission. Women collected and made or baked items to sell, set up booths, publicized each fair, and tabulated sales and expenses. *Godey's Lady's Book*, which generally avoided any mention of the war, all but gushed over the extravagant Philadelphia fair the editors attended in June 1864. This "superb exhibition" of saleable goods surpassed anything they had ever seen, "perhaps equal to anything of the sort ever displayed in Europe." The most "enduring source of satisfaction" was, of course, the money it raised for "our sick and wounded soldiers."[5]

As happens in most wars, the exigencies of the American Civil War drew more women into public life and into new positions of responsibility. With men engaged on the battlefront, females in the North and South took over management of their farms and homes and raised food to feed soldiers. An increased demand for workers brought thousands into the world of paid labor and occupations traditionally regarded as male. More women than ever before took factory jobs, producing the uniforms, boots, foodstuffs, and armaments the war demanded. Federal and state governments hired women as office clerks and scribes. They proved to be effective spies and couriers, hiding letters and official documents in their petticoats or corsets. Prompted by a desire for adventure and a compulsion to serve their country, an unknown number of women on both sides disguised themselves as soldiers and joined men on the battlefield. The identity of some was not discovered until they were wounded or killed in battle.

One of the most significant occupational changes that occurred during the Civil War was women's entry into nursing, with an estimated three thousand eventually serving as nurses, both paid and unpaid.[6] Formerly, Americans had considered this occupation ill-suited for women, believing that they should never expose themselves to bloody wounds, mangled bodies, and male nudity— even though women had always nursed male family members. In the past, men, including wounded soldiers, served as nurses in hospitals and on battlefields, but the Civil War necessitated a call for women. Traditional arguments were ignored in the chaos of a bloody conflict that eventually caused more than six hundred thousand deaths. Many women, especially those living near battlegrounds, undertook nursing as a matter of course, opening their homes to care for ill and wounded soldiers. Some, like Clara Barton, worked on the battlefront, while others served in hospitals, including Louisa May Alcott and Phoebe Yates Pember, who had charge of the nursing corps at the Confederacy's largest hospital, Chimborazo, outside Richmond, Virginia. Mary Ann "Mother"

Bickerdyke served tirelessly for four years, working in Union hospitals and on battlefields, accompanying the army as it moved south through Tennessee, Georgia, and Mississippi. Dorothea Dix, famous for her earlier crusade for prison reform and care of the insane, received an appointment as superintendent of the Union Army nursing corps. She ran a tight ship, establishing rigid standards that required female nurses under her to be a certain age and not too attractive, lest they regard nursing as a means to catch a husband.

Female nurses made a difference. Where they had charge of hospital care, mortality rates were reduced by as much as half, due to women's concerns over hygiene, fresh air and water, and healthful food. However, the job proved hazardous. Nurses endured long, exhausting days, consumed rancid food and polluted water, and experienced sentiments Louisa May Alcott described as "home sick, heart sick & worn out."[7] They often caught the very diseases they were treating. After only three months on the job, Alcott suddenly abandoned her position in a hospital outside Washington, D.C., having contracted a nearly fatal case of typhoid fever. That same disease claimed the life of the hospital's matron, Hannah Ropes.

The demand for female teachers also increased during the war. Women filled positions vacated by male teachers who left for military duty. Though a number of schools and colleges closed their doors, especially those in the Confederacy, a surprising number of female academies and schools remained open. In addition to teaching in private and public schools, hundreds of northerners ventured south to work as teachers and missionaries and ease former slaves' transition to freedom. One of the first such experiments took place on the Sea Islands of Georgia, an area occupied by Union soldiers in early 1862. Women who went there to educate and uplift former slaves believed that under the guidance of Christian and Yankee ideals, they could make a difference. As one female teacher explained, they could bring the "light of intelligence, mental and moral improvement" to the "once down-trodden and oppressed, but now free race." At the war's end and the emancipation of nearly four million slaves, women missionaries envisioned "a great field of labor opening."[8]

Naturally, the war affected women's rights activists and their families. "The war news occupies my whole thought," Antoinette Blackwell commented only a few weeks into the conflict. "I cannot write on any thing else and do not feel equal to sermonising of [*sic*] those topics." Elizabeth and her children managed to escape mob violence when the New York draft riots broke out on July 13, 1863. The melee occurred in their neighborhood, for they lived only two blocks from the Black Orphan Asylum, which rioters burned to the ground.[9] Responding to their patriotic duty, a number of men who were activists or related to activists joined the Union war effort, most notably Thomas Higginson. In November 1862, he took command of the First South Carolina Volunteers, a regiment made up of former slaves. Daniel and Henry Stanton, Jr., Elizabeth's two oldest sons, immediately volunteered for a New York regiment. Susan's brother Daniel served in the war with a Kansas cavalry unit. A grandson of Sojourner Truth and two of Frederick Douglass's sons joined the famous all-black Fifty-fourth Massachusetts Regiment led by Colonel Robert Gould Shaw. Martha Coffin Wright's son Willie signed up with the Army of the Potomac and was wounded at the Battle of Gettysburg. Yet not everyone felt such commitment. Like many privileged men in the North and South, Sam and Henry Blackwell each paid $300 for a substitute to serve in their place after Lincoln instituted conscription in March 1863.[10]

Activists continued to lecture, although their speeches addressed issues of antislavery rather than women's rights. In the winter of 1860–61, as southern states seceded and northern passions heightened about an impending national schism, Elizabeth and Susan traveled across the Northeast, eliciting negative reactions from those who opposed the emancipation of slaves. A concerned Henry Stanton, who typically exerted little control over his wife, warned Elizabeth that she and Susan were risking their lives by speaking to "mobocrats" who "would as soon kill you as not." He urged her to "keep quiet & let the Revolution go on."[11] From his vantage point in Washington, D.C., he sensed that the volatile situation was one to avoid.

Appearing on the lecture scene in 1861 was a new female speaker, Anna Dickinson. Born in 1842 into a Philadelphia Quaker family committed to the antislavery cause, Dickinson embraced it growing up. Her father died when she was two, and the family struggled to survive. Thanks to local philanthropy, Dickinson attended school for several years, but quit at fifteen in order to help support her family, working as a copyist and later as an adjustor at the U.S. Mint in Philadelphia. She encountered discrimination when applying for a teaching position. The school district offered to pay her half the salary men earned, so she refused the job. Though never formally committed to the women's movement, Dickinson delivered speeches on women's rights as well as on abolition and Republican politics. Her striking appearance, youth, passion, confidence, and gift for extemporaneous speaking captivated audiences. "This is indeed a girl of 19 to be proud of," observed Caroline Dall after hearing her speak. "She has logic, historical acuteness[,] clear argument—and a masterly treatment." Dickinson first attracted public attention with her lecture "The Rights and Wrongs of Women," which she delivered in Philadelphia in February 1861. She proved equally effective in rallying support for the Republican Party. The press

Anna Dickinson (Billy Rose Theatre Division, The New York Public Library for the Performing Arts, Astor, Lenox and Tilden Foundations)

seemed dazzled by this emerging superstar, reporting on her every movement, her many male admirers, the state of her health, and her physical appearance. At the height of her fame, Dickinson was earning the phenomenal salary of $20,000 a year.[12]

During Dickinson's years on the lecture circuit, she and Susan developed a close relationship. Susan was attracted to the young woman's personality, youth, and passion. By 1866, she addressed her as "My Dear Darling Annie," "Darling Dicky, Dicky," and "Chick a dee dee." She wrote of missing her "dear face" and yearned to spend more time together and share a bed where they could cuddle and whisper. "So Lovely child get rested, grow fat & strong & be a good brave girl," Susan advised her in July 1867. Such expressions of affection and physical attraction were not unusual in the nineteenth century when females often engaged in written and physical intimacies with one another. Most would later marry and bear children. This relationship lasted a few years, at least on Susan's part, but both were too busy and too committed to their work to spend much time together. In addition, Dickinson was twenty-two years younger than Susan and never as involved in the movement. Dickinson did bestow gifts on Susan, including a beautiful silk dress she sent for Susan's fiftieth birthday celebration.[13]

Despite the opportunities that were opening in paid and charitable work, a number of northern women began to express frustration, for they yearned to contribute more to the Union cause. "I long to be a man; but as I can't fight, I will content myself with working for those who can," Alcott wrote as the fighting began. Midway through the war, Elizabeth explained to others that "the women of the South are more devoted to their cause than we to ours. . . . They see and feel the horrors of the war; the foe is at their firesides; while we, in peace and plenty, live and move as heretofore." This sense of doing so little to support the Union troubled some women. Martha Wright's daughter Ellen queried a friend in August 1862, "Is it not stifling, irksome work, to remain quietly at home?"[14]

Two years into the war, northern women were given another opportunity to act. Elizabeth and Susan formed the Woman's Loyal National League (WLNL).[15] On April 10, 1863, Elizabeth called its first meeting, urging northern women to stand behind the Union and work to abolish slavery. In part, they acted out of a sense of frustration with Lincoln and his Emancipation Proclamation, which he formally issued on January 1, 1863. Their feelings were hardly unique. Many abolitionists expressed disappointment that the proclamation failed to eradicate slavery or rally Union military forces. As a political, wartime document, it equivocated on actually emancipating slaves, claiming to free slaves residing in the Confederacy—where Lincoln exerted no power—while maintaining slavery in areas occupied by Union soldiers. Several also expressed dissatisfaction that men were so "sadly wanting" in conducting the war, which had dragged on far too long. Elizabeth hoped several men in Lincoln's cabinet, whom she described as cases of "hopeless imbecility," would resign. She saw no reason why the nation should not depend on women "for our national as well as our individual and social salvation." In her eyes, the country could be no worse off than it was now.[16]

The WLNL held its first convention on May 14, 1863, in New York City. Elizabeth called the WLNL "the first and only organization of women for the declared purpose of influencing politics." Returning to public life after several years' absence, Lucy presided over that first meeting. Officers and members of the business committee included Elizabeth, Lucy, Martha Wright, Amy Post, Antoinette Blackwell, Ernestine Rose, and Angelina Grimké Weld. Women made up a majority of the audience. Characterizing their role as the "educator of the race," they insisted on their "God-given responsibilities" to abolish slavery. Elizabeth read aloud a letter she sent to President Lincoln, conveying support for his administration if he would pursue abolition.[17]

A contentious issue arose: whether to incorporate women's rights demands into the WLNL agenda. Some argued against this, since by doing so, the WLNL would discourage many from participating who supported abolition but not women's rights. Ernestine Rose countered this concern by reminding everyone that without the latter movement, they would not even be present and speaking courageously in public. Resolutions passed at the meeting included support for the Emancipation Proclamation, a demand for political and civil equality, and a statement that women would sacrifice anything to "secure the final and complete consecration of America to freedom." Despite these ringing statements, not everyone seemed satisfied with the meeting. An irritated Garrison declared the meeting "almost a dead failure—resolving itself, in fact, into a Woman's Rights Convention."[18]

Though some might have called this a shaky beginning, the WLNL was more official and more national in scope than any women's rights group had ever been. Susan and Elizabeth established an office in New York City and wrote its membership pledge: "We, the loyal women of _____, do hereby pledge ourselves loyal to justice and humanity and to the Government in so far as it makes the war a war for freedom." Artists created a badge depicting a slave breaking his own chains, and Elizabeth hoped that all would wear it. They considered the idea of hiring speakers to spark interest, and Susan suggested Lucy as an ideal spokesperson, even though she had done little public lecturing since the late 1850s. "I know the old fires are in her—or, if not the *old ones*—still brighter and grander ones.... The Committee will write her as soon as plans are fixed—& may the powers of all the good & true & earnest help her to say *yes*," a confident Susan insisted. Even without a corps of lecturers, word spread rapidly, and women in towns and cities throughout the North and Midwest organized WLNL branches.[19]

The WLNL outlined its central task: to gather a million signatures in a mammoth petition drive to demand the abolition of slavery. To defray the expenses of mass petitioning and mailings, women activists hoped to collect a penny from each signatory and secure franking privileges from sympathetic congressmen. Claiming the right to petition as their only effective political tool, Susan asserted, "Women can neither take the ballot nor the bullet to settle this question; therefore, to us, the right to petition is the one sacred right which we ought not to neglect." In defending female involvement in antislavery activities, Elizabeth reengineered a concept she and others had often rejected. Instead of denouncing the concept of women's separate sphere, she now invoked it. Because women were more moral and religious than men were and because slavery was a moral issue, women were the ones who should try to abolish it. After years of denying anyone's right to relegate women to a separate place, much less define it for them, a pragmatic Elizabeth now embraced the idea.[20]

Susan, appointed secretary of the WLNL, faced the daunting task of organizing this huge petition drive, which she undertook with her usual energy and drive. From Hovey funds, she was paid $12 in weekly salary. She eventually enlisted some two thousand volunteers to collect signatures. Newspapers like the *Liberator* and the *New York Tribune* gave the campaign positive coverage. By 1864, having collected some one hundred thousand signatures, women activists submitted their first petitions to Congress. At the war's end, they had nearly four hundred thousand names, an impressive number, though well below their ambitious goal. The outcome disheartened Susan, but as volunteers discovered, many people refused to sign, seeing no reason to stand behind an effort that appeared to duplicate the Emancipation Proclamation.[21] Others had no interest in or desire to support abolition, fearing the consequences of racial equality. They worried about blacks migrating northward, settling into white communities, and competing for jobs. Others rejected the radical nature of the WLNL and those involved in it. Most northern women preferred to support the war effort by nursing soldiers, rolling bandages, and knitting socks.

Despite all the good women activists were accomplishing, some of their wartime work met with negative press. Newspapers that had opposed the women's movement before the war remained skeptical and continued to criticize those who ventured into the public arena. Nor did all reformers find the WLNL's platform persuasive. Caroline Dall could not support its political agenda. She explained to Elizabeth that they should "not descend into vulgar politics" or dictate political beliefs to others. Lucretia abhorred the Civil War, would not support Lincoln, and hated to see war trumping women's rights efforts. "When our Meetings are forbidden, & doors closed against us, it is no time to stay away, & thus yield to the enemy," she explained.[22] But when the war ended in 1865 and the Thirteenth Amendment abolished slavery, Lucretia was elated. Though Lucy avoided most wartime activities and disliked politics, her antislavery beliefs overcame those sentiments. She supported the WLNL and made two speaking appearances, although she refused to serve as an official lecturer.

Wartime legislation affected women. A discouraging moment came in 1862 when a more conservative New York legislature rescinded some clauses in the state's 1860 Married Woman's Property Act, removing a mother's right to guardianship of her children and a widow's control of her late husband's estate. Susan was furious, but there was little she could do. On a more positive note, the Republican majority in Congress passed two significant pieces of legislation in 1862, the Homestead Act and the Morrill Land Grant Act. The Homestead Act encouraged settlement of the American West, offering up to 160 acres of surveyed public land to any adult man or single woman who would cultivate it, build a structure on it, and live on it for five years. After paying a small fee, the land was theirs. Having this access to land encouraged some women to move west, often accompanying adult family members with whom they hoped to amass land for a sizeable farm or ranch. The Morrill Land Grant set aside federal land to allow states to sell it and use the proceeds to build public institutions of higher learning. A number of these schools, especially in the West, were among the first colleges to admit women after the Civil War.

Once again, women found themselves drawn into politics, especially the 1864 presidential election. Elizabeth hoped that they could affect the outcome of this race. "We do not want an 'unknown man, pledged to nobody and nothing,'" she asserted. "Neither do we want one pledged to slavery, as President Lincoln has ever been." Several reformers opposed Lincoln's reelection, feeling he was ineffective and had avoided the issue of abolition for far too long. "He has proved his incapacity for the great responsibilities of his position," Elizabeth added. Nor did she and a number of others believe in a two-term presidency during wartime, and they preferred someone with military experience. The generals Benjamin Butler or John C. Frémont would be a far better choice. Lucy also disliked Lincoln for equivocating on abolition. But she aimed some of her deepest disappointment at Garrison, who, having eschewed politics in the past, now supported Lincoln and the Republican Party. "O, if he would only cry out as in the earlier days," she lamented. Though Lucy exhibited little confidence in any politician, she generally preferred Republicans to Democrats. Ultimately, women's political opinions mattered little. In September 1864, the Union victory over Confederate forces in Atlanta saved the day for Lincoln and the Republican Party.[23]

Personal issues affected female reformers' commitment to the war. In November 1862, while Susan was visiting home, her father suffered severe stomach pains; two weeks later he was dead. She mourned his passing for months. At times, the Blackwell-Stone marriage was in jeopardy, due in part to Henry's ill-advised investments and his difficulty in finding a lucrative occupation, exacerbating financial worries now that Lucy was not lecturing. Blackwell family members sensed tension between the two. Elizabeth Blackwell defined their marriage as one that "linked two excellent but unsuitable natures together." With both absorbed in women's rights, "there is never the shadow of peace or domestic enjoyment," observed another sister. At times, the burden of running a household during Henry's frequent absences overwhelmed Lucy. The year 1864 was particularly trying. Lucy visited her father, who was blind and suffering long stretches of poor health; he died that fall. She experienced periods of depression, her migraine headaches returned, and her confidence in her ability ever to lecture effectively dissipated. Her daughter Alice was sickly and needed her mother's constant attention. The couple rented an apartment in New York City, and Henry urged Alice and Lucy to move there. The idea held little appeal. Lucy yearned instead "to live in some quiet corner, free from criticism, or scrutiny, where I shall be able *perhaps,* to find that better self of me" and achieve "a life of worthy use." As her health and outlook gradually improved, she shared her thoughts with Susan. "I shall pray again for the return of that great impulse that drove me into the world, with words that must be spoken." Not until the war's end was Lucy fully able to return to public life. She began to lecture, and in the fall of 1865, Susan helped her outline a strategy for their next effort, including another petition drive for female suffrage. The family's financial situation eased when Lucy and Henry sold a portion of their New Jersey farm and paid off debts, thereby gaining some of the financial security they needed to be able to devote more time to reform.[24]

The Stantons experienced significant upheaval during the war. In 1861, Henry accepted an appointment as deputy collector of the Port Authority of New York and hired their son Neil as a clerk. Thanks to Elizabeth's inheritance from her late father's estate and Henry's new job, in May 1862 the Stantons moved from Seneca Falls to Brooklyn and then into Manhattan. Elizabeth now resided in a bustling city, a place more conducive to her personality and interests than upstate New York. Her commitment to women's rights underwent a major shift as she began to lecture, write more speeches and essays, and travel. Not only did the relocation motivate her activism, but she no longer had to devote every waking hour to her seven children. During the Civil War, Elizabeth reemerged as a visible figure in the movement.

But everything began to collapse when authorities discovered that Neil had accepted a bribe and forged his father's signature on some bonds. An investigation began when several bonds were discovered missing. Neil finally admitted wrongdoing. In December 1863, Henry resigned his post, but newspapers would not leave the scandal alone. Congress began its own investigation a month later and in June issued a report accusing Henry and Neil of negligence but not criminal behavior. The episode embarrassed Elizabeth, though she defended her son and husband, believing that the situation resulted from political struggles over plum patronage jobs. She pleaded with Horace Greeley to make little of this disgraceful event in his *Tribune*. "In this hour of the deepest sorrow of my life I ask not mercy, but justice," she entreated. Eventually Henry found work on Greeley's paper and then on Charles Dana's *New York Sun,* where he stayed for some twenty years. He also practiced law part-time. Elizabeth did not mention this event in her memoir or in the *History of Woman Suffrage*.[25]

With General Robert E. Lee's surrender to Ulysses S. Grant at Appomattox on April 9, 1865, the Civil War finally ended, bringing enormous relief to the entire country. The nation had survived the four bloodiest years in its history, although the assassination of President Lincoln only five days later sent shock waves across the entire country, North and South. Typical was Caroline Dall's despair on hearing the news of Lincoln's tragic death: "Oh God! do let me wake from this night mare & find it all a dream." Andrew Johnson now occupied the White House, a man whom some Americans began to sense lacked the necessary character and political acumen to handle the problems of Reconstruction and to restore the nation's solid foundation. A blunt Lydia Maria Child called him a "braying Ass" and felt that "every true lover of the country must want to creep into a knot-hole and hide himself, whenever the name of our President is mentioned." Elizabeth later observed that had Lincoln lived, he would have handled Reconstruction far better than Johnson did.[26]

The nation faced enormous challenges, including how to handle the eleven southern states that had seceded and how to treat and protect former slaves. Chaos, uncertainty, and enormous debates defined the postwar period, as states and Congress reexamined their laws and constitutions and argued over the meaning of citizenship and equal rights. In the midst of these heated discussions, women reformers sensed an opportunity finally to advance their cause. The war had "unsettled all our government foundations," Elizabeth observed, and she hoped that in their restoration, all "unjust proscriptions" would end. The nation could now have a government of "the WHOLE people" rather than one representing only white males. Weeks after the war ended, Elizabeth issued an appeal for suffrage: "No country ever has had or ever will have peace until every citizen has a voice in the government. Now let us try universal suffrage."[27] Having done so much to support the Union war effort and the antislavery cause, reformers believed that elected officials would at last reward them with the rights they had been demanding since Seneca Falls. Little did they imagine the enormous disappointments they would experience—and a new challenge: competing with freed black men for the right to vote.

The first of three Reconstruction amendments to the Constitution, the Thirteenth, which abolished slavery forever, passed a Republican-dominated Congress in January 1865. States ratified it the following December. This amendment suggested that Congress's primary concern was the condition of former slaves, not women's rights. In May 1865, Wendell Phillips made that clear at a meeting of the American Anti-Slavery Society. Demanding female suffrage at this point would dilute the most vital issues on the national agenda— the rights and freedom of former slaves. In a telling and often-quoted phrase, he avowed: "One question at a time. This hour belongs to the negro." The time was not ripe for female enfranchisement. A dispirited Elizabeth wrote Phillips, asking if he believed Negroes only included men.[28]

Using a public venue, Elizabeth in December 1865 fired off an essay to the *National Anti-Slavery Standard,* responding to Phillips's insistence that this was "the negro's hour." Now was the perfect time, she declared, for the nation to rectify past errors by enfranchising women and to create a true democratic republic. She articulated a theme she would employ often in the future— denouncing the favoring of black and immigrant men's right to suffrage over that of women. She and others had worked for over three decades to eliminate slavery, and the idea that women should "stand aside and see 'Sambo' walk into the kingdom first" appalled her. If black men voted before women, would they not add more voices "to hold us at bay"? And if black women could not vote, argued Elizabeth, their freedom would be another form of slavery. "It is better to be the slave of an educated white man, than of a degraded, ignorant black one!" she avowed.[29] While most white Americans at this time probably agreed with Elizabeth's thoughts on race, many parted company with her insistence on female suffrage.

Pronouncements like these that Elizabeth and others made at this point and later were unquestionably racist and xenophobic. While reading them arouses discomfort today, these were commonplace not only for someone of her background and education but also among a broad spectrum of society. Most Americans, whether living in the North or South, opposed black equality and did not want to see poor, uneducated immigrants enjoying the American dream. Chinese, Mexicans, Catholics, Native Americans, and the Irish were also victims of intolerance and violence. Many persons such as Elizabeth whom we admire in U.S. history expressed sentiments that we now judge—or should judge—by far different standards.

A significant number of reformers and most members of the Republican Party agreed with Phillips: black suffrage trumped a woman's right to vote. Even some women, including Abby Kelley Foster, agreed. In January 1867,

Lucy admonished her: "O Abby, it is a terrible mistake you are all making," for Lucy believed that only women could save the country. Thomas Higginson also identified black suffrage as the central issue of the day. In May 1866, he commented that he was losing "faith," though not "conviction," in the women's movement. Higginson's change of heart was due in part to Lucy's "entire absorption in her own household & admission that the mother of young children must during her prime of life be so absorbed." He and others were increasingly troubled by the indifference of most women and how willingly they seemed to accept their oppression. "Men can never secure woman's rights vicariously for them," he added. Women's indifference to the cause of women's rights irritated Wendell Phillips as well, and he urged that they be more forceful in demanding their rights. He agreed with Lucretia's assessment that women had launched "a cause which had its greatest enemy among its own victims." To many Americans, women seemed to be the greatest hindrance to their own advancement.[30]

Debates in Congress now addressed legislation to determine who should have the right to vote. Up to this point, states had determined voter eligibility. Republicans who controlled Congress were eager to add former male slaves to the voting lists, confident that nearly all would support the party of Lincoln. The U.S. House and Senate considered adding the word "male" to the Fourteenth Amendment, allowing the federal government to influence who could vote. Learning of this, Elizabeth, Susan, and Lucy immediately issued an appeal entitled "Women of the Nation" and addressed to them, warning them that with the addition of this one word, Congress might effectively exclude female voters. They denounced this move as a "desecration of the Constitution" and asked American women to petition for their right to suffrage and political representation. They also asked Congress to amend the Constitution so that states could never disenfranchise anyone on the basis of sex.[31]

Resuming a familiar task, women organized the Eleventh National Woman's Rights Convention, which met on May 10, 1866, in New York City. The meeting attracted well-known women's rights and antislavery activists, including Elizabeth, Susan, the Motts, Phillips, the minister Henry Ward Beecher, Martha Wright, and the Fosters. Since New York State was again revising its constitution and extending suffrage to black men, Lucretia agreed that this was "decidedly the fitting time for women to slip in" and "make what stir we can." At the convention, Susan endorsed a suggestion by the editor and reformer Theodore Tilton that they enlarge their mission and create a new organization by demanding universal suffrage. What women had been seeking for themselves, they now should demand for all. Out of this meeting a new organization emerged, the American Equal Rights Association (AERA), but it did not please everyone. "I for one have always gloried in the name of Woman's Rights, and pitied those of my sex who ignobly declared they had all the rights they wanted," Martha Wright declared, though she recognized the wisdom of this inclusive approach. By working together, Susan argued, they could secure "one grand, distinctive, national idea—*Universal Suffrage.*" They wrote a constitution for the new organization, printed stationery, and named Lucretia president and Elizabeth vice president, even though Lucretia's age and poor health made it difficult for her to participate.[32]

A division in the ranks quickly surfaced. Although the new association demanded suffrage for all, the issue became one of priority. Many members sensed that the nation was not ready to enfranchise both women and former male slaves. A newcomer to the movement, Henry Ward Beecher, the famous minister of Brooklyn's Plymouth Church and younger brother of Catharine and Harriet, spoke at length on this question. Eliciting much laughter and applause, he encouraged AERA members to champion women's rights; the nation should reward them for their Civil War work. In his mind, they had a duty, not merely a right, to vote. By adding female voices to the national agenda, they could offset the power of "the rising cloud of emancipated Africans" and the "great emigrant band of the Emerald Isle."[33] Others in attendance disagreed. Because slaves had been oppressed for centuries and freedmen now faced violence in the South, black males deserved suffrage first. Women should put their faith in the Republican Party, which presumably would support female enfranchisement once black male suffrage was firmly in place.

Some were wary of setting any priorities. Lucretia maintained that all humans deserved equal rights. Frances Ellen Watkins Harper, a well-known writer from Ohio, addressed this issue. She advocated black male suffrage but insisted on the rights of women, including their right to vote. Harper despaired over her inferior status as a free black woman. She was not allowed to ride on streetcars in Philadelphia, and on trains was segregated from whites by being forced to ride in the smoking car. Now a widow struggling to pay off her late husband's debts, Harper came to understand women's powerlessness after officials invaded her home and seized her possessions. "Justice is not filled so long as woman is unequal before the law," she asserted.[34]

Ignoring women's protests, Congress passed the Fourteenth Amendment in June 1866, and it went out to states for ratification, a process that took two years. On the surface, this amendment seemed to benefit women and former slaves, asserting in its first paragraph that "all persons born or naturalized in the United States . . . are citizens of the United States and of the State wherein they reside." No state laws could "abridge the privileges or immunities of citizens." Such language suggested to some that women might enjoy all the rights and privileges of citizenship, including the right to vote. This, however, was hardly the intent of radical Republicans, who sensed that privileging former male slaves was all the nation could bear. Thus, the amendment's second paragraph introduced wording that clearly discriminated against women. In three places, the word "male" appeared—the first time this word was included in the U.S. Constitution. The second clause said that if the right to vote were "denied to any of the male inhabitants" of a state, that state would lose a proportion of its representation in Congress, based on the number of men it had disenfranchised. Susan, Elizabeth, and others were aghast—the Fourteenth Amendment proved that Congress had turned its back on women.

In the fall of 1866, disenchanted with both Republicans and Democrats and knowing that New York State had no law prohibiting women from holding public office, Elizabeth ran for Congress as an independent in New York's Eighth Congressional District. She publicized her intent in several New York newspapers, basing her campaign on "*free speech, free press, free man,* and *free trade*— the cardinal points of democracy." Her concern was that freedmen in the South and millions of immigrants were gaining the right to vote and hold public office. They did not represent "property, education or civilization" but rather "pauperism, ignorance and degradation." To Elizabeth's way of thinking, women with "wealth, education, and refinement" should be able to vote and ensure the justice and safety of the nation. In this congressional race, a first for women, Elizabeth received twenty-four votes out of more than twenty-two thousand cast.[35]

Other activists campaigned for suffrage at the state level, as several states revisited and rewrote their constitutions. New York offered women this opportunity, scheduling another constitutional convention for 1867. Dozens of petitions inundated officials during early summer. Horace Greeley, a delegate to this constitutional convention and chair of a special committee on female suffrage, invited Elizabeth and Susan to speak. In late June, they did so. Elizabeth's sharp tongue was evident when Greeley reminded her that the "ballot and bullet" went hand in hand; women should be prepared to defend their country if they expected the right to vote. Elizabeth cultivated no male friendships that day (and lost Greeley's) by responding that women were ready to take up arms "just as you did in the late war by sending out substitutes." She added that it was "wiser and safer to enfranchise the higher orders of womanhood than the lowest orders of black and white, washed and unwashed, lettered and unlettered manhood." Women did not want the "lower orders of manhood placed over their heads." Men had made a mess of politics, and Elizabeth condemned the "wholesale corruption and fraud in our halls of justice and legislation" due to men's political action—or inaction. Men were to blame for the nation's ills.[36]

George William Curtis, a writer and editor, proposed an amendment demanding female suffrage and equal rights. In his speech, he cited Seneca Falls as the place where the struggle for women's rights began. Curtis summarized the reasons that so many people opposed female suffrage, including its revolutionary nature and the widespread indifference of most women. He countered that indifference was no reason to refuse to enfranchise women, since many men also did not vote or even want to vote. The idea that casting a ballot would unsex women made no sense, for "Nature is quite as wise as we are." Denying the belief that voting would "drag women down into the mire of politics," he retorted, "I would have them lift us out of it." Women, like men, were politically savvy and desired good government. Curtis's amendment and other speeches supporting female suffrage had little impact. Ultimately, the Committee on Suffrage claimed that his measure lacked adequate support, was too revolutionary, would foster "war" between the sexes, and would threaten domestic harmony. On the final count, Curtis's amendment lost resoundingly, 19 ayes to 125 nays. Elizabeth concluded that men were again uttering "stale platitudes from the effete civilizations of the Old World," and she was "filled with wonder at the apathy & indifference of our women." Once again, women reformers seemed to stand alone.[37]

For a brief moment, Massachusetts offered some hope. In April 1868, Lucy addressed the state legislature on the importance of women's suffrage. Several months later, reformers Julia Ward Howe and Wendell Phillips did the same. A year later, the state's Special Committee on Woman's Suffrage issued a carefully worded report. Committee members identified the writing of the Declaration of Independence and the abolition of slavery as the nation's two most historic events and envisioned "the full enfranchisement of woman" as the next great accomplishment. Massachusetts had a grand opportunity to enact female suffrage, a reform that would "purify and enlarge our influence." It offered numerous reasons to support women's suffrage. As taxpayers, women deserved the right to vote. Their interest in government and legal issues was keen. Voting would increase their sense of responsibility toward the nation. After devoted service to the war effort, women should not be denied a political voice. Finally, men questioned why people so often misquoted the Bible in order to subjugate women. If "thoroughly studied and correctly interpreted, so far from being in conflict . . . [it] aims at the establishment of perfect equality of all races and both sexes before human laws." The committee recommended an amendment that would give women the right to vote and hold office.[38] Such surprising support, however, did not convince the Massachusetts legislature to enfranchise women.

An exciting opportunity presented itself in February 1867, as the Republican-controlled Kansas legislature proposed two constitutional amendments for a statewide referendum in November. One asked that the word "male" and the other that the word "white" be removed from state qualifications for voting. The Kansas senator Samuel Wood invited activists to visit his state and campaign for the two bills. He would arrange their speaking engagements if they would pay expenses. Here was an opportune moment to make Kansas the first state in the Union "to realize a genuine Republic."[39] To AERA leaders, the state would serve as a test case for black and female suffrage, and they believed they could influence the outcome.

In late March 1867, Lucy and Henry led the way as the first AERA agents to campaign in Kansas. Leaving their daughter Alice in the care of her aunts, they spent three months trying to galvanize support for both propositions. Financial assistance for their travels, to the tune of $1,500, came from Jackson funds. The couple canvassed the entire state, covering twenty-five to forty miles a day by carriage, ferry, and wagon, speaking in schoolhouses, churches, sawmills, private homes, and outdoor venues. They brought 250 pounds of tracts to distribute. Kansas audiences were generally plain-spoken, "a queer mixture of roughness and intelligence, recklessness and conservatism," according to Henry. Yet despite the significance of both issues, many newspapers remained indifferent or denounced their efforts. One woman censured Lucy for "talking nigger and woman." Nevertheless, the two remained hopeful, exclaiming that "everywhere we go, we have the largest and most enthusiastic meetings," and concluded: "Any one of our audiences would give a majority for women."[40]

That optimism faded by late spring, for the going was tough and responses tepid. Fears that two issues on the ballot might divide blacks and women proved correct, for by May, Lucy realized that "the Negroes are all against us." Passing both bills seemed impossible. Lucretia had foreseen this, fearing that by linking the two amendments, women and blacks would compete to win suffrage before the other. Privately, Lucy felt that females should gain the right to vote before black men, who "will be just so much more dead weight to lift."[41]

While the couple campaigned in Kansas, the first anniversary convention of the AERA met in New York City on May 9 and 10, 1867. Reflecting the biracial nature of the organization, Lucretia Mott and Robert Purvis, an influential free black from Philadelphia, presided. Suffrage was on the minds of many attendees who had just spent two days at a meeting of the American Anti-Slavery Society.

The members of the AERA agreed to send a statement to Congress urging it to abandon any "prescriptive distinctions in rights of suffrage or citizenship, on account of color or sex." But reactions to such inclusiveness differed. Lucretia pushed for female enfranchisement, fearing that if black men won the right to vote first, they would use their political power to block female suffrage. Elizabeth concurred, asserting that she could not support black male suffrage, for she regarded black men as more autocratic than white men. Why, she wondered, was it acceptable to leave "the whole welfare of the nation to the lowest strata of manhood"? Congress should not grant suffrage to a "degraded, oppressed" group of men who "would be more despotic with the governing power than even our Saxon rulers are." Henry Ward Beecher spoke at length, admitting that many people feared former slaves, foreigners, and women as voters but insisting that universal suffrage was long overdue. Abby Kelley Foster described the widespread violence being perpetrated against blacks in the South and felt their gaining the right to vote was imperative. Female demands should not delay the needs of black men.[42]

Sojourner Truth, now in her eighties, spoke twice at this AERA convention, insisting that both black and white women must win full suffrage. In an extemporaneous style that elicited laughter, applause, and sympathy, a prophetic Truth commented: "There is a great stir about colored men getting their rights, but not a word about the colored women; and if colored men get their rights, and not colored women get theirs, there will be a bad time about it." In explaining why this struggle was so protracted and so difficult, she hit the nail on the head: "I know that it is hard for one who has held the reins for so long to give up."[43] Truth recognized two simple but key points. She raised the cry for black women's suffrage, an issue few white female rights activists articulated. White women tended to portray the issue as a choice between black men and educated white women. Truth also pointed out the difficulty of convincing men to relinquish any of their political monopoly.

In the summer of 1867, Elizabeth, Susan, and the Unitarian Universalist minister Olympia Brown followed Lucy and Henry to Kansas. Initially, they felt optimistic as crowds across the state welcomed them. Elizabeth relished the attention, and audiences were drawn to her wit, amiability, and pleasing appearance. She believed that Kansas, the "young and beautiful hero of the West," promised women and freed people real hope. Speaking at least once and sometimes twice a day, she asked Kansas voters to "take our names out of your constitutions and statute books and have no more special legislation for us. Let your codes be for persons, for citizens, throw all the Negroes and women overboard." Despite strong rhetoric and hundreds of speeches delivered by the three, they were dismayed when the Republican Party rejected women's suffrage and instead championed black male suffrage. At the same time, antisuffrage groups intensified their opposition, following them wherever they lectured. To Susan, however, this "low and scurrilous" tactic "helps us rather than hurts us." They also found themselves strapped for cash, lacking the funds that had supported Lucy and Henry. They struggled to raise $2,000 by accepting unsolicited donations and begging wealthy women like Ann Phillips for money. Often they engaged in the distasteful act of passing the hat after each public appearance.[44]

Betrayed by the Republican Party and desperate for cash, Elizabeth and Susan made a fateful decision to align with George Francis Train—a Democrat and a wealthy, extravagant, unstable dandy who offered to help them blitz Kansas and finance their campaign. Train had visions of grandeur, including a dream of someday occupying the White House. As the historian Ann Gordon aptly describes him, Train "occupied a space somewhere between brilliance and insanity." He traveled with Susan across Kansas, dressing in flashy outfits, uttering outrageously racist comments, and urging audiences to support female suffrage before black males gained the vote. There was no doubt that Train attracted large crowds. One newspaper described him as "masterly and exceedingly witty" and concluded that his lectures provided "rich and racy enjoyment." Elizabeth and Susan seemed delighted with Train's support. Susan assured him, "With your help we shall triumph."[45]

Back east, a number of activists, including Lucy, Henry, Lydia Maria Child, and Garrison, were horrified when they learned about this charlatan and his work on behalf of women's suffrage. They questioned why Elizabeth and Susan would compromise their reputations and the cause in order to befriend this known racist and align with the Democratic Party. The Train spectacle in Kansas was undermining AERA goals. Lydia Maria Child wondered why "Mrs. Stanton carries such a *Train* with her" and felt he made their undertaking look "ridiculous." Garrison minced few words, denouncing Train as a "ranting egoist"—"crack-brained, harlequin, and semi-lunatic." He warned Elizabeth and Susan that their action had subjected them to "ridicule and condemnation." In Garrison's eyes, African Americans "have not a more abusive assailant" than Train.[46] He and others became increasingly disenchanted with Elizabeth and Susan and their work on behalf of women's rights.

The two tried to deflect the barrage of criticism. They were willing to do almost anything to promote their agenda, even if it meant forming an ill-advised relationship with Train. They came to his defense. In late fall, Elizabeth called him "the most wonderful man of the century in some respects" and a "pure

Magee, 316 Chesnut St Phila

GEORGE F. TRAIN.

George Train (Library of Congress)

minded noble man . . . & an ardent & eloquent advocate of our idea" who had laid "his talents & wealth at our feet." Two years later, Susan wrote him, gushing, "My soul blesses you, as does the Good Father and all his Angels." She noted that men who had supported women's rights in the past, including Greeley, Garrison, and Phillips, had subsequently turned their backs on women by putting black male suffrage first. Following the Kansas referendum, Elizabeth and Susan made the situation even worse by traveling with Train as they lectured in Chicago, Louisville, Cincinnati, Boston, New York, and elsewhere.

Lucretia despaired over this direction in the movement. To her sister Martha, she expressed a desire to withdraw from all official duties, uneasy about the AERA and longing to return to female activism of the 1850s. "The several Conventions held were far more effective & all that we ought to have attempted," she observed. Elizabeth's racist comments also caused her discomfort: "Elizh. Stanton's sympathy for 'Sambo' is very questionable."[47]

Lucretia's worries were justified. For the next few years, Elizabeth continued to unleash her racism and antipathy toward black men, immigrants, and an uneducated male electorate. To an audience in Buffalo in December 1867, Elizabeth commented: "I am opposed to having another man allowed to vote until educated women are allowed too." Several months later, she challenged the Fifteenth Amendment, which Congress was considering as a measure to prevent states from disenfranchising anyone on the basis of race—but not gender. She denounced the enfranchisement of "another man of any race or clime until the daughters of Jefferson, Hancock, and Adams are crowned with all their rights." An essay, "Manhood Suffrage," she wrote in December 1868 cited reasons to oppose this amendment. If women had difficulty bearing the "oppressive laws of a few Saxon Fathers, of the best orders of manhood, what may she not be called to endure when all the lower orders, natives and foreigners...legislate for her and her daughters?" Elizabeth identified black men as women's worst enemies, pointing out that black men who had been voting in Washington, D.C., for two years had yet to support female suffrage.[48]

Returning east in the summer of 1867, Lucy and Henry observed the situation in Kansas with sinking spirits. By late October, they predicted that if women's suffrage passed, the margin would be small. Despite their hard work, Henry admitted, "*We are beat.*" And beat they were. The women's suffrage amendment in Kansas lost, 19,857 to 9,070. Black suffrage lost as well, but by a slightly smaller margin. Susan tried to make the best of the situation and urged Olympia Brown not to interpret this referendum as a defeat. "Let us hope and work to the brighter day," she urged. Yet, as the first statewide test of popular support for women's suffrage, the loss in Kansas was a major blow.[49]

In January 1868, Elizabeth and Susan undertook what they regarded as an exciting, new venture, founding and publishing a weekly newspaper, the *Revolution*, with financial backing from George Train and David Melliss, a financial writer for the *New York World*. The two women made the decision independently and did not promote the paper as a voice of the AERA. An announcement heralding the paper declared that it would become "the mouthpiece of millions, hoping to be emancipated." Elizabeth was elated: "My dream for years is at last to be realized." Since the movement seemed to lack the extensive press coverage that its conventions and other activities had generated in the 1850s, Susan and Elizabeth sensed the need for a paper that focused on women. Susan served as proprietor and Elizabeth and Parker Pillsbury as coeditors. Elizabeth wrote much of the copy. The first six-page issue appeared on January 8, 1868. They rented office space in New York City, tastefully decorated with carpets, tablecloths, shelves of books, calico screens, and pictures of Lucretia and Mary Wollstonecraft to provide inspiration. Some people questioned the paper's radical title, but the two women insisted that they wanted their paper to make a statement. Nothing was more revolutionary than the pursuit of women's rights.[50]

The *Revolution* addressed a wide range of topics, including suffrage, married women's property rights, education, laws and pending legislation, employment, equal pay for equal work, temperance, religion, marriage and divorce, moral reform—anything that affected the lives of American women. To meet their ambitious goal of one hundred thousand subscribers, Susan mailed sample copies to "liberal people who would be likely to appreciate our demands for women." For several months, the paper also carried Train's essays, letters, and poems and defended his Kansas work. Beginning in the fall of 1868, the *Revolution* serialized Wollstonecraft's *Vindication of the Rights of Woman*. Though the paper's primary intent was to enlighten supporters about women's rights, a few articles, like one entitled "To Women Who Do Not Wish to Vote," were aimed at the unconverted and urged women to demand an end to their enslavement and inferior status. At the end of the first year, the paper claimed several congressmen and foreigners as subscribers. Susan boasted that "no public journal ever achieved such a moral success before, in so short a time." With some pride, she added that other newspapers were now treating their paper with respect; even a handful of ministers expressed support.[51]

Despite such exuberance, the newspaper soon experienced problems. The reading public was not as enthusiastic as its two founders, and advertising revenues could not cover expenses, in part because Elizabeth refused to accept ads for products such as patent medicines, which she loathed.[52] Subscriptions peaked at three thousand, far below the goal. Some readers found the paper distasteful. To Garrison, the style was "coarse" and the subject matter "heterogeneous," though no doubt his negative feelings toward Elizabeth and Susan and antipathy toward Train influenced his reaction.[53] More important, funding from Train ceased when he departed for England. In January 1868, British authorities arrested him for transporting pro-Fenian literature and sent him to prison for ten months. Debts from the paper mounted. In May 1870, Elizabeth and Susan had no choice but to sell the *Revolution* to a newly formed joint stock company, with Laura Curtis Bullard as editor. The paper's demise devastated Susan, who felt that she was "signing my own death warrant." As a *feme sole*, Susan had been the only woman with the legal standing to sign a contract, meaning that all the paper's outstanding debts were in her name. Elizabeth told Susan that she and coeditor Parker Pillsbury lacked adequate funds to repay their share, and she never compensated Susan for the $10,000 they owed. Instead, Susan assumed the heavy debt, "every dollar of which I intend to pay." And she did so by lecturing for the next six years. While historian Elisabeth Griffith calls Elizabeth's behavior "unconscionable," there is no indication that Susan resented her friend. Despite questionable backing and the problems it encountered, the *Revolution* acquired some legitimacy and, for a brief time, served as a strong voice for the movement. Susan felt a sense of "joy" that she had shown that a radical women's newspaper was possible and hoped others would "reap where I had sown."[54]

Women continued to test the limits of their rights by engaging in acts of defiance and civil disobedience. Lucy and her mother-in-law went to the polls in November 1868 and tried to vote but were turned away. In Vineland, New Jersey, some 172 women, including four black women, voted in the same election, but did so symbolically by using their own ballots and ballot box. They defended their right to do so, claiming that the word "male" in the Fourteenth Amendment applied only to the eleven states in the former Confederacy. Even if their gesture had no impact on the outcome, their presence on voting day improved male behavior at the polls, encouraging men to extinguish cigars and cigarettes and act with greater decorum.[55]

The May 1868 annual convention of the AERA, held at New York's Cooper Institute, reintroduced the debate over suffrage for women versus black men and engendered greater discord. Lucretia resigned from office, leaving the movement, at least for the moment, without her sage counsel. She was in mourning for her beloved husband, James, who had died in January. Although Lucretia supported AERA goals, she wanted members to promote female issues, arguing that freed people were well supplied with more than enough advocates. The AERA meeting proved contentious on other issues. Lucy was in a testy mood, reflecting in part her lingering antipathy toward the debacle with Train. Lucy and Henry questioned Susan and Elizabeth's relationship with Train and Susan's expenditures in Kansas, and argued that the *Revolution* had "improperly stolen the thunder of the society" by eclipsing everything else. In response, Susan insisted that she had never misused funds and, in fact, had left Kansas in debt. The *Revolution* was a private venture, she countered, founded without any affiliation with the AERA.[56] Lucy then took on Douglass, after he roused "her every spark of latent fire" by avowing that women, unlike black men, had never been persecuted for demanding their rights. Several days later, Susan, still reeling from her confrontation with Lucy and Henry, nonetheless felt triumphant that Lucy's "anti-Train" argument had garnered little support. Commenting on the spat between Lucy and Douglass, she wrote that he "had stuck just enough pins into her soul" to cause Lucy to haul him "over the coals."[57]

The third AERA convention, in New York City on May 12, 1869, exposed deep fissures in the ranks. More than a thousand people attended, 90 percent of them female. States had ratified the Fourteenth Amendment ten months earlier and were now considering the Fifteenth Amendment, which Congress had passed in February. While the Thirteenth Amendment had abolished slavery and the Fourteenth protected citizenship, Republicans sensed that these two did not go far enough to ensure black male suffrage. The Fifteenth Amendment said that the right to vote could not be denied by any state on the basis of race. Now the AERA had to consider whether or not to support this amendment. Each side abandoned its sense of "equal." Elizabeth, Susan, and their backers opposed the amendment because it excluded women. Lucy, Douglass, Abby Kelley Foster, Henry Blackwell, and Henry Ward Beecher, among others, supported it, believing that after black males won suffrage, females would be next. Douglass decried Elizabeth's demeaning language when she used the term "Sambo" to refer to black men. Insisting that black men deserved the right to vote before women, Douglass detailed the many injustices, horrors, and humiliations that male slaves had endured for over two hundred years. When someone in the audience asked if female slaves hadn't experienced the same horrors, Douglass responded that if they had, it was due to race, not gender. By gaining the right to vote, Douglass insisted, black men would be able to protect their women.

Bickering defined this meeting. Susan challenged Douglass, arguing that women could not stand aside and wait while black men gained the right to vote. "If you will not give the whole loaf of suffrage to the entire people, give it to the most intelligent first," she demanded. Reluctantly, Lucy accepted the primacy of black male suffrage, but predicted that women would be able to cast ballots in the election of the president in 1872. Paulina Davis insisted that Congress not consider the Fifteenth Amendment without also passing a sixteenth amendment to enfranchise women. No more men should be enfranchised until enough women could vote and outweigh men's impact, Elizabeth added. Douglass's irritation was palpable; he labeled the AERA convention a women's rights, not an equal rights, meeting. Comments became more personal, as Stephen Foster accused Susan of misusing funds in Kansas and asked Elizabeth and Susan to relinquish their leadership positions because they opposed the Fifteenth

Amendment. The two did exactly that, withdrawing from the AERA. Two days later, they hastily formed what would become the National Woman Suffrage Association (NWSA).[58]

At the same time, Congress was debating women's suffrage, though with far less rancor. A handful of representatives suggested that they test the waters by giving women living in the western territories the right to vote. If the experiment failed, Congress could rescind such legislation, since it oversaw territorial governance. The Indiana congressman George W. Julian formally submitted this resolution, but it went nowhere. In December 1868, Senator S. C. Pomeroy of Kansas proposed a sixteenth amendment demanding female suffrage. The following March, Congressman Julian presented a joint resolution asking that "all citizens of the United States" enjoy the right of suffrage "equally without any distinction or discrimination whatever founded on sex." Simultaneously, he put forward a bill for women's suffrage in the District of Columbia. The majority in Congress, however, showed little interest, and both bills died.[59]

In the midst of the acrimony over suffrage, a split in the ranks of women activists was probably inevitable, especially with the creation of the NWSA. Two days after walking out of the AERA convention, Elizabeth and Susan held a hastily called and rather exclusive gathering to organize their new association. Their failure to issue an open invitation annoyed many reformers who felt they had been left out in the cold. Lucy and Henry were especially upset and took this as a personal affront. The new organization's first task was to begin a petition drive, "the largest the world has ever seen," asking the House and Senate to secure suffrage for all citizens "without distinction of sex." Elizabeth added her own touch of the dramatic, envisioning their petition decorated "with flowers and the American flag" and carried to Congress by several girls, each one representing a different state, territory, or district.[60]

That fall, in response to the formation of the NWSA, Lucy and Henry created a rival organization, the American Woman's Suffrage Association (AWSA), claiming that the NWSA did not reflect the views of many reformers. Unlike the NWSA, members of the AWSA stood behind the passage of the Fifteenth Amendment. The core identity of this association derived from the New England Woman Suffrage Association, which had formed a year earlier. The first president of the New England group was Julia Ward Howe, a wealthy Boston matron and popular writer, best known for her 1862 poem "The Battle Hymn of the Republic," which had served as the Union's Civil War anthem. Howe would play a central role in the AWSA and became one of Lucy's most stalwart supporters.

Julia Ward Howe, c.
1867 (The Schlesinger
Library, Radcliffe
Institute, Harvard
University)

Sympathy for women's rights came naturally to Howe, who knew firsthand what women endured in miserable marriages. Her prominent husband, Samuel Gridley Howe, was eighteen years her senior and domineering. He resented his wife's independent income, criticized her competence as a mother, undermined her self-esteem, and tried to prohibit her involvement in reform activities. Twice she considered divorcing him. Howe's commitment to women's rights emerged when friends convinced her to attend one of Lucy's lectures at the New England Woman's Club. Howe was reluctant, assuming that women's rights leaders were shrill, coarse, and masculine. On stage, however, stood a demure, cheerful woman with a musical voice. As Howe recalled, she went to hear Lucy "with a very rebellious heart. I came out very meek and have so continued ever since." When asked afterward to respond to Lucy's speech, Howe uttered, "I am with you." By the late 1860s, Howe ignored her controlling husband and did what she wanted. She committed her life to various reform issues, especially women's rights. She lectured, wrote, helped edit the *Woman's Journal,* and served as its foreign corresponding secretary. Howe's social prominence lent New England female activists enormous legitimacy and drew elite women into the cause.[61]

The AWSA held its first formal convention in Cleveland on November 24 and 25, 1869. Not wanting to fall prey to the criticism Susan and Elizabeth had experienced, Lucy made extensive preparations. She invited hundreds of men and women reformers. The convention's location promised strong participation from the Midwest. Lucy justified the formation of the new association on the grounds that "separate organizations, each in harmony with itself, will be more effective than is possible at present." In October, Lucy wrote Elizabeth and included a copy of her call to organize the AWSA:

> I wish I could have had a quiet hour with you to talk about it. I hope
> you will see it as I do. That with two societies each in harmony with itself,
> each having the benefit of national names, each attracting those who na-
> turally belong to it, we shall secure the hearty active cooperation of all the
> friends of the cause better than either could do alone. People will differ
> as to what they consider the best methods and means. The true wisdom is
> not to ignore but to provide for the fact. So far as I have influence,
> this soc. shall never be an enemy or critical of yours in any way. It will
> simply fill a field and combine forces, which yours does not.

Garrison expressed enthusiastic support for the AWSA, feeling that it would "inspire general respect and confidence, such as no similar association now does" and have a positive impact here and abroad. Delegates from twenty-one of the nation's thirty-seven states attended its first national convention, including southern representatives from Virginia and Mississippi. Interestingly, Susan was present at this meeting and charitably urged everyone to organize local societies under the NWSA or AWSA banner and work for a sixteenth amendment.[62]

Elizabeth was far less charitable and expressed displeasure over the emergence of a rival organization. In the pages of the *Revolution*, she responded to Lucy's plan with sharp words. She claimed that the AWSA, presumably long in planning, was the result of a "few dissatisfied minds." Everyone knew that leaders of this new organization had "been sedulously and malignantly working for two years to undermine certain officers in the National Association and their journal." Elizabeth "deplored" this division in the ranks, worried that it would shut out many people who would not want to choose one group over the other. The "Boston malcontents," she felt, seemed troubled by the "leadership and personalities" in the NWSA, since they were proposing nothing new. Elizabeth highlighted all the NWSA had accomplished and concluded that those who joined the AWSA "have probably been betrayed into this indiscretion." Paulina Davis was also upset with the new organization, sensing that its "purpose[,] aim and object is to destroy Elizabeth C Stanton and S B Anthony." Garrison read

Elizabeth's comments, which he felt were filled with "shuffling, tortuous, contradictory" prose, and called her remarks "slanderous" for "attacking and misrepresenting" her rivals.[63]

Despite Elizabeth's claim that the AWSA and NWSA were similar, the two groups exhibited some differences in their approaches to women's rights. The AWSA addressed most of its efforts to win suffrage at the state level. The NWSA, directing its primary appeal to Congress, demanded a constitutional amendment. The AWSA welcomed both male and female members and officers, while the NWSA initially only allowed female ones—although that rule would change. The NWSA campaigned for several women's issues, including additional grounds for divorce and more generous married women's property rights. The AWSA focused on suffrage. Its headquarters were in Boston; the NWSA was located in New York. The NWSA welcomed everyone to its meetings. Only delegates who represented recognized state organizations could vote at AWSA meetings, although any member present could speak. Reflecting its desire to keep power in the hands of women, Elizabeth became the first president of the NWSA, while the AWSA named Henry Ward Beecher as its leader.

Both organizations competed for prominent members. Each sought Lucretia's support, but she avoided taking sides, maintaining her fondness for all participants. Antoinette Blackwell tried to remain friends with everyone, though being the sister-in-law of Lucy and Henry, she joined the AWSA. Martha Wright's loyalty was to the NWSA. When invited to join the AWSA, Wright wrote Lucy, explaining why she said no. "I cannot agree with you that the cause will be better served by two. In *union* there is strength, & I feel persuaded that our cause will be weakened & the day of our success postponed, by unwise dissension, or the attempt to ostracise some of the truest & noblest pioneers, & most indefatigable workers in it." She hoped the two organizations could work together for a sixteenth amendment, and for a few years, she tried to end the rift. "The division is so senseless, all thinking so nearly alike, all working for the same end, nearly all loving one another, that I have no patience," Wright explained. Garrison's support of the AWSA was predictable, for he considered Elizabeth and Susan "untruthful, unscrupulous, and selfishly ambitious"—"I join my labors in behalf of woman with those whom I esteem and trust," he said. Some people felt conflicted, such as Isabella Beecher Hooker, younger sister of Catharine and Harriet, though she eventually joined the NWSA. Former male abolitionists, including Higginson and Phillips, joined the AWSA. A few reformers like Paulina Davis, Isabella Hooker, and Theodore Tilton tried to resolve differences between the two organizations. In April 1870, Tilton called a meeting with representatives of each association to discuss a merger. Lucretia also met with leaders, hoping they could unite their interests "in one common cause, and have one universal society." Apparently, delegates from the AWSA opposed every suggestion.[64]

Internal divisions and differences in approach were hardly the only problems. The press and the public, especially clergymen, continued to pound activists, denouncing female equality. Reflecting the attitudes of many Americans, Lewis Tayler, a biblical scholar and professor of Greek at the University of the City of New York, wrote a two-part article in December 1866, denouncing female suffrage and at the same time supporting black male suffrage. Citing scripture, Tayler claimed that the nation's patriarchal society was part of God's order and that men had the right to vote on behalf of their wives and daughters. *Godey's Lady's Book* maintained its traditional stance on women's rights, defending the primacy of home and stressing the perils women who stepped into the public arena faced. For instance, an 1868 article celebrated home as "heaven on earth." Here a man "finds his sweetest consolation," a place "to rest his weary limbs, and cheer his drooping spirits." What made home so delightful was "the sweet music of woman's voice...the soft whisper of woman's love." In closing, *Godey's* warned, "Fair daughters of Beauty, wander not from the paths of Prudence." Newspapers continued to present skeptical or negative coverage of women's rights efforts. The *Deseret News* of Salt Lake City derided female demands and listed all the rights women should cherish, including the "right to have her home in order whenever her husband returns from business" and the right "to be kind and forbearing whenever her husband is annoyed." Her most important right was "to remain a woman, without endeavoring to be a man."[65]

Horace Bushnell of Connecticut, a well-known Congregational minister who professed liberal ideas on some issues, was decidedly illiberal on women's suffrage. In his 1869 book *Women's Suffrage: The Reform against Nature,* Bushnell disparaged women's enfranchisement. He defended man's monopoly on voting, offering justifications such as man's greater height, his more muscular body, a "longer stride in his walk," and his larger brain. A woman was too delicate, her voice too soft, her hands too small to cast a ballot. If women voted, he cautioned, America was headed toward an "abyss" that would "make a final wreck of our public virtue." In short, Bushnell asserted, "there is nothing...to be gained for women's suffrage." Garrison found Bushnell's diatribe astonishing and wondered why brute strength was needed in order to vote. He predicted a "hornet's nest" of stinging criticism would follow, which, in his mind, Bushnell deserved.[66]

An equally sharp attack came from John Todd of western Massachusetts, a prominent Congregational clergyman. His brief treatise *Woman's Rights* presented all the hackneyed reasons used in the past to explain why women did not deserve equal rights or suffrage. Basing his arguments on the Bible, he explained that God never intended everyone to be equal. "He has given her *a physical organization* so refined and delicate that it can never bear the strain which comes upon the rougher, coarser nature of man." Todd enumerated the many occupations in which men excelled—as inventors, painters, intellectuals, lawyers, musicians, teachers, and doctors—ignoring the fact that few, if any, of these fields welcomed women. In his thinking, woman was created to be "queen of the home, its centre, its light and glory." She should celebrate her right to be exempted from a cruel, harsh world. Voting would mean "wading in the dirty waters of politics, draggling and wrangling around the ballot-boxes, e.g. mingling with the mobs and rowdies." He warned of severe consequences if women tried to become independent and self-supporting, directly contradicting God's will.[67]

Todd rightly predicted a "torrent of abuse" in response to his ideas. A fiery response came from the pen of Mary Abigail Dodge, a teacher and essayist, writing under the pseudonym Gail Hamilton. Her two-hundred-page book *Woman's Wrongs: A Counter-Irritant* used sharp, witty language to challenge Todd's arguments, claiming that his essay employed "impotent and sometimes ridiculous logic," "ill-directed denunciation," and "Scriptural misrepresentations." Emphasizing a woman's delicate nature, Hamilton argued, was useful when keeping her confined to a separate sphere, but not when holding her responsible for all the household drudgery and physical labor she had to perform each day. In keeping her out of "dirty political waters," Hamilton wondered who had made that environment so filthy. A woman overburdened by learning was a situation to celebrate, not denigrate, Hamilton added.[68]

Although not an advocate of female suffrage, Hamilton challenged Todd's "frivolous" arguments against enfranchising women, wondering why he regarded this as men's loss if women gained the right to vote. Women already formed political opinions and expressed them in public. Arguments that voting would take too much time and force women to sacrifice maternal duties made no sense, since casting a ballot took little effort. Women voters would not disrupt domestic harmony, for husbands and wives often held different opinions without upsetting the family. In language mirroring Elizabeth's, Hamilton added, "It is utterly irrational to have scores and hundreds of illiterate foreigners, just naturalized, go to the polls...while an educated and intelligent woman is not allowed to cast a vote." She denounced men like Todd who defined a woman's sphere by binding "manacles to her wrists" and confining her to her so-called divinely appointed arena.[69]

Personal crises continued to affect female reformers during these turbulent years. More than one historian has suggested that in the late 1860s, an impetuous, needy Henry Blackwell became romantically involved with Abby Hutchison Patton, a beautiful, charming woman married to a wealthy, influential New York City financier. Patton had been a member of the popular Hutchinson Family Singers, a group that often entertained at antislavery and women's rights conventions. The two couples were friends when Lucy and Henry lived in New Jersey. Whether Abby Patton and Blackwell's relationship was an intense flirtation or a full-blown affair is unclear, but Henry spent a good deal of time in New York City. Lucy may have suspected something, and at one point she wrote one of Henry's sisters, asking her to keep him away from Patton's office. His sisters seemed to suspect something, for in 1869, Emily Blackwell wrote that she anticipated that Abby Patton would end her relationship with Henry. Both Emily and her sister Elizabeth detected marital disharmony, which they attributed to Lucy's unflagging devotion to women's rights and Henry's "running after Mrs. P."[70] Whatever the reality, Lucy, probably acting on her own, decided the family should move to Boston. She bought a large home and completed the move in 1870, ending Henry's physical proximity to Abby. There in Dorchester, at the house they named "Pope's Hill," just outside Boston, Lucy found the peace she craved. Future letters between Lucy and Henry expressed mutual respect and affection, so the two must have come to terms with this difficult period.

Other reformers withdrew from the fray. The same year, Ernestine Rose, worn down by hard work and suffering from stress and rheumatism, left on a European vacation with her husband. The vacation became permanent; the couple settled in London, and Rose returned to the United States only once. George Train returned to the United States in 1869, ran for president as an independent in 1872, and engaged in global travel. In 1871, Paulina Davis published *The History of the National Woman's Rights Movement*. She spent long periods abroad, where she studied painting until crippled by arthritis. Abby Kelley Foster suffered years of poor health but resisted seeking medical advice. Finally, she saw a gynecologist who discovered an ovarian tumor. For two years, Kelley tried to cure it through special diet and exercise, but she grew worse. In July 1868, she finally agreed to surgery. The operation took place in her home (far safer than a hospital at that time). The doctor removed a thirty-five-pound mass, and Kelley proved extremely fortunate in not experiencing postsurgical infection from this risky procedure.[71] Nearing sixty, Foster never fully regained good health; she withdrew from most reform efforts.

Friends and acquaintances of the Stantons had long questioned what happiness, if any, Elizabeth derived from her marriage, since Henry was often away and showed little interest in her causes. Early on, Elizabeth claimed to have found the independence she needed in her marriage, reassuring a friend,

"You do not know the extent to which I carry my rights. I do in truth think and act for myself knowing that I alone am responsible for the sayings of E. C. S." She treasured the quiet of home and family and defended her marriage as happier than most. To her, Henry was a "highly cultivated liberal man" with whom she shared literary tastes and a love of music and fine oratory—a man of good humor, good health, and sunny personality. She admitted, however, that their views on religion were "as wide apart as the north and south pole" and that her activism and radical ideas annoyed him.[72] In 1869, Elizabeth purchased a home with her inheritance and moved to Tenafly, New Jersey. Henry continued to spend much of his time in New York City. Certainly to the public and to the Stanton children, the couple seemed estranged. Perhaps both Elizabeth and Henry were happiest when living apart.

Lucy, her husband, and Julia Ward Howe took on a new project in 1869: establishing a newspaper devoted to female issues. This venture was a significant departure from Lucy's public life of the 1850s, but she had been wrestling with poor health, stress, and Henry's alleged affair. Lecturing and extensive travel no longer fit her desire for a stable family life and "snug home," she admitted to Antoinette Blackwell. In need of $10,000 in seed money, founders spent months setting up the paper as a joint stock company and selling two hundred shares for $50 each, primarily to men associated with the New England Woman Suffrage Association. They incorporated a preexisting Chicago women's suffrage paper, the *Agitator*, and lured its well-regarded editor, Mary Livermore, to Boston to oversee the new paper, a position she held for two years. The first issue of the weekly *Woman's Journal* appeared on January 7, 1870.[73]

Arguably, activists' greatest accomplishment during the late 1860s was winning women's suffrage in two western territories. The Wyoming Territory became the first to enact female suffrage and allow women to hold public office. In November 1869, William Bright, a Virginian who had fought for the Union Army and settled in Wyoming a year earlier, introduced a bill demanding women's right to vote. The bill declared: "That every woman of the age of twenty-one years, residing in this territory, may, at every election to be holden [*sic*] under the laws thereof, cast her vote. And her rights to elective franchise and to hold office shall be the same under the election laws of the territory, as those of the electors."[74] After a month-long discussion, the territorial legislature quietly passed the bill. The all-Democratic body assumed that the law would embarrass the Republican governor of the territory, John A. Campbell, but he signed it into law without a word. Twenty years earlier, Campbell had attended the women's rights convention in Salem, Ohio; seated at the back of the hall, he could not help but be impressed by the women who were demanding their rights.

Several factors explain why female enfranchisement first became a reality in a western territory. In settling the Far West, women had no choice but to tackle the challenges of frontier life as men's equals. Fewer prescribed social traditions defined their lives there. Another factor was that Wyoming's population was only nine thousand, and men outnumbered women six to one. So women hardly seemed a political threat. And in the territories, only the legislature and the governor's signature were needed to enact such laws, while in states, bills on suffrage often had to pass two legislative sessions and then be put to the electorate in a statewide referendum. The Wyoming bill had little time to garner significant opposition, another factor in its favor. Its supporters regarded women's suffrage as a means to generate positive publicity for Wyoming. With the completion of the transcontinental railroad earlier that year, they hoped to encourage more easterners to move there, especially women and children. Reformers also influenced the outcome. In September, Anna Dickinson, returning home from a lecture tour in the Far West, addressed an audience in Cheyenne and impressed listeners with her charm and speaking ability. Another female lecturer, Redelia Bates of St. Louis, spoke there in early November.

Wyoming women went to the polls the following September; nearly all took advantage of their newly won right, belying the argument that women were indifferent to voting. Although they had little impact on the outcome of the election, their presence made for a more orderly process. A couple of months later, Wyoming resident Esther Morris became the nation's first female justice of the peace, a position she held for eight months. In 1871, when the Wyoming territorial legislature tried to overturn women's suffrage, Governor Campbell vetoed the bill. Wyoming achieved statehood in 1890 and entered the Union as the first state since New Jersey to allow women the right to vote.[75]

In February 1870, the Utah territorial legislature with its Mormon majority became the second territory to enact female suffrage, though unlike Wyoming, it did not give women the right to hold office. This law garnered the support of men who hoped it would counter widespread criticism of the Mormon practice of polygamy, which most Americans felt degraded women. In addition, Mormon women were already accustomed to limited decision-making, since they could vote on church matters, unlike women in mainstream Protestant denominations. Some men in Utah regarded female suffrage as a progressive step that was long overdue. A few felt that increasing the number of Mormon voters would allow their faith to continue to control territorial governance against growing numbers of non-Mormon settlers. In the East, many people who denounced polygamy anticipated that female suffrage in Utah would give Mormon women an opportunity to overturn this odious practice. This, of course, did not happen. Nonetheless, suffragists were thrilled when a second territory enacted female suffrage and hoped that eastern states would follow suit. Elizabeth and Susan, as part of their extensive lecture tour of the Far West in the summer of 1871, stopped in Salt Lake City, where they addressed three hundred Mormon women. In a five-hour session, they discussed marriage, birth control, women's rights, and divorce, and they lent support to the new suffrage law. Utah women enjoyed universal voting rights until 1887, when women's suffrage was nullified under a provision in the Edmunds-Tucker Act, the antipolygamy law Congress passed in anticipation of Utah's admission to the Union. Utah women regained their right to vote in 1895 with the writing of the state's new constitution.[76]

Even as the political chaos of the 1860s subsided and differences between the two suffrage organizations solidified, women activists knew much work lay ahead. Neither the federal government nor any state yet supported women's suffrage. The year 1869 marked a significant shift in the women's rights movement—the commitment, energy, optimism, and excitement women activists had shared during the 1850s had dissipated. Among female reformers, the dividing line was well established. While the initial split occurred due to disagreements over black male suffrage, that issue's relevance disappeared with the passage of the Fifteenth Amendment a year later. Instead, it seemed to be pride, jealousy, competition, and personal misunderstandings that generated the greatest amount of ill will between the two groups. Trying to understand the situation, Lucretia sensed that women exhibited "a strife for supremacy" as they promoted their own agendas.[77] Personal issues, more than institutional structure or goals, intensified the division.

Had American women united and worked together, one can only wonder if they would have won their right to vote sooner. Historians continue to debate the impact of this division in the movement. A few scholars perceive the split as a positive step, a vital part of the process as women struggled to define their goals and achieve equal rights. This suggests that competition and jealousy among leaders in the two organizations energized them and heightened their determination and commitment to the cause. I and a number of other scholars believe that women might have won suffrage years earlier had they been able to ignore differences and past mistakes and work together, rather than expending time and energy in jealous, competitive behavior.

This division in the women's movement and the resultant bad behavior are reactions that are all too typical of groups seeking to achieve larger goals. Often losing sight of what they most desire, they fight with one another rather than work together for a greater good. Such behavior becomes counterproductive, letting personal, often petty disagreements overwhelm a larger purpose. Women activists, especially the leaders who had been highly critical of male politicians and how they conducted themselves in the political arena, assumed that women could do better. Instead, they sometimes found themselves embroiled in trivial debates and misunderstandings as they fought for female suffrage. For the next twenty-one years, the AWSA and NWSA worked independently of one another as activists struggled against enormous odds—and all too often against each other—to win women's right to vote.

6

FRICTION AND
REUNIFICATION,
1870–1890

In January 1874, George Andrews, tax collector of Glastonbury, Connecticut, seized seven of the eight cows belonging to lifetime residents Julia and Abby Smith, for failing to pay their taxes. The Smith sisters refused to let this act go without a fight, and they undertook a campaign to challenge this injustice and gain public sympathy. The sisters had a strong grounding in protest and reform. Their principled father, a former minister, had studied law and served as justice of the peace. The Smith offspring were well educated; Julia taught briefly at Troy Female Seminary. Their mother's reformist bent and commitment to abolition exposed them to the oppression shared by slaves and women. Attending the Connecticut Woman Suffrage Association convention in 1869, the sisters learned about women who had been demanding "no taxation without representation." In the spring of 1873, they asked the town registrar to list them as voters. He, of course, refused. After attending the AWSA annual convention in New York City that fall, they returned home to find their taxes increased to $200. As Glastonbury's highest taxpayers, and at the ripe ages of eighty-one and seventy-six, respectively, Julia and Abby began their protest. For too long, men's decisions in spending town revenues had upset them. Appearing at the next town meeting, they announced their refusal to pay taxes until they could vote. In response, Andrews took their cows and sold them; a few months later, he sold eleven acres of their land.[1]

The story made great press, and sympathy for the sisters was immediate. The *Boston Daily Advertiser* maintained that the sisters were "doing a mightier work in behalf of their sex, or that portion of it which has a taste for public affairs, than all the rest in the country." *Harper's* likened the sisters' action to

Samuel Adams's resistance to the tyranny of King George III a century earlier. For months, the *Woman's Journal* covered the sisters' protest and printed letters from irate readers. Garrison expressed admiration for these "noble women," whose "calm, dignified, uncompromising manner" entitled them to the "warmest sympathy." Connecticut authorities were "not worthy to touch the hem of their garments." The sisters continued their protest for a few more years, testing the town's actions in court until Abby died in 1878, and Julia, now in her mid-eighties, married a lawyer—and eventually the taxes were paid.[2]

The Smith sisters' protest presaged much about the ensuing twenty years, as women activists continued to demand suffrage and an equal place in American society. What they and others now found was an established movement and a strong female support system. Those like Abby and Julia found themselves in good company when they joined an AWSA or NWSA affiliate. But many women without any organizational affiliation also did their part by engaging in individual or collective action. Reading a stirring essay or hearing a rousing speech motivated others. Like the Smiths, women could count on a more sympathetic press than in years past, especially the *Woman's Journal*. Nor was the battle entirely uphill. New opportunities opened. Some long-standing barriers to female advancement began to crumble, as women broke into fields formerly limited to men. Americans became more accepting of women's visibility and right to speak in public. No longer were activists and lecturers subjected to the ridicule they had faced years earlier. Despite division in the movement, the AWSA and NWSA inspired members to press for suffrage at the state and federal levels.

Activists replicated the Smiths' act of civil disobedience. Commemorating the centennial of the Boston Tea Party, on December 15, 1873, some three hundred people congregated in Faneuil Hall and Boston Harbor for a "New England Woman's Tea Party," demanding "no taxation without representation." The New England Woman's Suffrage Association (NEWSA) and the *Woman's Journal* publicized this gathering, calling taxation a "tyranny" against women and a slap in the face of democracy. Lucy, Julia Ward Howe, Wendell Phillips, Frederick Douglass, and Thomas W. Higginson were among the event's celebrated speakers. Nearly six hundred people joined a similar protest organized by the New York Woman's Suffrage Society, where Susan addressed the crowd, urging women nationwide to refuse to pay taxes until they could vote. Philadelphia celebrated with a similar tea party in January 1874.[3]

In 1872, Abby Kelley and Stephen Foster initiated their own protest by refusing to pay their taxes. The city of Worcester delayed taking action, for seizing this aging couple's possessions could turn them into martyrs for a cause.

Finally, in February 1874, the city announced plans to auction off the Fosters' household belongings to pay their tax bill. The couple made much of this, inviting friends and family to a "Convention on Taxation without Representation." Samuel May, Jr., presided, and Lucy applauded Abby's bravery. Garrison expressed his "profound respect" for the Fosters and hoped no self-respecting individual would buy their furniture. No one did, so the city confiscated the items. Friends then purchased the goods and returned them. With the headlines "Sale of the Foster Farm" and "Abby Kelley Foster Is Homeless," the *Woman's Journal* elicited immediate offers of assistance and temporary residence. A male sympathizer commended Abby on her stance against the "tyrannous exaction which enforces your taxation while it denies you the right of suffrage." This action reflected her lifetime of work, "ever rising with womanly energy against all infringement of human rights." The Fosters tried to keep their protest alive, but Stephen's poor health eventually forced the couple to settle.[4]

A number of courageous reformers adopted a different tactic by trying to vote, generating local responses and even a Supreme Court case. Hundreds of women during these years appeared at the polls on election days. The St. Louis attorney Francis Minor was the first to articulate what seemed like airtight arguments to prove that female voters had the law on their side. The Fourteenth Amendment, Minor argued, said that women could claim all the rights of citizenship; therefore, no state could deprive them of the right to vote. Susan later touted Minor's work, noting that no other man had "contributed to the woman suffrage movement so much valuable constitutional argument and proof."[5] In 1870, Sara J. Spencer, Sarah E. Webster, and some seventy women tried to register to vote in the District of Columbia. When authorities stymied their efforts, Spencer and Webster sued. They lost and appealed to the Supreme Court of the District—and lost again. The judge in the case agreed that women were capable of voting and that the Fourteenth Amendment gave them citizenship. But they could not vote until the law gave them the right to do so. Even with six hundred signatories on a petition and arguments by Francis Minor, their 1874 appeal to Congress went nowhere.[6] Another widely discussed trial occurred in Santa Cruz, California, in 1871. Ellen Van Valkenburg, a taxpaying widow and mother of three, applied for a writ of mandamus to force the county clerk to let her vote. After a three-day debate in court, the judge ruled against her, asserting that the Fourteenth Amendment guaranteed women civil, but not political, rights. "Physically they are persons; politically they are not," he averred.[7] A higher court upheld his ruling.

The most newsworthy voting attempt occurred in November 1872, when Susan and fourteen other women, including her three sisters, voted in Rochester,

New York. They were able to register, cast their ballots, and leave. An exuberant Susan shared the moment with Elizabeth: "Well I have been & gone & done it!—positively voted the Republican ticket." The fifteen women, however, had broken an 1870 federal law that made it illegal for anyone to vote who lacked that right. Authorities arrested Susan and brought her to trial. Anticipating a fight, she hired legal counsel and canvassed the county to protest the injustice, delivering her lecture "Is it a Crime for a U.S. Citizen to Vote?" A superior court judge heard her case in January 1873. As a female, she was deemed incompetent to testify. But when the judge asked if she had anything to say, Susan responded with a blistering speech that became one of her most famous. Yes, she had a great deal to say, objecting to this unfair trial without a jury of her peers. She claimed her right to vote under the Fourteenth Amendment. The judge, unmoved, instructed the jury to find her guilty. It did. Susan then refused to pay her $100 fine and court costs, asking the judge to incarcerate her so she could test the law in a higher court. He ignored the fine she owed, and the case stopped there. Only press coverage gave Susan the attention she sought.[8]

Another significant case dealing with female suffrage, *Minor v. Happersett* (1874), reached the U.S. Supreme Court. Virginia Minor, wife of Francis, tried to vote in the 1872 presidential election, but the registrar, Renee Happersett, turned her away. Since Virginia, as a married woman, did not have the legal right to bring suit, Francis sued the registrar for her. Virginia was no stranger to women's rights, having helped organize the Woman Suffrage Association of Missouri and served as its first president. Francis developed his wife's legal strategy, using the Fourteenth Amendment to claim that all citizens had the right to vote. When the couple lost in the lower court, they appealed to the U.S. Supreme Court, which agreed to hear the case. In a unanimous decision, the justices admitted that women were citizens but asserted that the Constitution, when written, had not given all citizens the right to vote. Being a citizen "has not in all cases been made a condition precedent to the enjoyment of the right of suffrage," they intoned. They also ruled that only states could convey voting privileges, which meant that the registrar had acted properly.[9] In reaching its decision, the Court did not consider the Fifteenth Amendment and the central role Congress had played in enfranchising black men. Apparently women did not deserve that same federal support. This decision proved a major setback; using the courts to demand women's constitutional right to vote seemed fruitless at this juncture.

Nevertheless, women continued to test their right to suffrage. In November 1880, dressed in their Sunday best, Elizabeth and Susan went to the polls and offered local officials a list of reasons why Elizabeth should vote. When an official refused, she was so upset she tried unsuccessfully to stuff the ballot in the box and then threw it, startling everyone around her and setting the town abuzz over her audacious act. Nonetheless, to ensure adequate publicity, she wrote an account of the event and sent it to the local paper. The *Woman's Journal* kept a running account of those who attempted to vote. A few actually succeeded; a Mrs. Annette B. Gardner, of Detroit, claimed she had "voted for years." In such cases, authorities at the polls, either lax or prosuffrage, ignored the law and made this possible. Lucy experienced a different problem when she took advantage of an 1879 bill that gave Massachusetts women the right to vote in district school elections. She paid her poll tax and tried to vote. Election officials refused to accept her payment or register her name because she insisted on being known as Stone, not Blackwell. For years she had been paying taxes and signing documents using her maiden name. A momentary mix-up allowed her to cast her ballot, but when officials discovered their error, they erased Lucy's name. She refused to budge on this issue, and for the rest of her life, she did not vote in school board elections. While no law required that a wife take her husband's last name, custom prevailed.[10]

In the midst of civil protests and legal challenges, a colorful, bewitching personality emerged and took the women's movement by storm. This fascinating character was Victoria Claflin Woodhull, whose life experiences and personal beliefs belied almost every trait attributed to the ideal woman. As Alice Stone Blackwell commented tactfully, Woodhull became a "synonym for licentiousness."[11] She was born in Homer, Ohio, in 1838 into an unstable, impoverished family. Unlike other reformers, who generally were well educated, Woodhull's limited schooling in no way impeded her future success. Traveling as part of her family's itinerant medicine show, Victoria at fifteen married a physician and alcoholic, Canning Woodhull, and bore two children. The marriage was never happy. She and her sister Tennessee began earning money as psychic healers, fortunetellers, and spiritualists, and by selling elixirs to help support the family. After divorcing her first husband but keeping his name, Woodhull married a radical anarchist, Colonel James Blood, in 1867—a marriage that lasted ten years.

Two years later, the entire Woodhull family (including Victoria's first husband) moved to New York City. Through their self-professed abilities as clairvoyants, Victoria and Tennie caught the eye of the railroad mogul Cornelius Vanderbilt, one of the wealthiest men in America. Victoria continued to reinvent herself as circumstances demanded, and the sisters soon became Vanderbilt's favored female companions, with Tennie becoming one of his several

Victoria Woodhull (Benjamin R. Tucker Papers, Manuscripts and Archives Division, The New York Public Library, Astor, Lenox and Tilden Foundations)

sexual partners. Sharing his knowledge of the stock market, Vanderbilt set up the two sisters to run the nation's first female brokerage firm, Woodhull, Claflin, and Company. Politics was the next step, and in the spring of 1870, Victoria announced plans to run for president of the United States, even though her age rendered her ineligible. She and Tennie also began publishing a newspaper, *Woodhull and Claflin's Weekly,* which covered financial news and Wall

Street fraud and advocated socialism and women's rights. Perhaps most controversial was their promotion of free love—eschewing sexual exclusivity and the constraints of marriage and proclaiming women to be as sexually passionate as men.[12]

Befriending the influential Massachusetts congressman Benjamin Butler, Woodhull gained a privilege no other woman had yet enjoyed—an invitation to speak before Congress. On January 11, 1871, she addressed the House Judiciary Committee. With Butler's assistance in writing her speech, she argued for a woman's right to vote under the Fourteenth Amendment. The same day, the NWSA was meeting in Washington, and many members crowded into the House gallery to hear Woodhull. Her speech thrilled them. Regarding Woodhull as a heroine for their cause, NWSA officers immediately invited her to their convention. Only days later, the Judiciary Committee rejected her plea for suffrage.

Woodhull's meteoric rise to fame was brief; adulation for her eroded quickly as scandal ensued. Vanderbilt remarried and showered less attention on the Claflin sisters. Woodhull's flirtation with socialism and free love repelled many Americans, and her "scruffy white-trash relatives," as the historian Richard Fox calls them, set off minor scandals, though this made Woodhull all the more intriguing in the public eye.[13] In 1872, she organized the People's Party and declared herself its presidential candidate. Without consulting him, she named Frederick Douglass as her running mate. Her unique campaign speeches addressed controversial issues covered in her *Weekly*.

Elizabeth found Woodhull's presidential candidacy an exciting alternative to staid male politicians who refused to support female suffrage. Even after learning about Woodhull's dubious past, Elizabeth defended her, insisting that no one should question someone else's private affairs. "Victoria Woodhull stands before us to day as one of the ablest speakers & writers of the century," she explained to Lucretia in the spring of 1872. "Her face[,] form[,] manners[,] & conversation, all indicate the triumph of the moral, intellectual, spiritual over the sensuous in her nature." Women in the past, Elizabeth warned, had been similarly skewered by others—with tragic results. "Men mock us with the fact, & say, we are ever cruel to each other." They needed to support one another if they were to succeed.[14]

Yet others were wary and began to distance themselves from Woodhull. Suffragists in Iowa and Michigan blamed Woodhull and her free love stance for their failed suffrage bills. Lydia Maria Child called Woodhull and her associates "a great blister to my spirit" and concluded that they were "doing immense harm to the real progress of women." A skeptical Susan found Woodhull's behavior alarming and opposed her third-party effort. By May 1872, Susan was completely disillusioned and anticipated potential harm if the NWSA stood behind Woodhull. "Our movement as such is so demoralized by the letting go the helm of ship to Woodhull," she bemoaned, believing NWSA members had rescued their organization in the nick of time.[15]

With her reputation in decline and her newspaper losing money, in October 1872 Woodhull exposed what became one of the greatest scandals of the nineteenth century, an affair between Henry Ward Beecher and Elizabeth Tilton, the wife of Theodore Tilton and one of Beecher's most devout parishioners. All three were women's rights advocates. Beecher and Theodore Tilton had been friends for fifteen years. Rumors had been circulating since 1870, when Elizabeth Tilton had admitted to her husband that she and Beecher had never engaged in "criminal intercourse" but in what she termed "a high religious love." She then retracted that statement in order to protect Beecher—and then retracted her retraction. A furious Tilton told his mother-in-law and several friends. Elizabeth and Susan learned of the affair from the Tiltons. Susan remained silent; Elizabeth did not, and the scandal began to leak. Woodhull heard about it, and before a convention of spiritualists in Boston, she spewed forth a torrent of criticism against powerful men who lied, cheated, and engaged in adultery. Beecher embodied the height of hypocrisy, she insisted, self-righteously denouncing free love in his sermons while committing adultery with a parishioner. Six weeks later, under the headline "The Beecher-Tilton Scandal Case," Woodhull's *Weekly* related all the details, with dramatic embellishments. Woodhull named two of her sources: Elizabeth Cady Stanton and Isabella Beecher Hooker,[16] Henry Ward Beecher's sister.

Henry Beecher ignored all charges until June 1873 and then declared his innocence. His wife, Eunice, who disliked the Tiltons, supported her husband throughout the scandal. Unsubstantiated rumors circulated that Theodore Tilton and Woodhull also had had an affair, that Beecher had engaged in adultery with other women, and that he had fathered one or more of Elizabeth Tilton's children. Elizabeth Cady Stanton concluded that Beecher would never be found guilty, no matter how strong the evidence. His Brooklyn church had too much riding on his prominence, and the public "would rather see every woman in the nation sacrificed than one of their idols of gold." She was right: a denominational "Committee of Investigation" examined charges against its famous minister and cleared him of any "unchaste or improper actions." Committee members concluded that "confidence and love for our pastor" had actually "heightened and deepened" because of the "unmerited sufferings which he has so long borne." In August 1874, Theodore Tilton sued Beecher for damages, and the case went to court the following January. The six-month trial created endless fodder for newspapers, as reporters exposed juicy details to hungry readers. Beecher's sisters disagreed over their brother's culpability. Harriet and Catharine defended Henry, while Isabella was certain he was guilty. Women's rights activists also disagreed. Leaders of the NWSA tended to support Beecher, while Lucy and Henry sympathized with Elizabeth Tilton as a woman wronged.[17]

Although the case for adultery seemed airtight, the civil trial resulted in a hung jury. One problem in reaching a verdict was Elizabeth Tilton's vacillating story. The public hounded Theodore Tilton, and he eventually fled to Europe after he and Elizabeth divorced. Elizabeth Tilton adopted a more pious existence, living with her mother and children, far from the public eye. Because she had exposed the Beecher-Tilton scandal, Woodhull was jailed twice for breaking the 1872 Comstock Law, which prohibited the dissemination or publication of sexually explicit material. She and her sister Tennie spent their final years in England, where Victoria met and married husband number three, a wealthy banker, and ably transformed herself into a lady. Beecher retained his ministerial post and lectured at home and abroad to pay his substantial legal fees. Some NWSA members questioned Elizabeth Cady Stanton's role, while the entire scandal disgusted AWSA leaders. Elizabeth only aggravated the situation when she told a reporter that some good had emerged from this outrageous event. "It has knocked a great blow at the priesthood," helped to equalize social standards for male and female behavior, and emphasized the need for women to be strong-minded and self-possessed.[18]

Women engaged in a more legitimate outlet to publicize their cause, participating in the 1876 Philadelphia Centennial Exhibition to celebrate the hundredth anniversary of the Declaration of Independence. The event was four years in the planning and slated to last six months. A Women's Centennial Executive Committee organized an exhibition to be displayed in the main building. With so many exhibitors demanding space, the committee decided to erect its own building in order to properly display female achievements. Members responded quickly and sent appeals to local committees in the states and territories. Within four months, they had raised enough money. The Women's Pavilion, listed as one of the outstanding structures of the Exhibition, covered two-thirds of an acre and cost nearly $40,000.[19] Inside were displays of women's domestic and artistic accomplishments that included a bust sculpted from butter, framed preserved flowers, a model kindergarten, eighty time-saving devices invented by women, and a display by the Woman's Medical College of Pennsylvania. Initially, Lucy opposed any involvement in the Exhibition, frustrated that female independence seemed years away. She relented, though, and helped to organize an exhibit of women's tax protests that also highlighted New

Jersey women, who had been enfranchised one hundred years earlier. To avoid any controversy, however, those in charge of the Women's Pavilion mounted this display in the library, an area cordoned off from visitors, so the exhibit was visible only at a distance.[20]

Bolder statements at the Centennial Exhibition were needed. The AWSA met in Philadelphia on July 3 to commemorate the day American women in New Jersey had first gained (though subsequently losing) the right to vote. Speakers included Lucy, Henry Blackwell, Julia Ward Howe, and Anna Dickinson, with entertainment provided by the Hutchinson Family Singers, who composed and performed songs such as "One Hundred Years Hence." On behalf of the NWSA, Susan asked Elizabeth to write a new Declaration of Rights and Sentiments. Perhaps women's demands seemed less startling now than in 1848, or perhaps Elizabeth's heart was not in it, for her statement lacked the dramatic impact of the Seneca Falls Declaration. But it effectively enumerated women's current frustrations, asserting that "one discordant note" of the Centennial was that "all women still suffer the degradation of disfranchisement." It complained that state constitutions defined voters as male, prevented women in jury trials from being judged by their peers, taxed women but would not allow them to vote, established different codes of behavior for men and women, and created vastly different state laws concerning marriage and divorce. A dozen women signed the Declaration, including Lucretia, Susan, and Elizabeth.[21]

Because fair officials refused women an opportunity to address the public, during the July 4 celebration Susan and four others barged into the main meeting hall after a reading of the Declaration of Independence. Susan handed a copy of their Declaration, reproduced on parchment and tied with red, white, and blue ribbons, to the official onstage. As they exited, the five women scattered copies of it over the audience, leaving people baffled by what had happened. Outside, Susan found an empty stage and, in the rain, addressed passers-by on the wrongs inflicted on women. Her actions generated positive responses from NWSA members. A pleased Elizabeth commented that "a splendid work has been accomplished here." Anne K. Irvine of Oregon, Missouri, was one among many who read about the protest and expressed their support, telling Susan that her act had "stirred the hearts of many women."[22] The press gave the event some coverage, though it is doubtful the public paid much heed to this fleeting moment.

Dress reform reengaged women's interest, although few embraced the issue with the enthusiasm they had shown during the bloomer craze of the 1850s. Some critics, especially female physicians, continued to worry about the harmful effects of tight lacing. Female medical students at the University of Michigan articulated their concerns in an article for the *Woman's Journal*. Among those who lectured and wrote on dress reform was Abba Goold Woolson, a teacher, author, and lecturer, who organized a series of free talks on the subject. Speaking in Boston in 1874 and then in other cities, Woolson and four female physicians sought to educate women on the harmful effects of "suicidal fashion." Of all women worldwide, Americans "suffer the most from the cruel tyrannies of dress," they asserted. A woman became victim of "a showy exterior," wasting her money and time "on decorating her person, instead of enlarging her mind." All should liberate themselves by rejecting the corset, an "instrument of human torture," and dress for comfort. By addressing the public, these advisors intended to create a "complete revolution" in female undergarments and reduce the pounds of material that engulfed female bodies and impeded circulation, breathing, and freedom of movement.[23]

Though Lucy had long ago discarded bloomers, she continued to wear sensible, well-made clothing. She instilled in her daughter Alice a similar appreciation for unrestricting undergarments. Sensitive to such matters, when Alice met Louisa May Alcott at an NEWSA meeting, she immediately focused on her appearance. Alcott's "looks greatly disappointed me," she wrote, for "she is positively unpleasant looking." Worst of all, "I think [she] laces." That a successful author like Alcott would wear a corset startled Alice. In another instance, when she visited the family physician, an advocate of dress reform, "she felt of my belt to see how I was dressed and greatly approved."[24]

Temperance also resurfaced as a national concern, with enormous implications, both positive and negative, for the women's suffrage movement. At an 1874 gathering in Cleveland, a group of women formed the Woman's Christian Temperance Union (WCTU), which soon became one of the most visible, powerful volunteer organizations of the late nineteenth century. Temperance advocates were much more aggressive than they had been during the antebellum period. Members of the WCTU tried to close down bars by praying, singing hymns, keeping lists of male customers, and smashing saloon windows to prevent the sale and consumption of alcohol. Within a few months, they had forced more than a thousand saloons and bars to close.

The WCTU experienced a new sense of energy and increased membership in 1879 when Frances Willard became its president. Born in 1839, Willard grew up on a Wisconsin farm and received an excellent education, graduating from North Western Female College in 1859. Although she was briefly engaged to one of several male suitors, her principal relationships were with other women. She taught at a number of schools, traveled and studied in Europe with a woman companion, and in 1871 became president of Evanston College for Ladies, associated with Northwestern University. Bureaucratic problems at the college caused her to resign three years later, and for a brief period, her life lacked focus. But Willard soon discovered a sense of purpose in the WCTU. Present at its inception, she aggressively rose through the ranks and served as president until her death in 1898. The historian Anne Firor Scott describes her as "a woman of immense ambition and organizational genius." Under Willard's leadership, the WCTU expanded rapidly, attracting tens of thousands of members, who formed local and state chapters nationwide. Willard's "Do everything" policy reflected her desire to have the WCTU support any issue or cause that would eradicate alcohol and uplift women's lives. The WCTU promoted water fountains in public spaces; the establishment of kindergartens, Sunday schools, and reform schools for girls; minimum wage laws; and higher education.[25]

Willard debated the wisdom of supporting female suffrage, and in 1876 she decided that if women could vote, they would have the political clout to rid the nation of alcohol and institute other essential reforms. While many WCTU members agreed that "the ballot given to women will be the greatest check upon the great evil of intemperance," others worried that adopting this radical measure could undermine their larger purpose.[26] Willard stuck by her decision. Tying prohibition to female suffrage brought significant benefits but also problems to both the women's movement and the temperance crusade. As WCTU members added numerical strength and new workers to the ranks of suffrage supporters, powerful opponents also emerged. Many men did not want anyone curtailing their right to drink. Saloon owners and manufacturers and distributors of alcohol denounced female suffrage, knowing that if women could vote, their livelihoods were at risk. Lucy and other activists soon identified temperance opponents as one of the major obstacles in their fight to win suffrage. In fact, the impact of the issue diminished only when states and the federal government enacted prohibition laws.

The relationship between the AWSA and NWSA continued on an uneasy path for years. Some misunderstandings between the two groups were aired in public. At the 1870 AWSA annual convention, Susan openly asked why the AWSA avoided issues like marriage and divorce laws. Lucy, having written a marriage protest, was only conditionally, not legally, married, she charged.[27] Thomas Higginson, who had married the couple, denounced Susan's careless remark. She apologized, but the damage was done. The *Woman's Journal* sometimes provided negative coverage of NWSA leaders and activities; for example, in 1880 an article accused the NWSA of campaigning for Democrats. Obviously hurt and angry, Susan informed a friend that the AWSA is "too weak and too wicked for anything or anybody decent— They *do nothing*—give no *plan* of work to the people—but growl."[28] Especially upsetting to Lucy was the NWSA establishing a branch in Boston in 1882, infringing on territory she claimed as hers.

Most spats occurred in private, but they reveal how a slight or insult could unleash nasty comments and recriminations. At the heart of the problem seemed to be an inability to forgive and move beyond past transgressions and misunderstandings and a clash of personalities, especially between Lucy and Susan. When both organizations campaigned for the Republican presidential candidate Ulysses S. Grant in 1872, leaders avoided one another. For years, Susan harbored bitter feelings toward her former friend, and Lucy in turn was often curt, even rude, to her. On one occasion, Lucy was collecting donations after a lecture. She raised the hat as she walked by Susan: "I don't want any of your money Miss Anthony!!" Susan retorted that lecturers should never reject any contribution. Lucy then lowered the hat, and Susan dropped in her half dollar. Determined to have the final word, Lucy responded, "Well you can be sure you give it to a good cause."[29]

On another level, Susan accused Lucy of establishing the AWSA on false premises, which she sustained "by keeping a whole cabinet of lies." In 1879, Susan opined that "Lucy, like the South, is incapable of understanding *magnanimous overtures*—(thousands of which have been made to her)—other than concessions—and acknowledgements of wrong on the part of the one who offers them." She pointed out that if the AWSA didn't exist, she, Elizabeth, and Lucy might be leading the movement together. Instead, Lucy's "*undermining* efforts" were destroying any chance for women's advancement. "Their *Journal* languishes—their society totters," she asserted.[30] Perhaps their former close friendship made the two especially sensitive to one another's actions and words, unleashing female behavior at its worst. Antoinette Blackwell, who remained friendly with both sides, likened the situation to a great "duel in the dark," even a "civil war." Martha Wright yearned for an end to the division and concluded that the situation resulted from the "large endowment of combativeness needed to make a reformer."[31]

Sporadic efforts to reconcile the two associations did take place. For several months in 1872 and 1873, Elizabeth wrote Lucy and Antoinette, urging them to ignore the past and consider uniting with the NWSA. The idea went nowhere. In November 1872, Elizabeth and her daughter Harriot called on Lucy and Alice in Dorchester, a visit that proved cordial. A year later, Elizabeth wrote Lucy, asking why she refused to recognize an organization "merely because you have a personal feud with its President [Susan]." She warned Lucy that she was harming herself more than anyone else by sustaining her organization. "Too grand a work awaits the women of this generation to spend any thought or feeling on personalities," she declared, asking Lucy to consider if it was "high principle" that caused her to treat Susan so badly.[32] Lucy made at least one gesture of reconciliation. In 1882, Eliza Jackson Eddy, daughter of Francis Jackson, died and bequeathed $48,250 to Susan and Lucy for their work. Lucy wrote Susan, who was coming to Boston to receive her share, and offered to meet her train. Susan rebuffed her. Elizabeth suggested a meeting with Susan, Lucy, Antoinette, and herself in December 1885 to discuss a plan of unity. Such a meeting was "out of the question," Lucy responded weeks later. Elizabeth had written the Boston educator George Cheyne Shattuck, a mutual friend, and called Lucy "the biggest liar and hypocrite she had ever seen." Lucy could not muster the "pretence of good fellowship" to meet with her.[33] Since this rivalry and ill will rarely filtered down to association members, those with no institutional memory and not privy to such unpleasant behavior naturally began to question the need for two associations.

Fortunately, larger issues consumed both organizations. The NWSA held most of its annual conventions in Washington, D.C. Susan served as chief organizer, even when not serving as president. Younger members appreciated her dedication and dogged pursuit of women's rights. Elizabeth presided over four conventions and attended one other, but displayed a limited interest in them, an indifference that rankled Susan. Martha Wright, whom Susan called a "tower of strength," briefly assumed a leadership role. Elected president of the NWSA in 1874, Wright died unexpectedly of pneumonia in early January 1875, which cut her tenure short.[34] Isabella Beecher Hooker proved a steadfast member, demonstrating a desire to organize and help underwrite several NWSA conventions. Initially, both Elizabeth and Susan resented Hooker's sense of entitlement and craving for the limelight, but they gradually became accustomed to the Beecher family traits.

Besides holding annual conventions, the AWSA and NWSA celebrated past events, though they disagreed over which ones deserved memorializing. The NWSA leaders commemorated the Seneca Falls Convention, since Lucretia, Elizabeth, and Martha Wright had been among its principle organizers. The NWSA members put on a grand thirtieth anniversary celebration of Seneca Falls on July 19, 1878. Over twelve hundred people filled Rochester's Corinthian Hall. Lucretia, now eight-five years old, was present, as were Sojourner Truth and Frederick Douglass. Expressing noble sentiments, Lucretia affirmed that if women could vote, they would elect to office "those who are pure in intention and honest in sentiment." Elizabeth paid homage to Douglass for his "steadfast, unwavering devotion" and support for female suffrage in 1848. Her lengthy speech highlighted women's many accomplishments. "We have aroused public thought to the many disabilities of our sex, and our countrywomen to higher self-respect and worthy ambition," she intoned. She urged them to continue their hard work, for much remained to be done. "It taxes and wearies the memory to think of all the conventions we have held," she said, "the Legislatures we have besieged, the petitions and tracts we have circulated, the speeches, the calls, the resolutions we have penned, the never ending debates we have kept up in public and private, and yet to each and all, our theme is as fresh and absorbing as it was the day we started." While women had made solid advances and challenged injustices outlined in the Declaration of Rights and Sentiments, men still refused to grant them political rights.[35]

This event was one of Lucretia's last public appearances. Advancing age and poor health had taken their toll. Nonetheless, she was amazingly productive until the end of her life. Besides her involvement in women's issues, she played an active role in the Pennsylvania Peace Society. She continued to entertain family and friends at her home outside Philadelphia and corresponded with a wide circle of acquaintances. Making the most of every waking moment, she often darned socks or sewed while conversing with family members and friends. She withstood a number of personal losses: two daughters, two younger sisters, a great-grandson, her husband James, and close friends predeceased her. Lucretia died quietly at her Pennsylvania home on November 11, 1880.

Only the most inspired accolades would do justice to this "peerless," ideal individual. Unable to attend Lucretia's memorial service, Elizabeth wrote her thoughts about her mentor and friend, noting how a mask of serenity always covered the countenance of a brave, passionate woman. She mentioned Lucretia's energy, her courteous nature, and her forthright reactions to injustice. To honor her, Elizabeth attended the 1881 NWSA convention, which served as another memorial to Lucretia. Here Elizabeth delivered a eulogy, calling her "the most remarkable woman of her time." She recalled how much Lucretia loved to talk and how she opened her home to everyone. Probably what most impressed Elizabeth was that "through all our conventions and discussions not one word to sting or exasperate anyone ever passed her lip." So admired was Lucretia that the first lady, Lucy Hayes, members of the Supreme Court and of the House and Senate, as well as hundreds of friends and family members, attended the service and paid their respects to this esteemed woman. Several years later, Lucy called Lucretia "one of the rarest and most excellent of women."[36]

In 1880, members of the Massachusetts Woman Suffrage Association joined Lucy and the AWSA in Worcester to celebrate the thirtieth anniversary of the first National Women's Rights Convention, which had been the occasion of Lucy's first presentation at a convention. Among those who had been at that meeting in 1850 were Lucy, Antoinette Blackwell, Abby Kelley Foster, Samuel May, Jr., and William Howard Channing.

Lecturing remained a mainstay of women's activism, and now it was Elizabeth who pursued a lucrative speaking career. With Henry living in New York City and the Stanton children nearly grown, her time had come. From 1869 to 1879, she traveled thousands of miles each year, speaking on behalf of women's rights. The historian Elisabeth Griffith estimates that during these ten years, Elizabeth was absent from home for eight months each year. Two agencies represented her and scheduled her speaking engagements. She justified the time away from home, explaining her need to earn money for her children's college tuitions. Just as important was the fact that she relished her celebrity status, independence, and ability to earn money. The work was exciting, despite the challenges. With her weight topping two hundred pounds, travel must have been difficult. One observer described Elizabeth as "plump as a partridge," and a blunt Alice Blackwell called her an "excessively fat little old lady with white curls."[37] Her bulk did little to curb her rhetoric or joy in the attention she received. In sharing one travel experience with Susan, Elizabeth described a "magnificent audience" in Chicago. Listeners packed stairwells and hallways, while others lined up outside the auditorium, hoping to find a seat. In small-town venues, some people traveled twenty miles on horseback just to hear her. "The people in the country towns are crazy to hear lectures," she observed.[38] Elizabeth was a star.

With her sunny outlook, Elizabeth retained a sense of optimism that often eluded Susan. After weeks on the road, Elizabeth wrote from Waynesville, Ohio, "What a satisfaction it is to talk to these earnest people. Well, Susan, I think we have done a good deal to make women feel some new self-respect and dignity. Perhaps the world is better that we have lived and so we will not mind the hotels and early hours." Elizabeth's faith in the movement and sense of its importance remained unshaken, despite past mistakes. "Our cause is too great to be permanently hurt by what any one individual or group of individuals may do," she commented. "For over thirty years some people have said from time to time that I have injured the suffrage movement beyond redemption; but it still lives. Train killed it, Victoria Woodhull killed it, the *Revolution* killed it. But with each death, it put on new life."[39]

In 1871, Susan and Elizabeth undertook a major lecture tour of the West, although the three months they spent together threatened their friendship.

Susan's speeches stuck to suffrage, but Elizabeth loved to introduce controversial topics such as marriage and divorce laws. When the two appeared onstage together, Susan paled in comparison to her lively friend. Audiences and the
press adored Elizabeth. Admirers sent her poems, gifts, and flowers. White-
haired and impeccably dressed, Elizabeth appeared as the respectable, kindly
grandmother, endowed with a talent for public speaking. Reporters commented
on differences between the two women, noting Anthony's rather shrill tone, her
walleye, and her gaunt appearance. One California paper referred to Susan as
"neither so refined nor so eloquent" as Elizabeth; another called Susan "hesi-
tating and halty in her style." Susan eventually decided to lecture on her own.
Two passionate women with healthy egos were too much for one stage.[40]

Extended travel and lecturing continued to be a mainstay of the movement,
as more states and territories debated and voted on female suffrage. In several instances, the issue never moved beyond the legislative assembly before
being rejected. But during this period, legislators in five states and territories—
Kansas, Michigan, Nebraska, Oregon, and Rhode Island—managed to pass a
women's suffrage bill that then went out for a statewide referendum. With each
popular vote looming, activists descended to campaign, as they had earlier in
Kansas. Most referenda took place west of the Mississippi, where a "broad,
liberal, and go-ahead spirit of the people" seemed to prevail.[41]

Yet the work undertaken in each state was exhausting, discouraging, and
expensive. Eastern reformers found they had to tread lightly to avoid fostering
resentment among local suffrage workers, who could take exception to out-
siders. Most disheartening was the outcome, for every state and territorial
referendum ended in defeat. Michigan held its popular referendum in 1874, and
both Susan and Elizabeth campaigned there. The amendment lost by fifteen
thousand votes, though Susan gave the loss a positive spin, calling the forty
thousand votes cast for women "a *grand triumph;—not a failure.*" Susan, Lucy, and
Henry spent time in Colorado in 1877, as the legislature considered extending
suffrage to women a year after Colorado became a state. In 1882, Nebraska
voters debated a bill to strike the word "male" from its constitution, and both
the AWSA and NWSA sent representatives, again including Susan, Lucy, and
Henry. On election day, Omaha women showed up at polling places armed with
free coffee and rolls to demonstrate the positive impact they could have on the
voting process. Their refreshments did little good; the proposal lost by a larger
majority than any other issue on the ballot.[42]

In 1885, Lucy and Henry campaigned in Indiana as the legislature debated
female suffrage. Here they "found a lot of women who had never heard
a suffrage speech." In campaigning out west, Lucy began to share Henry's

admiration for frontier women and the hardships they endured. She was cap-tivated by one young mother who brought her infant son to her lecture "and said she dedicated him that day to the suffrage cause. And as she nursed him from her own breast he will probably drink in all his mother's spirit." Though "good single hearted suffragists" and several newspapers supported female suffrage, the majority of male voters did not. When Rhode Island held its referendum in 1887, Alice and Henry campaigned there. Henry delivered sev-eral speeches, but Alice correctly discerned strong resistance and warned her mother, who was convalescing in the South, that the amendment had no chance of passing.[43]

Despite discouraging moments, East Coast reformers found a number of strong allies in the West. The movement was becoming national in scope, and suffrage organizations now existed in nearly all states and territories. One of the best-known western activists was Abigail Scott Duniway, who led the fight for suffrage in the Northwest. In 1852, when she was seventeen, she and her family traveled twenty-four hundred miles by wagon train from their Illinois farm to Oregon. Both her mother and younger brother died during the journey. (Dun-iway later wrote a fictionalized account of this experience, *Captain Gray's Journey*, published in 1859.) In Oregon, she taught school, married, and subsequently bore six children. When her husband suffered financial reversals and became permanently disabled in a farm accident, she supported the family by teaching school, running a successful millinery business, and writing novels and poems. She was well aware of married women's dependent state and their limited legal rights. After moving to Portland in 1871, she began to lecture and to publish a weekly newspaper, the *New Northwest*, to advance women's rights. Duniway managed Susan's 1871 speaking tour in the region, and an appreciative Susan described her as a "sprightly, intelligent young woman." The next year Duniway traveled east to attend a meeting of the NWSA, and she spoke at later con-ventions. Her fiery personality and independent ideas sometimes led her to clash with other reformers. Alice Blackwell heard her lecture in Boston and said she was "a lady I dont [*sic*] like at all." Duniway promoted local over federal action and opposed linking women's rights with prohibition. She campaigned for female suffrage throughout the Northwest for years, and she lived long enough to cast her ballot when Oregon women won the right to vote in 1914.[44]

To Susan, however, the state-by-state referendum approach seemed a futile endeavor. The work proved an uphill battle as female reformers lectured to audiences that often showed little interest. "The *states rights* plan getting women enfranchised—is *worse* than hopeless—And for our *men champions* & friends to longer bid us seek it there—is worse than *insult*," she concluded. Speaking in

Minnesota in December 1877 left Susan disheartened, for here she faced "the Whiskey ring & the religious bigots... *who cannot be educated—nor carried forward except by [s]heer party force.*" She disliked *"Irish Miners & Mountain Men, the Mexican Greasers and Negroes"* who staunchly opposed female suffrage. "How weary, how dusty, how forlorn," she grumbled and decided she could accomplish more by dealing directly with elected officials in Congress and state legislatures.[45] In fact, one argument Susan used when addressing Congress was to explain that it was more expeditious and far less costly to seek a federal amendment than for activists to campaign and appeal to male voters in each state. Obviously, male politicians paid scant attention to this argument.

Among the few men working for women's suffrage, Henry Blackwell now proved the most committed. Having had no luck establishing profitable sugar beet businesses in Maine and Santo Domingo, he found his place in women's rights work, a role that gained him much admiration. His optimism and ebullience provided a welcome balance to Lucy's more serious nature. Agreeing that female suffrage needed the backing of a political party, Henry attended a number of state and national conventions to convince Democrats and Republicans alike to add women's suffrage to their platforms, though he encountered limited success.[46]

By the late 1880s, as Lucy's health declined and she had to forgo long-distance travel, Henry campaigned in her stead. In 1889, he undertook a solo campaign in the Washington, North Dakota, and Montana territories as each sought admission to the Union. This seemed a propitious time to lobby for female suffrage. Leaving North Dakota in July, he was confident that he had made a difference, for many temperance workers and farmers endorsed women's suffrage. "If Dakota is saved it will be wholly due to my coming & I think I could surely save it by remaining two or three weeks longer," he boasted to Lucy. More challenging was Montana, which had never hosted a single suffrage meeting. Here, indifference and opposition from both parties was strong. Though he was impressed by the enterprising farmers he met, gambling and prohibition interests impeded his efforts. As he headed west to Washington, Henry learned that saloon interests controlled many local politicians. The situation appeared hopeless, for most delegates to the constitutional convention "seem to be in a conspiracy to shut women out." Female enfranchisement aroused so much antipathy that supporters were "shunned and avoided... as though it was dangerous to be seen conferring with them."[47] Henry awakened to the fact that politicians eschewed any radical issue, not wanting to muddy the waters as territories sought entry as states. All three territories achieved statehood—but without women's suffrage.

Alice Stone Blackwell
(Library of Congress)

Another Blackwell family member, Lucy and Henry's daughter Alice, also became a key player in the women's movement. After the family moved to the Boston area, Alice attended boarding school in Newburyport, then enrolled in the rigorous, progressive coed school Chauncy Hall in downtown Boston. Here she thrived, and at graduation she won a gold medal for English composition. She graduated Phi Beta Kappa from Boston University in 1881 and was elected class president. She then resided at home with her parents; she never married. Her principal roles were as an editor of the *Woman's Journal* and as a catalyst in merging the AWSA and NWSA.[48]

Being Lucy's daughter could not have been easy, although Alice called her upbringing "exceptional" and wrote when she was sixteen, "I am uncommonly proud of being Lucy Stone's daughter." As a parent, Lucy mixed high expectations with deep affection. She wrote to Alice frequently when she traveled and while Alice was at boarding school. "You know my dear I expect a great deal of you," she wrote from Michigan in 1869, but then tempered that with comments like "Here is a kiss for you, and a hug, and a cuddle, and a great deal of love."[49] She nicknamed Alice "Cubbe," "Alicekin," and "Soul of my Soul," even when Alice was an adult. But Lucy could be exacting and moody; as Alice noted in her diary: "Mama is . . . snarling all the time."[50] Alice adored her lighthearted, affectionate father, who read aloud to her at night and took her on boat outings and to the beach. Famous people were constantly in and out of their home and the *Journal* office. Alice's parents exposed her to Boston's rich cultural offerings, including lectures and musical performances. For years, she hoped to pay tribute to her mother, and she finally did, completing Lucy's biography in 1930.

From childhood on, Alice unconsciously became a feminist. She heard talks by reformers, dress advocates, writers, female physicians, and teachers. When a workman in their home learned she was Stone's daughter, he asked in a sneering manner if she supported women's rights. Alice responded yes, "in a loftily decided manner meant to stop impudence." On another occasion, her cousin Florence admitted that "she *didn't believe in woman's rights!*" Trying to remain calm, Alice asked why, and Florence answered that she had no desire to vote and felt married women should never pursue a profession. "I didn't take the trouble to argue with her, but told her she would come around when woman's rights became fashionable; which remark she took with great humor."[51]

During these two decades, activists continued to press Congress to pass a sixteenth amendment, or what became known as the "Susan B. Anthony Amendment." This declared simply: "The rights of citizens of the United States to vote shall not be denied or abridged by the United States or any State on account of sex." During the 1870s, the NWSA inundated Congress with petitions demanding this amendment, as well as female suffrage, in the District of Columbia. With each attempt, they found a few sympathetic senators and congressmen. In 1878, the Senate Committee on Privileges and Elections invited Elizabeth to speak. There she described women's tireless work in pursuit of suffrage and the importance of this not only to women but to the nation. Yet what should have been a privilege became a frustrating experience. The committee chair was hostile, and several members were apathetic, even disdainful, shuffling their feet, traipsing in and out of the chamber, chewing tobacco, and talking loudly when Elizabeth tried to speak.[52]

Male attitudes became somewhat more respectful by the early 1880s, and Congress gave suffrage more attention. A major step forward took place in 1882, when both the Senate and the House appointed a Special Select Committee on Woman Suffrage, thanks in part to last-minute maneuverings by

Senator George Hoar of Massachusetts. Each committee issued a favorable report on a suffrage proposal that year. The Senate Select Committee again debated a sixteenth amendment in 1884 and invited several women to testify. On March 7, 1884, as the NWSA annual convention ended, Susan and ten women she had selected addressed this committee. Each spoke for an allotted time, presenting fact-filled, compelling arguments on the need for female suffrage. They also denounced unequal wages and emphasized the good that would result if women could participate in government. They challenged those who insisted that Congress would only consider female suffrage if a majority of women supported it, for the same demand had never been made of men. Susan reminded senators that she and her colleagues had been appearing before Congress for fifteen years and submitting petitions for the past nineteen. She explained that the suffrage amendment rose above partisanship because it would uplift the entire nation. Privately, Susan perceived a weakness in her argument, realizing that female suffrage would have greater success and strong partisan support if women would vote as a block and support one party. This would never happen, she realized, for their political opinions were as varied as men's. At this point, neither Democrats nor Republicans saw much to gain by supporting female suffrage.[53]

Following this testimony, Senator Joseph Brown of Georgia, an ardent opponent of women's rights, presented his minority report with all-too-familiar arguments. The Creator had destined men and women to operate in separate spheres, he asserted. Men's greater physical strength allowed them to discharge duties that women could never tackle, including military service and construction work. Late-night political caucuses were suited to a man's world but ill-advised for a woman's. Reverting to decades-old rationalizations, Brown explained that while man faced the "sterner duties of life," a true woman discharged her duties at home. "She cheers his heart with words of kindness; if he is sick or languishing she soothes, comforts and ministers to him as no one but an affectionate wife can do." If she voted and participated in politics, who would perform her sacred duties? "Woman is a power behind the throne. . . . She rules not with a rod of iron, but with the queenly scepter; she binds not with hooks of steel, but with silken cords; she governs not by physical efforts, but by moral suasion and feminine purity and delicacy." Brown added that if white women voted, southern states would then have to give the vote to black women, "who have had much less opportunity to be educated than even the males of their own race."[54]

Appearing before the House Judiciary Committee the following day, Susan and another group spoke in support of a sixteenth amendment, making many of the same points women had made the day before. A Kentucky woman asserted that men were degrading women by keeping them in a servile, dependent position. A woman from the Midwest pointed out that hundreds of thousands of women had signed petitions demanding suffrage, yet men still insisted that women did not want to vote.

The "Susan B. Anthony Amendment" moved beyond committee and reached the floor of the Senate for the first time on December 8, 1886. The WCTU played a significant role, submitting an astonishing two hundred thousand signatures on petitions endorsing the bill. More than a hundred women packed the Senate balconies to witness the moment. Senator Henry W. Blair of New Hampshire expressed his support for the bill and challenged anyone to speak up who objected to it. He harkened back to a question raised years earlier: whether voting was a right or a privilege. Too many men circumvented that question, he asserted, by elevating women to a higher plane, using flattery to convince them that "the possession of mere earthly every-day powers and privileges" was unnecessary, even though men found political privileges "indispensable to their own freedom and happiness." Women had proven themselves men's intellectual equals, so no longer could anyone argue that they were unfit to vote. He pointed to the success of suffrage in the Wyoming, Utah, and Washington territories and in eleven states that allowed women to vote on school issues. Anyone who maintained that most women did not want to vote and therefore should not do so was uttering a specious argument, since many men never showed any interest in voting.[55]

Senator George Vest of Missouri accepted Blair's challenge, countering that suffrage would not enlarge woman's sphere but "would take her down from the pedestal where she is to-day, influencing, as a mother, the minds of her offspring, influencing by her gentle and kindly caress the action of her husband toward the good and true." He submitted a long list of men who opposed female suffrage and read a letter from a woman who opposed the amendment. Women, like men, would become corrupt and selfish if they could vote, he and other critics asserted, adding that women's most effective path to power was their gentle influence over men.[56]

Heated debates resumed on January 25, 1887, with principal support for the bill coming from senators Hoar of Massachusetts and Joseph Dolph of Oregon. As she had two years earlier, Susan invited more than a dozen women from around the country to speak, all of whom presented well-prepared, persuasive arguments. Southern senators were either absent or opposed to the bill. Senators Brown and Vest reiterated concerns about enfranchising black women and the harm voting would inflict on white women's most desirable feminine traits. Vest described female mobs who rebelled during the French Revolution, suggesting that similar chaos could erupt if American women voted. The debate finally ended, and for the first time in history, the Senate voted on a proposal to add this sixteenth amendment to the U.S. Constitution. Not surprisingly, the bill failed, with thirty-four nays, sixteen ayes, and twenty-six abstentions, revealing not only opposition but also apathy, since so many senators paired votes and absented themselves for the final tally. The sixteenth amendment would be introduced in Congress nearly every year until 1896, and then not reintroduced until 1913.[57]

Despite their failure to win a federal amendment, women were gaining minor political victories elsewhere. By 1889, two territories gave women full voting rights. Fifteen states and five territories allowed women to vote in school elections, and in some, to be elected to school boards. In these situations, male legislators agreed that mothers added an informed voice on school matters.[58] In 1887, after a three-year effort, Kansas became the first state in the union to allow women to vote in municipal elections. The next year, Oskaloosa, Kansas, claimed a first by electing a female mayor and an all-female city council.[59] Women in the Washington Territory enjoyed fleeting success. In November 1883, legislators there passed a bill to give women the vote, but the territorial supreme court rescinded that right four years later, arguing that the law was illegal because Congress had never given territories the right to confer suffrage. The fact that the Utah and Wyoming territories let women vote seemed immaterial. Washington State would not gain female suffrage until 1910. Yet these minor political gains did not sit well with all women. The most radical of them argued that men were merely trying to appease women by giving them limited political rights, though Lucy believed that every step toward full suffrage was an event to celebrate.

Newspapers continued to play a vital role in the movement. For the first time, women had a successful paper of their own. The *Woman's Journal*, published every Saturday from January 1870 to 1920 (it became the *Woman Citizen* in 1917), was now Lucy's major contribution to the movement. The first issue announced the paper's intent: to eliminate "a cargo of irrelevant opinions," to avoid partisan "warfare," and to focus on winning female suffrage. Lucy promised that the *Journal*'s work would be done as soon as "woman's disabilities are removed." Harriet Beecher Stowe, Julia Ward Howe, Henry Ward Beecher, Thomas W. Higginson, Antoinette Brown Blackwell, John Greenleaf Whittier, Charlotte Perkins Gilman, and Louisa May Alcott were among the many well-known writers whose contributions graced its pages. Lucy and Henry, assisted by Howe, Higginson, and later Alice, began editing the paper after Mary Livermore departed in 1872. While the *Journal* lacked the biting rhetoric of Susan and Elizabeth's *Revolution*, its less strident tone and broader coverage appealed to thousands of subscribers nationwide. The paper had a profound impact on the movement. Years later, during the final stages of the suffrage campaign,

Carrie Chapman Catt, president of the National American Woman Suffrage Association (NAWSA), called the *Woman's Journal* a "history-maker and history-recorder for the suffrage cause" and claimed that the success of their struggle was "not conceivable without the *Woman's Journal's* part in it."[60]

The *Woman's Journal* covered an astonishing breadth of information on activities and achievements at home and abroad. Predictably, it favored the interests of the AWSA and the NEWSA, although it covered some NWSA news, such as Susan's 1873 trial for attempting to vote, and made positive comments on the NWSA's annual meeting held in Boston in 1881. Features included updates on state suffrage referenda, news and suffrage reports from abroad, convention minutes of the AWSA and NEWSA, a children's column, complete texts of memorable speeches, short stories and poetry, and essays dealing with female education and employment. One series, "People You Should Know," provided biographical sketches of individuals crucial to the movement, such as Jane Swisshelm, Samuel May, Jr., the Grimké sisters, and Gerrit Smith. "News and Notes" informed readers of women's achievements: a Colorado woman who had mined alone for years; another woman's successful piano career; the appointment of female notary publics and school superintendents; debates at Harvard College on female suffrage; the opening of new female colleges and coed institutions; and a woman who trekked ninety miles on snowshoes. Articles described urban campaigns against prostitution, the evils of alcohol, and young seamstresses toiling in sweatshops. Lucy sometimes used her readers to advance the cause of women's rights. In November 1877, the AWSA executive committee mailed all *Journal* subscribers petitions urging Congress to pass a sixteenth amendment and urging states to pass female suffrage. Three months later, 120 petitions with more than six thousand signatures came back.[61] Supplementing the *Journal* was the *Woman's Column*, published from 1888 to 1904, a publication Henry conceived as a news service to dispense snippets of information on relevant issues to hundreds of newspaper editors nationwide.

Lucy often ran the paper single-handedly, especially in the late 1870s, when Henry's sugar beet businesses demanded his extensive travel. She raised money to support the *Journal*, found new advertisers and subscribers, wrote articles and editorials, hired writers, and edited all submissions. She and Henry had dreamed of vacationing in Europe together, but in the summer of 1879, Alice accompanied her father instead, because Lucy could not abandon the *Journal*. The stress associated with producing a weekly paper began to affect her health. On one particularly discouraging day, she confessed, "I am so tired to-day, body and soul, it seems as though I should never feel fresh again." Returning home to a cold, empty house, Lucy added, "It seemed as if the tiredness of a whole

Susan B. Anthony and Elizabeth Cady Stanton, c. 1870–1890 (The Schlesinger Library, Radcliffe Institute, Harvard University)

life came into my essence. . . . I do wish there was some way of carrying on the *Woman's Journal* without such a hard, constant tug."[62] But there was not, especially for someone as dutiful as Lucy.

Elizabeth and Susan also desired a "grand" newspaper to represent the NWSA. As Susan commented, "That righteous sheet," the *Woman's Journal,* "will not allow our name to deface its fair page." They found a paper to their liking, the *Ballot Box,* first published in April 1876 by the Toledo (Ohio) Woman Suffrage Association. Three months later, Elizabeth wrote the editor, sharing the good news that the NWSA executive committee deemed the *Ballot Box* "the best Woman Suffrage journal that we have yet had" and named it the official newspaper of the NWSA. By the spring of 1877, Susan was seeking new subscribers for this "live paper" that "represents our *National Society.*"[63] In May 1878, the paper became the *National Citizen and Ballot Box,* later shortened to *National Citizen,* and was published in Syracuse, New York, under a new editor, Matilda Joslyn Gage. When Susan and Gage became involved in writing the *History of Woman Suffrage* in 1881, they had less time to devote to the paper. Debts accumulated, and the *National Citizen* soon folded. In the late 1880s, NWSA leaders put their faith in the *Woman's Tribune,* edited by Clara Colby and published in Beatrice, Nebraska, from 1883 to 1910.

Though no NSWA publication ever equaled the enduring *Woman's Journal*, Elizabeth and Susan, with assistance from Gage, made a lasting contribution to the movement in their multivolume work *History of Woman Suffrage*. Lucretia had often encouraged Elizabeth to write the movement's history, and her death in 1880 prompted Elizabeth to see this project through. The *History* was an impressive production, though it presented a skewed view of the movement. Because all three editors were NWSA members, they emphasized their organization and the individuals they deemed worthy of inclusion. The AWSA received short shrift. Part of this reflected the fact that a few years earlier, Lucy had made all too clear her feelings that she would have nothing to do with any written history. In 1876, when Elizabeth was writing an encyclopedia article on "eminent women" in the suffrage movement, Lucy denied her request for biographical information. "In regard to the History of the Woman's Rights Movement, I do not think it can be written by any one who is alive to-day," she responded. "Your 'wing' surely are [*sic*] not competent to write the history of 'our wing,' nor should we be of yours." Elizabeth tried again, and Lucy refused, adding that she had never kept a diary or any records of her work. Three years later, a friend failed to convince Lucy to change her mind about the new project. "I must decline all and any participation in the suffrage history which Mrs. Stanton and Susan Anthony are preparing.... I am more than content to be left entirely out of any history those ladies may publish of suffrage work." She assumed that any history produced by the NWSA would ignore unfortunate past associations, including references to Train and Woodhull.[64]

In order to work on the *History* without interruption, Susan moved into Elizabeth's Tenafly home. The project proved to be an enormous undertaking. The first volume, published in 1881, took more than six months to complete and covered the movement up to 1860. For months, the three editors often worked twelve to fourteen hours a day, seven days a week. Susan had been collecting documents and newspaper clippings for years, and she and Elizabeth sorted through reams of material, as well as papers that Lucretia and Martha Wright had accumulated. The three editors gathered items from the *Congressional Record*, court cases, speeches, newspaper stories, convention reports, commentaries, and biographies of those they considered central to the movement. They corresponded with everyone involved, requesting updated information and answers to questions about specific events and conversations. They double-checked facts. They also had to raise money to publish the first volume. Susan solicited a number of friends and supporters. Amelia Willard, Elizabeth's housekeeper, donated $3,000. The three editors also charged each woman who wanted her picture in the volume $150. Elizabeth often found the work stimulating, but Susan soon yearned to be lecturing and campaigning rather than confined within four walls.

Dealing with individual contributors had its frustrations. Each wrote her own biographical entry, which meant that the three editors then had to shorten, delete, and edit, often resulting in bruised egos. Amelia Bloomer wrote to complain that her role appeared diminished, which necessitated a response from Elizabeth, who cited each page that included Bloomer's name and assured her that the third volume would contain more on her. "It is a most remarkable fact that each person, almost, feels that the cause *began with* their [*sic*] interest in it," a weary Susan noted. Several contributors found fault with their pictures and the limited space accorded them as the volumes appeared. "They seem to think the history was written specially to relate every incident of their lives," Elizabeth complained; she wished the "carping" and "growling" would cease.[65]

The three editors solicited Lucy for details of her life, and she again refused, prompting Susan to comment on her former friend's "narrow *pig-headedness*." In the judgment of the historian Ellen DuBois, Susan did not want to authenticate the AWSA by including any of its personalities and activities, and Lucy did not want to validate the *History* by providing information about herself and her organization. But it is also true that until late in life, Lucy shunned the limelight. Friends and family knew her to be self-effacing. She never wrote a memoir or autobiography and never wanted held in her honor the kind of huge birthday celebrations Susan and Elizabeth so enjoyed. Antoinette Blackwell, who knew her well, observed, "Lucy hates being written about." Alice agreed. Lucy's relationship with Elizabeth and Susan deteriorated further when she aired views in the *Woman's Journal* on the first volume of the *History*, asserting that no one should dare write a history while the movement was in progress. Nevertheless, Lucy did call the volume "interesting and handsome," and the paper ran advertisements for it. Yet Alice later called the *History of Woman Suffrage* "somewhat one-sided."[66]

Scarcely was the first volume in print when work on the second one began, covering the Civil War and postwar years. Gage had to abandon the project to care for her infirm husband. The daunting amount of material to be included in the second volume led Susan to wonder if they could ever complete the "Herculean task" of paring it down into a single book. At this juncture, in February 1882, Elizabeth's daughter Harriot sailed home from Europe to help her mother edit the volume, initiating her commitment to women's rights in this country. She had graduated with honors from Vassar College and attended the Boston School of Oratory. Harriot then worked as a governess in Germany and traveled throughout Europe. On this February voyage, she happened to meet her future husband, the Englishman William Henry Blatch, son of a wealthy brewer, whom she would marry later that year.[67]

Harriot quickly perceived the problem that her mother and Susan had created by ignoring anything connected with the AWSA. Without that coverage, Harriot realized, the *History* would be highly suspect, and she insisted on creating a more balanced work. Harriot then contacted Lucy and Julia Ward Howe. Both refused to contribute, so she pulled most of the material for her 120-page chapter on the AWSA and its leaders from the *Woman's Journal*. This chapter did much to redress what could have been a serious void in the book; it even included photos of Lucy and Howe. Still, this volume ignored events and personalities that reflected poorly on the NWSA and its leaders, including the episodes with Train and Woodhull, the Beecher-Tilton affair, and the 1869 split. The review of this volume in the *Woman's Journal* observed bluntly: "No one reading this book would get an accurate or adequate idea of the real history of the woman suffrage movement in this country from autumn of 1867 to 1871 and '72, its most critical and trying time."[68] The second volume appeared in 1882; it took another three years of intermittent work to produce the third.

Beyond the perimeters of the movement, perceptible advances for women were taking place, especially in education, career, and job opportunities, and public acknowledgment of their abilities. In their speeches and writings, Susan, Elizabeth, Lucy, and others began to comment on these developments, realizing that some of the demands in the 1848 Declaration of Rights and Sentiments were being met. More high schools, colleges, and jobs were opening to women, and they were taking advantage of these opportunities. For instance, the late nineteenth-century movement to establish coed public high schools allowed many more women access to a good, free education. Northerners helped to establish several schools to help educate newly freed blacks in the South, such as the coed Bennett Seminary (now an all-female college) in Greensboro, North Carolina, in 1873, and Spelman College, which opened as Atlanta Baptist Female Academy in 1881. Statistics soon revealed that females nationwide made up nearly 56 percent of all high school graduates.[69]

In higher education, scores of female colleges, coed colleges and universities, and normal schools for training teachers opened. Admittedly, privileged women were invariably the ones to benefit from higher education. Nevertheless, the number of women who attended college increased from eleven thousand in 1870 to eighty-five thousand in 1900, making up 35 percent of all college students by the end of the century. Lucretia and James Mott were instrumental in founding Swarthmore College, a Quaker institution located outside Philadelphia, which opened in November 1869. Lucretia called it "a perfect Establishmt [*sic*]" in fulfilling Quakers' commitment to coeducation. More colleges and universities welcomed women, especially out west, including public universities in Kansas, Indiana, and Minnesota in the late 1860s, and Michigan, Missouri, and California in 1870. The University of Wisconsin admitted women, as did Boston University, a private institution, in 1873. A number of academically rigorous female colleges were founded—Wellesley in 1875 and Bryn Mawr a decade later. Smith College, opening in 1875, was the nation's first women's college endowed by a woman. In the South, Goucher College, originally the Woman's College of Baltimore, opened in 1885, and Agnes Scott College in Decatur, Georgia, was founded four years later. Some men's colleges experimented with coordinate education. Cornell University built Sage College for women in the early 1870s, and Tulane University established Sophie Newcomb College adjacent to its New Orleans campus in 1886. Barnard opened in 1889 when Columbia's trustees refused to admit women, and Radcliffe, associated with Harvard, opened to women in 1894. Mississippi took a different tack in 1884, funding the nation's first all-female state-supported college—the Mississippi Industrial and Collegiate Institute, today known as Mississippi University for Women in Columbus.[70]

The first generation of female activists understood the importance of a college education and were determined that their daughters would benefit. Elizabeth hoped Margaret and Harriot would attend a coed institution, but one of her sisters who paid their tuitions insisted on Vassar College, which had opened in 1865 with the promise "to accomplish for young women what colleges of the first class accomplish for young men."[71] Alla Foster also graduated from Vassar. Alice attended Boston University, one of two women in her class of twenty-eight.

Even as women were making significant advances in education, critics still feared the social and physiological consequences of women becoming well educated. Traditionalists encouraged greater exposure to domestic skills, sensing that too many women were ill prepared for household management. Others exhibited alarm at the negative impact of academic life on young women. Probably the most famous—or infamous—commentary was that articulated by Edward Clarke, a physician and retired Harvard Medical School professor. Mistakenly regarding him as an ally, Julia Ward Howe invited him in December 1873 to address the New England Woman's Club of Boston on women in higher education. An expanded version of his talk later appeared as *Sex in Education; or a Fair Chance for the Girls*. Clarke worried that college women were overtaxing their brains and thus injuring the development of their reproductive organs. To Clarke, the female body was a fixed vessel. As a young woman engaged in serious study, the brain channeled energy away from her maturing body, perhaps sterilizing the "female apparatus." Lucy and Alice were in the audience the afternoon he spoke and noted the heated debate that followed his lecture. Harvard's president, Charles Eliot, was also present and agreed with Clarke's points, but, as the *Woman's Journal* noted, "the ladies without exception differed from his conclusion."[72]

Clarke's demeaning comments and unsubstantiated conclusions dismayed women activists, and for months thereafter, they responded with a flurry of attacks. The *Woman's Journal* published letters, book reviews, and impassioned responses from around the nation. The next year, Julia Ward Howe edited a collection of articles, *Sex and Education: A Reply to Dr. Clarke's "Sex in Education,"* challenging his premise. She included testimony from individuals at several female and coed colleges who touted the benefits of higher education. Eliza Bisbee Duffey, an author of popular books on marriage and home, wrote *No Sex in Education, or, An Equal Chance for Boys and Girls* the same year. Subsequent surveys conducted at coed and women's colleges revealed the positive impact of higher education on women and proved Clarke wrong.[73]

Even as the nation's job market expanded, in line with a rapidly developing industrialized economy, employment opportunities for women generally remained limited to occupations society deemed acceptable for them or jobs men avoided. Overall, more women were now part of the paid labor force, increasing from 14.7 percent in 1870 to 17.2 percent by 1890. Of course, that increase did not necessarily mean more women were pursuing fruitful careers; more likely it reflected the many impoverished women who had no choice but to engage in wage labor. Women made up the majority of teachers, nurses, laundresses, textile workers, maids, cooks, and seamstresses. The teaching profession had become feminized; by 1890, 72 percent of all schoolteachers were women, compared to 66 percent twenty years earlier. Few, though, were able to break into male-dominated fields such as architecture, engineering, science, and dentistry.[74]

More women pursued careers as authors, artists, actresses, and lecturers; many earned a comfortable income. Clara Barton and Frances Ellen Watkins became well known through the lecture circuit, touring the country with their accounts of their Civil War experiences. Women speakers were welcomed rather than vilified as in years past. Using her familiarity with the West, Abigail Scott Duniway wrote novels highlighting frontier women and turned tradition on its head by depicting strong women rescuing men in distress.[75] Louisa May Alcott became a household name with her bestselling *Little Women*, published in 1868. This novel and Alcott's subsequent books allowed her to support her family in comfort. Helen Hunt Jackson and Sarah Orne Jewett became well-known authors. Jackson's 1881 muckraking study *Century of Dishonor*, based on her personal investigation, was a bold indictment of the federal government's treatment of Native Americans. The theme of her novel *Ramona,* published in 1884, was Indian exploitation in early California. Jewett's popular books chronicled life in rural Maine. The sculptor Anne Whitney and the painter Mary Cassatt succeeded in the male-dominated art world, both studying abroad and later gaining fame at home. Maria Mitchell broke into the almost exclusively male field of astronomy with her 1847 discovery of the comet that bears her name. The following year, she became the first woman elected to the newly organized American Academy of Arts and Sciences in Boston; its next woman member was not elected until 1943. In 1865, she joined the faculty at Vassar College, where she was much admired as a professor and helped found the Association for the Advancement of Women in 1873.

New fields of employment opened to women, including office work and retail sales. This change reflected the nation's rapid industrial development in the late nineteenth century and a parallel growth in big business. Companies now demanded more systematic practices in order to tabulate statistics, keep track of profits and losses, and maintain records of every transaction. Supporting such needs were the inventions of new office machines such as the typewriter, adding machine, and telephone. In 1870, the census did not even list stenographers or typists. Two decades later, women held 64 percent of those jobs, for those with small, nimble fingers seemed well suited for office work. These jobs were respectable and fairly well paid. Women working in federal or state offices could earn up to $900 a year, compared to female teachers, who averaged $500. The growth of department stores and shops in the nation's burgeoning cities hastened the demand for sales clerks, and many women moved into this line of work. By 1890, some 120,000 females were clerking in stores.[76]

A few middle- and upper-class women were pursuing careers or finding jobs in a variety of professions. The number of women physicians increased from 525 in 1870 to 4,457 by 1890, representing 4.4 percent of all doctors. More women were able to pursue a medical degree by studying abroad or attending one of several all-female medical schools in this country, such as the Woman's Medical College of Philadelphia, the New York Infirmary for Women and Children, and the New England Female Medical College. Universities reluctantly admitted a few women to their medical programs; for example, the University of Michigan graduated eighty-eight women doctors by 1890. That same year, 115 African American women were practicing medicine. By the

1880s, twenty-two nursing schools provided training, and nursing was almost exclusively female by the end of the century.[77]

But some fields remained all but closed to women. By 1890, the nation had only 22 female architects, 124 engineers, 1,143 ministers, and 2 veterinarians. The legal profession still presented women with an uphill battle. In 1870, the nation had only five female lawyers, compared to nearly forty-one thousand male ones. Two decades later, that number had increased to 208 female lawyers, compared to some 90,000 males. Only a few law schools admitted women, and each one set a tiny quota. In 1868, the University of Iowa became the first institution to admit women to its law school. The next year, St. Louis Law School (Washington University), the University of Michigan, and the Union College of Law each admitted a handful of women.[78]

Those who tried to challenge the system faced huge obstacles. Myra Bradwell of Chicago was determined to practice law. After she was rejected by several law schools, the National University Law School (Northwestern) finally admitted her. On graduating, she applied to the Illinois bar, but it refused to license her on two counts: she was female and married. She sued, using the Fourteenth Amendment to argue that she should enjoy all the rights and privileges as a citizen of the United States. She lost and then appealed her case, *Bradwell v. Illinois* (1873), to the U.S. Supreme Court. The justices upheld the lower court's ruling, claiming that both law and nature recognized significant differences between a man and a woman. Woman's "timidity and delicacy" and society's well-established "family organization" meant that she had no right to pursue "a distinct and independent career from that of her husband." A state could determine who to admit to its bar. It was not "one of her fundamental rights and privileges to be admitted in every office and position, including those which required highly special qualifications and demanding special responsibilities." While Bradwell's case was pending, the Illinois legislature passed a bill to admit women to the state bar, finally giving her the right she sought.[79]

Belva Ann Bennett Lockwood faced similar barriers. She also attended National University Law School, graduating in 1873. After being admitted to the bar in Washington, D.C., she was denied the right to practice before the federal Court of Appeals. She brought her case to Congress, and after lengthy debates, Congress passed a law in February 1879 allowing women to argue before higher courts after practicing before state or territorial high courts for at least three years. Women activists were thrilled, and Susan wrote the first lady, Lucy Hayes, an ally of women's rights, asking her to be sure her husband signed the bill. Whether or not the president needed nudging, Lucy Hayes invited Lockwood to the White House to celebrate her victory. Lockwood became the first female attorney to argue before the U.S. Supreme Court, after being admitted to its bar in March 1879. In 1884 and again in 1888, Lockwood ran for president of the United States as the candidate of the National Equal Rights Party, organized by a group of Californians, and received over four thousand votes.[80]

But not everyone benefited from perceptible changes. The nineteenth-century women's movement, despite its achievements, did little to advance those most in distress. Women scraping by in miserable, poorly paid jobs needed support and greater economic opportunities. In her diary and letters, Elizabeth often expressed deep sympathy for low-paid workers who struggled to make ends meet. Yet in public, female reformers often addressed such concerns from a singular perspective, arguing that if women could vote, employment problems would cease. As an 1887 NWSA resolution read, "Only through the protection of the ballot can they [working women] secure equal pay for equal work." Though Susan was one of many who had experienced unfair wages firsthand, her solution for pay inequity was female enfranchisement. "With the ballot in the hands of all the millions of factory women and workingwomen in this nation, you can perceive at once that they have a power by which they, like the workmen of the nation, can decide what work they will do, what prices they will be paid, and what positions they will occupy."[81]

The *Woman's Journal* published a number of articles exposing wage inequities, female prostitution, the enslavement of Chinese women in San Francisco, and deplorable, often dangerous working conditions. But reflecting the perspective of privileged women who led the movement, articles in the *Journal* and other papers also addressed the issue by suggesting the need to improve the training of domestic servants. Except as mistresses and servants, the daily lives of elite and lower-class women rarely intersected. Understandably, few poor women embraced the cry of the movement as their own. For the most part, they did not hear speeches, attend conventions, or read the *Woman's Journal*. Those working in mills, factories, laundries, and other businesses occasionally tried to improve their lot by striking, but rarely with much success. In the 1880s, the Knights of Labor allowed female members, but overall, women had limited impact on the labor movement. Nor was the mainstream labor movement necessarily supportive of something as radical as female suffrage. In one unusual situation, some two hundred female parasol makers did try to make their feelings known, barging into the 1873 AWSA annual meeting to seek support for their desperate situation. A Miss Leonard spoke on their behalf, claiming that laboring women's primary need was "not for the ballot but for bread." The AWSA members took these concerns to heart, but without any political or economic power, they had no effective means to do anything but listen to such complaints.[82]

Personal issues continued to affect women's involvement in the cause. Susan's peripatetic lifestyle persisted; for years she lived without a home of her own. She remained in excellent health as she aged, and in her sixties, boasted that she had never been sick a day in her life. When not lecturing, Susan often stayed with Elizabeth, her sister Mary in Rochester, or with one of many friends. She evidenced no sign of slowing down and, in fact, seemed to bristle when anyone suggested that a new generation should take over. Relinquishing this work was unimaginable, and Susan felt little confidence in them. "I can not quite feel certain that our younger sisters will be equal to the emergency," Susan observed in 1882.[83] In the winter of 1883, she took time off for a European vacation, accompanied during part of the nine-month sojourn by Rachel Avery, one of her young followers, referred to as "Susan's nieces." The two spent time in England with Elizabeth and Harriot, visited Italy, and went on to France, where Theodore Stanton hosted them, and finally to Germany and Ireland. Wherever she ventured, Susan relished her preeminence as an American women's rights leader, feted at dinners and parties held in her honor. At a reception in Liverpool, Elizabeth, Susan, and several British suffragists discussed the idea of holding an international congress in the near future, something NWSA members had been discussing for a couple of years.

Lucy's life was now more sedentary in the comfort of her Dorchester home. Its proximity to Boston made for an easy train ride to the *Journal* office. Occasionally she hired a cook, housekeeper, gardener, or stable boy to give her more time to lecture and edit the *Journal.* Yet even with paid help, Alice knew her mother shouldered multiple burdens.

> It is a heavy load for poor Mamma—the *Journal* every week, the general supervision of the suffrage cause in Massachusetts, and the care of this big place, indoors and out—planning what we are to eat three times a day, keeping an absentminded daughter clothed and in running order, seeing that the geraniums are covered up if the evening threatens frost, that the various fruits are picked at the right time & kept without spoiling, etc etc. ad infinitum. I should think she would go cracked; but she pursues the even tenor of her way and shows no sign of breaking down.[84]

Offsetting the stress, Lucy found joy in the world close at hand. Alice recalled that her mother was always "keenly alive to the beauties of nature," and

Lucy Stone (Library of Congress)

Lucy joked that "there was a good farmer spoiled when I went into reform." She was known as an excellent homemaker. Even as she aged, she made her own bread and soap, dried herbs, put up dozens of jars of cherries, pears, jellies, and jams, and happily entertained friends and family for extended visits. While campaigning for suffrage in Nebraska in 1882, she missed her home surroundings and wrote Alice, wanting to know if her flowers were in bloom. But her priorities were straight, for she added that she "should not mind if they all spoiled if we could carry Nebraska."[85] The flowers bloomed; Nebraska's suffrage amendment lost.

Though she disliked calling attention to herself, Lucy attended Oberlin's fiftieth anniversary jubilee in July 1883. Her fame preceded her, a far cry from decades earlier when the college had prevented her from reading her prize-winning essay at graduation. Now she was the only female speaker on the dais and much admired. "Young women have kissed me," she later wrote, "and some brought their children, telling them to remember they had shaken hands with me—all for the love of our Cause, which they knew I had served."[86]

Lucy never lost her ability to sense irony in the hurdles women confronted. In one of the last essays she wrote, she examined the Massachusetts legislature's accomplishments during its 1889–1890 session. State politicians, she noted, had discussed the gypsy moth and woodchuck, measured the salable length for lob-sters and baby trout, set a fee for chickens, compared butter to margarine, pro-tected a man's right to vote when he changed residences, eliminated the poll tax, and determined a suitable punishment for theft. Given the opportunity to enact female suffrage, the men did nothing. When women demanded a law that would give them the right to guardianship of their children following a divorce, leg-islators turned them down. Wives also appealed to legislators to require that hus-bands reimburse their wives after borrowing money from them. The legislature denied women that right, although husbands could demand it of their wives.[87]

After a decade of public speaking, Elizabeth now took time to enjoy her family and pursue new projects. She helped Susan produce the third volume of the *History of Woman Suffrage*, covering 1876 to 1885, though Susan served as principal editor. Elizabeth made several trips to visit Harriot's family in England and Theodore's in Paris, often staying abroad for several months. There, her celebrity status and role in the American women's rights movement brought her numerous invitations. She met with British suffragists and attended elegant dinners and receptions. They invited her to lecture, and she happily complied. Her philosophy was to make the most of these years. For her grand seventieth birthday celebration, she wrote and delivered a speech entitled "The Pleasures of Age." In it, Elizabeth assured her many guests that old age was not some-thing to fear but to enjoy as long as one retained good health, moral purpose, and mental vigor. No woman should ever consider her work complete as long as she had energy and time to commit to worthwhile ventures. Nor should she ever feel too old to develop her talents fully. On a similar theme, Elizabeth advised her daughter Margaret to ignore those who complained about the "dangerous crises" of menopause. It was "nonsense" to equate this with a major disaster. "Just keep your heads & hands busy & your hearts warm with love of grand souls thoughts & labors & you will pass the line without knowing it."[88]

Even as she aged, Elizabeth never lost her desire to stir controversy. She simply could not avoid a challenge or curb her sharp tongue and pen. "I have always been in chronic condition of rebellion," she observed. Resolving to devote her "sunset" years to a radical project she had been contemplating for some time, Elizabeth sought to educate the public about the spurious authen-ticity of scriptural views of women. Having witnessed all the fruitless political arguments against women's rights proffered over the years, "I now see more clearly than ever that the arch enemy to woman's freedom skulks behind the altar." The public had tired of political rhetoric, and Elizabeth intended to set off "a hornets nest" by challenging the church, where women's "strongest enemies entrench themselves."[89]

Elizabeth had long ago given up on regular church attendance and for years asserted that she had little use for organized religion. She blamed women's inferior status in part on the Bible and on clergymen's adherence to scriptural passages that upheld female subordination. In 1885, she and Susan heard a sermon, "Woman and Scepticism" presented by W. W. Patton, the president of Howard University, in which he claimed that enlarging women's sphere would lead to widespread immorality. Because women were so emotional and thus "rushed to extremes," he argued that they should never participate in politics. At the conclusion, Susan hurried forward and told Patton that if his mother were still alive, she "should lay you across her knee and give you a good spanking for that sermon." Adopting a different tack, Elizabeth employed sarcasm to congratulate Patton. "I have been trying for years to make women understand that the worst enemy they have is in the pulpit and now you have illustrated the truth of it," she informed him. In her mind, a true religion should glorify both men and women by including "an equal share of the feminine element."[90]

In 1886, Elizabeth conceived a plan to gather every biblical reference on women and compile them into a single volume with accompanying commentary. "Women are told that they are indebted to the Bible for all the advantages and opportunities of life that they enjoy to-day," she explained, "hence they reverence the very book, that above all others, contains the most degrading ideas of sex." Harriot, who was visiting her mother, helped her identify those passages. Assisting them for a few weeks was Frances H. Lord, an English reformer, who visited in August 1886. Elizabeth wrote to dozens of friends and acquaintances, hoping to form a committee of twenty-five "distinguished" American and British women to help with this project. Nearly all rejected her request, claiming time constraints, a lack of interest, or fear of being associated with such a controversial undertaking. Even Elizabeth Smith Miller urged her cousin to put aside this idea and pursue more fruitful work. Failing to secure the assistance she needed, Elizabeth put her project on hold and sailed for England with Harriot. Not until 1895 did the first of two volumes of *A Woman's Bible* appear. The *New York Times* later called it the "crowning achievement" of Elizabeth's career; others were horrified that anyone would tamper with the word of God.[91]

As women gained legal and political rights and growing numbers joined the fight for suffrage, opponents became more visible and better organized. Certainly the appearance of formal opposition suggested something positive: women activists were making inroads and doing enough to alarm those who feared or rejected female equality and eschewed their right to vote. Female opponents who began to organize tended to be privileged and to be strongest in communities where suffragists were most active. Initially the "remonstrants," as they were called, conducted their work by petitioning and holding meetings to air their concerns. Unlike suffragists, they presented petitions to politicians in silence, believing that women should not address men in public. In 1869, two hundred women in Lancaster, Massachusetts, submitted a statement opposing a petition to the state legislature that demanded female enfranchisement. They argued that suffrage would "diminish the purity, the dignity and the moral influence of woman, and bring into the family circle a dangerous element of discord." Women in Elyria and Oberlin, Ohio, submitted a document entitled "Lorain Memorial Against Woman Suffrage" to their state legislature, for they saw no benefits in female suffrage. In Peoria, Illinois, in 1870, more than a thousand individuals signed and sent a petition to their state legislature opposing female enfranchisement, which they believed contradicted natural and divine law. As one Chicago newspaper noted, however, the irony in all these counter-protests was that suffrage opponents were mingling in the world of politics as they tried to influence legislators in order to prevent women from mingling in the world of politics.[92]

The first formal organization of remonstrants, the Woman's Anti-Suffrage Association of Washington, D.C., was founded in 1870 by Mrs. William (Ellen Ewing) Sherman, wife of the famous Union general, and Mrs. John (Madeline Vinton) Dahlgren, a widow and popular Washington hostess. The organization attracted other well-heeled members, including Catharine Beecher, Mrs. John (Margaret) Sherman, and Emma Willard's sister Almira Lincoln Phelps, a teacher. Phelps recruited new members by asking former pupils to oppose female suffrage. Mrs. William Sherman insisted that women did not want and actually would not accept suffrage. Members collected a thousand signatures on a petition to Congress, declaring that the right to vote would "threaten their peace and happiness." The NWSA leaders were upset but curious to hear Dahlgren's message, so they invited her to speak at their 1872 convention. Sensing that public lecturing would tarnish her image, Dahlgren declined. The same year, Catharine Beecher wrote *Woman's Profession as Mother and Educator: With Views in Opposition to Woman Suffrage*. Boston women formed the Boston Committee of Remonstrants in 1882, and up through the mid-1890s, members annually reminded state legislators that most women had no desire to vote. One of their biggest fears was the impact immigrant women would have on elections. The Committee published pamphlets, and some members (obviously no longer reticent about public speaking) testified before the state legislature, using arguments that had been uttered by men for forty years. Alice Blackwell regarded opponents as a challenge and admitted that "we had a great deal of fun with them" and their "extraordinary" arguments.[93]

Opponents of women's rights were correct: women were making progress and gaining the respect they had been seeking for forty years. Jeering crowds and scornful audiences were no longer the norm. Activists did not have to scour a community to find a church or public venue where they could hold a meeting. Events were held in New York City's Carnegie Hall and equally elegant auditoriums in other major cities throughout the country. Women's testimony before state legislatures and Congress was now a common occurrence. Newspapers coast-to-coast complimented their speeches and their conventions. Reporters referred to Elizabeth, Susan, and Lucy as "distinguished," "honorable," and "respected," and some news stories alerted readers to women's lengthy struggles in seeking the vote. Elizabeth observed that young girls, who had once been criticized for roller-skating, rolling hoops, and bicycling, were now publicly competing in sports and enjoying exercise at home and school.

Over the years, friction between the NWSA and the AWSA began to dissipate. Alice sensed that issues that had once divided the two organizations, such as their structure and basis of representation, seemed less important than in years past. Because Elizabeth had withdrawn from the daily proceedings and was spending more time abroad, the NWSA could focus more attention on winning the vote and less on divisive issues that she had endorsed. The success of the *Woman's Journal* no longer troubled NWSA leaders; they accepted its role as a voice of the movement. Notorious characters like Train and Woodhull were fading into history.[94] Most important, a new group of young, dedicated reformers with no memory of past problems was emerging. Alice's assessment and that of others was that only personalities stood in the way of uniting the two organizations.

Principal leaders of each association began to contemplate a merger. Relaxing in the South in 1887 to restore her health, Lucy began to consider a plan to negotiate with former enemies and unite the two groups. Age and poor health undoubtedly influenced her change of heart. Approaching her seventieth birthday, Lucy realized that this new generation had to take over. Alice "wants to have Union, to take the burden of work of the American from me, and to save it from coming on her, when I drop out." Lucy explained to her daughter:

> I have been thinking that there might be a union possible. . . . Miss Anthony
> intends to have a great celebration of the 40th anniversary of this movement[;]

if, after conferring with our auxiliary societies, it was thought best to do so, we might propose to make it a Jubilee Anniversary and union of the two National societies.... They are now doing very good work as an association, and apparently there is no reason why we should not unite. Besides, it would take away the feeling of grievance, etc. etc. and on the whole, perhaps be best. I have about come to the conclusion that this will be best for the Cause.... Its success and prosperity have always been more to me than any personal feeling, and any damage to it far more than any personal ill will to or mistreatment of myself. So I could always rejoice in good work no matter who did it.

Three months later, Lucy wrote Antoinette Blackwell, outlining a potential plan: that the two organizations retain some independence, hold one annual convention, and become auxiliaries of a United Suffrage Association. She recommended that she and Elizabeth serve as honorary members so a new generation could take over. Blackwell favored these ideas, hoping for the "marvelous harmony and sympathy of feeling" women had shared in the early years of the movement.[95]

That December, with the fortieth anniversary celebration of Seneca Falls ahead, a major breakthrough took place. Susan wrote to Lucy, expressing her desire to discuss a plan for unification. She offered to come to Boston accompanied by Rachel Foster and asked that Alice also be present so "that each of us may have a *suffrage daughter to help bring about the desired end.*" A stenographer could record their meeting. Susan, Lucy, Rachel, and Alice met on the last day of December 1887. Privately, Lucy felt that Susan did not deserve any special favors due to Susan's past transgressions, and Lucy worried that her "old grasping spirit" still wanted to take over. "She so much wishes to be president herself!"[96] Nonetheless, the four managed to carry on a fruitful discussion. The *Woman's Journal* carried minutes of this meeting, including conversations between Susan and Lucy over possible names, a new organizational structure, bylaws, and a constitution.

The first major public event that suggested the possibility of unification was the 1888 NWSA convention, a grand, week-long celebration of the fortieth anniversary of Seneca Falls, known as the International Council of Women. Albaugh's Opera House in Washington, D.C., was the setting for the meeting, held from March 25 to April 1. Railroad companies and hotels offered participants discounted rates.[97] As the date of the convention neared, however, a problem arose. Elizabeth, who was in England, indicated no desire to attend. Susan saw the celebration disintegrating. She fired off an appeal to Elizabeth, later claiming that this was one of the harshest missives she ever sent. Elizabeth, of all people, had to be present to commemorate Seneca Falls. Indeed, she had indicated a strong interest in holding a major international meeting. Elizabeth reluctantly agreed and sailed home, arriving in Washington in the midst of a blizzard and without a prepared speech. According to legend, Susan locked Elizabeth in her hotel room until she wrote one.[98]

This convention featured some eighty speakers from around the globe who represented fifty-three different organizations. A picture of "that loved, venerated woman," Lucretia Mott, hung above the stage, for Susan hoped that the audience would "feel that her benediction and her spirit are with us." She had invited all the signers of the 1848 Declaration of Rights and Sentiments she could locate; eight men and thirty-six women showed up. After Antoinette Blackwell's opening prayer, Isabella Beecher Hooker spoke, articulating the many reasons women should be enfranchised, and recounted Susan's 1872 arrest for attempting to vote.[99] Speakers addressed a range of issues, including suffrage, temperance, industrial labor, education, prostitution, religion, and the law. They provided updates on women in various professions and their participation in associations such as the Grange and the Knights of Labor. Women from India, France, Denmark, Italy, and other nations explained women's rights issues in their countries. Professional musicians enlivened the convention by entertaining the crowd on numerous occasions.

Though this event had an international focus, a "Conference of the Pioneers" honored Seneca Falls and the first generation of activists who were present, including Susan, Elizabeth, Lucy, Antoinette, Douglass, Henry Blackwell, and others. Mary Grew introduced the leaders and bequeathed the struggle to the movement's "young friends" in the audience who faced "glorious opportunities" ahead. She urged them to "be faithful unto death or victory."[100] Organizers had hoped to display the mahogany table on which Elizabeth had completed the Declaration of Rights and Sentiments, but the M'Clintocks, who owned it, felt that it was "too precious" to be shipped from Seneca Falls. Susan paid homage to Lucretia and noted the many remarkable changes that had occurred over the last four decades, including the passage of married women's property acts in nearly every state. Wives could now make contracts, could sue and be sued, and had easier access to divorce. Elizabeth's speech recalled historic moments in the movement, and she highlighted changes that Frederick Douglass later called "vast and wonderful." He spoke and compared past to present, observing that their cause once had few friends but now had many. Formerly an obscure topic, women's rights was now one the entire world knew about. Hyperbolic by even her own standards, Elizabeth added that Seneca Falls and the conventions that followed initiated "the greatest movement for human liberty recorded on the page of History: a demand for freedom to one-half the entire race." She encouraged everyone to work together in the struggle ahead. Her generation of reformers, now in the "sunset of life," needed younger women to carry on. Douglass recalled his role at Seneca Falls and rejoiced that Elizabeth and others could enjoy the current spectacle after a "tempestuous forty years of agitation." Susan paid tribute to her longtime friend, noting that Elizabeth had inspired everyone with "a daring voice and a determined hand." More than anyone else, Elizabeth understood how "to break the silence of woman." Even Lucy had an opportunity to shine, as she shared memories of her initial involvement in the movement.[101]

Despite all the enthusiasm, not everyone was impressed with the International Council of Women. Alice left the week-long meeting disenchanted and upset. While she admitted that "much good must have been done" due to the large attendance and impressive speeches, she labeled the week "disagreeable." Working behind the scenes, she sensed that the NWSA leaders did not really desire a union as much as she did. They had not formulated a merger plan as promised and were doing everything possible to silence any mention of Woodhull, Train, and free love. Alice felt defensive about her mother and admitted that Elizabeth's and Susan's behavior still upset her. "It is rather irritating to see unworthy women who hate your mother and have constantly maligned her, receiving a week's continuous ovation," she explained. Even Susan's introduction of her mother and request that she speak annoyed her. "It was one of those pieces of ostensible friendliness and real unfriendliness that are very riling to me. . . . I hate the Nationals." She also found it ironic that some two to three hundred women, most of whom supported the social purity crusade that sought to uplift the nation's morals, flocked to a White House reception, where they rubbed elbows with President Grover Cleveland, knowing full well that he had fathered a child out of wedlock.[102] Lucy and Alice declined the president's invitation, sensing they would be distracted.

Somehow problems dissolved, and Alice moved beyond her grumpy mood. In an almost anticlimactic move, on February 18, 1889, a document entitled "Open Letter to the Women of America" was issued, signed by Lucy, Julia Ward Howe, Mary Livermore, and Mary F. Eastman for the AWSA and Elizabeth, Susan, Belva Lockwood, Matilda Joslyn Gage, and Frances Willard for the NWSA. Transcending years of acrimony, misunderstandings, and jealousy, these women declared that they now wished "to work in harmony with all other Associations of like character—and as in union there is strength." Lucy offered to underwrite half the cost of a national convention to merge the two organizations and to commemorate the fortieth anniversary of the first National Woman's Rights Convention in Worcester. She hoped there would be time for "some reminiscences of 'pioneer times.'"[103] In November, announcements began to publicize this meeting that would initiate a new phase in the suffrage struggle.

Yet Susan was skeptical, privately wondering if an actual merger would take place. Writing to Olympia Brown, she wondered why Lucy, Henry, and the AWSA sought unity. She suspected that in presenting their plan, they secretly hoped the NWSA would back out and thus look bad in the public eye. To counter this, Susan was doing everything possible to exhibit a "cheerful welcome" to this proposal, knowing it would be "suicidal" for the NWSA if it rejected the unification plan. She insisted that Elizabeth become president of the new organization but predicted that AWSA leaders would balk and thus reveal their true colors. "I want them caught in their own trap," she gloated. In closing, she asked Olympia to keep her thoughts confidential and hinted that perhaps the AWSA had changed and would now support Elizabeth's presidency.[104]

Personal doubts aside, the first meeting of the National American Woman's Suffrage Association (NAWSA) met in Washington, D.C., from February 18 to 21, 1890. Three days before the event, a grand seventieth birthday celebration honored Susan, who was resplendent in a dark red velvet dress. A formal merger of the two organizations took place the first day of the convention. Elizabeth, accompanied by her daughters Margaret and Harriot, was elected president. While she exhibited only lukewarm interest in being involved, she was flattered by the honor and the admiration of association members. Susan became vice president. Everyone understood that Elizabeth would rarely be active, meaning that Susan would function as president in all but name. Lucy was elected chair of the executive committee. Alice and Henry were present, but a severe cough kept Lucy at home. Elizabeth's presidential address warned against religious influences, urged that the new organization work for suffrage, and asked that all members remain open to their own needs but also to those of "Colored women, Indian women, Mormon women, Christians and Infidels, and women from every quarter of the globe." Women activists had reunited at long last, understanding the importance of a strong, unified movement to invigorate and sustain a new generation of leaders. As Elizabeth wrote, "The next generation of women will reap the blessings we are now sowing, so let us work on in faith & hope to the end."[105]

EPILOGUE

"Make the World Better"

By 1890, the landscape for American women was a far cry from what it had been in 1848. Those who organized the Seneca Falls Convention never imagined that they would initiate a national women's rights movement and foster a social revolution: "the greatest and grandest reform of all time." Four remarkable, very human individuals—Lucretia, Elizabeth, Lucy, and Susan—as well as many other dedicated women and men, carried on from that first meeting, fighting for justice and equality and creating a women's movement that by 1890 breathed a life of its own.

The Seneca Falls Convention of 1848 and its Declaration of Rights and Sentiments could have been of little consequence. Instead, this meeting and its articulated concerns became a springboard, generating an enormous effort by determined activists who dedicated their lives to the cause of women's rights. The upheaval of the American Civil War, the profound disappointments during Reconstruction, the 1869 division of the movement, and some unfortunate personal decisions and associations were major setbacks. Throughout the struggle, a majority of Americans, including most women, opposed the movement's demands. Yet knowing their cause was just, these activists refused to give up.

In their quest to achieve equal rights for all women, these four sought to convince elected officials to alter or eliminate the many laws that oppressed women. They tried to change society's perceptions of women as innately inferior to men. They attempted to erase boundaries that confined women to a separate sphere and to convince Americans that women deserved the same opportunities men enjoyed. They tried to persuade clergymen that scriptural passages that silenced and oppressed women were exploitative and wrong. Women pleaded with men to share their political power. Most important, they pleaded with other women to believe in themselves and claim equal rights and all the benefits of citizenship.

Lucretia, Elizabeth, Lucy, and Susan were a remarkable foursome, different in personality, ability, and outlook, but each driven by unshakable dedication to the cause. All four had a profound impact on the struggle for female equality in the nineteenth century, a time when few Americans ever imagined the need for it. Though by 1890 women activists had not accomplished all that was articulated in the Seneca Falls Declaration of Rights and Sentiments and its Resolutions, and were still "rehearsing the same old arguments for women," they could celebrate significant advances. By 1890, this first generation of activists anticipated that a new group of women under the NAWSA could move forward and achieve their dream of universal suffrage.

With the formation of the NAWSA, female suffragists were now reunited, though their work had hardly ended. Lucy, Elizabeth, and Susan continued their efforts, though only Susan remained actively engaged in the movement.

By 1890, Lucy's health had declined significantly. She suffered from rheumatism and digestive and heart problems and could give no more than a day a week to the *Woman's Journal*. In addition, piqued by the prominent role Susan carved out for herself, Lucy played only a peripheral role in the NAWSA. She attended annual meetings, but most of the speeches she delivered were to local labor organizations, suffrage groups, college women's associations, and the New England Woman's Club. In 1891, she visited with Carrie Chapman Catt, the future president of the NAWSA, who came to Boston to meet this woman she so admired. The following year, when Lucy attended the NAWSA annual convention in Washington, D.C., she and Elizabeth testified before the House Committee on the Judiciary. Lucy's final public appearance was in May 1893 at the Woman's Congress, held in conjunction with the World Columbian Exposition in Chicago, the quadricentennial celebration of Columbus's arrival in the Americas. Alice accompanied her mother there. Though frail and suffering periodic pain, Lucy delivered what became her last major speech, "The Progress of Fifty Years," paying tribute to all that had been accomplished and urging listeners to carry on until women achieved their full rights.

Lucy knew she was dying. The medical diagnosis by several doctors, including her sister-in-law Emily, was stomach cancer. No effective cure existed, and Lucy refused all efforts to prolong her life, telling family and friends, "The kindest thing you can do is let me pass on." Her letters and Alice's diary reveal that in the last months of her life, she was in chronic pain, increasingly debilitated and unable to eat. She remained at home, where a stream of family and close friends visited during her final weeks. Many of them credited Lucy with their commitment to women's rights, and all noted her resolute, peaceful acceptance of death. Alice, who had been in Canada during July and August, came home to nurse her mother. She sat by her bedside and accumulated stories Lucy related about her childhood, her experiences at Mount Holyoke and Oberlin, and her initial involvement in women's rights. Several friends expressed regret that she would not live to see women vote, but Lucy told each one, "I shall know it in the next world." She instructed Alice on how to conduct their work and to care for Henry and their home when she was gone.[1]

Lucy passed away on October 18, 1893. According to Alice, the final words she whispered were "Make the world better!" To her father, Alice said, "We must try to keep Mamma's flag flying."[2] Eleven hundred people packed Boston's Church of the Disciple for her funeral, a service that reflected Lucy's wishes that the occasion be "bright and cheerful." She was cremated, and her ashes were buried at Forest Hills, outside Boston.[3] Henry wrote of his wife:

> The gentlest and most heroic of women has passed away. The woman who
> in her whole character and life most fully embodied our highest conceptions as
> daughter, sister, wife, mother, friend and citizen, no longer lives to disarm
> prejudice and convert even opposition into advocacy. . . . Dear Friends
> of woman suffrage everywhere, let the loving, unselfish life of our departed friend and leader be to us faith, courage and inspiration. In no way can
> we so cherish her memory as by promoting the cause that was to her
> more dear and sacred than any other.[4]

Lucy bequeathed everything to Henry and Alice and asked that they continue to work for women's rights.

After serving as NAWSA president for two years, Elizabeth resigned from her official post, in part because she wanted to pursue other interests but also because she found new members too conservative and timid. She spent more time with her family, wrote extensively, and pondered a philosophy for women. These thoughts she delivered in the most moving and powerful address she ever wrote—and one that still resonates today: "The Solitude of Self," presented in written form to the House Committee on the Judiciary in 1892 (see appendix B). She also read that essay at her final NAWSA convention and to the Senate Committee on Woman Suffrage two days later. The subject was one rarely heard in Congress. Elizabeth overshadowed every other speaker with her eloquence and profound message, emphasizing that "no matter how much women prefer to lean, to be protected and supported, nor how much men desire to have them do so, they must make the voyage of life alone." Women—and men—must be able to take care of themselves and know how to navigate solo through life because they would encounter situations where no one else could guide them. To handle these, Elizabeth urged women to develop strength and self-reliance. As Elizabeth, Lucretia, Lucy, Susan, and others had discovered, life presented women with enormous challenges but often no safety net to handle them. Armed with an education, a belief in themselves, and the ability to discover an inner strength, they would find that "solitude of self."

Susan did not like the essay; Elizabeth felt it was the best piece she had ever written. It so impressed Lucy that she printed it in its entirety in the *Woman's Journal.*[5] It is a timeless work that provides insight into how these women found the strength and confidence to carry on when so many challenges impeded their path.

Age did little to slow Elizabeth's pace or strong opinions. Women honored her at an elegant eightieth birthday celebration held at the Metropolitan Opera House in New York City in 1895. Some six thousand people were present. She produced the first volume of her *Woman's Bible* that year; the second volume appeared three years later. Reactions were both laudatory and critical, though the book sold well. Younger, more conservative women in the NAWSA were shocked by such a controversial publication and an outspoken woman who sought to "stir up the world." They feared the *Woman's Bible* would have a negative impact on their cause. At the 1896 NAWSA annual convention, members voted to censure the *Woman's Bible,* despite an appeal from Susan to tolerate free speech and Elizabeth's daring views. In 1898, Elizabeth published *Eighty Years and More,* a compilation and expansion of reminiscences she had written for the *Woman's Tribune* nearly a decade earlier. She admitted that she had no desire to die, for she found life "sweet," and she added, "There are many things I desire to do before I take final leave of this planet." As her eyesight dimmed, she hired readers in order to continue to enjoy a pastime that had sustained her throughout her life. Susan visited her at her apartment on the West Side of Manhattan in 1902, although the two were no longer as close as in former years. As Elizabeth had observed a few years earlier, "I get more radical as I grow older, while she [Susan] seems to get more conservative."[6]

Elizabeth hardly suffered a day of ill health before she died, quietly, from heart failure on October 26, 1902. Following her own advice in making the most of each day, she had written two essays earlier in the week and dictated a letter to President Theodore Roosevelt asking him to immortalize himself (as Lincoln had done when he emancipated the slaves, she pointed out) and endorse "the complete emancipation" of women. On learning of Elizabeth's death, Susan despaired, "How lonesome I do feel." She could speak few words at Elizabeth's funeral, but commented that "when the world stood against us, we stood together." She called her friend a "courageous" leader, the "philosopher and statesman" of the women's movement, and the one who "forged the thunderbolts and I fired them." Antoinette Blackwell delivered a tribute at the simple, private funeral Elizabeth had requested. At the head of her casket stood the mahogany table on which she had written the Seneca Falls Declaration of Rights and Sentiments. Many newspapers placed her obituary on their front pages and carried tributes for weeks thereafter.[7]

Susan was the last survivor among these four women. She remained active in the movement until 1900 and all the while kept up a demanding schedule. Wherever she traveled, she attracted female admirers who regarded her as the living embodiment of the women's movement. From 1892 to 1900, Susan served as president of the NAWSA. She toured the southern states in 1895. She spent nearly eight months in California, as women there fought a lively but unsuccessful campaign for female suffrage in 1896. There she lectured, held meetings, attended receptions and dinners, and found time to tour Yosemite Valley on horseback. She worked with Ida Husted Harper, a journalist and women's rights activist, to produce an authorized biography of herself, whose first volume appeared in 1898. When the presidency of the NAWSA passed on to her chosen successor, Carrie Chapman Catt, Susan seemed reluctant to let go, but age and declining health necessitated that step. Nevertheless, between 1900 and her death, she visited eighteen states and attended NAWSA annual meetings, including one in Portland, Oregon, in 1905. Catt, who founded the International Woman Suffrage Alliance in 1902, persuaded Susan to attend that organization's first official meeting in Berlin in June 1904.

Despite her seemingly indefatigable energy, Susan began to suffer poor health. She was determined to attend the February 1906 NAWSA annual convention in Baltimore but caught a bad cold en route from Rochester and was confined to bed. She was able to make only a brief appearance at the meeting. Afterward, her sister Mary and a nurse accompanied her home. Susan was too ill to attend her eighty-sixth birthday celebration, which was held at New York's Astor Hotel. Nearly four hundred women came anyway to honor this esteemed woman.

Her situation worsened, and she knew she was dying. On March 13, 1906, having fallen into a state of unconsciousness, Susan succumbed to heart disease and pneumonia. At her bedside were Anna Howard Shaw and her sister Mary. Susan bequeathed her entire estate of some $10,000 to the women's movement, a cause that had been her life. She received a full-page tribute, complete with photograph, in the *New York Times*. At her funeral in Rochester, an American flag draped her coffin, and an honor guard of young women from the University of Rochester accompanied it.[8]

Thanks to Lucy's wise investments and careful budgeting, Henry Blackwell lived on, enjoying a life of comfort as he aged. He no longer pursued his many ill-advised real estate and investment schemes that had so troubled Lucy but now devoted himself to women's causes and the *Woman's Journal*. He died in 1909.

Antoinette Blackwell was the only first-generation activist who was alive to see women's suffrage become a reality. In 1915, when she was over eighty years old, she and Alice rode in a huge suffrage parade in New York City. Though she experienced only moments of lucidity in the final months of life, Antoinette was able to cast her vote for Warren G. Harding in the 1920 presidential election. She died November 5, 1921.

A new generation took over the movement. Alice continued to play a fundamental role, editing and publishing the *Woman's Journal* until 1917. In 1902, Harriot Stanton Blatch with her husband and daughter Nora moved to the United States. On being exposed to the women's movement here, Harriot was appalled at its lackluster character, disorganization, and ineffective leadership. In England, Emmeline Pankhurst, her two daughters, and other ardent suffragists were holding public demonstrations and huge parades, disrupting government meetings, chaining themselves to fences, getting arrested, and engaging in hunger strikes. By comparison, the American effort seemed uninspired. The NAWSA faced significant problems and experienced internal disarray as the presidency shifted from Catt to Anna Howard Shaw in 1904 and then back to Catt in 1915. Shaw was an effective orator but lacked the management and organizational skills that were so essential to the movement. For six years, the NAWSA had its headquarters in Warren, Ohio, the home of the secretary-treasurer. Nevertheless, as the NAWSA floundered at the national level and some members resigned in frustration, thousands of energetic women in state suffrage organizations conducted effective, spirited work.

In New York State, Harriot brought her energy, determination, and knowledge of British tactics to the movement. Elizabeth would have been proud of her spunky daughter. Like her father, she loved politics and felt suffrage could be won through the political system rather than through moral suasion. Her first step was to organize those whom female reformers had generally ignored—laboring women. In 1906, she founded the Equality League of Self-Supporting Women, later renamed the Women's Political Union, to attract female wage and industrial workers to the movement. Thousands of wage-working women joined, as did well-known writers and activists like Charlotte Perkins Gilman, Florence Kelly, and Rosa Schniederman. Harriot also drew wealthy matrons into the cause, and their support gave the movement the financial security it needed. For instance, in 1909, Alva Vanderbilt Belmont funded the NAWSA's move back to New York City.[9]

Harriot and the League initiated fresh approaches, staging outdoor meetings and parades to generate excitement and support. They held their first major parade in New York City in February 1908. Suffragists nationwide began to duplicate these tactics and added advertising and poster campaigns, suffrage marching songs, automobile tours, and even motion pictures as they embraced mass marketing and the wonders of modern technology. In May 1908, Margaret and Harriot hosted a sixtieth-anniversary celebration of Seneca Falls to celebrate their mother's role in the movement, since in their minds, Susan was receiving most of the credit for the women's rights movement. The next year, Harriot invited Emmeline Pankhurst to lecture in the United States. Pankhurst addressed an audience of three thousand people at Carnegie Hall and spent a month generating excitement as she lectured throughout the country. With Harriot's vision, hard work, and the commitment she generated in so many others, it is little wonder that New York in 1917 was the only state in the East to give women the right to vote before the passage of the Nineteenth Amendment in 1920.[10]

The women's suffrage movement became increasingly energized in the second decade of the twentieth century. The progressive movement revitalized women, as did Catt's return to the NAWSA presidency in 1915. She developed her "winning plan," using any means possible to achieve suffrage in six years. Well-organized state suffrage campaigns resulted in fifteen states (nearly all in the West) giving women the right to vote before the Nineteenth Amendment was added to the Constitution. Also inspiring to American women were examples of other countries—including New Zealand, Australia, the Netherlands, Canada, and Austria—that gave women the vote. Women's dedicated service in World War I provided additional reason to demand suffrage.

The NAWSA focused more attention on winning a federal suffrage amendment. It now competed with a new organization, the Congressional Union (CU), founded in April 1913 by Alice Paul and Lucy Burns, who considered NAWSA tactics too tame. Both organizations pressured Congress, political parties, and President Woodrow Wilson to endorse women's suffrage. Paul and

Burns also tried to influence elections in which candidates opposed women's suffrage. The CU members adopted the radical techniques of the British suffragists. They interrupted party conventions, picketed the White House, and held parades, including a massive rally in Washington, D.C., the day before Wilson's inauguration. On May 21, 1919, the House passed the suffrage amendment; the Senate followed suit on June 4. It then went out to the states for ratification. On August 26, 1920, the Nineteenth Amendment giving women the right to vote was added to the U.S. Constitution. Seventy-two years after the Seneca Falls Convention, women had finally achieved their most radical demand.

One can hope that Lucretia, Elizabeth, Lucy, and Susan somehow knew that their vision, determination, and tireless efforts resulted in this hard-won victory. At her final NAWSA convention in 1906, Susan articulated what all four had believed throughout their long struggle on behalf of women: "Failure is impossible."

APPENDIX A

Declaration of Rights and Sentiments

When, in the course of human events, it becomes necessary for one portion of the family of man to assume among the people of the earth a position different from that which they have hitherto occupied, but one to which the laws of nature and of nature's God entitle them, a decent respect to the opinions of mankind requires that they should declare the causes that impel them to such a course.

We hold these truths to be self-evident: that all men and women are created equal; that they are endowed by their Creator with certain inalienable rights; that among these are life, liberty, and the pursuit of happiness; that to secure these rights governments are instituted, deriving their just powers from the consent of the governed. Whenever any form of Government becomes destructive of these ends, it is the right of those who suffer from it to refuse allegiance to it, and to insist upon the institution of a new government, laying its foundation on such principles, and organizing its powers in such form as to them shall seem most likely to effect their safety and happiness. Prudence, indeed, will dictate that governments long established should not be changed for light and transient causes; and accordingly, all experience hath shown that mankind are more disposed to suffer, while evils are sufferable, than to right themselves by abolishing the forms to which they are accustomed. But when a long train of abuses and usurpations, pursuing invariably the same object, evinces a design to reduce them under absolute despotism, it is their duty to throw off such government, and to provide new guards for their future security. Such has been the patient sufferance of the women under this government, and such is now the necessity which constrains them to demand the equal station to which they are entitled.

The history of mankind is a history of repeated injuries and usurpations on the part of man toward woman, having in direct object the establishment of an absolute tyranny over her. To prove this, let facts be submitted to a candid world.

He has never permitted her to exercise her inalienable right to the elective franchise.

He has compelled her to submit to laws, in the formation of which she had no voice.

He has withheld from her rights which are given to the most ignorant and degraded men—both natives and foreigners.

Having deprived her of this first right of a citizen, the elective franchise, thereby leaving her without representation in the halls of legislation, he has oppressed her on all sides.

He has made her, if married, in the eye of the law, civilly dead.

He has taken from her all right in property, even to the wages she earns.

He has made her, morally, an irresponsible being, as she can commit many crimes with impunity, provided they be done in the presence of her husband. In the covenant of marriage, she is compelled to promise obedience to her husband, he becoming, to all intents and purposes, her master—the law giving him power to deprive her of her liberty, and to administer chastisement.

He has so framed the laws of divorce, as to what shall be the proper causes of divorce; in case of separation, to whom the guardianship of the children shall be given; as to be wholly regardless of the happiness of women—the law, in all cases, going upon the false supposition of the supremacy of man, and giving all power into his hands.

After depriving her of all rights as a married woman, if single and the owner of property, he has taxed her to support a government which recognizes her only when her property can be made profitable to it.

He has monopolized nearly all the profitable employments, and from those she is permitted to follow, she receives but a scanty remuneration.

He closes against her all the avenues to wealth and distinction, which he considers most honorable to himself. As a teacher of theology, medicine, or law, she is not known.

He has denied her the facilities for obtaining a thorough education—all colleges being closed against her.

He allows her in Church as well as State, but a subordinate position, claiming Apostolic authority for her exclusion from the ministry, and, with some exceptions, from any public participation in the affairs of the Church.

He has created a false public sentiment, by giving to the world a different code of morals for men and women, by which moral delinquencies which exclude women from society, are not only tolerated but deemed of little account in man.

He has usurped the prerogative of Jehovah himself, claiming it as his right to assign for her a sphere of action, when that belongs to her conscience and her God.

He has endeavored, in every way that he could to destroy her confidence in her own powers, to lessen her self-respect, and to make her willing to lead a dependant and abject life.

Now, in view of this entire disfranchisement of one-half the people of this country, their social and religious degradation,—in view of the unjust laws above mentioned, and because women do feel themselves aggrieved, oppressed, and fraudulently deprived of their most sacred rights, we insist that they have immediate admission to all the rights and privileges which belong to them as citizens of these United States.

In entering upon the great work before us, we anticipate no small amount of misconception, misrepresentation, and ridicule; but we shall use every instrumentality within our power to effect our object. We shall employ agents, circulate tracts, petition the State and national Legislatures, and endeavor to enlist the pulpit and the press in our behalf. We hope this Convention will be followed by a series of Conventions, embracing every part of the country.

The Resolutions

Whereas, the great precept of nature is conceded to be, "that man shall pursue his own true and substantial happiness," Blackstone, in his Commentaries, remarks, that this law of Nature being coeval with mankind, and dictated by God himself, is of course superior in obligation to any other. It is binding over all the globe, in all countries, and at all times; no human laws are of any validity if contrary to this, and such of them as are valid, derive all their force, and all their validity, and all their authority, mediately and immediately, from this original; Therefore,

Resolved, That such laws as conflict, in any way, with the true and substantial happiness of woman, are contrary to the great precept of nature, and of no validity; for this is "superior in obligation to any other."

Resolved, That all laws which prevent woman from occupying such a station in society as her conscience shall dictate, or which place her in a position inferior to that of man, are contrary to the great precept of nature, and therefore of no force or authority.

Resolved, That woman is man's equal—was intended to be so by the Creator, and the highest good of the race demands that she should be recognized as such.

Resolved, That the women of this country ought to be enlightened in regard to the laws under which they live, that they may no longer publish their degradation, by declaring themselves satisfied with their present position, nor their ignorance, by asserting that they have all the rights they want.

Resolved, That inasmuch as man, while claiming for himself intellectual superiority, does accord to woman moral superiority, it is preeminently his duty to encourage her to speak, and teach, as she has an opportunity, in all religious assemblies.

Resolved, That the same amount of virtue, delicacy, and refinement of behavior, that is required of woman in the social state, should also be required of man, and the same transgressions should be visited with equal severity on both man and woman.

Resolved, That the objection of indelicacy and impropriety, which is so often brought against woman when she addresses a public audience, comes with a very ill grace from those who encourage, by their attendance, her appearance on the stage, in the concert, or in the feats of the circus.

Resolved, That woman has too long rested satisfied in the circumscribed limits which corrupt customs and a perverted application of the Scriptures have marked out for her, and that it is time she should move in the enlarged sphere which her great Creator has assigned her.

Resolved, That it is the duty of the women of this country to secure to themselves their sacred right to the elective franchise.

Resolved, That the equality of human rights results necessarily from the fact of the identity of the race in capabilities and responsibilities.

Resolved, therefore, That, being invested by the Creator with the same capabilities, and the same consciousness of responsibility for their exercise, it is demonstrably the right and duty of woman, equally with man, to promote every righteous cause, by every righteous means; and especially in regard to the great subjects of morals and religion, it is self-evidently her right to participate with her brother in teaching them, both in private and in public, by writing and by speaking, by any instrumentalities proper to be used, and in any assemblies proper to be held; and this being a self-evident truth, growing out of the divinely implanted principles of human nature, any custom or authority adverse to it, whether modern or wearing the hoary sanction of antiquity, is to be regarded as self-evident falsehood, and at war with the interests of mankind.

APPENDIX B

"Solitude of Self," by Elizabeth Cady Stanton

Address Delivered by Mrs. Stanton before the Committee of the Judiciary, U.S. Congress, January 18, 1892[1]

Mr. Chairman and gentlemen of the committee: We have been speaking before Committees of the Judiciary for the last twenty years, and we have gone over all the arguments in favor of a sixteenth amendment which are familiar to all you gentlemen; therefore, it will not be necessary that I should repeat them again.

The point I wish plainly to bring before you on this occasion is the individuality of each human soul; our Protestant idea, the right of individual conscience and judgment—our republican idea, individual citizenship. In discussing the rights of woman, we are to consider, first, what belongs to her as an individual, in a world of her own, the arbiter of her own destiny, an imaginary Robinson Crusoe with her woman Friday on a solitary island. Her rights under such circumstances are to use all her faculties for her own safety and happiness.

Secondly, if we consider her as a citizen, as a member of a great nation, she must have the same rights as all other members, according to the fundamental principles of our Government.

Thirdly, viewed as a woman, an equal factor in civilization, her rights and duties are still the same—individual happiness and development.

Fourthly, it is only the incidental relations of life, such as mother, wife, sister, daughter, that may involve some special duties and training. In the usual discussion in regard to woman's sphere, such as men as Herbert Spencer,

Frederic Harrison, and Grant Allen uniformly subordinate her rights and duties as an individual, as a citizen, as a woman, to the necessities of these incidental relations, some of which a large class of woman may never assume. In discussing the sphere of man we do not decide his rights as an individual, as a citizen, as a man by his duties as a father, a husband, a brother, or a son, relations some of which he may never fill. Moreover he would be better fitted for these very relations and whatever special work he might choose to do to earn his bread by the complete development of all his faculties as an individual.

Just so with woman. The education that will fit her to discharge the duties in the largest sphere of human usefulness will best fit her for whatever special work she may be compelled to do.

The isolation of every human soul and the necessary of self-dependence must give each individual the right, to choose his own surroundings.

The strongest reason for giving woman all the opportunities for higher education, for the full development of her faculties, forces of mind and body; for giving her the most enlarged freedom of thought and action; a complete emancipation from all forms of bondage, of custom, dependence, superstition; from all the crippling influences of fear, is the solitude and personal responsibility of her own individual life. The strongest reason why we ask for woman a voice in the government under which she lives; in the religion she is asked to believe; equality in social life, where she is the chief factor; a place in the trades and professions, where she may earn her bread, is because of her birthright to self-sovereignty; because, as an individual, she must rely on herself. No matter how much women prefer to lean, to be protected and supported, nor how much men desire to have them do so, they must make the voyage of life alone, and for safety in an emergency they must know something of the laws of navigation. To guide our own craft, we must be captain, pilot, engineer; with chart and compass to stand at the wheel; to match the wind and waves and know when to take in the sail, and to read the signs in the firmament over all. It matters not whether the solitary voyager is man or woman.

Nature having endowed them equally, leaves them to their own skill and judgment in the hour of danger, and, if not equal to the occasion, alike they perish.

The [*sic*] appreciate the importance of fitting every human soul for independent action, think for a moment of the immeasurable solitude of self. We come into the world alone, unlike all who have gone before us; we leave it alone under circumstances peculiar to ourselves. No mortal ever has been, nor mortal over [*sic*] will be like the soul just launched on the sea of life. There can never again be just such environments as make up the infancy, youth and manhood of this one. Nature never repeats herself, and the possibilities of one human soul will never be found in another. No one has ever found two blades of ribbon grass alike, and no one will never find two human beings alike. Seeing, then, what must be the infinite diversity in human character, we can in a measure appreciate the loss to a nation when any large class of the people in [*sic*] uneducated and unrepresented in the government. We ask for the complete development of every individual, first, for his own benefit and happiness. In fitting out an army we give each soldier his own knapsack, arms, powder, his blanket, cup, knife, fork and spoon. We provide alike for all their individual necessities, then each man bears his own burden.

Again we ask complete individual development for the general good; for the consensus of the competent on the whole round of human interest; on all questions of national life, and here each man must bear his share of the general burden. It is sad to see how soon friendless children are left to bear their own burdens before they can analise [*sic*] their feelings; before they can even tell their joys and sorrows, they are thrown on their own resources. The great lesson that nature seems to teach us at all ages is self-dependence, self-protection, self-support. What a touching instance of a child's solitude; of that hunger of heart for love and recognition, in the case of the little girl who helped to dress a Christmas tree for the children of the family in which she served. On finding there was no present for herself she slipped away in the darkness and spent the night in an open field sitting on a stone, and when found in the morning was weeping as if her heart would break. No mortal will ever know the thoughts that passed through the mind of that friendless child in the long hours of that cold night, with only the silent stars to keep her company. The mention of her case in the daily papers moved many generous hearts to send her presents, but in the hours of her keenest sufferings she was thrown wholly on herself for consolation.

In youth our most bitter disappointments, our brightest hopes and ambitions are known only to otherwise, even our friendship and love we never fully share with another; there is something of every passion in every situation we conceal. Even so in our triumphs and our defeats.

The successful candidate for Presidency and his opponent each have a solitude peculiarly his own, and good form forbide [*sic*] either in [*sic*] speak of his pleasure or regret. The solitude of the king on his throne and the prisoner in his cell differs in character and degree, but it is solitude nevertheless.

We ask no sympathy from others in the anxiety and agony of a broken friendship or shattered love. When death sunders our nearest ties, alone we sit in the shadows of our affliction. Alike mid the greatest triumphs and darkest tragedies of life we walk along. On the devine [*sic*] heights of human attainments, eulogized land worshiped as a hero or saint, we stand alone. In ignorance, poverty, and vice, as a pauper or criminal, alone we starve or steal; alone we suffer the sneers and rebuffs of our fellows; alone we are hunted and hounded thro dark courts and alleys, in by-ways and highways; alone we stand in the judgment seat; alone in the prison cell we lament our crimes and misfortunes; alone we expiate them on the gallows. In hours like these we realize the awful solitude of individual life, its pains, its penalties, its responsibilities; hours in which the youngest and most helpless are thrown on their own resources for guidance and consolation. Seeing then that life must ever be a march and a battle, that each soldier must be equipped for his own protection, it is the height of cruelty to rob the individual of a single natural right.

To throw obstacle in the way of complete education is like putting out the eyes; to deny the rights of property, like cutting off the hands. To deny political equality is to rob the ostracized of all self-respect; of credit in the market place; of recompense in the world of work; of a voice among those who make and administer the law; a choice in the jury before whom they are tried, and in the judge who decides their punishment. Shakespeare's play of Titus and Andronicus contains a terrible satire on woman's position in the nineteenth century—"Rude men" (the play tells us) "seized the king's daughter, cut out her tongue, out off her hands, and then bade her go call for water and wash her hands." What a picture of woman's position. Robbed of her natural rights, handicapped by law and custom at every turn, yet compelled to fight her own battles, and in the emergencies of life to fall back on herself for protection.

The girl of sixteen, thrown on the world to support herself, to make her own place in society, to resist the temptations that surround her and maintain a spotless integrity, must do all this by native force or superior education. She does not acquire this power by being trained to trust others and distrust herself. If she wearies of the struggle, finding it hard work to swim upstream, and allow herself to drift with the current, she will find plenty of company, but not one to share her misery in the hour of her deepest humiliation. If she tried to retrieve her position, to conceal the past, her life is hedged about with fears last [*sic*] willing hands should tear the view from what she fain would hide. Young and friendless, she knows the bitter solitude of self.

How the little courtesies of life on the surface of society, deemed so important from man towards woman, fade into utter insignificance in view of the deeper tragedies in which she must play her part alone, where no human aid is possible.

The young wife and mother, at the head of some establishment with a kind husband to shield her from the adverse winds of life, with wealth, fortune and position, has a certain harbor of safety, occurs against the ordinary ills of life. But to manage a household, have a desirable influence in society, keep her friends and the affections of her husband, train her children and servants well, she must have rare common sense, wisdom, diplomacy, and a knowledge of human nature. To do all this she needs the cardinal virtues and the strong points of character that the most successful stateman [*sic*] possesses.

An uneducated woman, trained to dependence, with no resources in herself must make a failure of any position in life. But society says women do not need a knowledge of the world, the liberal training that experience in public life must give, all the advantages of collegiate education; but when for the lock [*sic*] of all this, the woman's happiness is wrecked, alone she bears her humiliation;—and the attitude of the weak and the ignorant in [*sic*] indeed pitiful in the wild chase for the price of life they are ground to powder.

In age, when the pleasures of youth are passed, children grown up, married and gone, the hurry and hustle of life in a measure over, when the hands are weary of active service, when the old armchair and the fireside are the chosen resorts, then men and women alike must fall back on their own resources. If they cannot find companionship in books, if they have no interest in the vital questions of the hour, no interest in watching the consummation of reforms, with which they might have been identified, they soon pass into their dotage. The more fully the faculties of the mind are developed and kept in use, the longer the period of vigor and active interest in all around us continues. If from a lifelong participation in public affairs a woman feels responsible for the laws regulating our system of education, the discipline of our jails and prisons, the sanitary conditions of our private homes, public buildings, and thoroughfares, an interest in commerce, finance, our foreign relations, in any or all of these questions, here solitude will at least be respectable, and she will not be driven to gossip or scandal for entertainment.

The chief reason for opening to every soul the doors to the whole round of human duties an [*sic*] pleasures is the individual development thus attained, the resources thus provided under all circumstance to mitigate the solitude that at times must come to everyone. I once asked Prince Krapotkin, the Russian nihilist, how he endured his long years in prison, deprived of books, pen, ink, and paper. "Ah," he said, "I thought out many questions in which I had a deep interest. In the pursuit of an idea I took no note of time. When tired of solving knotty problems I recited all the beautiful passages in prose or verse I have ever learned. I became acquainted with myself and my own resources. I had a world of my own, a vast empire, that no Russian jailor or Czar could invade." Such is the value of liberal thought and broad culture when shut off from all the human companionship, bringing comfort and sunshine within even the four walls of a prison cell.

As women of times share a similar fate, should they not have all the consolation that the most liberal education can give? Their suffering in the prisons of St. Petersburg; in the long, weary marches to Siberia, and in the mines, working side by side with men, surely call for all the self-support that the most exalted sentiments of heroism can give. When suddenly roused at midnight, with the startling cry of "fire! fire!" to find the house over their heads in flames, do women wait for men to point the way to safety? And are the men, equally bewildered and half suffocated with smoke, in a position to more than try to save themselves?

At such times the most timid women have shown a courage and heroism in saving their husbands and children that has surprise [*sic*] everybody. Inasmuch, then, as woman shares equally the joys and sorrows of time and eternity, is it not the height of presumption in man to propose to represent her at the ballot box an [*sic*] the throne of grace, do her voting in the state, her praying in the church, and to assume the position of priest at the family alter [*sic*].

Nothing strengthens the judgment and quickens the conscience like individual responsibility. Nothing adds such dignity to character as the recognition of one's self-sovereignty; the right to an equal place, every where conceded; a place earned by personal merit, not an artificial attainment, by inheritance, wealth, family, and position. Seeing, then that the responsibilities of life rests [*sic*] equally on man and woman, that their destiny is the same, they need the same preparation for time and eternity. The talk of sheltering woman from the fierce sterns [*sic*] of life is the sheerest mockery, for they beat on her from every point of the compass, just as they do on man, and with more fatal results, for he has been trained to protect himself, to resist, to conquer. Such are the facts in human experience, the responsibilities of individual. Rich and poor, intelligent and ignorant, wise and foolish, virtuous and vicious, man and woman, it is ever the same, each soul must depend wholly on itself.

Whatever the theories may be of woman's dependence on man, in the supreme moments of her life he can not bear her burdens. Alone she goes to the gates of death to give life to every man that is born into the world. No one can share her fears, no one mitigate her pangs; and if her sorrow is greater than she can bear, alone she passes beyond the gates into the vast unknown.

From the mountain tops of Judea, long ago, a heavenly voice bade His disciples, "Bear ye one another's burdens," but humanity has not yet risen to that point of self-sacrifice, and if ever so willing, how few the burdens are that one soul can bear for another. In the highways of Palestine; in prayer and fasting on the solitary mountain top; in the Garden of Gethsemane; before the judgment seat of Pilate; betrayed by one of His trusted disciples at His last supper; in His agonies on the cross, even Jesus of Nazareth, in these last sad days on earth, felt the awful solitude of self. Deserted by man, in agony he cries, "My God! My God! Why hast Thou forsaken me?" And so it ever must be in the conflicting scenes of life, on the long weary march, each one walks alone. We may have many friends, love, kindness, sympathy and charity to smooth our pathway in everyday of life, but in the tragedies and triumphs of human experience each moral stands alone.

But when all artificial trammels are removed, and women are recognized as individuals, responsible for their own environments, thoroughly educated for all the positions in life they may be called to fill; with all the resources in themselves that liberal though [*sic*] and broad culture can give; guided by their own conscience and judgment; trained to self-protection by a healthy development of the muscular system and skill in the use of weapons of defense, and stimulated to self-support by the knowledge of the business world and the pleasure that pecuniary independence must ever give; when women are trained in this way they will, in a measure, be fitted for those hours of solitude that come alike to all, whether prepared or otherwise. As in our extremity we must depend on ourselves, the dictates of wisdom point of [*sic*] complete individual development.

In talking of education how shallow the argument that each class must be educated for the special work it proposed to do, and all those faculties not needed in this special walk must lie dormant and utterly wither for want of use, when, perhaps, these will be the very faculties needed in life's greatest emergies [*sic*]. Some say, Where is the use of drilling series in the languages, the Sciences, in law, medicine, theology? As wives, mothers, housekeepers, cooks, they need a different curriculum from boys who are to fill all positions. The chief cooks in our great hotels and ocean steamers are men. In large cities men run the bakeries; they make our bread, cake and pies. They manage the laundries; they are now considered our best milliners and dressmakers. Because some men fill these departments of usefulness, shall we regulate the curriculum in Harvard and Yale to their present necessities? If not why this talk in our best colleges of a curriculum for girls who are crowding into the trades and professions; teachers in all our public schools rapidly hiring many lucrative and honorable positions in life? They are showing too, their calmness and courage in the most trying hours of human experience.

You have probably all read in the daily papers of the terrible storm in the Bay of Biscay when a tidal wave such havoc on the shore, wrecking vessels, unroofing houses and carrying destruction everywhere. Among other buildings the woman's prison was demolished. Those who escaped saw men struggling to reach the shore. They promptly by clasping hands made a chain of themselves and pushed out into the sea, again and again, at the risk of their lives until they had brought six men to shore, carried them to a shelter, and did all in their power for their comfort and protection.

What especial school of training could have prepared these women for this sublime moment of their lives. In times like this humanity rises above all college curriculums and recognizes Nature as the greatest of all teachers in the hour of danger and death. Women are already the equals of men in the whole of ream [*sic*] of thought, in art, science, literature, and government. With telescope vision they explore the starry firmament, and bring back the history of the planetary world. With chart and compass they pilot ships across the mighty deep, and with skillful finger send electric messages around the globe. In galleries of art the beauties of nature and the virtues of humanity are immortalized by them on their canvas and by their inspired touch dull blocks of marble are transformed into angels of light.

In music they speak again the language of Mendelssohn, Beethoven, Chopin, Schumann, and are worthy interpreters of their great thoughts. The poetry and novels of the century are theirs, and they have touched the keynote of reform in religion, politics, and social life. They fill the editor's and professor's chair, and plead at the bar of justice, walk the wards of the hospital, and speak from the pulpit and the platform; such is the type of womanhood that an enlightened public sentiment welcomes today, and such the triumph of the facts of life over the false theories of the past.

Is it, then, consistent to hold the developed woman of this day within the same narrow political limits as the dame with the spinning wheel and knitting needle occupied in the past? No! no! Machinery has taken the labors of woman as well as man on its tireless shoulders; the loom and the spinning wheel are but dreams of the past; the pen, the brush, the easel, the chisel, have taken their places, while the hopes and ambitions of women are essentially changed.

We see reason sufficient in the outer conditions of human being for individual liberty and development, but when we consider the self dependence of every human soul we see the need of courage, judgment, and the exercise of every faculty of mind and body, strengthened and developed by use, in woman as well as man.

Whatever may be said of man's protecting power in ordinary conditions, mid all the terrible disasters by land and sea, in the supreme moments of danger, alone, woman must ever meet the horrors of the situation; the Angel of Death even makes no royal pathway for her. Man's love and sympathy enter only into the sunshine of our lives. In that solemn solitude of self, that links us with the immeasurable and the eternal, each soul lives alone forever. A recent writer says:

I remember once, in crossing the Atlantic, to have gone upon the deck of the ship at midnight, when a dense black cloud enveloped the sky, and the great deep was roaring madly under the lashes of demoniac winds. My feelings was [*sic*] not of danger or fear (which is a base surrender of the immortal soul), but of utter desolation and loneliness; a little speck of life shut in by a tremendous darkness. Again I remember to have climbed the slopes of the Swiss Alps, up beyond the point where vegetation ceases, and the stunted conifers no longer struggle against the unfeeling blasts. Around me lay a huge confusion of rocks, out of which the gigantic ice peaks shot into the measureless blue of the heavens, and again my only feeling was the awful solitude.

And yet, there is a solitude, which each and every one of us has always carried with him, more inaccessible than the ice-cold mountains, more profound than the midnight sea; the solitude of self. Our inner being, which we call ourself, no eye nor touch of man or angel has ever pierced. It is more hidden than the caves of the gnome; the sacred adytum of the oracle; the hidden chamber of eleusinian mystery, for to it only omniscience is permitted to enter.

Such is individual life. Who, I ask you, can take, dare take, on himself the rights, the duties, the responsibilities of another human soul?[1]

Notes

Introduction

1. Susan B. Anthony, "Remarks to the Fiftieth Anniversary of the American Anti-Slavery Society," December 4, 1883, in Elizabeth Cady Stanton and Susan B. Anthony, *Selected Papers of Elizabeth Cady Stanton and Susan B. Anthony,* vol. 4, *When Clowns Make Laws for Queens, 1880 to 1887,* ed. Ann D. Gordon (New Brunswick, N.J.: Rutgers University Press, 2006), 304.
2. Elizabeth Cady Stanton to Frederick Douglass, Johnstown, New York, May 27, 1884, in Stanton and Anthony, *Selected Papers,* 4:353–54.
3. Elizabeth Cady Stanton, "Third Decade Celebration at Rochester, New York," July 19, 1878, and Susan B. Anthony to Margaret Stanton Lawrence, n.p., after January 24, 1880, both in Elizabeth Cady Stanton and Susan B. Anthony, *The Selected Papers of Elizabeth Cady Stanton and Susan B. Anthony,* vol. 3, *National Protection for National Citizens, 1873 to 1880,* ed. Ann D. Gordon (New Brunswick, N.J.: Rutgers University Press, 2003), 387, 526.
4. I made the decision to use the familiar in referring to my four women in part because I have come to know them well and because using their first names make them seem more human.
5. I will be using the terms "women's rights" and "women's movement" throughout the text, although many of the primary sources I cite reflect the common use of "woman's" in the nineteenth century.

Chapter 1

1. Elizabeth Cady Stanton, *Eighty Years and More: Reminiscences 1815–1897* (n.p.: T. Fisher Unwin, 1898; reprint, New York: Schocken Books, 1971), 20.

2. Alice Stone Blackwell, *Lucy Stone: Pioneer of Woman's Rights* (Boston: Little, Brown, 1930; reprint, Charlottesville: University Press of Virginia, 2001), 3. Hannah Stone ultimately bore nine children.

3. Lucy Stone, "Reminiscences," September 1893, Blackwell Family Papers, Library of Congress, Washington, D.C., microfilm; and Joelle Million, *Woman's Voice, Woman's Place: Lucy Stone and the Birth of the Woman's Rights Movement* (London: Praeger, 2003), 6–7.

4. Blackwell, *Lucy Stone*, 9.

5. Harriet Jacobs's account of her experiences is *Incidents in the Life of a Slave Girl*, published in 1861.

6. For an interesting argument on women's secondary status and its relationship to age, see Corinne T. Field, "Are Women ... All Minors? Woman's Rights and the Politics of Aging in Antebellum United States," *Journal of Women's History* 12, no. 4 (2001): 113–37.

7. Field, "Are Women ... All Minors," 114.

8. Julia Cherry Spruill, *Women's Life and Work in the Southern Colonies* (Chapel Hill: University of North Carolina Press, 1938; reprint, New York: Norton, 1972), 263; and Laurel Thatcher Ulrich, *A Midwife's Tale: The Life of Martha Ballard, Based on Her Diary, 1785–1812* (New York: Knopf, 1990).

9. Marylynn Salmon, "Equality of Submersion? *Feme Covert* Status in Early Pennsylvania," in Carol Ruth Berkin and Mary Beth Norton, *Women of America: A History* (Boston: Houghton Mifflin, 1979), 109. The historian Joan Hoff Wilson believes women's legal status was better before 1776 than after. Norma Basch suggests that common law was sometimes stricter for American women than for English women.

10. James Otis, *The Rights of the British Colonies, Asserted and Proved*, 3rd ed. (Boston: J. Williams and J. Almon, 1766), 5, Eighteenth-Century Collections Online, http://galenet.galesgroup.com; Thomas Paine, "An Occasional Letter on the Female Sex," 1775, www.thomaspaine.org/Archives/occ.htm.

11. "Preceding Causes," in Elizabeth Cady Stanton, Susan B. Anthony, and Matilda Joslyn Gage, eds., *History of Woman Suffrage*, vol. 1 (New York: Fowler & Wells, 1881), 31.

12. Abigail Adams to John Adams, Braintree, Massachusetts, March 31, 1776, in Abigail and John Adams, *The Book of Abigail and John: Selected Letters of the Adams Family, 1762–1784*, ed. L. H. Butterfield, Marc Friedlander, and Mary-Jo Kline (Cambridge, Mass.: Harvard University Press, 1975), 121.

13. John Adams to James Sullivan, Philadelphia, May 26, 1776, in John Adams, *Papers of John Adams: February–August 1776*, vol. 4, ed. Robert J. Taylor (Cambridge, Mass.: Harvard University Press, 1979), 211. See also Judith Wellman, "Women's Rights, Republicanism, and Revolutionary Rhetoric in Antebellum New York State," *New York History* 69, no. 3 (July 1988): 353–84.

14. Celia Morris, *Fanny Wright: Rebel in America* (Cambridge, Mass.: Harvard University Press, 1984), 44–45; Harriet Martineau, *Society in America* (1837), http://xroads.virginia.edu/~HYPER/DETOC/fem/martineau.htm; and Alexis de Tocqueville,

Democracy in America, vol. 2, pt. 1 (1835; reprint, New York: Library of America, 2004), 695.

15. Linda K. Kerber, *Women of the Republic: Intellect and Ideology in Revolutionary America* (New York: Norton, 1980).

16. C. R. Carroll, "Woman," *Southern Literary Journal and Monthly Magazine* 3 (1836): 181.

17. Hannah Mather Crocker, *Observations on the Real Rights of Women* (Boston, 1818), 17, 20, in Early American Imprints, ser. 2, "Shaw—Shoemaker, 1801–1910," http://opac.newsbank/com/select/Shaw/43772; Mrs. A. J. Graves, *Woman in America: Being an Examination into the Moral and Intellectual Condition of American Society* (1841), in *Root of Bitterness: Documents of the Social History of American Women*, ed. Nancy F. Cott (New York: Dutton, 1972), 144; and Ella Gertrude Clanton Thomas, "Diary," April 11, 1855, in *The Secret Eye: The Journal of Ella Gertrude Clanton Thomas, 1848–1889*, ed. Virginia Ingraham Burr (Chapel Hill: University of North Carolina Press, 1990), 122. In her later years, after enduring a difficult marriage and much-reduced circumstances compared to her privileged upbringing, Thomas headed the Georgia Woman's Suffrage Association.

18. John S. C. Abbott, *The Mother at Home; or, The Principles of Maternal Duty Familiarly Illustrated* (New York: American Tract Society, 1833), 160, American Memory, Library of Congress, http://memory.loc.gov/cgi-bin/query/r?ammem.

19. "Domestic Duties," *Lady's Book* 12 (January 1836). This magazine later became *Godey's Lady's Book*.

20. *American National Biography*, s.v. "Hale, Sarah Josepha Buell," www.anb.org/articles/home.html; and "Code of Instruction for Ladies," *Lady's Book* 9 (October 1834). See also Mary Kelley, *Learning to Stand and Speak: Women, Education, and Public Life in America's Republic* (Chapel Hill: University of North Carolina Press, 2006), 53, 216.

21. Jane Kamensky, "The Colonial Mosaic, 1600–1760," in *No Small Courage: A History of Women in the United States*, ed. Nancy F. Cott (New York: Oxford University Press, 2000), 79; and Laura Thatcher Ulrich, *Good Wives: Image and Reality in the Lives of Women in Northern New England, 1650–1750* (New York: Oxford University Press, 1983).

22. Million, *Woman's Voice, Woman's Place*, 12.

23. Maria L. Giddings, "Report on the Common Law," in *Proceedings of the Woman's Rights Convention, Akron, Ohio, May 28 and 29, 1851*, American Memory, http://memory.loc.gov/cgi-bin/query/r?ammem/naw. Having been settled first by the Spanish and then the French, Louisiana adopted the Napoleonic Code, which was more generous to women and slaves than was English law. Some female reformers became aware of this exception. At the Akron convention, Giddings noted that a woman in Louisiana "whether married or not, enjoys all these rights and privileges. The wife there manages her own property—makes her own contracts, carries on business in her own name." She concluded, "Our northern statesmen hesitate and refuse to follow so noble an example." When challenging unjust laws, reformers like Elizabeth realized that state laws differed widely.

24. Elizabeth Cady Stanton and Susan B. Anthony, *The Selected Papers of Elizabeth Cady Stanton and Susan B. Anthony*, vol. 1, *In the School of Anti-Slavery 1840 to 1866*, ed. Ann D. Gordon (New Brunswick, N.J.: Rutgers University Press, 1997), 86 n. 13.

25. Antoinette Brown to Lucy Stone, Oberlin, Ohio, September 22, 1847, and Lucy Stone to Antoinette Brown, n.p., August 1849, both in Lucy Stone and Antoinette Brown Blackwell, *Friends and Sisters: Letters between Lucy Stone and Antoinette Brown Blackwell, 1846–1893*, ed. Carol Lasser and Marlene Deahl Merrill (Urbana: University of Illinois Press, 1987), 31, 56.

26. Marylynn Salmon, *Women and the Law of Property in Early America* (Chapel Hill: University of North Carolina Press, 1986), xv–xvi.

27. Thomas E. Buckley, *The Great Catastrophe of My Life: Divorce in the Old Dominion* (Chapel Hill: University of North Carolina Press, 2002), 8.

28. Million, *Woman's Voice, Woman's Place*, 12; and Alice Stone Blackwell, "Mother's Reminiscences," October 1893, Blackwell Family Papers, microfilm.

29. Stanton, *Eighty Years and More*, 32.

30. Buckley, *Great Catastrophe*, 100–101; Susanne Lebsock, *The Free Women of Petersburg: Status and Culture in a Southern Town, 1784–1860* (New York: Norton, 1984), 54–86; and Elizabeth Bowles Warbasse, *The Changing Legal Rights of Married Women, 1800–1861* (New York: Garland, 1987), 222–47.

31. *Proceedings and Debates of the Virginia State Convention of 1829–30* (Richmond: Samuel Shepherd, 1830), in Michael O'Brien, *Conjectures of Order: Intellectual Life and the American South, 1810–1860* (Chapel Hill: University of North Carolina Press, 2004), 1:266.

32. Richard Franklin Bensel, *The American Ballot Box in the Mid-Nineteenth Century* (Cambridge: Cambridge University Press, 2004), 20–22.

33. Caroline Wells Healey Dall, *Daughter of Boston: The Extraordinary Diary of a Nineteenth-Century Woman, Caroline Healey Dall*, ed. Helen R. Deese (Boston: Beacon Press, 2005), 81.

34. Lucy Stone also gave birth, after seven months, to a premature male child in 1859. The baby died either at birth or shortly thereafter.

35. Robert Dale Owen, "Marriage Contract with Mary Jane Robinson, April 2, 1832," in *Against the Tide: Pro-Feminist Men in the United States, 1776–1990: A Documentary History*, ed. Michael S. Kimmel and Thomas E. Mosmiller (Boston: Beacon Press, 1992), 75; Lucretia Mott to Josephine Butler, nr. Philadelphia, April 20, 1869, and Lucretia Mott to James Mott and children, c. June 19, 1849, Auburn, New York, both in Lucretia Coffin Mott, *Selected Letters of Lucretia Coffin Mott*, ed. Beverly Wilson Palmer (Urbana: University of Illinois Press, 2002), 415, 188; and James quoted by Lucy Stone, "The First National Convention," *Woman's Journal*, February 14, 1891.

36. Buckley, *Great Catastrophe*, 77–78.

37. Stanton and Anthony, *Selected Papers*, 1:163 n. 2; and Elizabeth Cady Stanton and Susan B. Anthony, *The Selected Papers of Elizabeth Cady Stanton and Susan B. Anthony*, vol. 2, *Against an Aristocracy of Sex, 1866 to 1873*, ed. Ann D. Gordon (New Brunswick, N.J.: Rutgers University Press, 2000), 246–47 n. 4.

38. Overall, while American women by the mid-nineteenth century were bearing fewer live children, the number of births did not reveal the number of pregnancies they experienced, since miscarriages and stillbirths were common.

39. "Rights of Married Woman," *Richmond Whig*, August 21, 1849, quoted in Buckley, *Great Catastrophe*, 186.

40. Judith Wellman, "Women's Rights, Republicanism, and Revolutionary Rhetoric in Antebellum New York State," *New York History* 69, no. 3 (1988): 371–72; and Warbasse, *Changing Legal Rights,* 100–108.

41. Eleanor Flexner, *Century of Struggle: The Woman's Rights Movement in the United States* (Cambridge, Mass.: Harvard University Press, 1975), 62–70.

42. Thomas Dublin, *Women at Work: The Transformation of Work and Community in Lowell, Massachusetts, 1826 to 1860* (New York: Columbia University Press, 1979), and Dublin, *Transforming Women's Lives: New England Lives in the Industrial Revolution* (Ithaca, N.Y.: Cornell University Press, 1994). See also Catherine Clinton and Christine Lunardini, *The Columbia Guide to American Women in the Nineteenth Century* (New York: Columbia University Press, 2000), 32–35.

43. Judith Sargent Murray, "On the Equality of the Sexes" (1790), www.hurdsmith.com/judith/equality.htm.

44. Mary Wollstonecraft, "Dedication," in *Vindication of the Rights of Woman* (1792), 5, www.bartleby.com/144/101html; Lucretia Mott to Elizabeth Neall Gay, Montgomery County, Pennsylvania, May 7, 1858, and Lucretia Mott to Elizabeth Cady Stanton, Philadelphia, March 16, 1855, both in Mott, *Selected Letters,* 272, 234.

45. Benjamin Rush, "Thoughts upon Female Education" (1787), http://sweb.berry.edu/academic/hass/csnider/berry/hum200/rush.htm. See also Kelley, *Learning to Stand and Speak,* 22; and Kerber, *Women of the Republic,* 210–12.

46. "Woman Physiologically Considered as to Mind, Morals, Marriage, Matrimonial Slavery," *Southern Quarterly Review* 2, no. 4 (1842): 279–99, quotation at 298.

Chapter 2

1. Lucretia Mott, "Addresses," in Paulina W. Davis, comp., *A History of the National Woman's Rights Movement* (New York: Journeymen Printers' Co-Operative Association, 1871), 31.

2. Lucretia Mott, "Proceedings of the AERA," May 1867, in Elizabeth Cady Stanton, Susan B. Anthony, and Matilda Joslyn Gage, *History of Woman Suffrage,* vol. 2 (New York: Fowler & Wells, 1882), 184; and Lucretia Coffin Mott to Elizabeth Cady Stanton, Philadelphia, March 16, 1851, in Lucretia Coffin Mott, *Selected Letters of Lucretia Coffin Mott,* ed. Beverly Wilson Palmer (Urbana: University of Illinois Press, 2002), 234 n. 3. The name of the school derived from the nine men who founded it and made a compact to run it as equal partners. See Otelia Cromwell, *Lucretia Mott* (Cambridge, Mass.: Harvard University Press, 1958), 15.

3. Margaret Hope Bacon, *Valiant Friend: The Life of Lucretia Mott* (New York: Walker, 1980); Dana Greene, "Quaker Feminism: The Case of Lucretia Mott," *Pennsylvania History* 48 (1981): 143–54; and *American National Biography,* s.v. "Mott, Lucretia Coffin," www.anb.org/articles/home.html.

4. Frederick Douglass, *The Life and Times of Frederick Douglass,* in Frederick Douglass, *Autobiographies* (New York: Penguin Books, 1994), 904.

5. Ralph Waldo Emerson, "Man the Reformer" (lecture delivered to the Mechanics' Apprentices' Library Association, Boston, January 25, 1841), in Ralph Waldo Emerson, *Nature: Addresses and Lectures* (New York: Literary Classics of the United States, 1983), 135.

6. Elizabeth Cady Stanton to Daniel Eaton, London, August 18, 1840, Papers of Elizabeth Cady Stanton and Susan B. Anthony, microfilm (Wilmington, Del: Scholarly Resources, 1991). This entire collection on microfilm is found in more than seventy libraries. I read them at Duke University and also at Davidson, thanks to interlibrary loan.

7. C. S. Griffin, *The Ferment of Reform, 1830–1860* (Arlington Heights, Ill.: Harlan Davidson, 1967), 33–45.

8. Frances Trollope, *Domestic Manners of the Americans*, 4th ed. (London: Whittaker, Treacher, 1832), 143–44, American Memory, Library of Congress, http://memory .loc.gov/cgi-bin/query/r?ammem.

9. *American National Biography*, s.v. "Finney, Charles Grandison."

10. *American National Biography*, s.v. "Miller, William"; and Mary A. Bull, "Woman's Rights and Other 'Reforms' in Seneca Falls," ed. Robert Reigel, reprinted in *New York History* 46 (January 1965): 43. Bull misidentified the date as October 14, 1843, but all other sources show October 22, 1844, as the day. No one knows how many people actually believed Miller's predictions, since followers never came together in one place or joined a church. Angelina Grimké Weld was briefly drawn to Miller's ideas during a difficult time in her life.

11. Elizabeth Cady Stanton, *Eighty Years and More: Reminiscences, 1815–1897* (n.p.: T. Fisher Unwin, 1898; reprint, New York: Schocken Books, 1971), 134.

12. Elizabeth Cady Stanton, quoted verbatim in a letter from Lucretia Mott to Richard D. and Hannah Webb, Philadelphia, February 25, 1842, in Mott, *Selected Letters*, 111.

13. Barbara Weisberg, *Talking to the Dead: Kate and Maggie Fox and the Rise of Spiritualism* (San Francisco: HarperCollins, 2004). Late in life, the Fox sisters admitted that their communications with the dead were a fraud.

14. Lucretia Mott to George and Celia Combe, Philadelphia, March 24, 1843, and March 2, 1846, in Mott, *Selected Letters*, 126–29, 137–41; and Bacon, *Valiant Friend*, 67.

15. O. Fowler, professor of phrenology, "Phrenological Character of Mrs. Elizabeth Stanton," January 10, 1853, Papers of Elizabeth Cady Stanton and Susan B. Anthony, microfilm; and Elizabeth Cady Stanton to Daniel Cady, New York, January 12, 1853, in Elizabeth Cady Stanton, *Elizabeth Cady Stanton as Revealed in Her Letters, Diary and Reminiscences*, ed. Theodore Stanton and Harriot Stanton Blatch (New York: Harper, 1922), 2:46–47. The brothers Orson and Lorenzo Fowler set up a successful phrenological practice on Nassau Street in New York City. As curious as phrenology might seem today, these "experts" rightly associated human behavior with the brain. Fowler published the *American Phrenological Journal*.

16. Anne Firor Scott, *Natural Allies: Women's Associations in American History* (Urbana: University of Illinois Press, 1992), 18.

17. Both women were prolific writers. Child was best known for her antislavery book *An Appeal in Favor of That Class of Americans Called Africans,* published in 1833.

Stowe's immensely popular novel *Uncle Tom's Cabin* was published in book form in 1852.

18. Carroll Smith Rosenberg, "Beauty, the Beast and the Militant Woman: A Case Study in Sex Roles and Social Stress in Jacksonian America," *American Quarterly* 23 (1971): 465.

19. *American National Biography*, s.v. "Mann, Horace."

20. Mary Kelley, *Learning to Stand and Speak: Women, Education, and Public Life in America's Republic* (Chapel Hill: University of North Carolina Press, 2006), 66–111.

21. Kathryn Kish Sklar, *Catharine Beecher: A Study in American Domesticity* (New Haven, Conn.: Yale University Press, 1973), and *American National Biography*, s.v. "Beecher, Catharine Esther." Catharine's siblings included Harriet Beecher Stowe, the suffragist and reformer Isabella Beecher Hooker, and the famous minister Henry Ward Beecher, who was also involved in women's rights.

22. Emma Willard, *Mrs. Willard's Plan of Female Education, An Address to the Public, Particularly to the Members of the Legislature of New-York, Proposing a Plan for Improving Female Education* (Middlebury, Vt.: J. W. Copeland, 1819), www.emmawillard.org/academics/library/theplan.php.

23. *American National Biography*, s.v. "Willard, Emma Hart"; and Stanton, *Eighty Years and More*, 37.

24. *American National Biography*, s.v. "Lyon, Mary." Lucy left because her sister Eliza died. She had to help care for her nieces and then decided to remain at home.

25. Ira V. Brown, "The Woman's Rights Movement in Pennsylvania, 1848–1873," *Pennsylvania History* 32, no. 2 (1965): 158. At this stage, Georgia Female College resembled a private female academy, with remedial courses for girls who lacked adequate preparation.

26. Horace Mann, "Dedication of Antioch College and Inaugural Address" (1854), in *Against the Tide: Pro-Feminist Men in the United States, 1776–1990: A Documentary History*, ed. Michael S. Kimmel and Thomas E. Mossmiller (Boston: Beacon Press, 1992), 133–34, quotation at 134.

27. "Lady Orators; or, the Oratress in Mourning," *Godey's Lady's Book* 55 (October 1857): 372.

28. Antoinette Brown, "Comments," in Elizabeth Cady Stanton, Susan B. Anthony, and Matilda Joslyn Gage, eds., *History of Woman Suffrage*, vol. 1 (New York: Fowler & Wells, 1881), 144; Andrea Moore Kerr, *Lucy Stone: Speaking Out for Equality* (New Brunswick, N.J.: Rutgers University Press, 1992), 31; and Lucy Stone to Mr. Thwing, Dorchester, Massachusetts, February 2, 1893, Blackwell Family Papers, Library of Congress, Washington, D.C., microfilm. Only a few coed colleges opened before the Civil War: Genesee College in Lima, New York, founded in 1850; McGrawville College in Cortland County, New York, which admitted students in 1849; and Antioch College in Ohio, which opened in 1854.

29. Lucy Stone Reminiscences, in Joelle Million, *Woman's Voice, Woman's Place: Lucy Stone and the Birth of the Woman's Rights Movement* (London: Praeger, 2003), 38; and Lucy Stone, "Address," *Proceedings of the Woman's Rights Convention, Held at Worcester, October 15, 16, 1851*, American Memory, http://memory.loc.gov/cgi-bin/query/r?ammem/naw.:@field.

30. Lucy Stone and Antoinette Brown Blackwell, *Friends and Sisters: Letters between Lucy Stone and Antoinette Brown Blackwell, 1846–93*, ed. Carol Lasser and Marlene Deahl Merrill (Urbana: University of Illinois Press, 1987), 5; and Million, *Woman's Voice, Woman's Place*, 49–51.

31. Antoinette Brown Blackwell, "Memoir of Lucy Stone, February 10, 1894, Read to the New Jersey State Suffrage Association," Blackwell Family Papers, microfilm. See also Stone and Blackwell, *Friends and Sisters*, 7; and *American National Biography*, s.v. "Blackwell, Antoinette Louisa Brown."

32. Alice Stone Blackwell, *Lucy Stone: Pioneer of Woman's Rights* (Boston: Little, Brown, 1930; reprint, Charlottesville: University Press of Virginia, 2001), 61–62.

33. "Lucy Stone at Oberlin College," James P. McKinney, Letter, *Woman's Journal*, June 14, 1902; and Blackwell, *Lucy Stone*, 63.

34. Stone and Blackwell, *Friends and Sisters*, 7; and Francis Stone to Lucy Stone, Gardner, Massachusetts, January 15, 1845, Blackwell Family Papers, microfilm.

35. "Teacher County License," Washington County, New York, February 25, 1843, Stanton and Anthony Papers, microfilm.

36. Ida Husted Harper, *The Life and Work of Susan B. Anthony* (Indianapolis: Hollenbeck Press, 1898), 1:45, 102; Susan B. Anthony, "Speech," in *Proceedings of the Woman's Rights Convention Held at the Broadway Tabernacle in the City of New York on September 6th and 7th, 1853*, American Memory, http://memory.loc.gov/cgi-bin/query/r?ammem/now:@field; and Betsy M. Cowles, "Report on Labor," in *Proceedings of the Woman's Rights Convention, Held at Akron, Ohio, May 28 and 29, 1851*, American Memory, http://memory.loc.gov/cgi-bin/query/r?ammem/rbnawsa:@field.

37. On the Blackwell family, see Elinor Rice Hays, *Those Extraordinary Blackwells: The Story of a Journey to a Better World* (New York: Harcourt, Brace & World, 1967). "Preceding Causes," in Stanton, Anthony, and Gage, eds., *History of Woman Suffrage*, 1:38. This medical college was the first in the nation to educate female physicians. Gregory's thoughts were contained in his book *Man-Midwifery Exposed and Corrected* (1848).

38. Elizabeth Blackwell to Lucy Stone, New York, June 1, 1854, Blackwell Family Papers, microfilm.

39. W. J. Rorabaugh, *The Alcoholic Republic: An American Tradition* (New York: Oxford University Press, 1979), 8 and table A1.2. Drinking during this period tended to be a male problem rather than a female issue. In polite society, most American women eschewed alcohol. However, medicines were heavily and legally laced with alcohol and drugs, and women often imbibed these to lessen pain or sorrow. Some women became addicted to snuff or to laudanum, an opium derivative.

40. Louise Noun, "Amelia Bloomer: A Biography," pt. 1, *Annals of Iowa* 47, no. 7 (1985): 575–617; Cheryl Schmidt, "Manuscript Collections: The Papers of Amelia Jenks Bloomer and Dexter Bloomer," *Annals of Iowa* 45, no. 2 (1979): 136–37; and *American National Biography*, s.v. "Bloomer, Amelia Jenks."

41. Kathleen Barry, *Susan B. Anthony: A Biography of a Singular Feminist* (New York: New York University Press, 1988), 19; and *American National Biography*, s.v. "Anthony, Susan Brownwell."

42. Elizabeth Cady Stanton and Susan B. Anthony, *The Selected Papers of Elizabeth Cady Stanton and Susan B. Anthony*, vol. 1, *In the School of Anti-Slavery, 1840 to 1866*, ed.

Ann D. Gordon (New Brunswick, N.J.: Rutgers University Press, 1997), xxvii–xxxi; and Susan B. Anthony to Lucy Anthony, Canajoharie, New York, February 17, 1849, Papers of Elizabeth Cady Stanton and Susan B. Anthony, microfilm.

43. Barry, *Susan B. Anthony*, 50–52; *American National Biography*, s.v. "Anthony, Susan B."; and "Susan B. Anthony," in Stanton, *Eighty Years and More*, 172 (quotation).

44. Harper, *Life and Work of Susan B. Anthony*, 1:54, 55.

45. *Lily*, May 1852; Stanton and Anthony, *Selected Papers*, 1: 204–5 n. 5, 204 n. 3. See also J.E.T., "Susan B. Anthony: Her Fight for Woman Suffrage," *New York Times*, March 18, 1906.

46. Lucy Stone to Paulina Wright Davis, Boston, May 20, 1853, *Una*, June 1853; Lucy Stone to Caroline Dall, n.p., May 17, 1853, Caroline Wells Healey Dall Family Papers, Massachusetts Historical Society, Boston; microfilm, Library of Congress, Washington, D.C.; "New York Correspondence," *National Era*, September 22, 1853; and Ian Tyrrell, "Women and Temperance in Antebellum America, 1830–1860," *Civil War History* 28 (1982): 147.

47. Maria W. Stewart, "An Address Delivered at the African Masonic Hall," Boston, February 27, 1833, http://afroamhistory.about.com/library/blmaria_stewart .htm; and Frederick Douglass, "The American Colonization Society," speech delivered at Faneuil Hall, Boston, June 8, 1849, in Frederick Douglass, *The Life and Writings of Frederick Douglass, Early Years, 1817–1849*, ed. Philip Foner (New York: International, 1950), 394.

48. Steven Mintz, *Moralists and Modernizers: America's Pre–Civil War Reformers* (Baltimore: Johns Hopkins University Press, 1995).

49. William Lloyd Garrison, "To the Public," *Liberator*, January 1, 1831; and *American National Biography*, s.v. "Garrison, William Lloyd."

50. A. Cheree Carlson, "Defining Womanhood: Lucretia Coffin Mott and the Transformation of Femininity," *Western Journal of Communication* 58 (Spring 1994): 89.

51. Maria W. Stewart, "An Address Delivered at the African Masonic Hall, Boston," February 27, 1833, and "Farewell Address," September 21, 1833, http:// afroamhistory.about.com/library/blmaria_stewart.htm; and Paula Giddings, *When and Where I Enter: The Impact of Black Women on Race and Sex in America* (New York: Bantam Books, 1985), 49–52.

52. Blanche Glassman Hersh, " 'Am I Not a Woman and a Sister?' Abolitionist Beginnings of Nineteenth-Century Feminism," in *Antislavery Reconsidered: New Perspectives on the Abolitionists*, ed. Lewis Perry and Michael Fellman (Baton Rouge: Louisiana State University Press, 1979), 261; Hersh, *The Slavery of Sex: Feminist-Abolitionists in America* (Urbana: University of Illinois Press, 1978), 13–14; and Stanton, Anthony, and Gage, eds., *History of Woman Suffrage*, 1:325–26. Lucretia Mott attended this meeting and was allowed to speak but not to sign its Declaration of Sentiments.

53. Lucretia Mott, quoted in Bacon, *Valiant Friend*, 187; Lucretia Mott to Phebe Post Willis, Philadelphia, March 1, 1834, in Mott, *Selected Letters*, 21, 24. See also Hersh, *Slavery of Sex*, 13; and Julie Roy Jeffrey, *The Great Silent Army of Abolitionism: Ordinary Women in the Antislavery Movement* (Chapel Hill: University of North Carolina Press, 1998), 44.

54. William Lloyd Garrison to George W. Benson, Brooklyn, New York, September 12, 1835, in William Lloyd Garrison, *The Letters of William Lloyd Garrison,* vol. 1, *I Will Be Heard! 1822–1835,* ed. Walter M. Merrill (Cambridge, Mass.: Harvard University Press, 1971), 527.

55. Angelina Emily Grimké, *An Appeal to the Christian Women of the South* (1836), in Sarah Grimké and Angelina Grimké, *The Public Years of Sarah and Angelina Grimké: Selected Writings, 1835–1839,* ed. Larry Ceplair (New York: Columbia University Press, 1989), 66. See also Gerda Lerner, *The Grimké Sisters from South Carolina: Pioneers for Woman's Rights and Abolition* (New York: Schocken Books, 1971; reprint, New York: Oxford University Press, 1997).

56. Sarah M. Grimké, *An Epistle to the Clergy of the Southern States* (1836), in Grimké and Grimké, *Public Years,* 92, 114.

57. Unidentified New England woman, quoted in Dorothy Sterling, *Ahead of Her Time: Abby Kelley and the Politics of Antislavery* (New York: Norton, 1991), 44.

58. Lucretia Mott, quoting Grimké's resolution to Elizabeth Cady Stanton, Philadelphia, March 16, 1855, in Mott, *Selected Letters,* 233 (first quotation), 236 n. 3 (second quotation); and Hersh, *Slavery of Sex,* 16–17.

59. "Ladies' Convention," *Liberator,* June 2, 1837.

60. Sarah M. Grimké and Angelina E. Grimké to "Clarkson," *Friend of Man,* April 5, 1837; Grimké and Grimké, *Public Years,* 119–21.

61. "Pastoral Letter of the General Association of Massachusetts," in Stanton, Anthony, and Gage, eds., *History of Woman Suffrage,* 1:81; and Sterling, *Ahead of Her Time,* 53.

62. Nancy Isenberg, *Sex and Citizenship in Antebellum America* (Chapel Hill: University of North Carolina Press, 1998), 46–47; and Ellen DuBois, "Women's Rights and Abolition: The Nature of the Connection," in Perry and Fellman, *Antislavery Reconsidered,* 244.

63. Blackwell, *Lucy Stone,* 25.

64. "The International Council," *Woman's Journal,* April 14, 1888; Hersh, *Slavery of Sex,* 20–22; John Greenleaf Whittier to Sarah and Angelina Grimké, New York City, August 14, 1837, in Grimké and Grimké, *Public Years,* 280; and John Greenleaf Whittier, "The Pastoral Letter," in Stanton, Anthony, and Gage, eds., *History of Woman Suffrage,* 1:84–86.

65. Sarah M. Grimké, letter 8, "On the Condition of Women in the United States," in Grimké and Grimké, *Public Years,* 223; letter 6, "Women in Asia and Africa," www.pin.net/~sunshine/book-sum/grimke3.html; letter 7, "Legal Disability of Woman," in Grimké and Grimké, *Public Years,* 231–37; Michael O'Brien, *Conjectures of Order: Intellectual Life and the American South, 1810–1860* (Chapel Hill: University of North Carolina Press, 2004), 1:268–69; and Grimké, letter 14, "Ministry of Women," in Grimké and Grimké, *Public Years,* 260.

66. Sarah M. Grimké, letter 15, "Man Equally Guilty with Woman in the Fall," and letter 8, "On the Condition of Women in the United States," both in Grimké and Grimké, *Public Years,* 272, 225.

67. Nehemiah Adams, "Pastoral Letter to the General Association of Massachusetts Congregational Churches," www.uua.org/uuhs/News/olympia.html; and Lerner, *The Grimké Sisters from South Carolina,* 189–90.

68. T. Gregory Garvey, *Creating the Culture of Reform in Antebellum America* (Athens: University of Georgia Press, 2006), 74–120.

69. Angelina E. Grimké, letter 12, "Human Rights Not Founded on Sex," in Grimké and Grimké, *Public Years*, 190, 195, 202–3.

70. Angelina Grimké to Theodore Weld and John Greenleaf Whittier, Brookline, Massachusetts, August 20, 1837, in *Letters of Theodore Dwight Weld, Angelina Grimké Weld, and Sarah Grimké*, vol. 1, *1822–1844*, ed. Gilbert H. Barnes and Dwight L. Dumond (New York: Appleton-Century, 1934), 429. Angelina's letters appeared a year later in Angelina Grimké, *Letters to Catharine E. Beecher* (Boston: Isaac Knopf, 1838).

71. Sarah and Angelina Grimké to Henry C. Wright, Brookline, Massachusetts, August 27, 1837, and Angelina E. Grimké to Theodore Dwight Weld, Groton, Massachusetts, August 12, 1837, both in *Letters of Weld, Weld, and Grimké*, 1:437, 415; and Angelina E. Grimké, "Speech to a Committee of the Massachusetts House of Representatives, February 21, 1838," in Grimké and Grimké, *Public Years*, 310–12. It is estimated that the sisters spoke to some forty thousand people and attended more than eighty-eight meetings. See Grimké and Grimké, *Public Years*, 141.

72. Angelina E. Grimké to Theodore Dwight Weld, Brookline, Massachusetts, April 29, 1838, in Grimké and Grimké, *Public Years*, 316.

73. Bacon, *Valiant Friend*, 77; Sterling, *Ahead of Her Time*, 62–66; and Angelina Grimké Weld, "Speech at Pennsylvania Hall," Philadelphia, May 16, 1838, in *Women's Rights Emerges within the Antislavery Movement, 1830–1870: A Brief History with Documents*, ed. Kathryn Kish Sklar (New York: St. Martin's, 2000), 153–56.

74. William Lloyd Garrison to Mrs. Sarah T. Benson, Boston, May 19, 1838, in William Lloyd Garrison, *The Letters of William Lloyd Garrison*, vol. 2, *A House Dividing against Itself, 1836–1840*, ed. Louis Ruchames (Cambridge, Mass.: Harvard University Press, 1971), 362–64, quotation at 363; Grimké and Grimké, *Public Years*, 302; Sterling, *Ahead of Her Time*, 63–66; and Lucretia Mott to Edward M. Davis, Philadelphia, June 18, 1838, in Mott, *Selected Letters*, 43.

75. This became an important source for Harriet Beecher Stowe's novel *Uncle Tom's Cabin*.

76. Henry Blackwell to Lucy Stone, Boston, June 21, 1853, in Lucy Stone and Henry B. Blackwell, *Loving Warriors: A Revealing Portrait of an Unprecedented Marriage*, ed. Leslie Wheeler (New York: Dial Press, 1981), 40; and Lucretia Mott to Elizabeth Cady Stanton, Philadelphia, October 3, 1848, in Papers of Elizabeth Cady Stanton and Susan B. Anthony, microfilm. Blackwell wrote his comments while wooing Lucy Stone. He used the Grimké-Weld marriage to contrast it with his more liberal views on what he hoped would be marriage with Lucy.

77. Stanton, Anthony, and Gage, eds., *History of Woman Suffrage*, 1:63. See also Hersh, "'Am I Not a Woman and a Sister?'" 270. This split helped women in the abolition movement. After the elimination of men who opposed female participation, Kelley and other female abolitionists could participate as full members. Lucretia Mott, Lydia Maria Child, and Maria Chapman became members of the Society's executive committee.

78. Susan B. Anthony, "On the Campaign for Divorce Law Reform," 1860. See About: Women's History, http://womenshistory.about.com/cs/quotes/a/ qu_s_b_anthony.htm.

Chapter 3

1. The female delegates who attended the 1840 London Anti-Slavery Convention were Lucretia Mott, from the American Anti-Slavery Society; Sarah Pugh, Abby Kimber, Elizabeth Neal, and Mary Grew, from the Philadelphia Female Anti-Slavery Society; and Ann Green Phillips, Emily Winslow, and Abby Southwick, from the Massachusetts Female Anti-Slavery Society. See Elizabeth Cady Stanton, Susan B. Anthony, and Matilda Joslyn Gage, eds., *History of Woman Suffrage*, vol. 1 (New York: Fowler & Wells, 1881), 54.
2. William Lloyd Garrison to Helen E. Garrison, New York, May 19, 1840, in William Lloyd Garrison, *The Letters of William Lloyd Garrison*, vol. 2, *A House Dividing against Itself, 1836–1840*, ed. Louis Ruchames (Cambridge, Mass.: Harvard University Press, 1971), 616.
3. Elizabeth Cady Stanton to Sarah and Angelina Grimké, London, June 25, 1840, Papers of Elizabeth Cady Stanton and Susan B. Anthony, microfilm (Wilmington, Del.: Scholarly Resources, 1991).
4. *American National Biography*, s.v. "Phillips, Wendell," www.anb.org/articles/index .html; and Irving H. Bartlett, *Wendell and Ann Phillips: The Community of Reform, 1840– 1880* (New York: Norton, 1979), 24.
5. James Brewer Stewart, *Wendell Phillips: Liberty's Hero* (Baton Rouge: Louisiana State University Press, 1986), 84–96.
6. Bartlett, *Wendell and Ann Phillips*, 28; and Wendell Phillips and George Bradburn, "Speeches at the World Anti-slavery Convention," in Stanton, Anthony, and Gage, eds., *History of Woman Suffrage*, 1:55, 56.
7. Henry Grew, "Speeches at the World Anti-slavery Convention," in Stanton, Anthony, and Gage, eds., *History of Woman Suffrage*, 1:55. See also The Rev. A. Harvey and Captain Wanchope, "Speeches at the World Anti-slavery Convention," *HWS* 1:59 and Blanche Glassman Hersh, "'Am I Not a Woman and a Sister?' Abolitionist Beginnings of Nineteenth-Century Feminism," in *Antislavery Reconsidered: New Perspectives on the Abolitionists*, ed. Lewis Perry and Michael Fellman (Baton Rouge: Louisiana State University Press, 1979), 275.
8. William Lloyd Garrison to Helen E. Garrison, London, June 29, 1840, in Garrison, *Letters of Garrison*, 2:654; and Lucretia Mott to her children, London, June 14, 1840, in "The Seneca Falls and Rochester Conventions," Department of Rare Books and Special Collections, University of Rochester Library, 1995 exhibition to commemorate the seventy-fifth anniversary of the passage of the Nineteenth Amendment, www.lib.rochester.edu/rbk/women/women.htm. See also Ira V. Brown, "The Woman's Rights Movement in Pennsylvania," *Pennsylvania History* 32, no. 2 (1965): 155.

9. Mott quotation in Margaret Hope Bacon, *Valiant Friend: The Life of Lucretia Mott* (New York: Walker, 1980), 93; and Lucretia Mott, "Comments," in *The Proceedings of the Woman's Rights Convention, Held at West Chester, Pennsylvania, June 2d and 3d, 1852* (Philadelphia: Merrihew and Thompson, 1852), American Memory, Library of Congress, http://memory.loc.gov/cgi-bin/query/r?ammem/rbnawsa.

10. Elizabeth Cady Stanton to Susan B. Anthony, Seneca Falls, New York, April 2, 1852, Papers of Elizabeth Cady Stanton and Susan B. Anthony, microfilm; and "The World's Anti-slavery Convention, London, June 12, 1840," in Stanton, Anthony, and Gage, eds., *History of Woman Suffrage*, 1:60, 61.

11. Sarah M. Grimké to Elizabeth Pease, December 20, 1840, in Sarah Grimké and Angelina Grimké, *The Public Years of Sarah and Angelina Grimké: Selected Writings, 1835–1839*, ed. Larry Ceplair (New York: Columbia University Press, 1989), 352.

12. Elizabeth Cady Stanton, "On the Social, Educational, Religious and Political Position of Woman in America," June 25, 1883, in Elizabeth Cady Stanton and Susan B. Anthony, *The Selected Papers of Elizabeth Cady Stanton and Susan B. Anthony*, vol. 4, *When Clowns Make Laws for Queens, 1880 to 1887*, ed. Ann D. Gordon (New Brunswick, N.J.: Rutgers University Press, 2006), 246–47; William Lloyd Garrison to Helen E. Garrison, London, June 29, 1840, in Garrison, *Letters of Garrison*, 2:655; and Elisabeth Griffith, *In Her Own Right: The Life of Elizabeth Cady Stanton* (New York: Oxford University Press, 1984), 23–34. Elizabeth described Edward Bayard with warmth and affection in her memoir, commenting that Tryphena and Edward acted as "counselors and advisors" to the Cady siblings. She called him a "great favorite in the family." See Elizabeth Cady Stanton, *Eighty Years and More: Reminiscences, 1815–1897* (n.p.: T. Fisher Unwin, 1898; reprint, New York: Schocken Books, 1971), 27.

13. "Memorial Service for Lucretia Coffin Mott," in Stanton and Anthony, *Selected Papers*, 4:37; Elizabeth Cady Stanton to Sarah and Angelina Grimké, London, June 25, 1840, Papers of Elizabeth Cady Stanton and Susan B. Anthony, microfilm; Lucretia Mott to Richard D. and Hannah Webb, Philadelphia, April 2, 1841, in Lucretia Coffin Mott, *Selected Letters of Lucretia Coffin Mott*, ed. Beverly Wilson Palmer (Urbana: University of Illinois Press, 2002), 93; Elizabeth Cady Stanton to Elizabeth Johns Neall, Johnstown, New York, November 26, 1841, Papers of Elizabeth Cady Stanton and Susan B. Anthony, microfilm; and Lucretia Mott to Richard D. and Hannah Webb, Philadelphia, February 25, 1842, in Mott, *Selected Letters*, 111. In the letter, Mott quotes Stanton verbatim in a letter she had written to her friend Elizabeth J. Neal.

14. Margaret Fuller, *Woman in the Nineteenth Century and Other Writings*, ed. Donna Dickenson (Oxford: Oxford University Press, 1994); and *American National Biography*, s.v. "Fuller, Margaret."

15. Lydia Maria Child to Louisa Loring, New York, February 8, 1845, in Lydia Maria Child, *Lydia Maria Child: Selected Letters, 1817–1880*, ed. Milton Meltzer and Patricia G. Holland (Amherst: University of Massachusetts Press, 1982), 219; Fuller, *Woman in the Nineteenth Century*, 61; and Fuller, *Woman in the Nineteenth Century*, pt. 3, pt. 1, www.vcu.edu/engweb/transcendentalism/authors/fuller. It is interesting

that someone who held strong views on women's independence would marry, though Fuller was hardly alone in that respect among nineteenth-century women reformers. For a thorough understanding of the life of Fuller—and her marriage—see Charles Capper, *Margaret Fuller: An American Romantic Life,* vol. 1, *The Private Years* (New York: Oxford University Press, 1994) and vol. 2, *The Public Years* (New York: Oxford University Press, 2007).

16. Elizabeth Cady Stanton and Susan B. Anthony, *The Selected Papers of Elizabeth Cady Stanton and Susan B. Anthony,* vol. 1, *In the School of Anti-Slavery, 1840 to 1866,* ed. Ann D. Gordon (New Brunswick, N.J.: Rutgers University Press, 1997), 86 n. 13.

17. Donald Yacovone, *Samuel Joseph May and the Dilemmas of the Liberal Persuasion* (Philadelphia: Temple University Press, 1991), 120–21; *American National Biography,* s.v. "May, Samuel Joseph"; and "Samuel Joseph May," www.mmuus.org/who-we-are/history/sjmay.html.

18. Samuel J. May, "The Rights and Condition of Women" (Syracuse, N.Y.: Stoddard & Babcock, 1846), American Memory, http://memory.loc.gov/cgi-bin/query/r?ammem/rbnawsa.

19. Judith Wellman, *The Road to Seneca Falls: Elizabeth Cady Stanton and the First Woman's Rights Convention* (Urbana: University of Illinois Press, 2004), 147–49; and Lori D. Ginzberg, *Untidy Origins: A Story of Woman's Rights in Antebellum New York* (Chapel Hill: University of North Carolina Press, 2005), 147–54.

20. Ginzberg, *Untidy Origins,* xvi–xvii. The six women were Eleanor Vincent, Lydia A. Williams, Lydia Osborn, Susan Ormsby, Amy Ormsby, and Anna Bishop. Future research may reveal similar acts at the local level.

21. Sarah Stone Lawrence to Lucy Stone, n.p., November 28, 1846 and March 28, 1847, Brookfield, Massachusetts, both in Blackwell Family Papers, Library of Congress, Washington, D.C., microfilm. Lucy's brothers were more supportive of her dreams and belief in women's rights.

22. Lucy Stone, "The International Council," extemporaneous speech, *Woman's Journal,* April 14, 1888. Hiram Powers's famous statue (1841) was on display in the Boston Common.

23. Brown, "Woman's Rights Movement in Pennsylvania,"155–56. It is interesting that Stanton lived in New York and Mott in Pennsylvania where these laws passed.

24. Stanton, *Eighty Years and More,* 82–83; and Lucretia Mott to Elizabeth Cady Stanton, Philadelphia, March 16, 1855, in Mott, *Selected Letters,* 236.

25. Wellman, *Road to Seneca Falls,* 65–87. I am grateful to Jack Shay, formerly a U.S. Department of the Interior interpreter at the National Woman's Rights Museum, Seneca Falls, for sharing his wealth of knowledge with an on-site, personal tour of Stanton's house.

26. Wellman, *Road to Seneca Falls,* 123–24, 108–19, and Jack Shay, tour.

27. Wellman, *Road to Seneca Falls,* 114–15, 84–86.

28. Mary A. Bull, "Woman's Rights and Other 'Reforms' in Seneca Falls," ed. Robert Reigel, reprinted in *New York History* 46 (January 1965): 45; and Wellman, *Road to Seneca Falls,* 128–29.

29. It may be that Mary Ann M'Clintock's two oldest daughters, Mary Ann and Elizabeth, were also there, but most sources state that only the five women were present.

30. Handwritten deed by Daniel Cady, June 23, 1847, Stanton and Anthony Papers, microfilm. Elizabeth worried that Henry might not be happy living in Seneca Falls, sensing he would miss the bustle of Boston. As it turned out, Elizabeth probably had more trouble adjusting, since Henry often left town to pursue political and reform activities.

31. Stanton, *Eighty Years and More,* 144–48, quotation at 147–48; "Elizabeth Cady Stanton," Women's Rights National History Project, www.cr.nps.gov/history/online_books/wori/shs3.htm; and Wellman, *Road to Seneca Falls,* 157–69.

32. Stanton, *Eighty Years and More,* 145.

33. Stanton, *Eighty Years and More,* 148.

34. Martha Coffin Wright to Lucretia Mott, October 1, 1848, quoted in Sherry H. Penney and James D. Livingston, *A Very Dangerous Woman: Martha Wright and Women's Rights* (Amherst: University of Massachusetts Press, 2004), 52, 54, 68, 2 (quotation).

35. "Quaker Influence," available at the website of the Women's Rights National Historical Park, www.nps.gov/wori/historyculture/quaker-influence.htm. According to this article, only weeks before the Seneca Falls Convention, the Hunts and M'Clintocks were among two hundred Friends (Quakers) who formed a more radical branch, the Progressive Friends. See also "Women in the Abolitionist Movement in Seneca County," in Judith Wellman, *Discovering the Underground Railroad, Abolitionism and African American Life in Seneca County, New York, 1820–1880,* (Waterloo, N.Y.: Seneca County Historian's Office, 2005–6); and Andrea Constantine Hawkes, "The Life of Elizabeth M'Clintock Phillips, 1821–1896: A Story of Family, Friends, and Community and a Self-Made Woman" (Ph.D. diss., University of Maine, 2005)

36. "Seneca Falls Convention," in Stanton, Anthony, and Gage, eds., *History of Woman Suffrage,* 1:67. For information on the Wesleyan Chapel, see "The Convention in Wesleyan Chapel," available at the website of the Women's Rights National History Project, www.cr.nps.gov/history/online_books/shs2.htm.

37. Stanton, Anthony, and Gage, eds., *History of Woman Suffrage,* 1:68–69, quotation at 68.

38. Lucretia Mott to Elizabeth Cady Stanton, Auburn, New York, July 16, 1848, in Mott, *Selected Letters,* 163. This mahogany table is in storage at the Smithsonian Institution in Washington, D.C. No one ever verified which of the three women suggested the Declaration of Independence as their model.

39. Lucretia Mott to Elizabeth Cady Stanton, Auburn, New York, July 16, 1848, in Mott, *Selected Letters,* 163.

40. Rheta Childe Dorr, *Susan B. Anthony: The Woman Who Changed the Mind of a Nation* (New York: Frederick A. Stokes, 1928), 48. Dorr was able to interview Woodward.

41. Bull, "Woman's Rights and Other 'Reforms,'" 48; Laura Curtis Bullard, "Elizabeth Cady Stanton," in *Our Famous Women: An Authorized Record of the Lives and Deeds of Distinguished American Women of Our Times,* ed. Elizabeth Stuart Phelps

Ward (n.p.: n.p., 1883; reprint, Freeport, N.Y.: Books for Libraries Press, 1975), 613; and "Seneca Falls Convention," in Stanton, Anthony, and Gage, eds., *History of Woman Suffrage*, 1:69. These handwritten notes of the proceedings have never been found.

42. Elizabeth Cady Stanton, "Address," in *Report of the Woman's Rights Convention, Held at Seneca Falls N.Y., July 19 and 20, 1848* (Rochester, N.Y.: John Dick, 1848), 6; Bull, "Woman's Rights and Other 'Reforms,'" 50; and *The First Convention Ever Called to Discuss the Civil and Political Rights of Woman; Seneca Falls, NY, July 19, 20, 1848*, 6, 7, in Elizabeth Cady Stanton and Susan B. Anthony, The Papers of Elizabeth Cady Stanton and Susan B. Anthony, microfilm (Wilmington, Del.: Scholarly Resources, 1991).

43. *First Convention Ever Called*, 7.

44. "Hints for Wives," *North Star*, in Sherry H. Penney and James D. Livingston, "Getting to the Source; Hints for Wives—and Husbands," *Journal of Women's History* 15 (summer 2003): 181–82; and E. W. Capron, quoted in Stanton and Anthony, *Selected Papers*, 1:84 n. 7. None of the speeches from the Convention were recorded or have survived, so we have no sense of everything the audience heard.

45. Bullard, "Elizabeth Cady Stanton," 613–14. Henry lectured in Canandaigua, New York. This may have been scheduled well in advance of the Convention, or Henry may have used it as an excuse to leave. See Wellman, *Road to Seneca Falls*, 277 n. 30.

46. Quoted in Harriot Stanton Blatch, *Challenging Years: The Memoirs of Harriot Stanton Blatch* (New York: Putnam, 1940), 106.

47. Frederick Douglass, *Narrative of the Life of Frederick Douglass, an American Slave* (Boston: Anti-Slavery Office, 1845; reprint, New York: Penguin Classics, 1986); and *American National Biography*, s.v. "Douglass, Frederick."

48. Frederick Douglass, speech at the 1888 International Woman's Convention, in Waldo E. Martin, Jr., *The Mind of Frederick Douglass* (Chapel Hill: University of North Carolina Press, 1984), 148; *Report of the Woman's Rights Convention, Held at Seneca Falls*, 11; Frederick Douglass, *The Life and Times of Frederick Douglass*, in Frederick Douglass, *Autobiographies* (New York: Penguin Books, 1994), 907; and Frederick Douglass, speech at the 1888 International Council of Women, in Frederick Douglass, *Frederick Douglass on Women's Rights*, ed. Philip S. Foner (Westport, Conn.: Greenwood Press, 1976), 14.

49. *Report of the Woman's Rights Convention, Held at Seneca Falls*, 12.

50. Wellman, *Road to Seneca Falls*, 231–32.

51. "The Rights of Women," *North Star*, July 28, 1848; and Stanton, *Eighty Years and More*, 149.

52. *Proceedings of the Woman's Rights Convention, Held at the Unitarian Church, Rochester, NY, August 2, 1848*, revised by Mrs. Amy Post (New York: Robert J. Johnston, 1870), title page; and Lucretia Mott to Thomas and Mary Ann M'Clintock, Auburn, New York, July 29, 1848, in Mott, *Selected Letters*, 164.

53. "The Syracuse Convention," in Department of Rare Books and Special Collections, University of Rochester Library, 1995 exhibition to commemorate the

seventy-fifth anniversary of the passage of the Nineteenth Amendment, www
.lib.rochester.edu/index.cfm?page=1800#syracuse; and Elizabeth Cady Stanton to
Amy Kirby Post, Grassmere, Seneca Falls, New York, September 24, 1848,
Stanton and Anthony Papers, microfilm. Little is known of Abigail Bush. She was
born around 1810 and, with her husband, became involved in antislavery activities through the Western New York Anti-Slavery Society. Chairing the 1848
Rochester meeting was her claim to fame. Her husband went to California
to seek his fortune in gold, and by the early 1850s, the Bush family had moved
there. See www.winningthevote.org./ABush.htm.

54. "The Rochester Convention, August 2, 1848," in Stanton, Anthony, and Gage,
eds., *History of Woman Suffrage*, 1:77; and Lucretia Mott and Maria Weston Chapman, "The Times That Try Men's Souls," in *Proceedings of the Woman's Rights
Convention, Held at the Unitarian Church, Rochester, NY*, 11, 12–13. See also *Rochester
Daily Advocate*, August 3, 1848.

55. Mr. Colton and Lucretia Mott, in *Proceedings of the Woman's Rights Convention, Held at
the Unitarian Church, Rochester, NY*, 5.

56. "Woman's Rights Convention," *North Star*, August 11, 1848; and *Rochester Daily
Advocate*, August 3, 1848.

57. Elizabeth Cady Stanton to Amy Kirby Post, Grassmere, Seneca Falls, New York,
September 24, 1848, Stanton and Anthony Papers, microfilm.

58. *Rochester Daily Advocate*, August 3, 1848.

59. "The Rights of Women," *North Star*, July 28, 1848; and "Woman's Rights Convention," *National Reformer*, August 3, 1848. The *Reformer*, because it had little
confidence in any elected officials, admitted that its comment on female speakers
seemed like "faint praise."

60. "Woman's Rights Convention," *Seneca County Courier*, July 21, 1848.

61. Wellman, *Road to Seneca Falls*, 210, citing Timothy Terpstra, "The 1848 Seneca
Falls Woman's Rights Convention" (master's thesis, University of Mississippi,
1975).

62. Stanton, *Eighty Years and More*, 149.

63. "Women Out of Their Latitude," *Albany (NY) Mechanics Advocate*; "The Women
of Philadelphia," *Philadelphia Public Ledger and Daily Transcript*; and "Woman's
Rights Convention," *New York Herald*, all in Stanton, Anthony, and Gage,
eds., *History of Woman Suffrage*, 1:802, 804, 805; *Syracuse Recorder*, August 3, 1848;
and *Oneida Whig*, August 1, 1848.

64. Terpstra, "The 1848 Seneca Falls Woman's Rights Convention"; Nancy A. Hewitt,
"Seneca Falls, Suffrage and the South: Remapping the Landscape of Women's
Rights in America, 1835–1965," unpublished paper. I thank Nancy Hewitt for a
copy of her essay.

65. Dana was the father of Richard Henry Dana, Jr., who wrote *Two Years before the
Mast*. No copy of his speech exists.

66. Lucretia Coffin Mott, "Discourse on Woman, 1849," in Karlyn Kohrs Campbell,
ed., *Man Cannot Speak for Her: Key Texts of the Early Feminists* (Westport, Conn.:
Greenwood Press, 1989), 2:71–97, quotation at 74; A. Cheree Carlson, "Defining
Womanhood: Lucretia Coffin Mott and the Transformation of Femininity,"

Western Journal of Communication 58 (spring 1994): 85–97; Stanton and Anthony, *Selected Papers,* 1:168–69 n. 4; and Bacon, *Valiant Friend,* 134–36.

67. Elizabeth Blackwell to Mrs. Emily Collins, Philadelphia, August 12, 1848, in Stanton, Anthony, and Gage, eds., *History of Woman Suffrage,* 1:90; and Elizabeth Blackwell to Henry Blackwell, September 17, 1853, in Andrea Moore Kerr, *Lucy Stone: Speaking Out for Equality* (New Brunswick, N.J.: Rutgers University Press, 1992), 79.

68. Barbara Anne White, *The Beecher Sisters* (New Haven, Conn.: Yale University Press, 2003), 74–75.

69. "Address by ECS on Woman's Rights," September 1848, in Stanton and Anthony, *Selected Papers,* 1:94. Stanton later wrote in the margin of that speech: "I give this manuscript to my precious daughters, in the hope that they will finish the work which I have begun." Wellman, *Road to Seneca Falls,* 214.

70. Lucretia Mott to Elizabeth Cady Stanton, Philadelphia, October 3, 1848, and Paulina Wright to Elizabeth Cady Stanton, Philadelphia, September 19, 1848, both in The Papers of Elizabeth Cady Stanton and Susan B. Anthony, microfilm.

71. Mott, *Selected Letters,* xxv; Lucretia Mott to Edmund Quincy, Philadelphia, August 24, 1848, in Mott, *Selected Letters,* 166; and Stanton, Anthony, and Gage, eds., *History of Woman Suffrage,* 1:68.

72. Elizabeth Cady Stanton and Susan B. Anthony, *The Selected Papers of Elizabeth Cady Stanton and Susan B. Anthony,* vol. 2, *Against an Aristocracy of Sex, 1866 to 1873,* ed. Ann D. Gordon (New Brunswick, N.J.: Rutgers University Press, 2000), 424 n. 14; and "Catharine A. F. Stebbins," http://winningthevote.org/CStebbins.html.

73. Emily Collins, "Reminiscences," in Stanton, Anthony, and Gage, eds., *History of Woman Suffrage,* 1:88–95, quotation at 88. In 1879, in part because of the work of women like Collins, Louisiana gave women the right to vote and hold office for school board (94).

Chapter 4

1. *Report of the Woman's Rights Convention, Held at Seneca Falls, N.Y., July 19 and 20, 1848* (Rochester, N.Y.: John Dick, 1848), 10; and *The First Convention Ever Called to Discuss the Civil and Political Rights of Women, Seneca Falls, N.Y., July 19, 20, 1848* in Papers of Elizabeth Cady Stanton and Susan B. Anthony, microfilm (Wilmington, Del.: Scholarly Resources, 1991).

2. Elizabeth Cady Stanton, "Letters to the Convention," in *Proceedings of the Ohio Women's Convention, Held at Salem, April 19th and 20th, 1850* (Cleveland: Smead & Cowles, 1850), 15, 18, Papers of Elizabeth Cady Stanton and Susan B. Anthony, microfilm.

3. Antoinette Brown to Lucy Stone, Rochester, New York, April 14, 1852, in Lucy Stone and Antoinette Brown Blackwell, *Friends and Sisters: Letters between Lucy Stone and Antoinette Brown Blackwell, 1846–1893,* ed. Carol Lasser and Marlene Deahl Merrill (Urbana: University of Illinois Press, 1987), 114.

4. *American National Biography,* s.v. "Davis, Paulina Kellogg Wright," www.anb.org/articles/index.html; and "Paulina Kellogg Wright Davis," available at the website of

the National Women's Hall of Fame, www.greatwoman.org/home.php. For the comment on her manikin, see "Addresses," in *Report of the Proceedings of the Twentieth Anniversary of the National Woman's Rights Movement, Apollo Hall, 1870,* American Memory, Library of Congress, http://memory.bc.gov/ammemory/browse/.

5. "Rights of Woman," *Liberator,* September 6, 1850; and Paulina Wright Davis to Elizabeth Cady Stanton, Providence, Rhode Island, July 7, 1850, Papers of Elizabeth Cady Stanton and Susan B. Anthony, microfilm. Some historians call the Worcester convention the event that initiated a nationwide effort to address women's rights. Davis, who played a leadership role there and again in 1851, called this meeting the most important one in the women's rights struggle. Other female reformers heralded Seneca Falls as the starting point.

6. "Speech of Paulina Wright Davis," in *The Proceedings of the Woman's Rights Convention, Held at Worcester, October 23rd & 24th, 1850* (Boston: Prentiss & Sawyer, 1851).

7. Joelle Million, *Woman's Voice, Woman's Place: Lucy Stone and the Birth of the Woman's Rights Movement* (London: Praeger, 2003), 107–8; "Newspaper Accounts of the 1850 Convention," and "Woman's Rights Convention at Worcester, Mass.," *New York Daily Tribune,* October 25, 1850, www.assumption.edu/whw/old/ newspaper%20accounts_htm.

8. "Woman's Rights Convention," *New York Herald,* October 25, 1850, and "Women's Rights Convention," *New York Daily Tribune,* October 24, 1850, in Worcester Women's History Project, www.assumption.edu/whw/old/on-line %20archive.html. See also John F. Clymer, *This High and Holy Moment: The First National Woman's Rights Convention, Worcester, 1850* (Fort Worth, Tex.: Harcourt Brace, 1999).

9. *Proceedings of the Woman's Rights Convention, Held at Worcester, October 23rd & 24th, 1850.*

10. Alice Stone Blackwell, *Lucy Stone: Pioneer of Woman's Rights* (Boston: Little, Brown, 1930; reprint, Charlottesville: University Press of Virginia, 2001), 98; Andrea Moore Kerr, *Lucy Stone: Speaking Out for Equality* (New Brunswick, N.J.: Rutgers University Press, 1992), 59–60; and Million, *Woman's Voice, Woman's Place,* 105–6.

11. "Worcester Convention," in Elizabeth Cady Stanton, Susan B. Anthony, and Matilda Joslyn Gage, eds., *History of Woman Suffrage,* vol. 1 (New York: Fowler & Wells, 1881), 222–26; and Dorothy Sterling, *Ahead of Her Time: Abby Kelley and the Politics of Antislavery* (New York: Norton, 1991), 264–65, 267. Harriot Hunt was a practicing physician, although she never attended medical school but trained as an apprentice—quite common at the time.

12. Elizabeth Cady Stanton, *Eighty Years and More: Reminiscences 1815–1897* (n.p.: T. Fisher Unwin, 1898; reprint, New York: Schocken Books, 1971), 163; and editor's note, Elizabeth Cady Stanton and Susan B. Anthony, *The Selected Papers of Elizabeth Cady Stanton and Susan B. Anthony,* vol. 1, *In the School of Anti-Slavery, 1840 to 1866,* ed. Ann D. Gordon (New Brunswick, N.J.: Rutgers University Press, 1997), 182–83.

13. Elizabeth Cady Stanton to Susan B. Anthony, Seneca Falls, August 20 [?], 1857, in Stanton and Anthony, *Selected Papers,* 1:351; Elisabeth Griffith, *In Her Own Right: The Life of Elizabeth Cady Stanton* (New York: Oxford University Press, 1984), 74; Harriot Stanton Blatch, *Challenging Years: The Memoirs of Harriot Stanton*

Blatch (New York: Putnam, 1940), 15; Kathleen Barry, *Susan B. Anthony: A Biography of a Singular Feminist* (New York: New York University Press, 1988), 64–65; and Stanton quotation, in Stanton, Anthony, and Gage, eds., *History of Woman Suffrage*, 1:459. Perhaps indicative of their relationship and class issues was Susan addressing Elizabeth as "Mrs. Stanton" in her letters and Elizabeth using "Susan" when writing to her.

14. Paulina Wright Davis, "Address to 1851 Convention, Worcester," Worcester Women's History Project, www.assumption.edu/whw/old/Davis_1851_Address.html.

15. "Woman's Rights Convention," *North Star*, October 9, 1851; Abby Kelley Foster, "Speech to 1851 Convention," www.assumption.edu/whw/old/AKFoster_1851-speech; and Lucy Stone, "The First National Convention," *Woman's Journal*, February 14, 1891.

16. Abby H. Price, "Address," in *Proceedings of the 1850 Woman's Rights Convention*, October 23, 1850, www.assumption.edu/whw/old/Proceedings.htm; Lucretia Mott to Martha Coffin Wright, road side, July 6, 1858, in Lucretia Mott, *Selected Letters of Lucretia Coffin Mott*, ed. Beverly Wilson Palmer (Urbana: University of Illinois Press, 2002), 274–75 and 277 n. 2; Martha Coffin Wright to Susan B. Anthony, Auburn, New York, June 8, 1858, in Stanton and Anthony, *Selected Papers*, 1:372–73; and "News of the Day," *New York Times*, May 14, 1858. Andrews's comments do not appear in the convention report in Stanton, Anthony, and Gage, eds., *History of Woman Suffrage*.

17. "National Convention at Cincinnati, Ohio," in Stanton, Anthony, and Gage, eds., *History of Woman Suffrage*, 1:164–65; and Kerr, *Lucy Stone*, 90. See also Ellen DuBois, "Women's Rights and Abolition: The Nature of the Connection," in Lewis Perry and Michael Fellman, eds., *Antislavery Reconsidered: New Perspectives on the Abolitionists* (Baton Rouge: Louisiana State University Press, 1979), 245–47.

18. "National Convention at Cincinnati, Ohio," in Stanton, Anthony and Gage, eds., *History of Woman Suffrage*, 1:163–66, quotation at 165; and Kerr, *Lucy Stone*, 90.

19. "Women's Rights Convention at Worcester, Mass," *New York Daily Tribune*, October 24, 1850, www.assumption.edu/whw/old/NY_TribuneI.html; Frances D. Gage, "Reminiscences," in Stanton, Anthony, and Gage, eds., *History of Woman Suffrage*, 1:115–17; Nell Irvin Painter, *Sojourner Truth: A Life, A Symbol* (New York: Norton, 1996), 125; and *American National Biography*, s.v. "Truth, Sojourner." It was at the Akron, Ohio, convention that Sojourner allegedly delivered her "Ain't I a Woman" speech, which historians realize she never presented in the manner that has been widely mythologized. At the time, no one recorded her speech verbatim. It appears in volume 1 of Stanton, Anthony, and Gage, eds., *History of Woman Suffrage*, written by Frances D. Gage years later. The essence of the speech may be correct, but the actual words were not Truth's. For one thing, Gage used a southern dialect, something Sojourner would not have spoken, since she spent her life in the North. See Frances D. Gage, "Reminiscences," 115–16. Gage describes her rendition as a "graphic picture" of the moment (115).

20. "National Convention in Philadelphia," in Stanton, Anthony, and Gage, eds., *History of Woman Suffrage*, 1:380–82, quotation at 380; and Wendell Phillips to Elizabeth Pease, quoted in Margaret Hope Bacon, *Valiant Friend: The Life of Lucretia Mott* (New York: Walker, 1980), 137.

21. "The Syracuse National Convention," in Stanton, Anthony, and Gage, eds., *History of Woman Suffrage*, 1:541; Paulina Wright Davis to Elizabeth Cady Stanton, Providence, Rhode Island, December 12, 1851, Papers of Elizabeth Cady Stanton and Susan B. Anthony Papers, microfilm; Lucretia Mott to Lucy Stone, Philadelphia, August 16, 1852, in Mott, *Selected Letters,* 219; Letter from Angelina Grimké Weld, "The Syracuse National Convention," in Stanton, Anthony, and Gage, eds., *History of Woman Suffrage*, 1:540; and Wendell Phillips to Lucy Stone, Northampton, Massachusetts, August 20, 1852, Blackwell Family Papers, Library of Congress, Washington, D.C., microfilm.

22. "National Convention in Philadelphia," in Stanton, Anthony, and Gage, eds., *History of Woman Suffrage*, 1:375–76; and Lucretia Mott to Elizabeth Neall Gay, Philadelphia, October 9, 1854, in Mott, *Selected Letters*, 233 n. 5.

23. "The Syracuse National Convention" and "Cleveland National Convention," both in Stanton, Anthony, and Gage, eds., *History of Woman Suffrage*, 1:535–37, 124. See also *Proceedings of the National Woman's Rights Convention Held at Cleveland, Ohio* (Cleveland: Gray, Beardsley, Spear, 1854), 162, American Memory, http://memory .loc.gov/cgi-bin/query/r?ammem/naw:@field.

24. Mary Anne W. Johnson, "President's Address," June 2, 1852, in *The Proceedings of the Woman's Rights Convention Held at West Chester, Pennsylvania* (Philadelphia: Merrihew and Thompson, 1852), American Memory, http://memory.loc.gov/cgi-bin/ query/r?ammem/rbnawsa.

25. Frances D. Gage, "Remarks of Frances D. Gage," in *Proceedings of the National Woman's Rights Convention Held at Cleveland, Ohio*, and "National Convention at Cincinnati, Ohio," in Stanton, Anthony, and Gage, eds., *History of Woman Suffrage*, 1:164. Harriot Hunt celebrated Seneca Falls at the 1859 convention as well. See *Report of the Woman's Rights Meeting at Mercantile Hall, May 27, 1859* (Boston: S. Urbino, 1859), American Memory, http://memory.loc.gov/cgi-bin/query/r? ammem/rbnawsa).

26. Wendell Phillips, speech at "The Second National Convention in Worcester," in Stanton, Anthony, and Gage, eds., *History of Woman Suffrage*, 1:227; Mott, *Selected Letters*, 209 n. 4; Lucretia Mott to George Combe, Philadelphia, May 21, 1852, in Mott, *Selected Letters*, 215; and "Woman's Rights Convention," *Liberator*, October 24, 1851, Papers of Elizabeth Cady Stanton and Susan B. Anthony, microfilm.

27. Lucretia Mott to Elizabeth Cady Stanton, Philadelphia, September 11, 1851, in Stanton and Anthony, *Selected Papers*, 1:186–87; and Lucretia Mott to William Lloyd Garrison and Helen Benson Garrison, Philadelphia, September 11, 1851, in Mott, *Selected Letters*, 209. See also Bonnie S. Anderson, *Joyous Greetings: The First International Women's Movement, 1830–1860* (Oxford: Oxford University Press, 2000).

28. "Proceedings of the National Woman's Rights Convention, Worcester, 1851," in Stanton, Anthony, and Gage, eds., *History of Woman Suffrage*, 1:234–36, 229–30, quotation at 236; Ernestine Rose, "Woman's Rights Convention," *New York*

Herald, October 25, 1850; and "The Seventh National Woman's Rights Convention," in Stanton, Anthony, and Gage, eds., *History of Woman Suffrage*, 1:644–47. The two women imprisoned at St. Lagare in Paris were Jeanne Deroine and Pauline Roland.

29. "Mob Convention in New York City," in Stanton, Anthony, and Gage, eds., *History of Woman Suffrage*, 1:570.

30. Lucy Stone, "The First National Convention," *Woman's Journal*, February 14, 1891; and Wendell Phillips, "Shall Women Have the Right to Vote?" delivered at "The Second National Convention in Worcester," October 1851, in Votes for Women: Selections from the National Woman Suffrage Association, American Memory, http://memory.loc.gov/cgi-bin/query/r?ammem/naw:@field.

31. Henry Blackwell, speech at the "Cleveland National Convention, October 5, 6, 7, 1853," in Stanton, Anthony, and Gage, eds., *History of Woman Suffrage*, 1:126–27; and *Proceedings of the National Woman's Rights Convention Held at Cleveland, Ohio.*

32. "Woman's Rights," *North Star*, September 3, 1852; Stanton and Anthony, *Selected Papers*, 1:213 n. 4; and "The Syracuse National Convention," in Stanton, Anthony, and Gage, eds., *History of Woman Suffrage*, 1:527, 539.

33. *Proceedings of the Woman's Rights Convention held at the Broadway Tabernacle, in the City of New York, on . . . September 6th and 7th, 1853* (New York: Fowler & Wells, 1853); William Lloyd Garrison, "Mob Convention in New York," in Stanton, Anthony and Gage, eds., *History of Woman Suffrage*, 1:549; and "Woman's Rights Convention," *Una*, September 1853.

34. "Mob Convention in New York," *New York Times,* September 8, 1853, and "Mob Convention," both in Stanton, Anthony, and Gage, eds., *History of Woman Suffrage*, 1:557; "Mobs," *Una*, October 1853; and Bacon, *Valiant Friend*, 2, 3.

35. Lucretia Mott to Lucy Stone, Montgomery County, July 1, 1857, in Mott, *Selected Letters*, 259.

36. Mott, *Selected Letters*, 277 n. 2.

37. Elizabeth Cady Stanton to Susan B. Anthony, Seneca Falls, New York, July 20, 1857, and Elizabeth Cady Stanton to Daniel Cady, New York, January 12, 1853, in Elizabeth Cady Stanton, *Elizabeth Cady Stanton as Revealed in Her Letters, Diary and Reminiscences*, ed. Theodore Stanton and Harriot Stanton Blatch (New York: Harper, 1922), 2:70, 46; and "Tenth National Woman's Rights Convention," in Stanton, Anthony, and Gage, eds., *History of Woman Suffrage*, 1:716–22, 717 (quotation).

38. "Tenth National Woman's Rights Convention," in Stanton, Anthony, and Gage, eds., *History of Woman Suffrage*, 1:732, 735, 731. See also Suzanne M. Marilley, *Woman Suffrage and the Origins of Liberal Feminism in the United States, 1820–1920* (Cambridge, Mass.: Harvard University Press, 1996), 55.

39. "Lucy Stone," *Cayuga Chief,* reprinted in *Una*, June 1854; "Lucy Stone," *Syracuse Weekly Chronicle,* quoted in *San Antonio Ledger*, June 6, 1853; "Lucy Stone on Woman's Rights," *Sunday Morning Republican*, December 18, 1853; Elizabeth Cady Stanton, "Letter to the Editor," *New York Semi-Weekly Tribune*, December 1, 1854; Susan B. Anthony to Lucy Stone, Rochester, May 1, 1853, in Stanton and Anthony, *Selected Papers*, 1:219; and "The National Woman's Rights Convention at Syracuse," *Frederick Douglass Paper*, September 17, 1852.

40. Susan B. Anthony, "Remarks to Women's New York State Temperance Society," October 14, 1852, in Stanton and Anthony, *Selected Papers*, 1:208.

41. Lucy Stone to Susan B. Anthony, New York City, January 25, 1854, Blackwell Family Papers, microfilm; Amelia Bloomer, "Women Voting in Nebraska—A Triumph, Almost," *Lily*, March 1, 1856; Susan B. Anthony to Lucy Stone, Rochester, New York, May 1, 1853, in Stanton and Anthony, *Selected Papers*, 1:220; and Susan B. Anthony to Lucy Stone, Rochester, New York, January 31, 1854, Papers of Elizabeth Cady Stanton and Susan B. Anthony, microfilm.

42. William Lloyd Garrison to Abby Kelley Foster, Boston, August 12, 1851, Abby Kelley Foster Papers, American Antiquarian Society, Worcester, Massachusetts.

43. Caroline Healey Dall, *Daughter of Boston: The Extraordinary Diary of a Nineteenth-Century Woman*, ed. Helen R. Deese (Boston: Beacon Press, 2005), 251. Dall dedicated her book of lectures, *The College, the Market, and the Court; or, Woman's Relation to Education, Labor and Law* (Cambridge, Mass.: Lee and Shepherd, 1867; reprint, New York: Arno Press, 1972), to Lucretia, calling her "the best example that I know of what all women may and should become."

44. Alice Stone Blackwell, "Diary," September 30, 1893, Blackwell Family Papers, microfilm. The story of Margaret Garner is the basis for the novel *Beloved* by Toni Morrison and the opera *Margaret Garner*, music by Richard Danielpour, libretto by Toni Morrison.

45. Paulina Wright Davis to Elizabeth Cady Stanton, Providence, Rhode Island, September 1, 1852, Papers of Elizabeth Cady Stanton and Susan B. Anthony, microfilm.

46. Elizabeth Cady Stanton, "Women's Temperance Meeting, Albany, January 1852," and Stanton, "Temperance—Woman's Rights," July 1852, both in Stanton and Anthony, *Selected Papers*, 1:191–92, 201–4, 203 (quotation).

47. Elizabeth Cady Stanton, *Address to the Legislature of New-York* (Albany: Weed, Parson, 1854), American Memory, http://memory.loc.gov/cgi-bin/query/r?ammem/rbnawsa.

48. Million, *Woman's Voice, Woman's Place*, 136–38; Massachusetts, Constitutional Convention (1853), Committee on Qualification of Voters, "Convention. No. 97" (Boston: The Committee, 1853), American Memory, http://memory.loc.gov/cgi-bin/query/r?ammem/rbnawsa:@field; Elizabeth Cady Stanton, "On Divorce," delivered to the Judiciary Committee of the New York Senate, February 8, 1861, in Karlyn Kohrs Campbell, ed., *Man Cannot Speak for Her: Key Texts of the Early Feminists* (Westport, Conn.: Greenwood Press, 1989), 2:235–50. According to Glenda Riley, New York and South Carolina retained their "restrictive policies" on divorce as World War II ended. Not until 1966 did New York make the first significant alteration to its divorce laws since 1787. See Glenda Riley, *Divorce: An American Tradition* (New York: Oxford University Press, 1991), 156–57.

49. Frances W. Kaye, "The Ladies' Department of the *Ohio Cultivator*, 1845–1855: A Feminist Forum," *Agricultural History* 50 (1976): 414–23.

50. Robert C. Williams, *Horace Greeley: Champion of American Freedom* (New York: New York University Press, 2006), 275–76; and "The Woman's Rights Convention

at Worcester," *New York Christian Enquirer*, in Stanton, Anthony, and Gage, eds., *History of Woman Suffrage*, 1:243.

51. "The Worcester Convention," *Lily*, November 1850; "Convention," *Massachusetts Spy*, October 30, 1850; "The National Woman's Rights Convention of Syracuse," *Frederick Douglass Paper*, September 17, 1852; "Address to the Legislature of the State of New York," *Frederick Douglass Paper*, March 3, 1854; and "The Woman's Convention," *Syracuse Journal*, carried in the *National Era*, September 23, 1852.

52. "Woman's Rights Convention. Awful Combination of Socialism, Abolitionism, and Infidelity," *New York Herald*, October 25, 1850; Sterling, *Ahead of Her Time*, 266; and "The Rights of Woman—Syracuse Convention," *New York Daily Times*, October 15, 1852. The *New York Daily Times* carried the *London Times* story.

53. Frances D. Gage, "How Fares Our Cause," *Una*, August 1854; and "Woman's Rights and Duties," *Middletown (CT) Constitution*, November 6, 1850.

54. "Tenth National Woman's Rights Convention" (New York City, May 11, 1860), in Stanton and Anthony, *Selected Papers*, 1:418–31, quotation at 419; *New York Evening Post*, May 23, 1860; and *New York Observer*, May 17, 1860.

55. "Women's Temperance Meeting," *Utica Evening Telegraph*, April 28, 1853.

56. "Woman's Rights: Circulate the Petitions," n.d., Papers of Elizabeth Cady Stanton and Susan B. Anthony, microfilm; and Sarah Pugh, *A Memorial of Sarah Pugh: A Tribute of Respect from her Cousins* (Philadelphia, 1888), quoted in Bruce Dorsey, *Reforming Men and Women: Gender in the Antebellum City* (Ithaca, N.Y.: Cornell University Press, 2002), 170. See also Julie Roy Jeffrey, *The Great Silent Army of Abolitionism: Ordinary Women in the Antislavery Movement* (Chapel Hill: University of North Carolina Press, 1998), 86–93; and Susan Zaeske, *Signatures of Citizenship: Petitioning, Antislavery, and Women's Political Identity* (Chapel Hill: University of North Carolina Press, 2003), 3, 179–81.

57. *Proceedings of the Ohio Women's Convention, held at Salem, April 19th and 20th, 1850*, 15; Mott, *Selected Letters*, 204 n. 5; Elizabeth Cady Stanton to Mary Ann White Johnson and the Ohio Woman's Convention, April 7, 1850, in Stanton and Anthony, *Selected Papers*, 1:168 n. 1; and Nancy Isenberg, *Sex and Citizenship in Antebellum America* (Chapel Hill: University of North Carolina Press, 1998), 15–17.

58. Two petitions, in "Circulate the Petition," June 22, 1854, Stanton and Anthony Papers, microfilm. A local newspaper called this the first convention of women "designed to influence political action." "Woman's Rights Convention," *Albany Evening Transcript*, February 16, 1854, Papers of Elizabeth Cady Stanton and Susan B. Anthony, microfilm.

59. Henry B. Stanton to Elizabeth Cady Stanton, Albany, New York, 1851, Papers of Elizabeth Cady Stanton and Susan B. Anthony, microfilm; Million, *Woman's Voice, Woman's Place*, 136–37; and Lucy Stone to Elizabeth Cady Stanton, n.p., August 14, 1853, in Stanton and Anthony, *Selected Papers*, 1:226 n. 7.

60. Elizabeth Cady Stanton to Mary Ann White Johnson and the Ohio Woman's Convention, April 7, 1850, in Stanton and Anthony, *Selected Papers*, 1:165; "Dr. Hunt's Protest of 1852," "The Syracuse National Convention," and "Woman's Rights Convention, Rochester," in Stanton, Anthony, and Gage, eds., *History of Woman Suffrage*, 1:259–60, 520, 582.

61. Lucy Stone, "Protest of Taxation without Representation," *Orange (NJ) Journal,* January 18, 1858, www.scc.rutgers.edu/njwomenshistory.

62. Sarah M. Grimké, letter 11, "Dress of Women," in Sarah Grimké and Angelina Grimké, *Letters on the Equality of the Sexes,* in *The Public Years of Sarah and Angelina Grimké: Selected Writings, 1835–1839,* ed. Larry Ceplair (New York: Columbia University Press, 1989), 227, 230; Mrs. R. B. Gleason, "Woman's Dress," *Lily,* March 1851, 17; and "Comments," *Magnolia* 4 (1842): 46.

63. "Mrs. Kemble and Her New Costume," *Lily,* December 1, 1849; "Bloomerism in the Mills," *Lily,* July 1851; "The Lowell Bloomer Institute," *Lily,* November 1851; and Million, *Woman's Voice, Woman's Place,* 114–16.

64. "Female Attire," *Lily,* March 1851, 21; and Danny O. Crew, *Suffragist Sheet Music* (London: McFarland, 2002), 21, 24, 28. See also Paul Fatout, "Amelia Bloomer and Bloomerism," *New-York Historical Society Quarterly* 36 (1952): 361–74.

65. Griffith, *In Her Own Right,* 72.

66. "Mrs. Swisshelm," *Lily,* September 1851, and "Mrs. Swisshelm Again," *Lily,* October 1851; and Paulina Wright Davis to Elizabeth Cady Stanton, Monroe, July 20, 1852, and Providence, Rhode Island, September 1, 1852, Papers of Elizabeth Cady Stanton and Susan B. Anthony, microfilm.

67. *Harper's* 4, no. 20 (January 1852); "Full-Dress for Home," *Harper's* 4, no. 21 (February 1852): 432; Elizabeth Cady Stanton to Henry Stanton, Peterboro, New York, April 11, 1851, Papers of Elizabeth Cady Stanton and Susan B. Anthony, microfilm; Elizabeth Cady Stanton, "My Diary," March 10, 1889, in Stanton, *Elizabeth Cady Stanton as Revealed,* 2:257; and Anne Coone, "The Bloomer Costume," *Rochester History* 57 (1995): 18–24.

68. Elizabeth Cady Stanton to Lucy Stone, Seneca Falls, February 16, 1854, Papers of Elizabeth Cady Stanton and Susan B. Anthony, microfilm; and Susan B. Anthony to Lucy Stone, Albany, New York, March 7, 1854, in Stanton and Anthony, *Selected Papers,* 1:262.

69. E. C. S., "Legislative Doings," *Lily,* May 1850; E. C. S., "I Have All the Rights I Want," *Una,* March 1855; and Elizabeth Cady Stanton, "Mrs. Dall's Fraternity Lecture" (Seneca Falls, New York, November 16, 1860), in Stanton and Anthony, *Selected Papers,* 1:447.

70. Elizabeth Cady Stanton to Susan B. Anthony, Seneca Falls, New York, January 16, 1854, Papers of Elizabeth Cady Stanton and Susan B. Anthony, microfilm; and Lucretia Mott to Elizabeth Cady Stanton, Philadelphia, March 16, 1855, in Mott, *Selected Letters,* 233.

71. "A Voice from Virginia," *Lily,* December 1853.

72. Paulina Wright Davis to Elizabeth Cady Stanton, "Prospectus," Providence, Rhode Island, 9th [n.d.] 1852, Papers of Elizabeth Cady Stanton and Susan B. Anthony, microfilm; and "Prospectus," *Una,* February 1, 1853.

73. Paulina W. Davis to Caroline Dall, Providence, Rhode Island, May 19, 1853, Caroline Wells Healey Dall Family Papers, Massachusetts Historical Society, Boston, microfilm; "Our Salutatory," *Una,* January 1855 (quotation); and Paulina Wright Davis to Caroline Dall, Providence, Rhode Island, November 16 and 17, 1854, Caroline Dall Papers, microfilm. See also Dall, *Daughter of Boston,* 224, 237;

Helen R. Deese, "Caroline Healy Dall and the American Women's Rights Movement, 1848–1875," *American Nineteenth Century History* 3 (2002): 1–28; and Deese, "'My Life Reads Like a Romance': The Journals of Caroline Healy Dall," *Massachusetts Historical Review* 3 (2001): 116–37.

74. "The Woman's Advocate," *Lily*, September 1, 1855, 117; Linda Steiner, "Finding Community in Nineteenth-Century Suffrage Periodicals," *American Journalism* 1 (1983): 2–3; Frank Luther Mott, *A History of American Magazines, 1850–1865*, vol. 2 (Cambridge: Cambridge University Press, 1938), 50–52; and Sylvia Hoffert, *When Hens Crow: The Woman's Rights Movement in Antebellum America* (Bloomington: Indiana University Press, 1995), 87–91.

75. "Woman's Rights Tracts," in *Proceedings of the Syracuse Convention*, last page; and "Woman's Rights Tracts," *Una*, February 1853, 16.

76. John Weiss, "The Woman Question," *Christian Examiner and Religious Miscellany*, January 1854, 8, 17.

77. "1857 Report of the Assembly Committee on Women's Rights," *New Jersey Assembly, Minutes of Votes and Proceedings*, 1857 (Flemington, 1857), 552–54, www.scc.rutgers.edu/njwomenshistory.

78. "Female Education," *Southern Presbyterian Review* 14 (April 1861): 60–91, quotation at 63; Louisa S. McCord, "Woman's Progress," in Louisa S. McCord, *Selected Writings*, ed. Richard C. Lounsbury (Charlottesville: University Press of Virginia, 1997), 178; and "Female Prose Writers of America," *Southern Quarterly Review* 21 (1852): 118.

79. Susan B. Anthony to John J. Ormond, n.p., October 2, 1859, in Stanton and Anthony, *Selected Papers*, 1:396–97.

80. "National Convention in Philadelphia," October 18, 1854, in Stanton, Anthony, and Gage, eds., *History of Woman Suffrage*, 1:380; Susan B. Anthony, "The Woman's Rights Convention, Penn Yan, NY," *Yates County Whig*, January 10, 1855, Papers of Elizabeth Cady Stanton and Susan B. Anthony, microfilm; and Abby Kelley Foster, "Speech at the 1851 Convention," www.assumption.edu/whw/old/AKFoster_1851_speech.

81. Elizabeth Cady Stanton, "To the Women of the State of New York," *Frederick Douglass Paper*, December 22, 1854; and Stanton, "Paper for the Yearly Meeting of the Friends of Human Progress" (June 6, 1857), in Stanton and Anthony, *Selected Papers*, 1:344.

82. Thomas Wentworth Higginson, "Women and the Alphabet," available at the website of the Worcester Women's History Project, www.assumption.edu/wwhp.; and Higginson, "Ought Women to Learn the Alphabet," *Atlantic Monthly*, February 1859.

83. Paulina Wright Davis to Elizabeth Cady Stanton, Providence, Rhode Island, December 12, 1851, Papers of Elizabeth Cady Stanton and Susan B. Anthony, microfilm.

84. Lucy Stone to Antoinette Brown, Walnut Hills, Ohio, July 11, 1855, in Stone and Blackwell, *Friends and Sisters*, 144; Susan B. Anthony to Lucy Stone, Rochester, New York, December 13, 1853, Papers of Elizabeth Cady Stanton and Susan B. Anthony, microfilm; James Mott to Lucy Stone, Philadelphia, December 9, 1856, Blackwell Family Papers, microfilm; and "Lucy Stone at Musical Fund Hall, Philadelphia," *Frederick Douglass Paper*, February 17, 1854.

85. Kerr, *Lucy Stone*, 110–11. Other abolitionists hated Senator Stephen Douglas. Garrison described him as a "desperate demagogue and Iscariot traitor to liberty." See William Lloyd Garrison to Samuel G. Howe, and Others, Committee, Boston, November 12, 1855, in William Lloyd Garrison, *The Letters of William Lloyd Garrison,* vol. 4, *From Disunionism to the Brink of War, 1850–1860,* ed. Louis Ruchames (Cambridge, Mass.: Harvard University Press, 1975), 359.

86. Elizabeth Cady Stanton to Susan B. Anthony, Seneca Falls, April 2, 1852, Papers of Elizabeth Cady Stanton and Susan B. Anthony, microfilm.

87. Elizabeth Cady Stanton to Susan B. Anthony, Peterboro, New York, September 10, 1855, in Stanton, *Elizabeth Cady Stanton as Revealed,* 2:59.

88. Two of Henry's sisters, Elizabeth and Emily, were among the first women in this country to graduate from medical school. His other sisters became a writer, a poet, and a newspaper correspondent. Family members often called him Harry, but for the sake of consistency, I refer to him by his given name.

89. *American National Biography,* s.v. "Blackwell, Henry," and Harriet Beecher Stowe, quoted in Blackwell, *Lucy Stone,* 170.

90. Henry Blackwell to Emily Blackwell, June 3, 1850, quoted in Kerr, *Lucy Stone,* 65; Henry Blackwell to Sam Blackwell, n.p., n.d., in Lucy Stone and Henry B. Blackwell, *Loving Warriors: A Revealing Portrait of an Unprecedented Marriage,* ed. Leslie Wheeler (New York: Dial Press, 1981), 34; "Marriage of Lucy Stone under Protest, 1855," in Stanton, Anthony, and Gage, eds., *History of Woman Suffrage,* 1:260–61; and "Marriage of Lucy Stone under Protest," *Una,* June 1855, 87. See also Elinor Rice Hays, *Those Extraordinary Blackwells: The Story of a Journey to a Better World* (New York: Harcourt, Brace & World, 1967).

91. Lucy Stone to Susan B. Anthony, n.p., n.d., quoted in Kerr, *Lucy Stone,* 88; and Elizabeth Cady Stanton to Susan B. Anthony, Seneca Falls, June 10, 1856, Papers of Elizabeth Cady Stanton and Susan B. Anthony, microfilm.

92. F. D. Gage, "Lucy Stone," *Lily,* June 1855.

93. Blackwell, *Lucy Stone,* 170–71; and Elizabeth Cady Stanton to Rebecca R. Eyster, Seneca Falls, May 1, 1847, in North American Women's Letters and Diaries, www.alexanderstreet4.com/cgi-bin/asp/nawld/getdoc.pl?/projects.

94. Antoinette Brown Blackwell, "Lucy Stone at Oberlin College," *Woman's Journal,* February 10, 1894.

95. Abby Kelley Foster to Stephen Foster, Worcester, September 9, 1847, and Stephen Foster to Abby Kelley Foster, Worcester, April 11, 1850, Abby Kelley Foster Papers; and Sterling, *Ahead of Her Time,* 316–17.

96. Elizabeth Cady Stanton to Antoinette Brown Blackwell, Seneca Falls, New York, March 13, 1861, in Stanton and Anthony, *Selected Papers,* 1:462; and Elizabeth Cady Stanton to Lucretia Mott, Seneca Falls, New York, October 22, 1852, Papers of Elizabeth Cady Stanton and Susan B. Anthony, microfilm.

97. Elizabeth Cady Stanton to Abigail Kelley Foster, Grassmere, Seneca Falls, New York, January 12, 1851, in Stanton and Anthony, *Selected Papers,* 1:178; Susan B. Anthony to Lucy Stone, Rochester, New York, December 13, 1853, Papers of Elizabeth Cady Stanton and Susan B. Anthony, microfilm; and Lucy Stone to

Elizabeth Cady Stanton, n.p., August 4, 1853, in Stanton and Anthony, *Selected Papers*, 1:244.

98. Elizabeth Cady Stanton to Susan B. Anthony, Seneca Falls, New York, April 2, 1852, Papers of Elizabeth Cady Stanton and Susan B. Anthony, microfilm; and Elizabeth Cady Stanton to Susan B. Anthony, Seneca Falls, New York, June 10, 1856, in Stanton, *Elizabeth Cady Stanton as Revealed*, 2:66.

99. Susan B. Anthony to Lucy Stone, Rochester, New York, May 1, 1853, Papers of Elizabeth Cady Stanton and Susan B. Anthony, microfilm; Susan B. Anthony to Antoinette Brown Blackwell, at home, April 22, 1858, and Elizabeth Cady Stanton to Antoinette Brown Blackwell, Seneca Falls, New York, March 13, 1861, both in Stanton and Anthony, *Selected Papers*, 1:360, 462.

100. Griffith, *In Her Own Right*, 80.

101. Susan B. Anthony to Caroline Nichols, n.p., c. Fall 1856, Papers of Elizabeth Cady Stanton and Susan B. Anthony, microfilm; Lucy Stone to Susan B. Anthony, Viroqua, Wisconsin, July 22, 1856, in Stanton and Anthony, *Selected Papers*, 1:327; "Kansas and Woman's Rights," *Lily*, June 1, 1856, 84; and Elizabeth Cady Stanton to Elizabeth Smith Miller, Seneca Falls, New York, November 15, 1856, Papers of Elizabeth Cady Stanton and Susan B. Anthony, microfilm.

102. Jessie Benton Frémont, *The Letters of Jessie Benton Frémont*, ed. Pamela Herr and Mary Lee Spence (Urbana: University of Illinois Press, 1993), 67; and Martha Wright to Susan B. Anthony, Auburn, New York, July 14, 1856, in Stanton and Anthony, *Selected Papers*, 1:326. See also Melanie Susan Gustafson, *Women and the Republican Party, 1854–1924* (Urbana: University of Illinois Press, 2001), 19–20.

103. Susan B. Anthony to Wendell Phillips, Rochester, New York, July 3, 1854, Papers of Elizabeth Cady Stanton and Susan B. Anthony, microfilm.

104. William Lloyd Garrison to Henry C. Wright, Boston, June 27, 1859, in Garrison, *Letters of Garrison*, 4:634.

Chapter 5

1. Martha Coffin Wright to Susan B. Anthony, Philadelphia, March 31, 1862, and Susan B. Anthony to Lydia Mott, Rochester, New York, after April 10, 1862, both in Elizabeth Cady Stanton and Susan B. Anthony, *The Selected Papers of Elizabeth Cady Stanton and Susan B. Anthony*, vol. 1, *In the School of Anti-Slavery, 1840 to 1866*, ed. Ann D. Gordon (New Brunswick, N.J.: Rutgers University Press, 1997), 473, 475.

2. Grace Brown Elmore, *The Heritage of Woe: The Civil War Diary of Grace Brown Elmore, 1861–1868*, ed. Marli F. Weiner (Athens: University of Georgia Press, 1997), 73, 21.

3. Jeanie Attie, *Patriotic Toil: Northern Women and the American Civil War* (Ithaca, N.Y.: Cornell University Press, 1998); and Judith Ann Giesberg, *Civil War Sisterhood: The U.S. Sanitary Commission and Women's Politics in Transition* (Boston: Northeastern University, 2000).

4. Caroline Healey Dall, "Diary," Boston, February 20, 1862, in Caroline Healey Dall, *Daughter of Boston: The Extraordinary Diary of a Nineteenth-Century Woman*, ed. Helen R. Deese (Boston: Beacon Press, 2005), 314; Louisa May Alcott, "Diary," May 1861, in Louisa May Alcott, *The Journals of Louisa May Alcott*, ed. Joel Myerson and Daniel Shealy (Boston: Little, Brown, 1989), 105; and Louisa May Alcott to Mrs. Joseph Chatfield Alcox, n.p., early December 1862, in Louisa May Alcott, *The Selected Letters of Louisa May Alcott*, ed. Joel Myerson and Daniel Shealy (Boston: Little, Brown, 1987), 80.

5. "The Great Central Fair: Philadelphia," *Godey's Lady's Book* 69 (September 1864).

6. Catherine Clinton, *The Other Civil War: American Women in the Nineteenth Century* (New York: Hill and Wang, 1984), 81–84.

7. Louisa May Alcott, "Diary," Union Hotel Hospital, Georgetown, D.C., January 1863, in Alcott, *Journals*, 113.

8. Mrs. Amanda Turpin, "Female Influence," *Williamsport Christian Recorder,* August 20, 1864.

9. Antoinette Brown Blackwell to Susan B. Anthony, Millburn, New Jersey, April 30, 1861, in Stanton and Anthony, *Selected Papers*, 1:466; and Elizabeth Cady Stanton to Nancy Smith, Johnstown, New York, July 20, 1863, in Elizabeth Cady Stanton, *Elizabeth Cady Stanton as Revealed in Her Letters, Diary and Reminiscences*, ed. Theodore Stanton and Harriot Stanton Blatch (New York: Harper, 1922), 2:94.

10. Stanton and Anthony, *Selected Papers,* 1:476 n. 4, 536 n. 1

11. Henry B. Stanton to Elizabeth Cady Stanton, Washington, D.C., January 12, 1861, in Stanton and Anthony, *Selected Papers*, 1:454–55.

12. "Anna Dickinson," *New Hampshire Sentinel*, March 16, 1865; and Caroline Healey Dall, "Diary," Boston, April 20, 1862, in Dall, *Daughter of Boston*, 315. See also J. Matthew Gallman, *America's Joan of Arc: The Life of Anna Elizabeth Dickinson* (New York: Oxford University Press, 2006); *American National Biography*, s.v. "Dickinson, Anna Elizabeth," www.anb.org/articles/home.html; and Giraud Chester, *Embattled Maiden: The Life of Anna Dickinson* (New York: Putnam, 1951).

13. Susan B. Anthony to Anna E. Dickinson, New York, July 12, 1867, in Elizabeth Cady Stanton and Susan B. Anthony, *The Selected Papers of Elizabeth Cady Stanton and Susan B. Anthony*, vol. 2, *Against an Aristocracy of Sex, 1866 to 1873*, ed. Ann D. Gordon (New Brunswick, N.J.: Rutgers University Press, 2000), 79; and Jean H. Baker, *Sisters: The Lives of America's Suffragists* (New York: Hill and Wang, 2005), 74–77.

14. Louisa May Alcott, "Diary," April 1861, in Alcott, *Journals*, 105; Elizabeth Cady Stanton, "To the Women of the Republic," New York, April 24, 1863, in Stanton and Anthony, *Selected Papers*, 1:483; and Ellen Wright to Lucy McKim, n.p., August 15, 1862, quoted in Wendy F. Hamand, "The Woman's National Loyal League: Feminist Abolitionists and the Civil War," *Civil War History* 35 (1989): 39.

15. Historians identify this organization by slightly different names. Many use the name here in the text—which these women usually used—but some scholars, as well as Stanton, Anthony, and Gage in *History of Woman Suffrage,* call it the Woman's National Loyal League.

16. "The Great Uprising of the Women of the North, *New York Herald*, May 12, 1863.

17. "Meeting of the Loyal Women of the Republic," May 14, 1863, in Stanton and Anthony, *Selected Papers*, 1:491.

18. "Meeting of the Loyal Women of the Republic," May 14, 1863, in Stanton and Anthony, *Selected Papers*, 1:488; and William Lloyd Garrison to Helen E. Garrison, New York, May 14, 1863, in William Lloyd Garrison, *The Letters of William Lloyd Garrison*, vol. 5, *Let the Oppressed Go Free, 1861–1867*, ed. Walter M. Merrill (Cambridge, Mass.: Harvard University Press, 1979), 154.

19. Elizabeth Cady Stanton to Elizabeth Smith Miller, New York, September 1, 1863, in Stanton, *Elizabeth Cady Stanton as Revealed*, 2:95; and "Meeting of the Women's Loyal National League," May 15, 1863, and Susan B. Anthony to Elizabeth Cady Stanton, Worcester, Massachusetts, October 10, 1863, both in Stanton and Anthony, *Selected Papers*, 1:494, 502–3.

20. Susan B. Anthony, "Speech to the American Anti-Slavery Society," December 4, 1863, and "Meeting of the Women's Loyal National League," May 29, 1863, both in Stanton and Anthony, *Selected Papers*, 1:506, 498; and "The Woman's National Loyal League: Mammoth Petition," Elizabeth Cady Stanton, Susan B. Anthony, and Matilda Joslyn Gage, eds., *History of Woman Suffrage*, vol. 2 (New York: Fowler & Wells 1882), 50–54. The WLNL petition read: "The undersigned, women of the United States above the age of 18 years, earnestly pray that your honorable body will pass, at the earliest practicable day, an act emancipating all persons of African descent held to involuntary service or labor in the United States."

21. Hamand, "The Woman's National Loyal League," 44; and Susan B. Anthony to Charles Sumner, New York, March 1, 1864, in Stanton and Anthony, *Selected Papers*, 1:511–12.

22. Elizabeth Cady Stanton to Caroline Healey Dall, New York, May 7, 1864, in Stanton and Anthony, *Selected Papers*, 1:518–19; and Lucretia Mott to Lydia Mott, near Philadelphia, January 22, 1861, in Lucretia Coffin Mott, *Selected Letters of Lucretia Coffin Mott*, ed. Beverly Wilson Palmer (Urbana: University of Illinois Press, 2002), 306. Stanton's letter quotes from Dall's letter, trying to make sense of what Dall had written.

23. Elizabeth Cady Stanton to Caroline Healey Dall, New York, May 7, 1864, and Elizabeth Cady Stanton to Caroline Healey Dall, New York, c. April 22, 1864, both in Stanton and Anthony, *Selected Papers*, 1:521, 514; and Lucy Stone to Susan B. Anthony, West Brookfield, Massachusetts, July 12, 1864, Blackwell Family Papers, Library of Congress, Washington, D.C., microfilm. Elizabeth later changed her opinion of Lincoln, wishing that women had had someone to work on their behalf as he had done for slaves.

24. Elizabeth Blackwell to George Washington Blackwell, n.p., August 23, 1862, quoted in Andrea Moore Kerr, *Lucy Stone: Speaking Out for Equality* (New Brunswick, N.J.: Rutgers University Press, 1992), 114; Marian Blackwell to Elizabeth Blackwell, n.p., December 3, 1871, quoted in Baker, *Sisters,* 32; Lucy Stone to Henry Blackwell, West Brookfield, July 22, 1864, in Lucy Stone and Henry B. Blackwell, *Loving Warriors: A Revealing Portrait of an Unprecedented Marriage*, ed. Leslie Wheeler (New York: Dial Press, 1981), 196; and Lucy Stone to Susan B. Anthony,

West Brookfield, Massachusetts, July 12, 1864, Blackwell Family Papers, microfilm.

25. Elizabeth Cady Stanton to Horace Greeley, New York, January 18, 1864, in Stanton and Anthony, *Selected Papers*, 1:509; and Elisabeth Griffith, *In Her Own Right: The Life of Elizabeth Cady Stanton* (New York: Oxford University Press, 1984), 113–15.

26. Caroline Healy Dall, "Diary," Boston, April 19, 1865, in Dall, *Daughter of Boston*, 347; Lydia Maria Child to Sarah Shaw, Wayland, Massachusetts, September 7, 1866, in Lydia Maria Child, *Lydia Maria Child: Selected Letters, 1817–1880*, ed. Milton Meltzer and Patricia G. Holland (Amherst: University of Massachusetts Press, 1982), 463, 464; and Stanton, "My Diary," May 16, 1896, in Stanton, *Elizabeth Cady Stanton as Revealed*, 2:318.

27. "First Anniversary of the American Equal Rights Association," Papers of Elizabeth Cady Stanton and Susan B. Anthony, microfilm (Wilmington, Del.: Scholarly Resources, 1991); and Elizabeth Cady Stanton, "Universal Suffrage," *National Anti-Slavery Standard*, July 29, 1865, in Stanton and Anthony, *Selected Papers*, 1:551.

28. Stanton and Anthony, *Selected Papers*, 1:549 n. 2.

29. Elizabeth Cady Stanton, "This Is the Negro's Hour," December 26, 1865, in Stanton and Anthony, *Selected Papers*, 1:564–65.

30. Lucy Stone to Abby Kelley Foster, New York, January 24, 1867, in Stone and Blackwell, *Loving Warriors*, 216; Thomas W. Higginson to Elizabeth Cady Stanton, Newport, Rhode Island, May 2, 1866, in Stanton and Anthony, *Selected Papers*, 1:578; and Lucretia Mott to Wendell Phillips, Philadelphia, April 17, 1866, in Mott, *Selected Letters*, 371 and 372, fn 5.

31. "Appeal by Elizabeth Cady Stanton and Susan B. Anthony," December 26, 1865, and "To the Senate and House of Representatives," December 30, 1865, both in Stanton and Anthony, *Selected Papers*, 1:566–67. Although Lucy was one of the three signatories, her name is not included in the title.

32. Lucretia Mott to Wendell Phillips, Philadelphia, April 17, 1866, and Lucretia Mott to Elizabeth Cady Stanton, Philadelphia, April 22, 1866, both in Mott, *Selected Letters*, 371, 372; Martha C. Wright, "Eleventh National Woman's Rights Convention," in Stanton, Anthony, and Gage, eds., *History of Woman Suffrage*, 2:175; and Susan B. Anthony, "Eleventh National Woman's Rights Convention," May 10, 1866, in Stanton and Anthony, *Selected Papers*, 1:585.

33. Henry Ward Beecher, "Woman's Duty to Vote," May 10, 1866, in George William Curtis and Henry Ward Beecher, *The Speeches of George William Curtis and Henry Ward Beecher* (New York: National American Woman Suffrage Association, 1898), American Memory, Library of Congress, http://memory.loc.gov/cgi-bin/query/r?ammem/naw.

34. Frances Ellen Watkins Harper, "We Are All Bound Up Together," in *Women's Rights Emerges within the Antislavery Movement, 1830–1870: A Brief History with Documents*, ed. Kathryn Kish Sklar (New York: St. Martin's, 2000), 196–98.

35. "Elizabeth Cady Stanton for Congress," in Stanton and Anthony, *Selected Papers*, 1:593–94; and Melanie Susan Gustafson, *Women and the Republican Party, 1854–1924* (Urbana: University of Illinois Press, 2001), 36.

36. Elizabeth Cady Stanton, "Comments before the Committee on Suffrage," June 27, 1867, Papers of Elizabeth Cady Stanton and Susan B. Anthony, microfilm; and Elizabeth Cady Stanton, "Female Suffrage Committee," June 19, 1867, in Stanton and Anthony, *Selected Papers*, 2:72–73.

37. George William Curtis, "Equal Rights for Women: A Speech in the Constitutional Convention of New York," July 19, 1867, in Curtis and Beecher, *Speeches*, American Memory, http://memory/loc.gov/cgi-bin/query/r?ammem/rbnawa; Elizabeth Cady Stanton, "Constitutional Convention," July 18, 1867, in Stanton and Anthony, *Selected Papers,* 2:81; and Elizabeth Cady Stanton to Anna E. Dickinson, New York, August 6, 1867, in Stanton and Anthony, *Selected Papers*, 2:86.

38. Commonwealth of Massachusetts, General Court, Joint Special Committee on Woman's Suffrage, "Report," May 24, 1869, American Memory, http://memory.loc.gov/cgi-bin/query/r?ammem/nawbib.

39. "Meeting of the American Equal Rights Association in New York," May 9, 1867, in Stanton and Anthony, *Selected Papers*, 2:62.

40. Henry Blackwell to Friends, Junction City, Kansas, April 21, 1867, in Stone and Blackwell, *Loving Warriors*, 217; Lucy Stone to Susan B. Anthony, Atchison, Kansas, May 9, 1867, in Stanton and Anthony, *Selected Papers*, 2:57; and Griffith, *In Her Own Right*, 127–30.

41. Lucy Stone to Susan B. Anthony, Atchison, Kansas, May 9, 1867, Blackwell Family Papers, microfilm.

42. "Memorial of the American Equal Rights Association to the Congress of the United States," New York, May 10, 1867, in Mott, *Selected Letters*, 38; "Meeting of the Equal Rights Association in New York," May 9, 1867, in Stanton and Anthony, *Selected Papers*, 2:60–68, 63 (quotation); and Henry Ward Beecher, "Speech," in *Proceedings of the First Anniversary of the American Equal Rights Association* (May 9 and 10, 1867) (New York: Robert J. Johnston, 1867), Papers of Elizabeth Cady Stanton and Susan B. Anthony, microfilm.

43. Sojourner Truth, "Speech of May 9, 1867," in Karlyn Kohrs Campbell, ed., *Man Cannot Speak for Her: Key Texts of the Early Feminists* (Westport, Conn.: Greenwood Press, 1989), 2:252–54, first quotation at 252, second at 253.

44. Elizabeth Cady Stanton, "Kansas State Referendum Campaign Speech, Lawrence, Kansas, 1867," in Campbell, *Man Cannot Speak for Her*, 2:259–77, first quotation at 263, second at 274; Susan B. Anthony to Anna Dickinson, Lawrence, Kansas, September 23, 1867, Papers of Elizabeth Cady Stanton and Susan B. Anthony, microfilm; and "To the Public" Office of the American Equal Rights Association, New York, July 1867, in Mott, *Selected Letters*, 390–91 and nn. 1, 2. Exacerbating the situation was the fact that a Massachusetts court had recently ruled in favor of Jackson family members who claimed the money given in the late 1850s to support reform efforts belonged to them.

45. Stanton and Anthony, *Selected Papers*, 2:95 n. 11; "Laing's Hall—Geo. Francis Train," *Leavenworth Commercial*, October 21, 1867, Papers of Elizabeth Cady Stanton and Susan B. Anthony, microfilm; and Susan B. Anthony to George Francis Train, Lawrence, Kansas, October 9, 1867, in Stanton and Anthony, *Selected*

Papers, 2:95. The historian Kathleen Barry maintains that Henry Blackwell arranged for Train to come to Kansas, sensing that their effort needed the backing of the Democratic Party, since Republican support was gone. She suggests that this was both a surprising and somewhat underhanded action on Henry's part—to push Train on Anthony. Yet both Stanton and Anthony continued to travel with Train, welcomed his money to start the *Revolution*, and gave him space in the paper. See Barry, *Susan B. Anthony: A Biography of a Singular Feminist* (New York: New York University Press, 1988), 175–76.

46. Lydia Maria Child to Samuel E. Sewall, Wayland, Massachusetts, March 21, 1868, in Child, *Lydia Maria Child: Selected Letters*, 478; and William Lloyd Garrison, "Letter to Susan B. Anthony," *Revolution*, January 29, 1868.

47. Elizabeth Cady Stanton to Edwin A. Studwell, Buffalo, New York, November 30, 1867, and Susan B. Anthony to George F. Train, New York, January 1, 1870, both in Stanton and Anthony, *Selected Papers*, 2:116, 288; and Lucretia Mott to Martha Coffin Wright, Brooklyn, New York, January 21, 1868, in Mott, *Selected Letters*, 399.

48. *Buffalo Daily Courier*, December 3, 1867, in Mott, *Selected Letters*, 401 n. 9; E. C. S., "Frank Blair on Woman's Suffrage," *Revolution*, October 1, 1868; Elizabeth Cady Stanton, "Manhood Suffrage," December 24, 1868, in Stanton and Anthony, *Selected Papers*, 2:195; and E. C. S., "Women and Black Men," *Revolution*, February 4, 1869.

49. Henry Blackwell to Lucy Stone, Lawrence, Kansas, October 25, 1867, Blackwell Family Papers, microfilm; Stone and Blackwell, *Loving Warriors*, 222; and Susan B. Anthony to Olympia Brown, Leavenworth, Kansas, November 7, 1867, Papers of Elizabeth Cady Stanton and Susan B. Anthony, microfilm.

50. "The Revolution," December 10, 1867, Papers of Elizabeth Cady Stanton and Susan B. Anthony, microfilm; Elizabeth Cady Stanton to Ellen D. Eaton, New York, December 17, 1867, Papers of Elizabeth Cady Stanton and Susan B. Anthony, microfilm; and "Among the Strong Minded: A Visit to the 'Revolutionary' Headquarters," *Macon (GA) Weekly Telegraph*, May 7, 1869.

51. S. B.A., "One Hundred Thousand Subscribers," *Revolution*, April 16, 1868; Julia Couch, "To Women Who Do Not Wish to Vote," *Revolution*, November 5, 1868; and "Close of the Volume," *Revolution*, December 31, 1868.

52. Griffith, *In Her Own Right*, 132–33.

53. William Lloyd Garrison to Elizabeth Pease Nichol, Roxbury, Massachusetts, September 26, 1869, William Lloyd Garrison, *The Letters of William Lloyd Garrison*, vol. 6, *To Rouse the Slumbering Land, 1868–1879*, ed. Walter M. Merrill and Louis Ruchames (Cambridge, Mass.: Harvard University Press, 1981), 129.

54. Griffith, *In Her Own Right*, 144–45, quotation at 145; Barry, *Susan B. Anthony*, 257–60; and Ida Husted Harper, *The Life and Work of Susan B. Anthony*, (Indianapolis: Hollenbeck Press, 1898), 1:360–64, quotation at 362.

55. "Female Suffrage," *Flake's Galveston (TX) Bulletin*, November 18, 1868; and in Mott, *Selected Letters*, 410–11 n. 5.

56. "Meeting of the AERA in New York," May 14, 1868; Susan B. Anthony to Thomas W. Higginson, New York, May 20, 1868; and Susan B. Anthony to Anna

Dickinson, New York, May 22, 1868, all in Stanton and Anthony, *Selected Papers*, 2:135–39 (quotation at 138), 141–43.

57. Susan B. Anthony to Anna E. Dickinson, New York City, May 20, 1868, in Stanton and Anthony, *Selected Papers*, 2:142.

58. "The May Anniversaries in New York and Brooklyn," May 12–14, 1869, in Stanton, Anthony, and Gage, eds., *History of Woman Suffrage*, 2:378–402; "Remarks by Susan B. Anthony to the AERA in New York, May 12, 1869," in Stanton and Anthony, *Selected Papers*, 2:238; and Stone and Blackwell, *Loving Warriors*, 224–25.

59. P. P., "Annual Meeting of the American Equal Rights Association Address," *Revolution*, May 20, 1869; and "The Sixteenth Amendment," in Stanton and Anthony, *Selected Papers*, 2:236.

60. E. C. S., "Petitions," *Revolution*, May 20, 1869.

61. Howe quoted in Alice Stone Blackwell, *Lucy Stone: Pioneer of Woman's Rights* (Boston: Little, Brown, 1930; reprint, Charlottesville: University Press of Virginia, 2001), 267; Deborah Bickman Clifford, *Mine Eyes Have Seen the Glory: A Biography of Julia Ward Howe* (Boston: Little Brown, 1978), 174–75; and *American National Biography*, s.v. "Howe, Julia Ward."

62. Lucy Stone to Esther Pugh, Boston, c. 1869, and Lucy Stone to Elizabeth Cady Stanton, Boston, October 19, 1869, both in Blackwell Family Papers, microfilm; and William Lloyd Garrison to Elizabeth Pease Nichol, Roxbury, Massachusetts, September 26, 1869, and "To the American Woman Suffrage Association," Boston, November 22, 1869, both in Garrison, *Letters of Garrison*, 6:130, 153.

63. Elizabeth Cady Stanton, "The Cleveland Convention," October 28, 1869, and Susan B. Anthony to Elizabeth Smith Miller, n.p., before November 13, 1869, both in Stanton and Anthony, *Selected Papers*, 2:276–78, 283 n. 1; and William Lloyd Garrison to Isabella Beecher Hooker, Roxbury, Massachusetts, November 12, 1869, in Garrison, *Letters of Garrison*, 6:146, 145.

64. Martha Coffin Wright to Susan B. Anthony, quoting the letter she sent to Stone, Auburn, New York, November 4, 1869, in Stanton and Anthony, *Selected Papers*, 2:280; Martha Wright to William Lloyd Garrison, Jr., quoted in Sherry H. Penney and James D. Livingston, "Expectant at Seneca Falls," *New York History* 84, no. 1 (2003): 46; William Lloyd Garrison to Theodore Tilton, Roxbury, Massachusetts, April 5, 1870, in Garrison, *Letters of Garrison*, 6:174; and Lucretia Mott to Theodore Tilton, on the road, March 18, 1870, in Mott, *Selected Letters*, 437.

65. Comments on Lewis Tayler in a letter from Lydia Maria Child to Theodore Tilton, n.p., before January 17, 1867, in Lydia Maria Child, *A Lydia Maria Child Reader*, ed. Carolyn Karcher (Durham, N.C.: Duke University Press, 1997), 396 n. 1; "The Anglo-Saxon Home," *Godey's Lady's Book* 77 (July 1868); and "List of Women's Rights Which Have Been Overlooked," *Deseret News*, Salt Lake City, December 10, 1862. Tayler's articles appeared in the *Independent* on December 6 and 20, 1866.

66. Horace Bushnell, *Woman's Suffrage: The Reform against Nature* (New York: Scribner's, 1869), www.public.coe.edu; and William Lloyd Garrison to Samuel May, Jr., Roxbury, Massachusetts, July 23, 1869, in Garrison, *Letters of Garrison*, 6:126.

67. John Todd, *Woman's Rights* (Boston: Lee and Shepard, 1867), American Memory, http://memory.loc.gov/cgi-bin/query/D?nawbib.
68. Gail Hamilton [Mary Abigail Dodge], *Woman's Wrongs: A Counter-Irritant* (Boston: Ticknor and Fields, 1868), www:onlinebooks.library.upenn.
69. Hamilton, *Woman's Wrongs.*
70. Baker, *Sisters*, 35–36; and Kerr, *Lucy Stone*, 143–44, quotation at 144.
71. Dorothy Sterling, *Ahead of Her Time: Abby Kelley and the Politics of Antislavery* (New York: Norton, 1991), 348, 349. Information about Train causes some to suggest that his global travels made him the inspiration for Jules Verne's novel *Around the World in Eighty Days.*
72. Elizabeth Cady Stanton to Isabella Beecher Hooker, New York, September 8, 1869, in Stanton and Anthony, *Selected Papers*, 2:264.
73. Lucy Stone to Antoinette Brown Blackwell, Eastport, Maine, October 31, 1869, in Stone and Blackwell, *Loving Warriors*, 230; Stanton and Anthony, *Selected Papers*, 2:292 n. 1; and Wendy Hamand Venet, *A Strong-Minded Woman: The Life of Mary Livermore* (Amherst: University of Massachusetts Press, 2005), 161–66. When Livermore stepped down from her post as editor, she became a popular speaker, traveling nationwide and lecturing on a variety of topics, including women's rights, education, labor, and politics (201–8).
74. "State Suffrage Laws," American Memory, http://memory.loc.gov/cgi-bin/query/D?awh:1:./temp/~ammem.
75. T. A. Larson, "Woman Suffrage in Wyoming," *Pacific Northwest Quarterly* 56 (April 1965), 57–63; and Beverly Beeton, *Women Vote in the West: the Woman Suffrage Movement, 1869–1896* (New York: Garland, 1986).
76. Carol Cornwall Madsen, ed., *Battle for the Ballot: Essays on Woman Suffrage in Utah, 1870–1896* (Logan: Utah State University Press, 1997); Beeton, *Women Vote in the West*; and Griffith, *In Her Own Right*, 150.
77. Lucretia Mott to Martha Coffin Wright, roadside, July 16, 1870, in Mott, *Selected Letters*, 446.

Chapter 6

1. Linda Kerber, *No Constitutional Right to Be Ladies: Women and the Obligations of Citizenship* (New York: Hill and Wang, 1998), 81–92.
2. Press quotations in Julia E. Smith, *Abby Smith and Her Cows* (Hartford, Conn.: n.p., 1877; reprint, New York: Arno Press, 1972), 14, 28; and William Lloyd Garrison to Abby Kelley Foster, Boston, February 16, 1874, in William Lloyd Garrison, *The Letters of William Lloyd Garrison* vol. 6, *To Rouse the Slumbering Land, 1868–1879*, ed. Walter E. Merrill and Louis Ruchames (Cambridge, Mass.: Harvard University Press, 1981), 299. For details of the case as well as additional press coverage and the trial, see Smith, *Abby Smith and Her Cows,* and Julia E. Smith, "Protest of Julia E. Smith," *Woman's Journal,* May 7, 1881. In this letter, Julia explained that Horace Smith was occupying and farming the land and had offered to pay the taxes. She turned the bill over to him, but reassured readers that she had not compromised her principles.

3. "New England Woman's Tea Party," *Woman's Journal*, December 20, 1873; and "The Philadelphia Tea Party," *Woman's Journal*, January 3, 1874.

4. William Lloyd Garrison to Abby Kelley Foster, Boston, February 16, 1874, in Garrison, *Letters of Garrison*, 6:298; "Sale of the Foster Farm," *Woman's Journal*, April 29, 1876; John T. Sargent to Abby Kelley Foster, Boston, February 15, 1874, Abby Kelley Foster Papers, American Antiquarian Society, Worcester, Massachusetts; and Dorothy Sterling, *Ahead of Her Time: Abby Kelley and the Politics of Antislavery* (New York: Norton, 1991), 367–72.

5. Elizabeth Cady Stanton and Susan B. Anthony, *The Selected Papers of Elizabeth Cady Stanton and Susan B. Anthony*, vol. 2, *Against an Aristocracy of Sex, 1866 to 1873*, ed. Ann D. Gordon (New Brunswick, N.J.: Rutgers University Press, 2000), 275 n. 1.

6. "Sara J. Spencer vs. The Board of Registration and Sarah E. Webster vs. The Judges of Election, Argument of the Counsel of the Plaintiffs, Supreme Court of the District of Columbia 1871," American Memory, Library of Congress, http://memory.loc.gov/cgi-bin/query/r?ammem/rbnawsa; "Right of Suffrage in the District of Columbia," *Woman's Journal*, November 18, 1871; and Francis Miller, "Argument before the Judiciary Committee of the House of Representatives, upon the Petition of 600 Citizens," January 21, 1874 (Washington, D.C.: Gibson, 1874).

7. Susan B. Anthony to the editor, *Revolution*, writing from Portland, Oregon, September 4, 1871, in Stanton and Anthony, *Selected Papers*, 2:444–45 and (quotation) 447 nn. 5–7.

8. Susan B. Anthony to Elizabeth Cady Stanton, Rochester, New York, November 5, 1872, Papers of Elizabeth Cady Stanton and Susan B. Anthony, microfilm (Wilmington, Del.: Scholarly Resources, 1991). See also "Woman's Rights. The Case of Susan B. Anthony," *Philadelphia Inquirer*, June 19, 1873; "New York City and State," *Philadelphia Inquirer*, June 20, 1873; "Miss Anthony's Defense," *Woman's Journal*, February 15, 1873; *An Account of the Proceedings on the Trial of Susan B. Anthony on the Charge of Illegal Voting* (Rochester, N.Y.: Daily Democrat and Chronicle Book Print, 1874); and Eleanor Flexner, *Century of Struggle: The Woman's Rights Movement in the United States* (Cambridge, Mass.: Harvard University Press, 1975), 165–67. The trial proved unusual in the way it failed to adhere to proper judicial procedures. Reports of Susan's speech appeared in several newspapers in Ontario County, including the *Ontario County Times* and the *Geneva Gazette*. See Stanton and Anthony Papers, microfilm.

9. *Minor v. Happersett (1874)*, in *Women's Suffrage in America: An Eyewitness History*, ed. Elizabeth Frost-Knappman and Kathryn Cullen-DuPont (New York: Facts on File, 1992), 391–96, quotation at 396. See also *Minor v. Happersett*, Supreme Court of the United States, 88 U.S. 162; 21 Wall. 162, October 1874 Term, www.law.umkc.edu.

10. Elizabeth Cady Stanton to Theodore Weld Stanton, Tenafly, New Jersey, November 2, 1880, and Edward R. Furlong, "Account of Elizabeth Cady Stanton Attempt to Vote at Tenafly, New Jersey, November 3, 1880," both in Papers of Elizabeth Cady Stanton and Susan B. Anthony, microfilm; Elisabeth Griffith, *In Her Own Right: The Life of Elizabeth Cady Stanton* (New York: Oxford University

Press, 1984), 171; "Notes and News," *Woman's Journal*, January 18, 1873; and Alice Stone Blackwell, *Lucy Stone: Pioneer of Woman's Rights* (Boston: Little, Brown, 1930; reprint, Charlottesville: University Press of Virginia, 2001), 174–76.

11. Blackwell, *Lucy Stone*, 223.

12. *American National Biography*, s.v. "Woodhull, Victoria Claflin," www.anb.org/ articles/15/15-00771-article.html; Lois Beachy Underhill, *The Woman Who Ran for President: The Many Lives of Victoria Woodhull* (Bridgehampton, N.Y.: Bridge Works, 1995); and Barbara Goldsmith, *Other Powers: The Age of Suffrage, Spiritualism, and the Scandalous Victoria Woodhull* (New York: Knopf, 1998), 139, 149.

13. Richard Wightman Fox, *Trials of Intimacy: Love and Loss in the Beecher-Tilton Scandal* (Chicago: University of Chicago Press, 1999), 154.

14. Elizabeth Cady Stanton to Lucretia Mott, New Castle, Delaware, April 1, 1872, in Stanton and Anthony, *Selected Papers*, 2:427–28.

15. Lydia Maria Child to Lucy Osgood, Wayland, Massachusetts, February 12, 1872, in Lydia Maria Child, *Lydia Maria Child: Selected Letters, 1817–1880*, ed. Milton Meltzer and Patricia G. Holland (Amherst: University of Massachusetts Press, 1982), 504; and Susan B. Anthony, "Diary," May 12, 1872, in Stanton and Anthony, *Selected Papers*, 2:494. See also Diana Pounds, "Suffragists, Free Love, and the Woman Question," *Palimpsest* 72 (1991): 2–15; and Melanie Susan Gustafson, *Women and the Republican Party, 1854–1924* (Urbana: University of Illinois Press, 2001), 46–47.

16. "Mr. Tilton's Sworn Statement," and "What Elizabeth Cady Stanton Knows," in *Beecher-Tilton Investigation: The Scandal of the Age* (Philadelphia: Barclay, 1874), 28, 59. See also Debby Applegate, *The Most Famous Man in America: The Biography of Henry Ward Beecher* (New York: Doubleday, 2006); *American National Biography*, s.v. "Woodhull, Victoria Claflin"; Fox, *Trials of Intimacy*; and Goldsmith, *Other Powers*.

17. Blanche Butler Ames to Adelbert Ames, Lowell, Massachusetts, October 3, 1872, in North American Women's Letters and Diaries, www.alexanderstreet2.com/ WLDLive; "The Committee's Report," in *Beecher-Tilton Investigation*, 127; Applegate, *Most Famous Man*, 391–455; and Elizabeth Cady Stanton to Isabella Beecher Hooker, Tenafly, New Jersey, November 3, 1873, Papers of Elizabeth Cady Stanton and Susan B. Anthony, microfilm.

18. "A Talk with Mrs. Stanton," *New York Sun*, before July 17, 1875, Papers of Elizabeth Cady Stanton and Susan B. Anthony, microfilm; and *American National Biography*, s.v. "Woodhull, Victoria Claflin."

19. Lucy Stone to Nettie Blackwell, Dorchester, Massachusetts, May 21, 1876, 188, in Lucy Stone and Antoinette Brown Blackwell, *Friends and Sisters: Letters between Lucy Stone and Antoinette Brown Blackwell, 1846–1893*, ed. Carol Lasser and Marlene Deahl Merrill (Urbana: University of Illinois Press, 1987), 187 n. 4, 188; Blackwell, *Lucy Stone*, 252–53; and Mary Frances Cordato, "Toward a New Century: Women and the Centennial Exhibition, 1876," *Pennsylvania Magazine of History and Biography* 107, no. 1 (1983): 113–35.

20. *Memorial of the International Exhibition at Philadelphia, 1876* (Philadelphia: Thomas Hunter, n.d.).

21. Andrea Moore Kerr, *Lucy Stone: Speaking Out for Equality* (New Brunswick, N.J.: Rutgers University Press, 1992), 195; "Declaration of Rights of the Women of the United States," July 4, 1876, American Memory, http://memory.loc.gov/cgi–bin/ampage.

22. Elizabeth Cady Stanton to Isabella Beecher Hooker, Philadelphia, July 5, 1876, Papers of Elizabeth Cady Stanton and Susan B. Anthony, microfilm; and Anne K. Irvine to Susan B. Anthony, Oregon, Missouri, July 11, 1876, *Ballot Box*, August 1876. Dozens of letters of support appeared in this issue.

23. Abba Goold Woolson, ed., *Dress-Reform: A Series of Lectures Delivered in Boston, on Dress as It Affects the Health of Women* (Boston: Roberts, 1874), vii, xv, 86–87, 135. The four doctors were Mary J. Safford-Blake, Caroline E. Hastings, Mercy B. Jackson, and Arville B. Haynes. See *Woman's Journal*, May 17, 24, and 31, June 21, and September 20, 1873, for examples of other essays and speeches.

24. Alice Stone Blackwell, "Diary," May 28, 1873, and "Diary," December 16, 1872, in Alice Stone Blackwell, *Growing Up in Boston's Gilded Age: The Journal of Alice Stone Blackwell, 1872–1874* (New Haven, Conn.: Yale University Press, 1990), 174, 133.

25. Anne Firor Scott, *Natural Allies: Women's Associations in American History* (Urbana: University of Illinois Press, 1992), 94–101, quotation at 96; *American National Biography*, s.v. "Willard, Frances Elizabeth Caroline"; and Ruth B. A. Bordin, *Frances Willard: A Biography* (Chapel Hill: University of North Carolina Press, 1986).

26. "Female Suffrage," *Philadelphia Inquirer*, November 24, 1871.

27. "Remarks" (Susan B. Anthony to the AWSA), Cleveland, November 23, 1870, *Woman's Journal*, December 3, 1870; and Blackwell, *Lucy Stone*, 218–20. Susan had no basis for her accusation other than the "Protest" Lucy and Henry had written and made public after their wedding. This document did not negate the ceremony, only declared their rejection of marriage laws that oppressed wives.

28. Susan B. Anthony to Elizabeth Boynton Harbert, Rochester, New York, August 5, 1880, Papers of Elizabeth Cady Stanton and Susan B. Anthony, microfilm.

29. Susan B. Anthony to Harriet Jane Hanson Robinson, Tenafly, New Jersey, October 24, 1880, Papers of Elizabeth Cady Stanton and Susan B. Anthony, microfilm.

30. Susan B. Anthony to Laura De Force Gordon, Cedar Rapids, Iowa, February 9, 1871; Susan B. Anthony to Harriet Jane Hanson Robinson, Rochester, New York, August 12, 1879; and Susan B. Anthony to Laura De Force Gordon, Williamsport, Pennsylvania, November 17, 1870, all in Papers of Elizabeth Cady Stanton and Susan B. Anthony, microfilm.

31. Antoinette Brown Blackwell to Elizabeth Cady Stanton, Somerville, New Jersey, December 21, 1874, Papers of Elizabeth Cady Stanton and Susan B. Anthony, microfilm; and Martha Coffin Wright to Ellen Wright Garrison, n.p., May 14, 1873, quoted in Sherry H. Penney and James D. Livingston, *A Very Dangerous Woman: Martha Wright and Women's Rights* (Amherst: University of Massachusetts Press, 2004), 207.

32. Elizabeth Cady Stanton to Lucy Stone, Tenafly, New Jersey, December 28, 1873, Papers of Elizabeth Cady Stanton and Susan B. Anthony, microfilm. See also "Why There Are Two National Woman Suffrage Associations," *Woman's Journal*,

December 3, 1870. The article quoted material published in *Harper's* that explained reasons for the division.

33. Lucy Stone to Antoinette Brown Blackwell, Boston, March 26, 1882, and Lucy Stone to Antoinette Brown Blackwell, Dorchester, Massachusetts, January 10, 1886, both in Stone and Blackwell, *Friends and Sisters*, 237, 250, and 237–38 n 4. Elizabeth's relationship with Lucy seemed to blow hot and cold, perhaps influenced by Susan and also by Elizabeth's level of involvement in the NWSA.

34. Penney and Livingston, *A Very Dangerous Woman*, 218.

35. Lucretia Mott, "Remarks," *Woman's Journal,* July 27, 1878, reprinted in *Lucretia Mott: Her Complete Speeches and Sermons*, ed. Dana Greene (New York: Edwin Mellen Press, 1980), 393; and Elizabeth Cady Stanton, "Thirty Years Old," *Rochester Union and Advertiser*, July 19, 1878, Papers of Elizabeth Cady Stanton and Susan B. Anthony, microfilm. Lucy wanted to rewrite history to promote the 1850 Worcester convention, for in 1888 she wrote Nette: "I think we ought to puncture the bubble that the Seneca Falls meeting was the first public demand for suffrage." Lucy Stone to Antoinette Brown Blackwell, Dorchester, Massachusetts, Winter 1888, Stone and Blackwell, *Friends and Sisters*, 255.

36. "Memorial Service for Lucretia Coffin Mott," in Elizabeth Cady Stanton and Susan B. Anthony, *Selected Papers of Elizabeth Cady Stanton and Susan B. Anthony,* vol. 4, *When Clowns Make Laws for Queens, 1880 to 1887*, ed. Ann D. Gordon (New Brunswick, N.J.: Rutgers University Press, 2006), 36, 37; Elizabeth Cady Stanton, "My Diary," November 14, 1880, in Elizabeth Cady Stanton, *Elizabeth Cady Stanton as Revealed in Her Letters, Diary and Reminiscences*, ed. Theodore Stanton and Harriot Blatch Stanton (New York: Harper, 1922), 2:178; and Lucy Stone, "The First National Convention," *Woman's Journal*, February 14, 1891. See also "Lucretia Mott," *Christian Recorder*, November 25, 1880; and Griffith, *In Her Own Right*, 176.

37. Observer's quotation in Griffith, *In Her Own Right*, 161, 163; and Alice Stone Blackwell, "Diary, November 2, 1872," in Blackwell, *Growing Up in Boston's Gilded Age*, 122.

38. Elizabeth Cady Stanton to Susan B. Anthony, Chicago, February 16, 1875, Papers of Elizabeth Cady Stanton and Susan B. Anthony, microfilm. After a decade of lecturing, Elizabeth admitted to being weary and now happy to enjoy home. Stanton, "My Diary," December 27, 1880, in Stanton, *Elizabeth Cady Stanton as Revealed*, 2:181.

39. Elizabeth Cady Stanton to Susan B. Anthony, Waynesville, Ohio, December 1878, Papers of Elizabeth Cady Stanton and Susan B. Anthony, microfilm; and Elizabeth Cady Stanton to Isabella Beecher Hooker, Tenafly, New Jersey, May 10, 1880, North American Women's Letters and Diaries, www.alexanderstreet4.com/cgi-bin/asp/nawld/getloc.pl?/projects.

40. Griffith, *In Her Own Right*, 149–51; and Stanton and Anthony, *Selected Papers*, 2:435 n. 2.

41. A. J. B., "The Work in the West" (Dayton, Ohio), *Woman's Journal*, September 3, 1870.

42. Susan B. Anthony to Isabella Beecher Hooker, Tenafly, New Jersey, January 20, 1875, Papers of Elizabeth Cady Stanton and Susan B. Anthony, microfilm; and "Arguments before the Judiciary Committee of the House of Representatives,"

Forty-eighth Congress, March 8, 1884, American Memory, http://memory
.loc.gov/cgi-bin/query/r?ammem/naw:@field.

43. Lucy Stone to Alice Stone Blackwell, Warsaw, Indiana, October 27, 1885, and
Alice Stone Blackwell to Lucy Stone, Boston, March 12, 1887, both in Blackwell
Family Papers, Library of Congress, Washington, D.C., microfilm.

44. Susan B. Anthony to the editor, *Revolution,* September 4, 1871, Papers of Elizabeth
Cady Stanton and Susan B. Anthony, microfilm; and Alice Stone Blackwell,
"Diary," May 28, 1872, in Blackwell, *Growing Up in Boston's Gilded Age,* 78. See also
American National Biography, s.v. "Duniway, Abigail Jane Scott"; Debra Shein,
"Abigail Scott Duniway Exhibit Text," www.libweb.uoregon.edu/exhibits/
archive; and Ruth Barnes Moynihan, *Rebel for Rights: Abigail Scott Duniway* (New
Haven, Conn.: Yale University Press, 1983).

45. Susan B. Anthony to Benjamin F. Butler, St. Charles, Minnesota, December 30,
1877, Papers of Elizabeth Cady Stanton and Susan B. Anthony, microfilm;
and Susan B. Anthony to Isabella Beecher Hooker, Onawa, Iowa, November 11,
1877, in Elizabeth Cady Stanton and Susan B. Anthony, *The Selected Papers of
Elizabeth Cady Stanton and Susan. B. Anthony,* vol. 3, *National Protection for National
Citizens, 1873 to 1880,* ed. Ann D. Gordon (New Brunswick, N.J.: Rutgers University Press, 2003), 338.

46. Blackwell, *Lucy Stone,* 248.

47. Henry Blackwell to Lucy Stone, Bismarck, North Dakota, July 10, 1889; Henry
Blackwell to Lucy Stone, Helena, Montana, July 14, 16, and 18, 1889; Henry
Blackwell to Lucy Stone, Tacoma, Washington, July 20, 1889; and Henry Black-
well to Lucy Stone, Olympia, Washington, July 21, 1889, all in Blackwell
Family Papers, microfilm. See also T. A. Larson, "The Woman Suffrage Move-
ment in Washington," *Pacific Northwest Quarterly* 2 (1976): 49–62; and Leslie
Wheeler, "Woman Suffrage's Gray-Bearded Champion," *Montana* 31, no. 3
(1981): 2–13.

48. *American National Biography,* s.v. "Blackwell, Alice Stone."

49. Alice Stone Blackwell to Kitty Blackwell, October 29, 1872, in Blackwell, *Growing
Up in Boston's Gilded Age,* 244; and Lucy Stone to Alice Stone Blackwell, Grand
Rapids, Michigan, November 30, 1869, and January 31, 1870, both in Blackwell
Family Papers, microfilm.

50. Alice Stone Blackwell, "Diary," February 11, 1872, in Blackwell, *Growing Up in
Boston's Gilded Age,* 31.

51. Alice Stone Blackwell, "Diary," April 5, 1871, and December 26, 1873, in
Blackwell, *Growing Up in Boston's Gilded Age,* 57, 214–15.

52. Griffith, *In Her Own Right,* 168–69.

53. "Arguments before the Select Committee on Woman Suffrage in the Senate,
March 7, 1884," American Memory, http://memory.loc.gov/cgi-bin/query/
r?ammem/naw:@field. In 1884, the House did not renew its Select Committee on
Woman Suffrage.

54. Senator Joseph Brown, "Minority Opinion, Arguments before the Judiciary
Committee of the House of Representatives, March 8, 1884," American Memory,
http://memory.loc.gov/cgi-bin/query/r?ammem/naw:@field.

55. Senator H. W. Blair, "Debate on Woman Suffrage in the Senate of the United States," December 8, 1886, 2nd session, 49th Congress, American Memory, http://memory.loc.gov/cgi-bin/query/r?ammem/naw:@field.

56. Blair, "Debate on Woman Suffrage in the Senate of the United States."

57. Blair, "Debate on Woman Suffrage in the Senate of the United States."

58. As of 1883, women could vote in school elections in Colorado, Dakota Territory, Kansas, Kentucky, Massachusetts, Minnesota, Michigan, Nebraska, New Hampshire, New York, Oregon, and Vermont. See Stanton and Anthony, *Selected Papers*, 4:262 n. 13.

59. "Progressive Kansas," *Woman's Journal*, April 28, 1888.

60. "Woman and Man," *Woman's Journal*, January 15, 1870; and Blackwell, *Lucy Stone*, 237, 243 (Catt quotation).

61. "The National Suffrage Association," *Woman's Journal*, June 4, 1881; and, in Stanton and Anthony, *Selected Papers*, 3:339 n. 8.

62. Blackwell, *Lucy Stone*, 239–40.

63. Susan B. Anthony to Sarah Landgon Williams, Philadelphia, June 7, 1876, 228; Elizabeth Cady Stanton to Sarah Langdon Williams, Tenafly, New Jersey, July 22, 1876; and Susan B. Anthony to Laura De Force Gordon, Newman, Illinois, March 18, 1877, Papers of Elizabeth Cady Stanton and Susan B. Anthony, microfilm. One can't help but imagine that Susan must have been somewhat resentful of Lucy's success with the *Woman's Journal* since Susan's paper, the *Revolution*, failed to achieve what she had hoped.

64. Elizabeth Cady Stanton to Lucy Stone, July 30, 1876, Tenafly, New Jersey; Lucy Stone to Elizabeth Cady Stanton, Dorchester, Massachusetts, August 3, 1876; and Lucy Stone to Mrs. Robinson, Boston, March 4, 1879, all in Blackwell Family Papers, microfilm.

65. Susan B. Anthony to Barbara J. Thompson, Rochester, New York, August 18, 1881, and Elizabeth Cady Stanton to Amelia Bloomer, Tenafly, New Jersey, November 10, 1885, both in Papers of Elizabeth Cady Stanton and Susan B. Anthony, microfilm. See also Stanton, "My Diary," September 30, 1885, in Stanton, *Elizabeth Cady Stanton as Revealed*, 2:226.

66. Susan B. Anthony to Harriet Hanson Robinson, Rochester, New York, August 12, 1879, Papers of Elizabeth Cady Stanton and Susan B. Anthony, microfilm; Ellen Carol DuBois, *Harriot Stanton Blatch and the Winning of Woman Suffrage* (New Haven, Conn.: Yale University Press, 1997), 49; Antoinette Brown Blackwell to Susan B. Anthony, Somerville, New Jersey, August 14, 1876, Papers of Elizabeth Cady Stanton and Susan B. Anthony, microfilm; Blackwell, *Lucy Stone*, 226; and L. S., "The History of Woman Suffrage," *Woman's Journal*, June 11, 1881.

67. Griffith, *In Her Own Right*, 174–75.

68. "Woman Suffrage History," *Woman's Journal*, March 10, 1883. Harriot's chapter is at the end of Elizabeth Cady Stanton, Susan B. Anthony, and Matilda Joslyn Gage, eds., *History of Woman Suffrage*, vol. 2 (New York: Fowler & Wells, 1882), 756–863. The only evidence that she authored the chapter is in a footnote, 756.

69. U.S. Department of Commerce, Bureau of the Census, *Historical Statistics of the United States, Colonial Times to the 1970s* (Washington, D.C.: Government Printing Office, 1975), 379.

70. Mary F. Eastman, "The Education of Woman in the Eastern States," May Wright Sewall, "The Education of Woman in the Western States," and Christine Ladd Franklin, "The Education of Woman in the Southern States," all in Annie Nathan Meyer, *Woman's Work in America* (New York: Holt, 1891; reprint, New York: Arno Press, 1972), 3–53, 54–88, 89–106.

71. "Vassar College," *Godey's Lady's Book* 72 (August 1866).

72. "Domestic Service in Schools for Young Ladies," *Godey's Lady's Book* 70 (January 1865); and "Higher Education for Women," *Woman's Journal*, May 17, 1873.

73. Rosalind Rosenberg, *Beyond Separate Spheres: Intellectual Roots of Modern Feminism* (New Haven, Conn.: Yale University Press, 1982), 5–14.

74. See U.S. Bureau of the Census, Department of the Interior, *The Statistics of the Population of the United States . . . Compiled from the Original Returns of the Ninth Census, 1870* (Washington, D.C.: Government Printing Office, 1872), table 29, 703–15; and U. S Census Office, Department of the Interior, *Report on Population of the United States at the Eleventh Census: 1890* (Washington, D.C.: Government Printing Office, 1897), 306–10.

75. Debra Shein, "Abigail Scott Duniway," in Feminist Voices & Vision, Abigail Scott Duniway exhibit, www.libweb.uoregon.edu/exhibits/archive. See also Moynihan, *Rebel for Rights.*

76. U.S. Bureau of the Census, *The Statistics of the Population of the United States . . . Ninth Census, 1870*, table 29; and U.S. Census Office, Department of Labor, *Report on Population, 1890* (Washington, D.C.: Government Printing Office, 1895), table 79.

77. U.S. Census Office, Department of Labor, *Report on Population, 1890*, table 79; and Harriet Sigerman, "Laborers for Liberty," in *No Small Courage: A History of Women in the United States*, ed. Nancy F. Cott (New York: Oxford University Press, 2000), 323.

78. U.S. Census, *Report on Population, 1890*, table 79.

79. *Bradwell v. Illinois, 1873*, in Frost-Knappman and Cullen-DuPont, eds., *Women's Suffrage in America*, 390–91; and Sigerman, "Laborers for Liberty," 323–25. Sources differ on the date for this case; some list December 1872 and others 1873.

80. "Lockwood, Belva Ann Bennett McNall," in *Notable American Women: A Biographical Dictionary* (Cambridge, Mass.: Harvard University Press, 1971), 2:413–16; and *American National Biography*, s.v., "Lockwood, Belva Ann Bennett McNall." As Victoria Woodhull was not thirty-five in 1872 when she ran for president and could not campaign because she was in jail, Lockwood was the first viable female candidate to run for president.

81. "Resolutions of the NWSA," January 27, 1887, in Stanton and Anthony, *Selected Papers*, 4:549; and Susan B. Anthony, "Woman Suffrage—Arguments before the Committee on the Judiciary," January 24, 1880, Papers of Elizabeth Cady Stanton and Susan B. Anthony, microfilm.

82. "American Woman Suffrage Association. Fourth Anniversary and Fifth Annual Meeting," *Woman's Journal*, October 18, 1873. See also Kerr, *Lucy Stone*, 192–93.
83. Susan B. Anthony to Clarina Howard Nichols, en route Omaha, after September 2, 1882, in Stanton and Anthony, *Selected Papers*, 4:175.
84. Alice Stone Blackwell, "Diary," Dorchester, September 28, 1879, in Blackwell, *Growing Up in Boston's Gilded Age*, 237–38.
85. Blackwell, *Lucy Stone*, 7, 233; and Lucy Stone to Alice Blackwell, Grand Island, Nebraska, October 12, 1882, Blackwell Family Papers, microfilm.
86. Lucy Stone to Alice Stone Blackwell, Oberlin, Ohio, 1886, Blackwell Family Papers, microfilm.
87. Lucy Stone, "Some Things the Massachusetts Legislature of 1889 and 1890 Did for Men, Who Have Votes, Contrasted with What It Did for Women, Who Have No Votes," Blackwell Family Papers, microfilm.
88. Elizabeth Cady Stanton, "The Pleasures of Age," New York, November 12, 1885; and Stanton to Margaret Stanton Lawrence, Tenafly, New Jersey, November 15, 1885, both in Papers of Elizabeth Cady Stanton and Susan B. Anthony, microfilm.
89. Elizabeth Cady Stanton to Frederick Douglass, Johnstown, New York, May 27, 1884, in Stanton and Anthony, *Selected Papers*, 4:353; and Elizabeth Cady Stanton to Benjamin F. Underwood, Tenafly, New Jersey, October 19, 1885 and Elizabeth Cady Stanton to Antoinette Brown Blackwell, Tenafly, New Jersey, April 27, 1886, both in Papers of Elizabeth Cady Stanton and Susan B. Anthony, microfilm.
90. Elizabeth Cady Stanton, "My Diary," January 25, 1885, in Stanton, *Elizabeth Cady Stanton as Revealed*, 2:224; and "Women and Scepticism," *Washington (DC) National Republican*, January 26, 1885, Papers of Elizabeth Cady Stanton and Susan B. Anthony, microfilm.
91. Elizabeth Cady Stanton, "The Woman's Bible," August 9, 1886, in Stanton and Anthony, *Selected Papers*, 4:510; and "Elizabeth Cady Stanton Dies at Her Home," *New York Times*, October 27, 1902.
92. Thomas J. Jablonsky, *The Home, Heaven, and Mother Party: Female Anti-suffragists in the United States, 1868–1920* (Brooklyn, N.Y.: Carlson, 1994), 1–3; "Marshalling Their Forces" and "Woman Suffrage in Illinois," *Woman's Journal*, April 23 and 30, 1870.
93. "Mrs. Gen. Sherman and 1,000 Other Ladies against Woman Suffrage," *Woman's Journal*, January 28, 1871; Jablonsky, *The Home, Heaven, and Mother Party*, 4; and Alice Stone Blackwell, "Objections Answered" (1915), http://douglassarchives.org. See also Mary M. Huth, "Kate Gannett Wells, Anti-Suffragist," *University of Rochester Library Bulletin* 34 (1981), www.lib.rochester.edu/index.
94. Blackwell, *Lucy Stone*, 229.
95. Lucy Stone to Alice Stone Blackwell, Thomasville, Georgia, April 12, 1887, and Lucy Stone to Antoinette Blackwell, Dorchester, Massachusetts, July 23, 1887, both in Blackwell Family Papers, microfilm; and quotation in Elizabeth Cazden, *Antoinette Brown Blackwell: A Biography* (Old Westbury, N.Y.: Feminist Press, 1983), 223.
96. Susan B. Anthony to Lucy Stone, Philadelphia, December 12, 1887, Blackwell Family Papers, microfilm; Lucy Stone to Mrs. Campbell, Boston, March 17, 1888,

in Lucy Stone and Henry B. Blackwell, *Loving Warriors: A Revealing Portrait of an Unprecedented Marriage*, ed. Leslie Wheeler (New York: Dial Press, 1981), 313; and Lucy Stone to Antoinette Brown Blackwell, Dorchester, Winter 1888, in Stone and Blackwell, *Friends and Sisters*, 255.

97. So important was this convention that within months after it ended, the proceedings were published in a four-hundred-page volume. See National Woman Suffrage Association, *Report of the International Council of Women* (Washington, D.C.: Rufus H. Darby, 1888). The volume contains only one picture, placed at the front: it is signed "affectionately thine, Lucretia Mott."

98. Griffith, *In Her Own Right*, 192–94.

99. "The International Council," *Woman's Journal*, April 14, 1888; and Isabella Beecher Hooker, "The Constitutional Rights of the Women of the United States," delivered at the International Council of Women, Washington, D.C., March 30, 1888, American Memory online, http://memory.loc.gov/cgi-bin/query/r?ammemm/rbnawsa:@field.

100. Quoted in Cazden, *Antoinette Brown Blackwell*, 221.

101. "The International Council," *Woman's Journal*, April 14 and March 31, 1888.

102. Alice Stone Blackwell to Kitty Blackwell, Dorchester, Massachusetts, April 8, 1888, Blackwell Family Papers, microfilm; and "Received at the White House," *Washington Post*, March 31, 1888. President Grover Cleveland fathered a child out of wedlock, a fact well known when he ran for president—and a topic that generated much gossip. Despite this, he won. Women involved in the social purity crusade were trying to improve the morals of America, which meant dealing with prostitution, adultery, the double standard, and any activity that promoted illicit sex.

103. "Open Letter to the Women of America," February 18, 1889, and Lucy Stone to Susan B. Anthony, Boston, December 11, 1890, both in Blackwell Family Papers, microfilm.

104. Susan B. Anthony to Olympia Brown, n.p., March 11, 1889, Papers of Elizabeth Cady Stanton and Susan B. Anthony, microfilm.

105. Elizabeth Cady Stanton, "Address of Mrs. Stanton," *Woman's Journal*, March 1, 1890; and Elizabeth Cady Stanton to Elizabeth Pease Nichol, Basingstoke Hants, England, January 10, 1883 in Elizabeth Cady Stanton and Susan B. Anthony, *The Selected Papers of Elizabeth Cady Stanton and Susan B. Anthony: When Clowns Make Laws for Queens, 1880 to 1887*, vol. 4, ed. Ann D. Gordon (New Brunswick, N.J/: Rutgers University Press, 2006), 212.

Epilogue

1. Alice Stone Blackwell, "Diary," September 19, 1893, 52, Blackwell Family Papers, Library of Congress, Washington, D.C., microfilm.

2. Alice Stone Blackwell, "To Henry B. Blackwell," in *What I Owe My Father*, ed. Sydney Strong (New York: Holt, 1931), 46.

3. Alice Stone Blackwell, *Lucy Stone: Pioneer of Woman's Rights* (Boston: Little, Brown, 1930; reprint, Charlottesville: University Press of Virginia, 2001), 282, 287, 284.

For background, see Andrea Moore Kerr, *Lucy Stone: Speaking Out for Equality* (New Brunswick, N.J.: Rutgers University Press, 1992), 227–45. Lucy would have been upset had she seen the *New York Times* headline, which read: "Lucy Stone Blackwell Buried." *New York Times*, October 22, 1893.

4. Blackwell, *Lucy Stone*, 285–86.

5. Elizabeth Cady Stanton, "My Diary," January 20, 1892, in Elizabeth Cady Stanton, *Elizabeth Cady Stanton as Revealed in Her Letters, Diary and Reminiscences*, ed. Theodore Stanton and Harriot Stanton Blatch (New York: Harper, 1922), 2:281; and "The Solitude of Self," *Woman's Journal*, January 23, 1892.

6. Elisabeth Griffith, *In Her Own Right: The Life of Elizabeth Cady Stanton* (New York: Oxford University Press, 1984), 210–16; and Stanton, "My Diary," January 9, 1889 and October 6, 1898, in Stanton, *Elizabeth Cady Stanton as Revealed*, 2:254, 335.

7. Elizabeth Cady Stanton, "Letter to Theodore Roosevelt," New York, October 25, 1902, in Stanton, *Elizabeth Cady Stanton as Revealed*, 2:368–69; "Tribute from Miss Anthony," *New York Times*, October 27, 1902; and Griffith, *In Her Own Right*, 218.

8. "Honor Susan B. Anthony Who Is Ill at Home," *New York Times*, February 21, 1906; and Kathleen Barry, *Susan B. Anthony: A Biography of a Singular Feminist* (New York: New York University Press, 1988), 352–55.

9. Harriot Stanton Blatch, *Challenging Years: The Memoirs of Harriot Stanton Blatch*, with Alma Lutz (New York: Putnam, 1940; reprint, Westport, Conn.: Hyperion, 1976), 91–134; Eleanor Flexner, *Century of Struggle: The Woman's Rights Movement in the United States* (Cambridge, Mass.: Harvard University Press, 1975), 250–52; and Robert P.J. Cooney, Jr., *Winning the Vote: The Triumph of the American Woman Suffrage Movement* (Santa Cruz, Calif.: American Graphic Press, 2005), 104–10, 114. Alva was married to William Vanderbilt, grandson of Cornelius.

10. *American National Biography*, s.v. "Blatch, Harriot Stanton," www.anb.org/articles/index.html. States that gave women full suffrage before 1920 were Wyoming, Colorado, Idaho, Washington, Utah, California, Arizona, Oregon, Nevada, Montana, Kansas, New York, South Dakota, Oklahoma, and Michigan. With two exceptions, all were in the West.

Appendix B

1. This document is reprinted from the original and thus contains typographical and other errors. It is available at the website of the Women's Rights National History Project, www.nps.gov/wori/historyculture/solitude-of-self.htm.

Acknowledgments

This book could never have become a reality without the scores of scholars who have written biographies and histories of the womn's rights movement or edited letters, journals, and papers of the principal players included here. I am so grateful for their scholarship. As a reluctant convert to web-based research, I am now more enthusiastic, having discovered many documents, convention reports, speeches, and pamphlets full-text, online, especially material from the Library of Congress.

It is no easy task for an editor to take on a project mid-stream, but Tim Bent, executive editor for Oxford's history trade publications, did just that, with amazing grace, humor, encouragement, and meticulous editing. I shall never forget our first meeting, when he related how his memorable high school history teacher, Carol Kammen, drilled into her students the significance of the Seneca Falls Convention. I have tried to keep that vivid image alive while engaged in this project. To Tim, I extend profound thanks.

I also want to thank Peter Ginna for inviting me to join the Pivotal Moments series and for overseeing the initial stages of this project. In addition, I thank series co-editors and historians James McPherson and David Hackett Fischer for their helpful and thoughtful comments. It is a pleasure and an honor to be associated with the inspiring historians in this series. Dayne Poshusta and Joellyn Ausanka at Oxford have been models of patience in assisting with book production.

At Davidson College, I am profoundly grateful for generous research support from the Mary Reynolds Babcock Professorship and the Boswell Family Faculty Fellowship, allowing me a year off to complete this book. I thank Dean

Clark Ross for his constant support; Ann Douglas and Bobbie Campbell for their careful reading and editing of the manuscript; Cynthia Lewis for helpful writing hints; colleagues Vivien Dietz and Trish Tilburg for their insights into British and European history and John Wertheimer on legal history; the staffs at Davidson College Library (with special thanks to Sharon Byrd and Susanna Boylston for research assistance and to interlibrary loan librarian Joe Gutenkanst, who continually works miracles) and Information Technology Services specialist Kristen Eshelman; Andrew Kengeter for research assistance; and finally, Margaret Sprinkle for all her help in preparing this manuscript.

Farther afield, I thank Jack Shay for informative tours, sharing his wealth of knowledge at the National Woman's Rights Museum and the Elizabeth Cady Stanton home in Seneca Falls, New York; guides at the Susan B. Anthony home in Rochester, New York; my dear friend Beth Curry for research assistance and inspiration; Nancy Hewitt and Carol Lasser for sharing research and conversations on this topic; Celia Wright for her gracious hospitality in Washington, D.C.; and librarians at the Manuscript Room of the Library of Congress, the Duke University Library, the Boston Public Library, and the American Antiquarian Society in Worcester, Massachusetts. I also thank Rick Swegan, his wife, Debra Dinnocenzo, and their daughter, Jennimarie, for sharing insights into the M'Clintock family. Rick and Jennimarie are descendents of Mary Ann and Thomas. And I am ever grateful to my loyal friends and colleagues who saw less of me this past year than I would wish.

I am continually blessed by my family—son Blair, daughter Carrie, and daughter-in-law Kay—and their steadfast belief in this project and their unshakable commitment to women's equality; and always by Bruce, who has been my most dedicated, helpful critic and chief editor but, most important, my best friend and number one supporter throughout this project and throughout our married life.

It is to my students—past and present—that I dedicate this book. They make college teaching such a rewarding profession, keeping me energized and young at heart by making each day in the classroom a time of joy and excitement. I hope they and others find in this story what I have discovered.

Index

Note: Page numbers in *italics* refer to illustrations. The initials "SFC" refer to the convention at Seneca Falls.